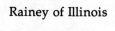

Rainey of Illinois

RAINEY OF ILLINOIS

A Political Biography
1903-34

Robert A. Waller

60
Illinois Studies in the Social Sciences

UNIVERSITY OF ILLINOIS PRESS
Urbana   Chicago   London

© 1977 by the Board of Trustees of the University of Illinois
Manufactured in the United States of America

Library of Congress Cataloging in Publication Data

Waller, Robert A.   1931-
  Rainey of Illinois.

  (Illinois studies in social sciences; 60)
  Bibliography: p.
  Includes index.
  1. Rainey, Henry Thomas, 1860-1934. 2. Legislators
— United States — Biography. 3. Illinois — Politics and
government — 1865-1950. 4. United States — Politics and
government — 1865-1933. I. Title. II. Series.
E748.R22W34   328.73′092′4 [B]   77-23859
ISBN 0-252-00647-X

To Peg, Tom, and Jim

Contents

Preface

During the first third of the twentieth century, Illinois produced
numerous leaders who left their imprint upon state and national
history. Some individuals like Governor Frank O. Lowden are known
for their administrative reforms. Others like "Uncle Joe" Cannon,
Speaker of the House of Representatives, and "Big Bill" Thompson,
mayor of Chicago, played a controversial role in political affairs.
Some like Jane Addams of Hull House pioneered in the struggle for
social reform. Still more have exerted an influence which is un-
deservedly neglected; such is the case with Henry Thomas Rainey.
This political biography rescues Congressman Rainey from the
obscurity to which he has been relegated thus far.

No other son or daughter of Illinois has been privileged to
give thirty years of service to district, state, and country in a
national legislative capacity. Democrat Henry T. Rainey of
Carrollton made such a contribution. With the exception of a
narrow defeat in the 1920 Harding landslide, Rainey's legislative
career uninterruptedly spans the years from 1903 until his death
in 1934. This political era embraces the clashes, conflicts, and
controversies represented in the expressions rural versus urban,
wet versus dry, Chicago versus downstate, native stock versus
immigrant, and federal versus state. Initially as a member of the
Labor Committee, later as a member of the Ways and Means Committee,
still later as majority leader, and finally as Speaker of the House,
Rainey was a participant in these struggles.

During his political career Rainey endeavored to shape public
thought and action in the interest of reform. The United States of
the early twentieth century was in the process of revitalizing its
faith in liberalism. The liberals regarded man as a rational
creature. Man could use his intelligence to overcome human and
natural obstacles in reaching his greatest fulfillment without
resorting to violence against the established order. During the
nineteenth century, liberalism had evolved as a doctrine emphasizing
the fullest development of the individual free from governmental
restraints. Conversely, the twentieth-century liberal requested
that the government intervene and correct the abuses of society
with a positive program of action.

In the early twentieth century, the term for the accomplishment of this purposeful change is progressivism. Definitions are
as numerous as there are proponents.[1] Nevertheless, there is
general agreement that progressivism is an application of the

liberal creed. The composite progressive would be an individual who works for a wider achievement of political, economic, and social equality; who combines zeal for service with a curiosity for facts; who strives for the gradual displacement of the obsolete with the new; and who contentedly takes small constructive steps within a broader framework of education and motivation. The progressive seeks to conserve the Jeffersonian ideal of a society emphasizing equality and human worth, but he envisions its achievement through an increased concern on the part of government for the supervision and care of men.

During the Rainey years, the reform movement was especially concerned with economic and political equality. Nationally the progressive program centered around the problem of those interstate organizations of capital known as trusts. Reformers delved into the relationship between a capitalistic economy and a political democracy. Among those aspects which especially interested Henry T. Rainey were regulation of transportation, conservation of resources, determination of tariff and tax rates, and establishment of programs beneficial to laborers, farmers, and veterans. He focused upon the economic aspects of reform; he provided his vote but not his voice in the support of political reform. While he was interested in the social aspects of reform, subsequent generations have given this facet greater attention.

An examination of scholarly writing concerning the early twentieth century reveals little mention of Rainey. The combination of lady luck, a famous name, or a major incident never operated to connect him with a legislative landmark. In part this historical neglect is the result of being overshadowed by such dominant presidential personalities as Woodrow Wilson and Franklin D. Roosevelt whenever his party controlled the White House. Historians of Illinois have been preoccupied with concerns such as the intraparty struggles and the depression when contemporaries Edward F. Dunne and Henry Horner occupied the State House. At other times Rainey's absence from the record is the consequence of being a member of the ineffectual minority party. The Democratic proponents of progressivism were submerged when their party directed the executive department and were neglected during the years of Republican ascendancy when insurgency drew the public's attention. This latter statement seems especially true of members of the House of Representatives. While numerous studies have been made of leadership in the Senate, only recently is attention being directed to the lower chamber.

An examination of the Rainey career is significant. The longevity of his public life makes him an important proving ground for the continuity yet transitoriness of legislative focuses from the turn of the century through the early New Deal. This study also reveals his role as a reformer, his interpretation of the components of reform, and his relation to the reform movement and its leaders. Loyalty led this intensely partisan Democrat to attempt to change the party from within rather than from outside the organization. On numerous occasions, however, he charted an independent course rather than follow conservative leadership. In addition, this investigation offers insights into the nature of

Illinois politics and facts about neglected aspects of the state's
history, especially the development of the Illinois waterway.
Rainey's successful rise from membership in Congress representing
a traditionally one-term district to the Speakership of the House
deserves closer scrutiny.

This biography of Henry T. (as he preferred to be called) has
been gleaned from a diversity of sources. Unfortunately, much of
the Rainey correspondence was lost over the years; however, a
collection filling twenty-six letter boxes is deposited in the
Manuscripts Division of the Library of Congress. Supporting manu-
script materials retained by his contemporaries have been consulted.
Likewise, the records of friends and foes in the Columbia Oral
History Project were examined. Rainey's public legislative beliefs
are expressed in the *Congressional Record* and related government
publications. An especially valuable source has been the record
preserved in his hometown newspapers, the Carrollton *Gazette*
(Democratic) and the Carrollton *Patriot* (Republican). Other
newspaper and periodical sources have supplemented the contemporary
coverage of his career. Autobiographies, memoirs, reminiscences,
and published works of his legislative colleagues have also been
useful sources of information in completing his story.

Today the term "politician" often conjures images of personal
corruption, political chicanery, blatant opportunism, or moral
decay. Politics is decried as a disreputable profession; political
history is denegrated as dull, insignificant, and meaningless. This
state of affairs is indefensible given the role of government in
our lives and the process of legislation by which policies are
formulated. From the insights of historians and social scientists
can come a better appreciation and understanding of the part played
by the politician and of the contribution made by the democratic
political process in fostering mankind's development in a civilized
society. Toward this goal, an analytic description of the Rainey
activities complements our knowledge of the nation's growth and
development in the first third of the twentieth century. The
sidelights into local and state history illuminate these microcosms
of our heritage in relation to national events. Congressman Rainey's
public service provides a perspective from which to examine the
political process from elections through issues to leadership roles.

Any study of this magnitude incurs an indebtedness to numerous
institutions and individuals, among them many libraries and librari-
ans. While the University of Illinois Library was the principal
center for this research, special thanks are also due to the staffs
at the Manuscripts Division of the Library of Congress, the Columbia
University Oral History Project, the Franklin D. Roosevelt Library,
the Herbert Hoover Presidential Library, and the Carrollton Public
Library. The Graduate College Research Board at the University
of Illinois-Urbana Campus provided research support, and the
extensive services of David R. Huehner and Vicki Ann Vogel are
acknowledged.

In the preparation of this biography I have incurred intellectual obligations to numerous teachers and colleagues. In
particular I wish to thank Professor Richard W. Hantke of Lake

Forest College for transmitting his love of history as a discipline
and Professor Clyde F. Snider of the University of Illinois for
transmitting has knowledge of social science concepts and political lore.

In its original form the study was undertaken as a dissertation
under the direction of Professor J. Leonard Bates. His care,
comments, and criticisms provided an invaluable guide. Thanks are
also due to Professor Robert M. Sutton, Director of the Illinois
History Survey, for imparting a love of Illinois history and
providing encouragement from conception to completion. The
support of the Board of Editors of the Illinois Studies in the
Social Sciences is greatly appreciated. Special thanks are due
my wife, Joan, who has shared me with Congressman Rainey for more
years than either of us would care to admit. Due recognition
should be accorded her unlimited understanding, enduring patience,
and constructive assistance. While acknowledging the contribution
of many friends, the author remains solely responsible for any
errors of fact or interpretation which may remain.

Robert A. Waller

Urbana, Illinois
December, 1976

NOTES

1. Dewey W. Grantham, Jr., "The Progressive Era," 227-251,
places the movement in its broad perspective, while Peter G. Filene,
"An Obituary for 'The Progressive Movement,'" 20-34, doubts that a
"movement" ever existed. Four sets of core values have been determined by G. Edward White, "The Social Values of the Progressives,"
62-76.

1

Sage of Walnut Hill

"I think I am in line for the Speakership and will be a candidate."[1]
With this terse announcement in November, 1932, Congressman
Henry T. Rainey of Illinois' twentieth district indicated his avail-
ability for this nation's third highest elective political office.
Although a veteran of twenty-eight years in the national legislature,
Henry T. was virtually unknown to the general public. The news
journals endeavored to familiarize readers with the colorful personality then occupying the post of majority leader for the Democrats
in the Seventy-second Congress and now aspiring to the position of
leadership for the entire House of Representatives.[2] The nation
did become better acquainted with this son of the Illinois prairie
whom reporters dubbed the Sage of Walnut Hall, an allusion to his
home and farm in Carrollton.

In his congressional service, Henry T. Rainey made a memorable
impression upon his constituents and colleagues, if not the general
public. In personal appearance he was a big man, standing over six
feet tall and weighing 275 pounds. He had wide shoulders topped by
a bull-like neck and a massive head crowned with tousled hair that
stuck out in all directions. A contemporary newspaper reporter
described him as having "a big, open, boyish face, with a tremen-
dously strong jaw, a generous mouth, firm but not thin lipped, fine
hazel eyes, deep set under dark eyebrows, full depth of the face
between the cheek bones and the well-formed ears, set rather far
back, and [a] somewhat small and upturned nose, which tells a tale
of inquisitiveness and pugnacity."[3] Flowing black bow ties were a
characteristic feature of his wearing apparel. In his later years
the mane turned silver and he acquired the habit of smoking a bulldog pipe. In conducting his affairs, Rainey commanded the respect
of the citizens in the twentieth district and the politicians in
Washington. His rural neighbors noted his friendliness and
hospitality at Walnut Hall, his concern and contribution to scientific agriculture, and his thoughtfulness and thoroughness in
meeting constituent needs.[4] In Congress he was known for his
kindness and courtesy to all regardless of political party or
station in life, for his conscientious and patient toil in behalf
of the common people, and for his aggressive and able advocacy
of popular government.[5]

Rainey's ability in persuasion contributed to his success with
agriculturalists and politicians. The greatest art, he believed,
was the gift of oratory, the ability to make an instantaneous

impression on the minds of men. He eschewed telling funny stories
because they allegedly detracted from the message in the address.
It was his belief that the listeners should be challenged with a
thesis which must be considered seriously before accepting or
rejecting it.[6] He spoke simply with a grammatical precision
befitting a student of the classics. His delivery was soft and
amiable, yet it had carrying power and was persuasive. On the floor
of the House he could be a formidable opponent—direct and quick in
attack, gifted in locating an opponent's weakness. The effectiveness of his formula is attested by his success on the Chautauqua
circuits, lyceum programs, and lecture platforms. With the advent
of radio as a force in politics, he was frequently called upon to
present party positions in well-modulated tones. In part his
legislative longevity was due to effective speaking in political
and public circles.

Rainey's philosophical bent was attuned to the reform ferment
at the turn of the century. When asked to express his philosophy of
life, he reportedly summarized it in simple fashion as service to
others. Early in his career, he urged upon youth the obligation
to search for progress as a duty to themselves, their parents, and
the state. At the close of his career, he persevered in this
dedication to public service saying: "I think any man who is worth
his salt feels that way. He has a sense of worth and achievement;
he establishes his self-respect only as his ambitions and efforts
are for the good of others."[7] The literature of the reform era is
replete with appeals for service, sacrifice, and love of mankind.
Unfortunately the congressman who practiced this belief so successfully did not provide posterity with a more precise description of
his personal and public philosophy.

An inquiry into Henry T. Rainey's background and early years
provides a microcosm of the broad generalizations made about the
origins of progressive leaders. Many of the characteristics attributed to early twentieth-century reformers are exhibited. Such
factors as family background, locale, education, occupation, religion, and interests contributed to an atmosphere conducive to reform
ideas.[8] In terms of heredity and environment Rainey was oriented
toward progressive concerns.

Rainey's pioneer stock was a part of this heritage. His
maternal grandfather, Samuel Thomas, was the first settler north
of Macoupin Creek in Greene County, Illinois. After the pacifica-
tion of the Indians following the Wood River Massacre in 1814 and
his marriage to Elizabeth Isley in 1816, Samuel Thomas decided to
make a home in this virgin territory. On November 9, 1818, about
a month before Illinois achieved official statehood, he established
a homestead amidst a beautiful grove near a clear spring, the
traditional frontier prerequisites for a prairie home. His posses-
sions included a rifle, an ax, a horse, and a wife—in that order
of importance according to community tradition. Here the Thomas
family prospered and multiplied. On May 3, 1838, Catherine (Kate)
M. Thomas, the youngest of twelve children, was born.[9]

The paternal grandfather, William C. Rainey, was also an early
settler in the Prairie State. At an early age he emigrated from

Pennsylvania to Kentucky, where he married Susan Clay. Among their eight children was John, who was born at Lexington on July 15, 1825.. Between 1831 and 1833 the Rainey family moved to the vicinity of Carrollton, Illinois (a struggling new community named for John Carroll of Carrollton, the bold signer of the Declaration of Independence). Grandfather Rainey served as an officer in the Mexican War of 1846 to 1848 and fought at Buena Vista. Subsequently he served in a South American army as a mercenary soldier. Family folklore maintains that he brought asparagus and rhubarb plants from the Amazon Valley and introduced them to the community.[10]

Both grandfathers transmitted to Henry T. Rainey a love of farming and an interest in politics. Samuel Thomas added to his original eighty acres of land and became one of the wealthy men of the county. He was widely known for his herds of fine cattle and was credited with initiating many new agricultural ideas. As a farmer and real estate dealer, William C. Rainey acquired extensive holdings of land northeast of Carrollton.[11] Politically Grandfather Thomas bequeathed a Democratic party heritage rooted in the principles of Andrew Jackson. "Major" Rainey was a leader in the community's Democratic political circles and frequently served as justice of the peace for the locality.

As a result of this sequence of events, the parents of Henry Rainey were raised in the Carrollton vicinity. Few details of the early life of John Rainey and Catherine Thomas are available. On September 9, 1859, the second child of William C. Rainey and the youngest daughter of Samuel Thomas were married. John Rainey farmed 226 acres about three miles from the city limits and speculated in real estate. An active participant in local government, he served intermittently as town trustee and city councilman. John Rainey died on April 15, 1887, and Kate Rainey on September 14, 1911.[12] She lived long enough to see her eldest son serve his first terms in Congress.

Henry Thomas Rainey was born on August 20, 1860. There followed a brother who was named William C. and a sister, Susie E. Unquestionably, Kate Rainey entertained the usual motherly aspirations for her oldest son, although it is not recorded that she beheld him as a future president.[13] Such a dream, if ever held, would reach the realm of possibility for at the pinnacle of his career he occupied the most important legislative position in the land.

The Speaker-to-be received his early education in the Carrollton public grade school and continued his academic pursuits in the newly built high school. The high school curriculum had just been reorganized and each student followed a rigid pattern of mathematics, science, history, and literature. The only option was the opportunity to substitute Latin or German in place of the equivalent English studies. Rainey took the English courses. He is listed among the nine members of the class of 1878, the fourth to be graduated.[14] At the time of graduation he was approaching his eighteenth birthday.

As was customary then, it was decided that he should attend an academy in order to prepare for college entrance. Knox Academy

at Galesburg was selected. After completion of this preparatory
year, it was natural that Rainey should continue at Knox College
in the same city. His freshman and sophomore years were spent on
the Siwash campus, as Knox is familiarly known. While attending
there, Rainey and his classmates became best known for their
extracurricular pursuits. Knox College tradition holds that no
class, before or since, has equaled the incorrigibles of '83 "in
class color, excess of animal spirits, nor in the ability,
amounting to positive genius, of disrupting the traditions, morale
and discipline of both the faculty and the student body of Knox
College."[15] This frolicsome approach to higher education and an
unsuccessful confrontation with the faculty concerning student
rights determined that one of Knox College's foremost alumni would
pursue his academic goals elsewhere.

One additional facet of Knox College life, however, left a
heavy impress upon Henry T. Rainey. Here he met Ellenora (Ella)
McBride, the future Mrs. Rainey, who was pursuing a degree in
education. She had been born in Princeton, Illinois, on December
7, 1860. At the time of her college attendance her parents,
William Henry and Mary Jane (Allen) McBride, were living in Wyanet.
She was a member of the class of 1880.[16] Between studies and
pranks, "Pete" (his college nickname) Rainey found time to woo and
win his bride-to-be. Following his completion of college and law
school, they were married. Ella McBride deserves attention in her
own right as a leading woman reformer and an influential helpmate.

The transfer of Rainey from Knox at the end of his sophomore
year was a foregone conclusion. He followed a number of his
acquaintances to Amherst College in Massachusetts. In his new
surroundings he was a serious student and devoted excess energies
to the more legitimate channels of athletics and public speaking.
A fellow classmate's recollection of Rainey will highlight the
difference between Knox and Amherst. Walter T. Field recalled
him as being "quiet, unassuming, earnest, and industrious." Field
also remembered that he was an excellent speaker and that friends
came naturally, although he did not seek them. That his classmates held him in high regard is suggested by his election to the
class office of historian, but he declined the honor. Later in
the year he was appointed to a committee to collect the class
statistics, and he did serve in this capacity.[17]

While at Amherst Rainey acquired an interest in athletics
which remained throughout his life. At the time he became a
leader of the Democratic Congresses in the 1930s, his collegiate
athletic prowess was brought to the nation's attention. Fifty
years after the events, the nation's press portrayed him as a
heavyweight boxing champion and a trackman able to run the
100 yard dash in ten and one-quarter seconds. The only verifi-
able evidence of his athletic abilities is the fact that he took
second place in a boxing exhibition held as a part of the
college's annual gymnasium program.[18] The exaggerations in later
life should not diminish the fact that he maintained an interest
in vigorous exercise. At the age of seventy he was still walking
the two miles to the House office building. His recreational

interests included an eight- to ten-mile hike on Sundays in the
woods or parks in the Washington area. Rainey justly deserved
his reputation for a robust constitution; he attributed his lifelong freedom from sickness to the habits of exercise acquired at
Amherst.

A half-century after graduation Henry Rainey singled out those
in the academic circles of Amherst who most influenced his later
life. He paid special tribute to President Julius H. Seelye's
high conception of duty and called it the most ideal example of
public service he had ever known. Seelye had served one term in
the House before becoming president of Amherst. Rainey credited
Professor Heman H. Neil with instilling the love of books and dis-
cernment in their selection which enabled him to build his own
private library at Walnut Hall. In a similar vein he praised the
Greek lectures of Professor Richard H. Mather as being instrumental
in developing art as a source of pleasure and discrimination.[19] It
was to these men that the national political figure attributed part
of his success.

The closing ceremonies for the Amherst class of 1883 included
a class-day ceremony at which the class prophecy was read. At the
fiftieth class reunion it was remembered that the observations were
especially clairvoyant with respect to Rainey, although they were
intended to be facetious at the time. It had been predicted that
"Pete" Rainey would become "a statesman and the popular champion of
the 'poor serving girl' who works ten hours 'amidst the rattle of
machinery, in the glare of the furnace.'"[20] In a limited fashion
this statement did provide a forecast of the kind of reform which
would engage Rainey in his political career. At the time of graduation, however, the attainment of a law degree was a more urgent
problem.

Following his graduation with a bachelor of arts degree, he
entered Union College of Law in Chicago, now Northwestern University
School of Law. He received a bachelor of law from that institution
in 1885. He is reported to have graduated as the valedictorian in
a class of forty-two. In 1886 Rainey received a master of arts
from Amherst. The candidate for such a degree obtained it by filing
a petition once he was a graduate of three years' standing and had
attended two years of professional training. After the completion
of law school, he was a successful candidate for admission to the
Illinois bar.[21] He then began the active practice of his profession
in Carrollton.

For the remainder of the nineteenth century, Henry T. Rainey's
professional contributions were as a community lawyer. Essentially
he conducted practice alone during the years before 1900. As was
true of many prairie lawyers, he served as the local attorney for
such railroad interests as the Chicago and Alton and the Chicago,
Burlington and Quincy, whose lines pass through Greene County. His
first major legal opportunity came in 1887 with his appointment as
master in chancery for Greene County. In this capacity, he was an
officer of the court assisting the judicial process by finding the
facts in a contested case and by executing the decisions rendered.
He retained this position for six years. He continued to practice

alone until 1900 when he formed an advantageous partnership with
Norman L. Jones, later to become chief justice of the Illinois
Supreme Court. This arrangement began a lifelong friendship and a
period of mutual help in advancing each other's political careers.[22]
Their practice together terminated officially in 1914 when Rainey's
duties as congressman and Jones's election to the circuit court
bench made their continued association impractical. Nevertheless,
their political reinforcement in local, state, and federal matters
continued.

The financial security afforded by a promising legal career
made possible Rainey's marriage to Ella McBride. By this time the
McBrides lived in Nebraska and the wedding took place in their home
at Harvard on June 27, 1888.[23]   Their first home was a small but
modern cottage on North Main Street in Carrollton. Throughout their
lifetime they made Carrollton their home, although they necessarily
had extensive stays in Washington. As Rainey's law practice expanded, the fees were directed toward two objectives—the gratification
of his boyhood ambition to purchase a farm and the indulgence of his
wife in her desire to help others less fortunate than she.[24]

In addition to legal matters, Henry T. devoted attention to
such community interests as the public schools, the local library,
and the farm community. During the academic year 1895-96, he was
president of Carrollton's board of education. The civic improvement with which most Carrolltonians immediately identify Rainey is
the public library. He is credited with originating the movement
creating the Carrollton Public Library, and he served as a member
of the board of directors from its inception on July 1, 1901, until
July 1, 1911. His most significant contribution was serving as
chairman of the finance committee in the protracted negotiations
for support from Andrew Carnegie. His lifelong interest in farming
was typified by his connection with the Greene County Fair Association. He, along with Leroy McFarland and S. E. Simpson, incorporated the organization in 1895. Rainey served as president for many
years, and when congressional duties forced him to decline the
presidency, he continued as a member of the board of directors.[25]
Such concern for all aspects of formal and informal education
proved to be an abiding interest throughout his career.

A natural bent for politics was reinforced by Rainey's
acquaintance with William Jennings Bryan prior to Bryan's move
from Jacksonville, Illinois, to Lincoln, Nebraska, in 1887. Their
early years offer numerous parallels. Bryan was born in Salem on
March 19, 1860, and then attended school in Jacksonville. Following graduation from Illinois College in 1881 and Union College of
Law in 1883, Bryan returned to Jacksonville to begin his professional practice.[26]   As a result of these circumstances the men were
friends, but the issue which brought them both prominence was free
silver. For Bryan it brought national attention as a presidential
candidate, and for Rainey it meant increased stature in local and
state politics. Under the leadership of Governor John Peter
Altgeld, the Democrats called a special state convention for the
sole purpose of passing free-silver resolutions. On June 5, 1895,
a group of 1,076 delegates gathered at Springfield to hear addresses

by party notables, among them Bryan. Rainey was a delegate from his congressional district. The convention adopted a resolution recommending a strong educational program for free silver and advocated independent action on sixteen to one regardless of the national party's stand. Rainey was among those selected to attend a national silver convention, but the proposed conference was never called.[27] Nevertheless, this baptism of fire marked the beginnings of Rainey's life work in politics.

Although the future congressman had been active previously in county Democratic circles, he now expanded his interest in political affairs. While attending the 1896 Republican national convention in St. Louis, as an observer, Rainey encountered Bryan in his capacity as a reporter for some Nebraska newspapers. Rainey also attended the Democratic convention in Chicago as an observer, but Bryan came as the head of a contesting free-silver delegation from Nebraska. Following Bryan's nomination after the Cross of Gold speech, Rainey worked hard for his election on the free-silver plank. He had been selected as the presidential elector from his congressional district, but the November election results prevented him from exercising that privilege in Bryan's behalf. In a lengthy letter to Bryan, Rainey expressed his disappointment but not discouragement over the defeat of the free-silver movement. It was the old story, he wrote, of "'right forever on the scaffold, wrong forever on the throne,' but in this case the scaffold sways the future as it never has before." Perennial optimist that he always was, Rainey noted the Democratic gains in Greene County and freely predicted that, with Bryan as the leader and free silver as the issue, the 1900 general election would reverse the outcome. Under the auspices of the Democratic national committee in that election, Rainey stumped the states of Ohio, Indiana, and Illinois in Bryan's behalf. Nevertheless, the popular verdict was the same. Rainey's letter of regret to the twice-defeated candidate received this reply: "I am gratiful [sic] to you for your work and your expressions of good will. We have made the best fight we could for principles which we believe to be American, and we must continue to do our duty as we see it, regardless of temporary reverses."[28] The issue of free silver was to lie dormant for a generation, but the other principles for which Bryan fought were to gain increasing attention from congressional candidate Rainey.

This interest in politics was shared by the future congressman's influential helpmate. In addition, Mrs. Rainey contributed an intense concern for a wide range of social service and philanthropic activities. Following her graduation from Knox College in 1880, she embarked upon a career of public service; it has been suggested that she was among the first to use the expression "social welfare."[29] Her activities at the local, state, and national levels exemplify this concern for the welfare of others.

At the local level, both Raineys were interested in promoting community clubs devoted to social and self-improvement. As founder and first president of the Ladies Mutual Improvement Club, she stressed literary refinement and social service activities. Another of the clubs in which she participated was the East End Reading Club

whose study included current events, education, literature, and
philanthropy. In founding the largest club in Carrollton, the
Art League, Mrs. Rainey fostered an appreciation for art and
architecture. As a result of these activities, she became involved
with the area Federation of Women's Clubs, serving as district
president in 1904 to 1905. In a seminal speech before the state
federation of this group, she urged that women's groups cease their
lobbying activities on behalf of legislative measures and focus
instead upon pre-election campaign promises extracted from candidates for public office.[30] Ultimately this became the strategy for
the prohibition forces and other pressure groups. Both Raineys
were active, he as president and she as secretary, in the University Extension Club. The only coeducational club of the Carrollton
community, it stimulated interest in educational advancement
through participation in University of Illinois extension courses.
Participation in such local groups as these by thousands of
individuals all over the nation made possible a ferment for reform
and the growth of a national progressive movement.

By the turn of the century, Mrs. Rainey's involvement with
programs of social welfare had gained statewide importance. As
secretary of the Illinois State Conference of Charities and Correc-
tions, she was in a position to promote her special interest in
the prevention and cure of juvenile delinquency. That organization's campaign reached fruition when the state legislature enacted
a law permitting the establishment of a home for delinquent boys at
St. Charles. Mrs. Rainey was appointed on July 19, 1902, by Governor
Richard Yates as a member of its board of trustees. Her appointment
was renewed by Governor Charles Deneen. She was the only woman on
the seven-member board. During her service she made a trip to
Europe to study similar institutions in France and Germany. Upon
her return she inaugurated a successful fight for the cottage system
of rehabilitation. Mrs. Rainey continued to serve on the board
until December 31, 1909, when an independent, centralized board was
established to supervise St. Charles School for Boys and the sixteen
other state charitable institutions.[31]

As the Rainey interests centered in Washington, she became
active in a number of philanthropic and social service organizations in that area. Among her friends she was known as a live wire
because of her boundless energies and great enthusiasm. Mrs. Rainey
was active in the National Civic Federation, in Neighborhood House
(a social settlement in Washington), and in Associated Charities
(an organization offering direct aid to the poor in the city of
Washington). Although the Raineys had no children of their own,
they were both intensely interested in children. She was a patron
to both the Boy and Girl Scout movements. In 1912 she served as
the first president of the Washington Council of Girl Scouts.
Questions relating to child labor, especially compulsory education,
were her pet interest. Trained as an educator, Ella was elected
national vice-president of the Mother's Congress, the predecessor of
the Parent-Teacher Association. As a result of these pursuits a
contemporary described Ella Rainey as "one of the really interesting
and certainly one of the most practical women in the congressional

circle."[32]

Mrs. Rainey carried her ideas of social uplift and her concept of democratic community into Washington society. As a charter member of the Woman's Congressional Club, she noted that the purposes of the club were "to make Congressional society less artificial, to enable members of Congress and their families to meet on a plane of absolute social equality, to make closer and pleasanter friendships than could otherwise exist, and to brighten up the dull monotony of official life and duties." The club helped democratize Washington's otherwise stratified social structure, and it still plays this role in the life of official Washington. Additionally, she was an officer in the Illinois State Society of Washington, a nonpolitical organization whose object was to foster and encourage a social and fraternal spirit among Illinoisans in the national capital.[33] She favored total abstention from alcoholic beverages and abhorred bridge as a waste of time. While fond of social life, she did not allow its distractions to warp her sense of practicality. The action was in the political arena.

From 1903 to 1934 Ella Rainey was inseparably associated with her husband's political career. During that time she officially served as his legislative and research secretary, thus reversing the usual procedure by first marrying him and then becoming his secretary. She helped handle his voluminous correspondence, met constituents and party leaders, and supervised a staff of secretaries and clerks. During the throes of the Great Depression, a frequent criticism directed at Congress was the charge of nepotism. Foremost among the critics of this practice was columnist Drew Pearson. In the case of the wife of the then Democratic majority leader, however, Pearson admitted that the money was well earned because Mrs. Rainey had a reputation as a hard and able worker. Senator Estes Kefauver subsequently cited the Raineys as one of the famous and successful congressional man-and-wife teams.[34] On numerous occasions Henry T. Rainey stated that the smartest move he ever made was marrying such a talented helpmate. Unquestionably she contributed a considerable measure to Rainey's political success. The triumph and recognition accorded her husband by his elevation to the Speakership was partly hers.

The Raineys' position in Washington society was greatly altered by his election as Speaker of the House. Before this they had lived simply and modestly in a small apartment on Sixteenth Street. Both worked long hours during a six-day week and avoided social commitments except on Sundays. Now they found themselves beckoned from the sidelines into the whirl of Washington society. In the social hierarchy only the President, Vice-president, and Chief Justice outranked them. Since the Roosevelts and Garners rarely went out, and Chief Justice and Mrs. Charles Evans Hughes only on Saturday nights, the Raineys faced a heavy load of receptions, teas, cocktail parties, and dinners. One arbiter of Washington society characterized the Speaker as "a wonderful department store Santa Claus with his white hair, rosy cheeks, comfortably upholstered figure, and benevolent but sleepy look." Mrs. Rainey was credited with supplying "most of the enthusiasm and ambition" for both of

them.[35]   Although the Raineys now lived at the Sheraton Park Hotel,
they continued an unpretentious existence in the newly opened social
world. These new social obligations did not interfere with their
long hours at an increasingly burdensome legislative task.

The embodiment of the Rainey philosophy when combined with
practice may be found in Walnut Hall, their country estate just east
of Carrollton. The farm received its name from the spreading, three-
story, red brick mansion with imposing white columns and solid black
walnut woodwork throughout the house. Its three large porches and
sixteen rooms, plus five in the basement, provided ample room for
the Raineys and their hobbies. In addition, it served as a mecca
for visiting delegations of Democratic politicians and the "plain
peepul." The Raineys had a tradition that whenever they were home
a flag flew from a ninety-foot pole in front of the house. This
was the signal that guests were most welcome.[36]   From the time the
Raineys bought the place in 1909, they endeavored to make it attractive for themselves and their neighbors.

As their principal hobby, the Rainey's began collecting antiques
with which to furnish Walnut Hall. Their home and grounds were an
antiquarian's delight. Of special note in the legislator's office
was a quaint, carved oak desk which had occupied a place on the
Senate floor as early as 1840. Another unique feature was a plaque
bearing the Great Seal of the United States which had hung on the
inaugural stand in 1933. One of Henry T.'s special hobbies was
collecting Currier and Ives prints. Some fifty of these covered
two sides of his bedroom. During the Great War, he had collected
the forty war posters issued by the government to stimulate patriotism. Henry T. took special pride in the library. It contained a
private collection of more than 2,800 volumes, which were utilized
as a circulating library among the farm boys in the area. The
dominant piece of furniture in this room was a mammoth desk once
used by Stephen A. Douglas, Rainey's political idol. As a part of
his library collection, Rainey kept a file of Douglas materials
which he had been able to accumulate over the years. Although the
"Little Giant" and the "Sage of Walnut Hall" were separated by a
lifetime in years, they were joined by a common heritage in the
Illinois country. Visitors to Walnut Hall were usually shown the
library and treated to some new Douglas anecdote which Rainey had
recently acquired.[37]

In keeping with the Rainey belief in recreational activities,
the surroundings near the main house were made equally attractive
through their industrious efforts. The spacious grounds were
devoted to park-like facilities which the Raineys made available
to the public, especially families and youth groups. The recreational facilities included a playground and wading pool for children,
a small golf course, tennis courts, bridle paths, and one lake for
swimming, another for boating and fishing. Also available were a
tea-house, a flower garden with fountains and statuary, and camping-
picnic grounds. An unusual feature of the park was a herd of
Japanese Sika-Siko (sacred) deer. The herd was bred from a buck
and two does originally obtained from the Washington zoo in exchange
for one porcupine.[38]   The Raineys and Walnut Hall were noted for a

gracious hospitality which was extended to the humble and great alike. Without benefit of an interior decorator or a landscape gardener, they had created a comfortable atmosphere in which to foster the better life for themselves and their neighbors.

For at least a generation historians have attempted to determine those characteristics which distinguished twentieth-century reformers from their conservative counterparts. This brief description of the Raineys provides a gauge against which to measure these historical generalizations. In terms of his middle-class family background, midwestern locale, college education, legal career, Protestant religion, and social service interests, Rainey fits the categorization of a typical progressive.[39] In his case these influences were reinforced by a wife who also filled the expected mold. Recently, however, these allegedly distinct and special characteristics have been seriously questioned. Biographical and statistical studies have revealed that most liberal reformers did not differ markedly from the standpat conservatives or the moderates when compared on such factors as age, origins, geographical distribution, occupation, education, religious and fraternal associations, and previous political affiliation and experience.[40]

Other theses have been advanced to explain the origins of an individual's progressivism. Among the most provocative is the "status revolution" hypothesis which attributes progressive political activities to man's notion of status anxiety.[41] Subsequent examination of the applicability of this explanation has cast doubt on its general validity in providing the rationale for the progressive movement.[42] Still other interpretations emphasize the nineteenth-century heritage in the continuance of the farmers' revolt,[43] the response of the urban-immigrant classes to modernization,[44] and the reaction of the business elites.[45] In the Rainey career these elements are decidedly missing as a major explanation for his progressive proclivities.

In searching for the foundation and motivation in Rainey's interest in reform measures, the traditional explanations are inadequate. This analysis suggests that the individual and the issues may deserve more attention in ascertaining an appropriate answer about his motivation in particular and progressivism in general. In Rainey's case, his religious convictions provide an ill-defined but significant role. An inquiry into religious affiliation at the turn of the century revealed that members of the Protestant Episcopal church supplied 21 percent of the social reform workers but constituted only 2 percent of the total population.[46] Reformers cannot operate in a vacuum and thus are influenced by the issues which arise with the advent of industrialization and urbanization. Likewise, they cannot operate effectively without community acquiescence or endorsement.[47] Thus, it is necessary to investigate the political arena in which Rainey operated, the major legislative issues with which he became involved, and the leadership roles which he came to occupy. An investigation into this triumvirate of concerns will facilitate a judgment on the public service career of the Sage of Walnut Hall.

NOTES

1. Washington *Post*, Nov. 17, 1932, 1:2.

2. *Time*, XX (Dec. 19, 1932), front cover and 8-10; *Newsweek*, I (March 11, 1933), 10.

3. Henry N. Hall, St. Louis *Post Dispatch* Washington correspondent, in the Carrollton *Gazette*, May 22, 1933, 1:3 (hereafter cited as the *Gazette*).

4. W. F. Hardy, "'Mr. Speaker' as the Country Squire," 1.

5. *Memorial Services . . . of Henry T. Rainey*, *passim*.

6. His philosophy of public speaking is most clearly outlined in Carrollton *Patriot*, Dec. 6, 1923, 1:1 (hereafter cited as the *Patriot*).

7. Commencement address in *Patriot*, June 2, 1905, 1:1; *Memorial Services . . . Henry T. Rainey*, 39.

8. See George E. Mowry, *The California Progressives*, esp. 86-104.

9. *Atlas Map of Greene County*, 23, 26.

10. *History of Greene County*, 321, 494; Miss Mary K. Rainey, Detroit, Nov. 16, 1962, to the author.

11. *Atlas Map of Greene County*, 26, 44; *Plat Book of Greene and Jersey Counties*, 53.

12. *History of Greene County*, 338, 494-495; *American Biography*, 156; *Gazette*, Sept. 14, 1911, 1:5, and Sept. 21, 1911, 1:4; *Patriot*, Sept. 14, 1911, 1:1.

13. Ethel Thomas Barnes to Henry T. Rainey (hereafter the abbreviation HTR will be used in the footnotes), Chicago, March 12, 1934, in the Rainey Papers (hereafter abbreviated RP). (Unless otherwise indicated, all references to the RP will be in the regular chronological file rather than in a subject file.)

14. *History of Greene County*, 333-334, 344.

15. For further detail concerning these activities consult Chapter 1, "The Saga of the Class of 1883," by Thomas Gold Frost, *Tales from the Siwash Campus*.

16. Agness G. Gilman and Gertrude M. Gilman, *Who's Who in Illinois, Women-Makers of History*, 194; Durward Howes (ed.), *American Women*, 557-558; and Winfield S. Downs (ed.), *Encyclopedia of American Biography*, 35-36.

17. Walter T. Field, "The Amherst Illustrious: Speaker Rainey," 23; *Amherst Student*, XVI (Oct. 14, 1882), 37; (Feb. 10, 1883), 119; and (June 26, 1883), 234.

18. *Amherst Student*, XVI (May 19, 1883), 186, and a scrapbook entry under the date of May 16, 1883, giving the results of the sparring exhibition. The latter information was supplied by E.

Porter Dickinson (Reference Librarian), Amherst, May 22, 1963, to the author.

19. HTR quoted and paraphrased by Allen T. Treadway, "The Amherst Illustrious: The Congressional Leaders—Rainey, '83 and Snell, '94," 210-211.

20. Prophecy from the Class Book as quoted by Field, "The Amherst Illustrious," 23.

21. Charles O. Paullin, "Henry Thomas Rainey," 617; no present records verify the class rank according to Prof. Kurt Schwerin, Librarian of Northwestern University School of Law, Chicago, May 6, 1970, to the author; MA requirements as listed in *Amherst College Catalogue of 1885-1886*, furnished by E. Porter Dickinson, Amherst, May 31, 1963, in a letter to the author.

22. John M. Palmer (ed.), *The Bench and Bar of Illinois*, II, 1113-14; Ed Miner, *Past and Present of Greene County*, 260-262.

23. There is considerable confusion about the date of their marriage. Various biographical sketches place it between June, 1887, and June, 1889. The date given appears in the *Marriage Records for Clay County, Nebraska*, Book 3, page 364, as attested by County Judge Lisle Hanna, Clay Center, Neb., May 10, 1963, in a letter to the author.

24. Doris B. Whitney, "Highlights in the Career of the Late Speaker of the House, Henry T. Rainey" (carbon copy of typescript in Carrollton Public Library, dated Oct. 23, 1951), 1.

25. Miner, *Past and Present of Greene County*, 262; "The Minutes of the Directors of the Public Library and Reading Room of the City of Carrollton, Illinois," 2-112, 202-203; for fair association information see *Gazette*, Nov. 13, 1913, 1:4; July 22, 1914, 1:3; and Nov. 24, 1915, 2:4.

26. Reminiscences expressed in a speech delivered at a dinner of the Bryan National Memorial Association in Lincoln, Neb., on March 19, 1926, as printed in *Congressional Record* (hereafter cited as *CR*), 69:1 (March 18, 1926), 5865 (hereafter these remarks will be cited as Rainey's Bryan Memorial Speech).

27. Chicago *Tribune*, June 5, 1895, 1:7 and 2:1-7; June 6, 1:7, 2:1-7, and 3:1-5; and June 7, 2:3-4. See also Charles R. Tuttle, *Illinois Currency Convention*, 80-81; Harvey Wish, "John Peter Altgeld and the Background of the Campaign of 1896," 506-510.

28. Rainey's Bryan Memorial Speech in *CR*, 69:1 (March 18, 1926), 5866; HTR to Bryan, Carrollton, Nov. 6, 1896, in Bryan Papers, Box 9; Bryan to HTR, Lincoln, Neb., Dec. 1, 1900, as published in *Gazette*, Dec. 7, 1900, 1:3.

29. AP writer Sigrid Arne in the Cincinnati *Times-Star* of March 23, as quoted by *Gazette*, March 30, 1933, 1:6.

30. As reported in *Patriot*, Oct. 20, 1905, 4:3.

31.   John W. Cook, *Educational History of Illinois*, 512–513.

32.   Isabel Joyce, "Women of the Democracy," 78.

33.   Mrs. HTR, "The Women's Congressional Club," 265–271; O. F. James, "The Illinois State Society of Washington, D.C.," 569–570.

34.   [Drew Pearson], *More Merry-Go-Round*, 417, 431–432; Estes Kefauver and Jack Levin, *A Twentieth-Century Congress*, 215–216.

35.   Vera Bloom, *There's No Place Like Washington*, 95–98.

36.   W. F. Hardy, "'Mr. Speaker' as the Country Squire," 1, 3; John Drury, *Old Illinois Houses*, 44–45.

37.   An excellent description of this facet of the Rainey life may be found in an eight-page letter from HTR to W. P. Miller, Washington, May 8, 1924, in RP, "McNary Haughen" file.

38.   Federal Writers' Project, *Illinois: A Descriptive and Historical Guide*, 484.

39.   George E. Mowry, *The California Progressives*, Chap. 4, and his *The Era of Theodore Roosevelt, 1900–1912*, 85–105; Alfred E. Chandler, Jr., "The Origins of Progressive Leadership" in Elting E. Morison (ed.), *The Letters of Theodore Roosevelt*, VIII, Appendix III, 1462–65.

40.   E. Daniel Potts, "The Progressive Profile in Iowa," 257–268; Jack Tager, "Progressives, Conservatives, and the Theory of the Status Revolution," 162–175.

41.   Richard Hofstadter, *The Age of Reform*, Chap. 4, "The Status Revolution and Progressive Leaders," 131–172.

42.   Richard B. Sherman, "The Status Revolution and Massachusetts Progressive Leadership," 59–65.

43.   John D. Hicks, *The Populist Revolt*, 404–423; Mowry, *The Era of Theodore Roosevelt*, 3–35.

44.   J. Joseph Huthmacher, "Urban Liberalism and the Age of Reform," 231–241; John D. Buenker, "The New-Stock Politicians of 1912," 35–52.

45.   Samuel P. Hays, "The Politics of Reform in Municipal Government in the Progressive Era," 157–169; James Weinstein, "Organized Business and the City Commission and Manager Movements," 166–182.

46.   W. D. P. Bliss, "The Church and Social Reform Workers," 123–124.

47.   For suggestive treatment of this inquiry model see David P. Thelen, "Social Tensions and the Origins of Progressivism," 323–341. Superb overviews of interpretations of the progressive movement may be found in William G. Anderson, "Progressivism: An Historiographical Essay," 427–452, and David M. Kennedy, "Overview: The Progressive Era," 453–468.

2

A "Little Giant" in Local Politics

The length of Henry T. Rainey's congressional tenure provides an
unusual opportunity for insight into American political history
because it allows examination of the electoral process from local,
state, and national perspectives. When a member of the House of
Representatives goes to Washington, he represents himself, his
constituents, and his party. More than any other elected public
official, a member of the lower house of Congress must address himself to this triumvirate of concerns. This aggregation of influences
plus the biennial obeisance of the congressman to his electorate
enables the investigator to integrate the local political problems
with state and national developments for a better understanding of
all three. In Rainey's case the task was compounded because he so
frequently bore the burden of representing the minority party. His
term of service includes the administration of seven Presidents of
the United States, only two of whom were Democrats, and seven
Governors of Illinois, again only two of whom were members of his
party. This chapter places emphasis upon the local scene during
the first third of his career, with sidelights into state and
national affairs.

In responding to these challenges, Rainey's political model
was Stephen A. Douglas, the "Little Giant" of the Illinois prairies.
In addition to representing the same general geographic area in the
national legislature, Rainey took philosophic pride in emulating
the principles of popular democracy in which Douglas believed. In
supporting the resurgence of interest in Douglas, it was Rainey's
wish that "some day we can honor Douglas in this country without
detracting from the position Lincoln occupies and must always
occupy. They will rank throughout time as two of our greatest
citizens and statesmen." To a fellow Douglas fancier, Rainey wrote
that the country and the world were "just beginning to appreciate
his great career and the great service he rendered his country."[1]
The parallels in the careers of Douglas and Rainey were not lost on
newspaper editors, for Henry T. was occasionally described as the
area's twentieth-century version of the "Little Giant."

Regardless of the example to be followed, the ability of a
particular individual to maintain himself in office is partially
dependent upon two major considerations almost wholly outside his
control. These factors are the geographic integrity of the district
and the partisan inclinations of the constituency.[2] Henry T. Rainey
was fortunate in both of these elements.

Throughout his career the boundary lines for the twentieth
congressional district remained unchanged. Following the census

in 1900 the Illinois legislature reapportioned the state so that
Greene County was included in a ten-county district along the Illinois
River valley. In spite of a state constitutional mandate that redistricting be accomplished every decade, this was the last effective
reapportionment for the next half-century. Rural fear of urban
domination precluded any changes by the Illinois General Assembly.[3]
After the 1910 census the membership in the House of Representatives
was increased from 391 to 435 members. The size of the Illinois
delegation was increased from twenty-five to twenty-seven, but
redistricting was avoided by electing two members at large. The
state constitutional convention of 1920 proposed to resolve the
apportionment imbalance, but the voters rejected the new document
in November, 1922. Following the 1930 census, the legislature
reapportioned the state into twenty-seven districts, but the Illinois
Supreme Court ruled the changes unconstitutional. The congressional
district boundaries returned to the lines drawn in 1901 and there
the matter rested until the 1950s.[4] Rainey exploited this geographic
integrity to the fullest in his three and one-half decades of
electioneering.

Equally significant for his longevity were the Democratic
political inclinations of his constituency. The party of Jefferson
and Jackson could expect 55 percent of the two-party vote at most
elections, and thus the area was deemed a safe rather than a swing
district. The popular conception of Illinois politics envisions a
Democratic and metropolitan Chicago arrayed against a Republican
and rural/suburban downstate. This misconception fails to account
for the diversity of politics within the state. The rural areas show
varying portions of Democratic-Republican strength roughly relating
to the sectional origins of settlement. The southern portion of·
the state is inclined to favor Democracy while the northern half,
excepting Chicago, remains staunchly Republican under even the most
adverse political conditions. A study of twentieth-century voting
trends reveals the pervasiveness of tradition in determining voting
patterns even though the state's population doubled, women were
granted the right to vote, and mass communication offered everyone
the opportunity for information. Because of the migration patterns
from the South, Democratic candidates tended to poll well in the
middle and lower courses of the Illinois River.[5] As an illustration
of this point, Greene County had returned a Democratic presidential
majority in every quadrennial election of its history until the
Herbert Hoover landslide of 1928. Such a sinecure was almost without
precedent outside the Solid South. Subsequent events suggest that
this relative political security enabled Rainey to pursue a policy
of congressional liberalism with considerable independence.

As a result of these fortuitous circumstances, the Democratic
congressional nomination in the twentieth district was a highly
coveted prize. Initially, Rainey's efforts to become the nominee
were frustrated. It was the custom for each county to present a
favorite-son candidate and then come to an agreement at a district
convention. The honor was passed around so that no incumbent
served consecutive terms. Rainey tried for the county endorsement
in 1894 but was defeated. In 1896 and 1898 he received the primary

endorsement from Greene County's Democrats, but neither of these
campaigns proved to be serious bids in the district as a whole.
A more concerted effort was made in 1900, and it was crowned with
success in 1902.

The eight counties comprising the district in 1900 each presented
a favorite-son candidate for nomination. Rainey chose not to alienate
other contenders by campaigning in their counties. He was unopposed
in the Greene County primary and thus carried the county's eleven
votes to the congressional convention in Jacksonville. Because
Greene County had not received the nomination since 1856, the Rainey
supporters were optimistic that this recognition would now be
afforded them. Thirty-seven votes were needed to nominate a candidate. After four days of voting and a total of 824 ballots, the
convention appeared to be hopelessly deadlocked. On the fifth day,
according to the correspondent for the St. Louis *Republic*, the
Rainey forces arranged a deal whereby a combination of votes would
provide him with the victory margin. Congressman William Elza
Williams became aware of the arrangement and moved for adjournment
in order to prevent the nomination. The Jersey County delegation,
a party to the Rainey deal, then accidentally (or purposely) voted
for the adjournment motion and the Rainey opportunity for nomination
was reduced.[6] After 971 ballots the delegates could only resolve to
meet again for another round of deliberations.

When the convention reconvened, 400 Greene County folks visited
Jacksonville in order to "'root' for Rainey," but their presence only
broke the monotony of the proceedings. After 2,095 ballots, the
impasse was still unresolved. Candidate Rainey had shown his maximum strength to be 33 votes, four shy of the required number because
the votes promised from Jersey County were not delivered. On the
2,452nd ballot, a Rainey-inspired combination secured the nomination
for Thomas Jefferson Selby, a state's attorney and dark-horse candidate from Calhoun County. Although the Greene County delegation had
not been able to secure the nomination for their candidate, they
retained the good will of the contesting delegations. In a letter
of thanks solidifying the support he had received, Rainey paid
special attention to the disenfranchised women by writing: "I feel
particularly grateful to the ladies . . . and I feel that with such
fair adherents I ought to have been successful."[7] Once women
attained the right to vote, there is little doubt that the handsome
Rainey capitalized on his physical attractiveness to women in
establishing his electoral domain. In spite of the defeat of 1900,
Rainey attempted to lay the groundwork for a successful convention
fight in subsequent years.

As the time for the next biennial donnybrook drew near, the
political ground rules were changed slightly. During the county
nominating primaries the Australian or secret ballot was used for
the first time throughout the state. Also, the Illinois General
Assembly had reapportioned the state by redrawing district lines
and renumbering the areas. There were ten counties included in
the new twentieth district. Although Rainey encountered opposition
within Greene County for the favorite-son status, his primary
victory was convincing. The formidable district convention was a

greater obstacle. Negotiation between rival county claimants pre-
ceded the district convention in Jacksonville. The Calhoun delegation to whom Rainey had yielded two years previously figured
prominently in the final balloting in his behalf. In addition to
this return favor, the Jacksonville *Journal* noted that the successful combination involved deals concerning support for judicial
candidates, members of the state board of equalization, and state
legislative positions.[8] During the early evening of the second day
at the 257th ballot and on his forty-second birthday, Henry T. Rainey
had virtually achieved his political objective of a seat in Congress.

Rainey immediately let it be known that he did not intend to
be bound by the one-term tradition in existence since the Civil War.
At a victory rally he told a crowd of well-wishers that it might be
the disposition of the district to elect him for a series of terms.
Among the editorials supporting him after the nomination, there was
frequent mention of eliminating the "one terming," as it was called.
The Jacksonville *Courier* put it this way: "no one expects fruit
from a tree the first year it is planted. And so it is with a
member of congress if he is to do good work--he must have time to
get rooted in the congressional orchard before we have any right to
look for good results."[9] Rainey's success came at a fortuitous time
since opposition to deadlocked conventions and rotation of offices
was developing. These concerns were revived two years from then
when both traditions were permanently shattered.

After the campaign for the nomination was successfully concluded, the canvass for election was anticlimatic. In making more
than fifty speeches throughout the district, Rainey focused upon
three issues: anti-imperialism, anti-militarism, and Republican
incompetency (topics reminiscent of Bryan's 1900 platform). His
election bid was not seriously contested by the Republican candidate,
James H. Danskin. As became customary before general elections, the
Democratic *Gazette* gave Republican readers very explicit instructions
about voting a split ticket. Rainey's success in gathering support
from Republican ranks contributed to his political longevity. He
outpolled Danskin by a 2 to 1 margin in Greene County while his
two-party majority in the district was 5,000-plus votes. The 642
votes cast for the Prohibition candidate were indicative of a
significant trend which would bear watching. Rainey ran substantially stronger in his congressional district than the rest of the
Democratic ticket.[10] His ability to provide coattails for the
regular ticket was pronounced throughout the Rainey years. This
election victory in 1902 marked the beginning of a long and successful political career.

The twentieth congressional district would occupy much of
Rainey's attention in the next three decades. His interests often
stemmed from those of "his people" back home. The ten counties
included Brown, Calhoun, Cass, Greene, Jersey, Mason, Menard, Morgan,
Pike, and Scott (see accompanying map). This district extends along
both sides of the Illinois River from below Peoria to near Alton.
A portion of the boundaries of all the counties except Menard are
formed along this river. In addition, Calhoun, Pike, and Jersey
have a common boundary with the Mississippi River. The special

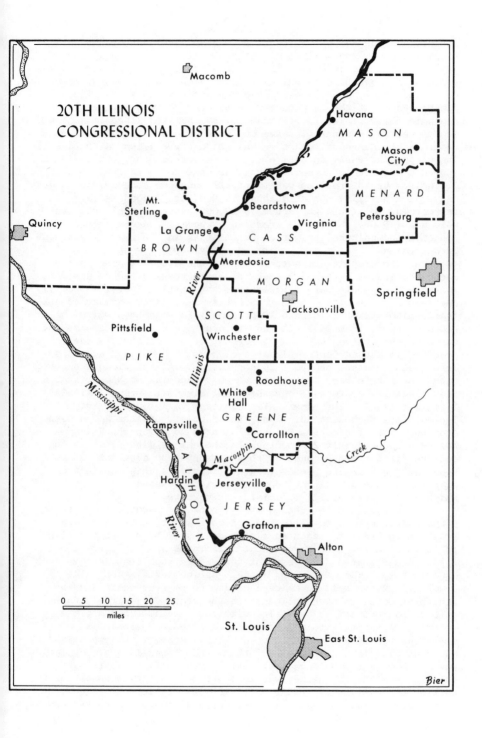

20TH ILLINOIS
CONGRESSIONAL DISTRICT

attention which Rainey was to give to such river matters as navigation, flooding, and pollution came naturally. The principal occupation of the region was farming. An adequate rainfall and growing
season made possible the cultivation of such crops as corn, wheat,
oats, and fruit, and the pasturage for a dairy industry. The per-
capita wealth of the area tended to be average or below on most
economic scales. The farms tended to be isolated since less than
10 percent in 1930 were located on "hard" roads. Except for the
railroad brotherhoods, union organizations were alien to the district.
Throughout the early decades of the twentieth century, this district
showed a decline in population such as came to characterize southern
Illinois. Urban problems were virtually unknown because the largest
city, Jacksonville, was only about 15,000, the second largest,
Beardstown, fell into the 5,000 to 10,000 class, and all the rest
were under 5,000.[11] The congressman's special concern for the
economic and cultural plight of rural areas in the 1920s was almost
predetermined.

The demographic characteristics of the district also influenced the issues with which the area's congressman had to deal. By
ancestry the people were largely from the British Isles; especially
numerous were the Irish. In 1900 German immigrants were an identi-
fiable minority of less than 10 percent. Foreign-born whites of the
new migrations from southern and eastern Europe at the turn of the
century constituted less than 4 percent of the total. Negroes,
pocketed in Menard County almost exclusively, comprised slightly
less than 1 percent of the 1920 population. Almost without exception, the forefathers of the native white population had emigrated
from Virginia, Kentucky, Tennessee, and Missouri during Illinois'
formative years. The numerically dominant religious elements
included the Methodist Episcopal, the Baptist, and the Roman Catholic
churches. The Protestant Episcopal church to which the Raineys
belonged counted only 200 members in the entire district. Throughout the first three decades of this century, the district was resoundingly dry in its prohibition sentiment.[12] This combination
of physical and social environment provided constraints within
which any elected public official must operate.

The predominantly rural complexion of the twentieth congressional district did not preclude interest in urban problems and
programs in order to reach an accommodation. The nature of Illinois
politics with its Chicago-downstate cleavages and its rural-urban
splits necessitated an adjustment to some metropolitan desires such
as home rule, labor laws, and social justice legislation. The
Democratic stronghold in Chicago needed to be courted if a downstater expected to have influence in the state capital. In Rainey's
case he was primarily identified with the federal crowd and the
reformist minority within state party circles. While it was a
matter of political convenience for him to support welfare measures
aimed at alleviating problems of the metropolitan masses, conviction
was an important consideration. Unlike many of the liberals of
the Progressive era, Rainey was more attuned to the needs of the
working classes.[13] As traditional with Democratic politicians, he
stressed such issues as taxes, tariffs, and trusts which transcended

specific constituent interests. The course of Rainey's legislative
career was determined by this combination of geographic circumstances,
economic foundations, national origins, religious opinions, political
options, and private convictions.

Biennially a member of the House of Representatives is required
to subject his management of these forces to the electorate. Under
the lame-duck system the first-term congressman operated with a
severe handicap. He had barely been sitting in Congress a few months
when the party members were expected to pass upon his bid for renomination and the electorate upon his request for re-election. Because
of the one-term tradition in his district, Rainey's initial hold on
his congressional seat was especially tenuous. As an indication of
his conscientious attention to duty, Rainey made a trip to Washington
before the term began so that he might familiarize himself with the
routine of congressional work. While Rainey was establishing a
record of service and a promise of continued performance, newspapers
in the district were criticizing the tradition of rotating the
office. As Washington correspondent for the Montgomery *News* and the
Edwardsville *Intelligencer*, Clint Bliss decried the notion that the
congressional seat was a political sinecure to be passed among the
county war horses. After praising Rainey's brief stint, Bliss concluded that it would be foolish for the party to abandon him in view
of the services he could perform if his term were continuous.[14]
Similar expressions may be found in other newspapers in the district,
but the attitude of the politicos in the district nominating convention was unknown.

The district's congressional convention of 1904 provided a
sharp contrast to the political orgies of the preceding years.
Rainey was unanimously endorsed by the Greene County Democratic
Central Committee and his name was placed in nomination by the
convention chairman, J. M. Riggs of Scott County. Ex-Congressman
William Elza Williams of Pike County seconded the nomination and
this was the signal for other county favorite sons to withdraw in
favor of a unanimous ballot for Rainey. A first-ballot nomination
represented both a radical departure in the deadlock district and
a compliment to the fledgling congressman's political savvy. In
another show of Rainey strength, the convention adopted a resolution
favoring a district-wide primary to select future congressional
candidates. While the three least populous counties opposed this
procedure as a dilution of their influence, the Rainey-supported
measure permitting complete popular participation in the nomination
process was approved by a vote of 44 to 32.[15] Once the party
nomination and electoral reform were secured, Rainey relied chiefly
upon the customary Democratic plurality to assure election, but
this was nearly a fatal mistake in 1904.

The results provided Rainey's narrowest margin of victory in
his fifteen successful campaigns. Although Rainey lost only two
counties in the district, the margins in the other eight were so
slight that he had a majority of only 1,642 votes in the major party
balloting. The Prohibitionist candidate showed increasing
strength.[16] The closeness of this contest would not be forgotten;
it would be some time before he allowed the district to shift for

itself without his personal attention. Carter H. Harrison, former
mayor of Chicago and political ally of Rainey in state politics,
recalled that Rainey "eked out" a scant victory in an overwhelmingly
Democratic district. Henry T. himself subsequently described the
situation as one in which he barely survived.[17] Admidst the general
popularity of the Republican President, Theodore Roosevelt, Henry
T. Rainey was the only remaining member of what had been a seven-man
Illinois Democratic congressional delegation. This rather unusual
circumstance was an asset to Rainey's career for it focused attention
on him. Many were interested in what Illinois' lone Democrat thought
on legislative issues and political questions.

Although renomination and re-election in 1906 seemed pre-ordained,
Roosevelt's popularity had made serious political inroads in the
district. Democratic opinion became solidly entrenched behind Rainey
when potential candidate and former Congressman Williams announced
that he would not oppose the incumbent. In his letter of declination
Williams attributed his decision to the favorable sentiment toward
Rainey and the desire not to interfere with the accomplishment of
Rainey's deep waterway proposals. Except for the formalities of a
district-wide primary ballot and an endorsement from the congressional
convention, the renomination campaign was ended. Following a roll
call of county delegations making the nomination unanimous, Rainey
made an acceptance speech calling for common honesty within and
without the party. He announced his unalterable opposition to ship
subsidies and campaign contributions by corporations and his unflag-
ging support of a tariff for revenue only, an eight-hour day, and a
lakes-to-gulf deep waterway.[18] These were the planks in the personal
platform on which he based his campaign for re-election.

The first use of the district-wide primary ballot had demonstrated an apathy on the part of Democratic voters. In order to
stimulate interest in the campaign, William Jennings Bryan responded
favorably to Rainey's request for assistance. Bryan's influence was
especially great in this district because he had attended preparatory
school and college in Jacksonville. His early law practice there
had acquainted him with much of the area. Because of Bryan's feud
with Roger Sullivan, the Illinois party boss, Rainey's district was
only one of two in the state where Bryan would make personal appear-
ances in behalf of candidates. At Pittsfield, Jacksonville, and
Carrollton in mid-October, the Great Commoner launched the re-election
campaign. Bryan provided a strong endorsement of Rainey and argued
that President Roosevelt's popularity had been gained by adopting
Democratic principles. Subsequently, Bryan used the pages of his
journal of opinion, the *Commoner*, to indicate that the Illinoisan
deserved support because of his vigorous opposition to trusts, his
favorable views on labor, and his admirable river improvement
program.[19]

After this advice, the decision was in the hands of the people.
In the district Rainey carried every county and had a comfortable
5,000-vote margin over his Republican opponent, Jacob G. Pope, who
had campaigned on the hope that the farmers' interests in Washington
would be better served if he were elected.[20] The electorate did
not accept this argument. The strategy of combatting the apathy so

common to off-year elections by bringing Bryan into the district
had been fruitful. The voters had renewed Rainey's legislative
life.

1908 was an unusual election year for Carrollton's "Little
Giant" because he became engaged in a severe primary battle. At
first it seemed that he would again be unopposed for the nomination.
Part of Rainey's electoral success stemmed from his judicious treatment of war veterans and their widows. Certainly it was more than
coincidence that his first and long-time private secretary was
Sam Murdock, an ex-soldier who was active in the affairs of the
Grand Army of the Republic. The renomination campaign was inaugurated by resolutions from local GAR posts praising Rainey's untir-
ing efforts in behalf of old soldiers.[21] The illusion of a constituency satisfied with Rainey's performance of personal tasks
was shattered in late May by notice that there was to be a contest
for renomination.

Former Congressman William Elza Williams announced his
candidacy by issuing a broadside containing a series of charges
against Rainey. Williams had withdrawn from the 1906 primary in
the interest of waterway legislation, but this time his candidacy
meant a no-holds-barred contest. The Williams indictment charged
that Rainey was falsely representing himself as the champion of a
deep waterway when the credit should go to Williams. Williams also
wished to claim credit for favoring Jacksonville with a public
building, a political euphemism for a post office. He accused
Rainey of voting for the "mileage grab" of the Fifty-ninth Congress
and for salary increases to congressmen. The last assertion was
that Rainey did not enjoy the favor of the *Commoner* and thus of
William Jennings Bryan.[22] This arraignment served as Williams's
public declaration of the basis for his opposition to Rainey's
renomination.

With characteristic thoroughness and a wealth of documentation,
Rainey proceeded to demolish each of Williams's allegations. He
candidly admitted that little had been accomplished toward the deep
waterway but thought that even the bitterest of enemies would give
him credit for trying. He asserted that he never posed as the
originator of the deep waterway idea but merely as an aid to its
growth and development. Rainey categorically denied that Williams
had ever introduced bills giving him claim to the title of deep
waterway advocate. The incumbent proved that the credit for the
Jacksonville post office went to a former representative, Thomas
Jefferson Selby; Rainey said he never claimed the credit for himself. While admitting that he had voted for the so-called "mileage
grab," he suggested that the line of argument applied to others,
not himself, because he had actually gone home toward the end of
the second session and returned to Washington in time for the
opening of the new session. He flatly denied voting for the salary
increases. Rainey accused Williams of garbling the *Commoner*'s
position and cited several instances of complimentary notices from
the paper. Henry T. categorically stated he would never again under
any circumstances be a candidate for Congress if Bryan refused his
approval.[23] With but one addition, these charges and countercharges

formed the basis of the appeal of both candidates to the party
faithful.

About a month before the primary balloting, Williams introduced his final thrust. He urged that it was time to switch horses because Rainey had been in Congress long enough. It was time for a change and that change, of course, was William Elza Williams. Rainey easily countered this argument by quoting from one of Williams's few remarks while in Congress. Williams had said that his district was in the unfortunate habit of swapping horses every two years and thus did not get its fair share of pension benefits.[24] Rainey needed no more assistance than the opposition's own words to blunt that line of attack.

Rainey's thirty-year public career is singularly free from any taint of corruption or malfeasance in office. The single exception to that statement concerns the "mileage grab" charge. The Fifty-eighth Congress ended at twelve o'clock noon on March 4, 1905. The subsequent Congress began on exactly the same hour of the same day. Nevertheless, the House included in the general deficiency appropriation bill an item appropriating $190,000 to pay mileage to senators and representatives for their journeys home and back during Theodore Roosevelt's "constructive recess." Rainey was among the House majority favoring the bill, but the Senate did not approve the measure, so it never became law. At the time *Collier's* drew attention to the disgrace and placed Rainey's name on "The Mileage Roll of Dishonor." The Chicago *Tribune* and the Chicago *Record-Herald* deplored this disheartening raid on the treasury and publicized the names of the offenders. In 1906 when Henry T. was part of a good government group endeavoring to reform Democratic state politics, Chicago boss Roger Sullivan taunted him as the "mileage steal" congressman. The matter was a campaign issue in 1908, and as late as 1910 Rainey was still being chastised for that vote.[25] While his explanation for voting the way he did seems plausible, it would have been more prudent to forego the ten cents per mile. Even so, this mistake is in marked contrast to such legislative scandals as that associated with William Lorimer's election to the United States Senate in 1909.

The "mileage grab" issue paled in the primary beside the broader question of the arrogance of certain corporations in conducting business. The Rainey-Williams primary fight drew national attention because the incumbent was represented as the staunch opponent of these predatory interests. In noting certain overtones in the intraparty struggle, Louis F. Post of the Chicago *Public* stated that Rainey's antitrust record had inspired an effort to defeat him in the primaries. The editor specifically named the Waltham Watch Company and the Standard Oil Company as being desirous of his defeat. The Johnston (Pa.) *Daily Democrat* endeavored to convey the East's interest in the affair by observing "you never hear of money being spent by [the] thousands to unhorse a congressman who gives a fine impression of being a knot on a log." In like manner the El Paso (Tex.) *News* attributed the strenuous effort to defeat him to a plutocracy composed of the watch, beef, and oil trusts.[26] Though it would be difficult to prove, there is a haunting suspicion that some business interests actually were working actively for Rainey's political demise. Whether this was the primary motivating factor in the Williams candidacy is beyond the evidence available.

At the district level the political pace quickened as the August primary approached. There was a preponderance of editorial support in behalf of the incumbent. Samplings indicate that Rainey had support for renomination from all over the district, from Republican and Democratic ranks, and from town as well as farm areas. The editor of the White Hall *Republican* typified the support with this inevitable pun: "It will have to be a mighty Rainey day when voters go back on so faithful a servant as the present incumbent has proven himself to be." In order to harness the outpouring of editorial and testimonial support, Rainey operated an official campaign bureau. He had never resorted to this device previously. With his wife in charge of quarters over the Carrollton bank, the bureau operated from the middle of June to the middle of August. The bureau served as a letter-answering service and mailed out an estimated 200,000 pieces of literature.[27]

After the most strenuous local campaign to date, the Rainey forces were ready for the verdict of fellow party members. The vote was a complete vindication of his record. There had been predictions of a 2 to 1 majority but no one openly dreamed of a 4 to 1 avalanche. Rainey carried every precinct but three in the ten county area. A letter of congratulations from the vanquished completed the saga of the 1908 renomination campaign.[28] This was the most severely contested of all Rainey's renomination efforts. Although there would be occasional opponents, Rainey would never again be seriously threatened from within the party.

The Rainey political activities in the fall of 1908 were a veritable three-ring circus—his efforts in behalf of the national and state ticket, his campaign for a waterway amendment to the state constitution, and his own re-election. As the Illinois member of the party's congressional campaign committee, he made speeches throughout the Midwest. He also helped the state campaign by serving on the advisory committee of the Democratic State Central Committee and by addressing political gatherings across the state. In addition, he delivered lantern lectures in behalf of the non-partisan deep waterway project. Such attention as Rainey gave the district was focused upon his support of the Illinois waterway proposal which would directly benefit his constituency. His Republican opponent, meanwhile, was concentrating on the prohibition question in an area which was 90 percent antisaloon territory. Candidate James H. Danskin of Jacksonville campaigned on the twin issues of local option and national legislation forbidding the shipment of liquor into dry territory.[29] While the incumbent was stumping the state on the nonpartisan issue of a deep waterway, his challenger was endeavoring to base his appeal on bipartisan support of dry legislation. This concern for the prohibition question portended the single issue campaign conducted in 1910.

The 1908 election results were not all that Rainey had hoped they would be. His own re-election was secured and the

constitutional amendment carried easily, but for a third time William
Jennings Bryan failed to achieve the presidency. In his district
Rainey outpolled Bryan by 1,600 votes. Rainey's personal margin of
victory over his Republican opponent was increased to 6,297 votes.[30]
The persevering Rainey had gained another two-year lease on his
congressional seat in spite of an intraparty struggle and a strenuous
tripartite campaign.

During the 1910 election year, Rainey was again involved in all
three levels of politics—national, state, and local. He was
appointed chairman of the five-man executive committee of the
National Democratic Congressional Committee and served as a member
of the literature committee of that body. In an article for *The
National Monthly*, a new Democratic magazine edited by Norman E.
Mack, Rainey warned that the Republican party was preparing to make
political capital out of the taking of the census. He asserted
that a small army of Republican workers, paid out of the federal
Treasury, would be arrayed against every northern Democratic
congressional candidate. The campaign committee and the candidates
had their work cut out for them in opposing this scheme, but the
Payne-Aldrich tariff outrage, he wrote, would help the Democrats
offset this advantage.[31] By focusing on the tariff issue nationally,
Rainey hoped to secure the first successful Democratic congressional
canvass since 1892.

As his contribution to party harmony in Illinois, Rainey agreed
to preside at the Democratic state convention in East St. Louis.
Since this was an off-year election and no gubernatorial candidate
was being selected, the factional splits within the party were not
readily in evidence. Rainey's keynote address emphasized the
importance of tariff reform to the party's state and national
success. The only action of the convention bearing on this study
was the adoption of a party statement favoring personal liberty
laws with respect to the prohibition question.[32] This particular
plank produced repercussions in Rainey's own election campaign since
wet versus dry was more important locally than protective or revenue
tariffs.

In local matters the twentieth district sinecure seemed safe.
His primary renomination was unopposed and his Republican opponent
was James H. Danskin, whom he had beaten on two previous occasions.
All appeared quiet in the home district when suddenly the prohibition issue was thrust into the election.

In the month prior to the November balloting, the wet/dry
question became the dominant issue for voter consideration.
On behalf of Morgan County's executive committee of the Anti-
Saloon League, Dr. Edward Bowe warned Rainey that he should not
have been associated with the "political marauders" at the East
St. Louis convention who opposed statewide prohibition. Candidate
Danskin challenged Rainey to debate the personal liberty plank
since Danskin stook squarely "for all the purposes and plans of
the anti-saloon league, including the protection of 'dry' territory
from interstate shipments." The late October edition of *The
Illinois Issue*, official voice of the Illinois Anti-Saloon League,
carried a lengthy editorial urging all those interested in

prohibition to vote for Danskin and against Rainey. The basis for
this advice was that Danskin freely and frankly endorsed a federal
law to protect dry territory from shipment of alcohol in interstate commerce. Rainey, however, had declined comment even though
given two opportunities to express himself. Since the twentieth
district was more than four-fifths dry, the editorial argued that
it was entitled to a congressman who would openly act in accord
with this overwhelming temperance sentiment. Voters were urged to
put principle above party. The concluding argument disclosed the
new Anti-Saloon League strategy of concentration on federal activity
in behalf of prohibition. The editorial said: "It is time that
not only members of the legislature but members of our national
congress shall be true representatives of the people on the things
that the people are most vitally interested in."[33] Rainey's
district was the only one in Illinois singled out for attention
in this campaign, although a comparable effort had been made
against "Uncle Joe" Cannon of Danville in 1908.

There was little time in which Rainey could attempt an effective reply to these charges. He endeavored to do so by a circular
letter sent to Democratic voters and all newspapers in the district.
Rainey attributed this sudden campaign against him to certain large
corporations and certain high government officials who wished to
capitalize on Democratic apathy in order to defeat him. He asserted
that the Anti-Saloon League charges were "malicious and untruthful"
because he had supported every measure they endorsed. In fact, he
claimed to have made nearly fifty speeches in the Northwest
advocating "People's Rule" measures such as the league supported.
Rainey minimized his connection with the personal liberty plank
since he was not a member of the platform committee and he argued
that county or local option was preserved under the Democratic platform. Because he was singled out for criticism, Rainey asserted
that the league was simply a tool in the hands of the predatory
interests which he had antagonized. Rainey vowed that he would
continue to oppose such interests if given the opportunity.[34] This
effort had to suffice in the time that was available to him.

The criticism of Rainey's attitude on the temperance question
completely overlooked one of the ceremonial duties he had performed
in 1905. It was Rainey who delivered the formal speech of acceptance
when the state of Illinois presented a statue of Frances E. Willard
to Congress for placement in Statuary Hall. She was the first
woman to be so honored. Rainey had provided eloquent praise for
the first national president of the Women's Christian Temperance
Union.[35] Apparently the voters had not forgotten this gesture as
well as his actions when it came time to express themselves at the
polls.

On November 8 the voters of the twentieth congressional district
marked their choice. It was decidedly pro-Rainey. In Greene County
the favorite son held a 3 to 1 margin. Rainey's two-party majority
of 7,233 votes was a most comfortable margin. The Prohibition party
had been polling substantial votes in Rainey's previous campaigns.
In this instance, the bedrock prohibitionist voters who chose
neither party candidate totaled 550.[36] The Rainey success was part

of a brightening Democratic outlook. The House of Representatives
in the Sixty-second Congress would contain a Democratic majority for
the first time in eighteen years. For the first time in his career,
Rainey would be a part of the legislative majority.

The campaign raised against Rainey was part of the initiation
of a larger strategy to secure national legislators sympathetic to
the cause of prohibition. The long-range effect may have pleased
the prohibitionists because Rainey's subsequent voting record left
no doubt about his favorable public stand on the issue. On each of
the subsequent key votes for prohibition, the twentieth district's
representative was recorded as voting yea. During the early years
of Bryan's tenure as Secretary of State, Rainey praised his peace-
ful revolution in substituting grape juice for wine at diplomatic
dinners. In 1916 an old copper whiskey still of Samuel Thomas's
was uncovered and sold for scrap metal as an aid to the preparedness campaign. The *Patriot* editorialized: "The change in public
sentiment is illustrated by the fact that while the grandfather
was a highly respected maker of whiskey, the grandson has indicated
his opposition to the liquor business by introducing various bills
in congress putting penalties and restrictions upon the making of
whiskey." The strength of his conviction was momentarily questioned
in 1919 during the voting on the Volstead Act providing for prohibition's enforcement. Henry T. Rainey, Democrat of Carrollton,
voted for the measure, while John W. Rainey, Democrat of Chicago,
voted against the implementation of the Eighteenth Amendment. The
confusion over the two Raineys caused some initial consternation
among the former's dry constituents, but the voting record was
clarified satisfactorily.[37] During the 1920s he was a staunch but
silent supporter of prohibition, lending his vote but not his voice
to the cause. His voting record remained unquestioned until the
tax situation of the 1930s altered his approach to the question.

During the 1912 campaign Rainey was largely content to serve
the interests of others. His renomination was uncontested in the
Democratic primary, and E. E. Brass became his Republican opponent
on the strength of twenty write-in votes from Menard County. Since
his personal situation indicated an unobstructed path through
November's election, Rainey focused upon the presidential contest.
Rainey was zealous in defending Bryan's continued leadership within
the Democratic party. To H. N. Wheeler, editor of the Quincy
Journal and Bryan critic, Rainey wrote that Bryan was loyal to
principles, not men. He did not think Bryan could control the
1912 national convention, but he did believe that it would not be
possible for the Democratic party to elect any man who did not
have Bryan's enthusiastic support. Both of these observations
proved remarkably accurate. Rainey attributed "the present progressive movements so apparent and becoming so irresistable [*sic*]
in both political parties" as being "due more to his leadership
and to his rugged political honesty than to any other source."
The Bryan magic had lost none of its appeal according to Rainey.
Henry T. was also supportive of Champ Clark and his exercise of the
Speaker's power. He indicated to Wheeler that the Speaker had
the right not only to suggest but also to lead on questions of

fundamental Democratic belief. Clark was expected to do it, Rainey wrote.[38]

As this defense of party leaders indicates, the Illinois congressman exhibited considerable interest in the nominating campaign. The Woodrow Wilson forces sent him a feeler, but he remained noncommital. The Bryan wing of the party was at this time inclined toward Champ Clark of Missouri. On the occasion of Clark's birthday, Rainey delivered a speech from the floor of the House booming the Speaker for the presidency. Their congressional districts shared a common border of over 100 miles along the Mississippi River, and thus Rainey could speak as a neighbor in praise of Clark's qualifications. In the first use of the presidential primary in Illinois, Clark's "houn' dawg" (his political emblem) carried Greene County by 3 to 1 and received a statewide endorsement as well. Rainey attended the national convention as an interested bystander. He would later recall being thrilled when Bryan addressed the convention, and he believed that the Great Commoner was alone responsible for the nomination of Governor Woodrow Wilson of New Jersey.[39] Rainey should not have been displeased at the selection of Wilson, although there is no indication that he gave it serious thought prior to the reform governor's nomination.

In the 1912 campaign a record of adherence to progressive policies was an asset. Rainey delighted in presenting his party to the voters as "the conservative party of progress." He objected to the title "progressive Democracy" being used by the Quincy *Journal* because: "There is only one kind of Democracy at the present time. If a man is not a progressive he is not a Democrat. There is no division of Democrats into progressives and non-progressives. Those men who are not progressives are not Democrats although they may be masquerading as such." In evaluating Rainey's own performance, Mark Sullivan of *Collier's* was very complimentary, although the congressman was criticized for his extreme partisanship. In rating the Illinois Democratic congressional delegation, Lynn Haines, later executive secretary of the nonpartisan National Voters' League, listed Rainey as partly progressive.[40] Rainey's opposition to Cannonism, attack upon trusts and tariffs, support for eight-hour bills, and economy in government contributed to his favorable record from the liberal perspective.

Rainey's personal campaign for re-election in 1912 was distinguished only because it was a three-cornered affair. The newly formed Progressive party of Theodore Roosevelt had entered Dr. B. O. Aylesworth of Chandlerville in the contest. The Progressives sought a joint debate with Rainey on the "Relative Merits of the Democratic and Progressive Platforms," but he declined. Henry T. indicated that his campaign plans were already fully matured and that such a debate would be inappropriate since "the best planks in the progressive platform are based upon the teachings and practices of the democratic party." He suggested that it was not platform difference that called the new party into existence but the struggle over the nomination, and that issue could best be fought in the Republican party. After the Progressives had sufficiently debated

with the Republican candidate about the methods by which Taft got
the nomination, then all three could debate from the same platform.[41]
No three-cornered public debate ever took place. With the Republicans split, Rainey showed little concern about his own campaign.
The election results clearly indicate that Rainey had correctly
assessed the situation. For the first time the local Republican
newspaper had placed Henry T. on its recommended ticket. The
spirited presidential contest between Taft, Roosevelt, and Wilson
attracted many voters. Greene County was Democratic by a 3 to 1
margin and Rainey outpolled the ticket leaders. An analysis of
the vote in Greene for President, governor, and congressman indicates that Rainey drew his additional strength about equally from
Republicans and Progressive party adherents.[42] As a result of
the split within Republican ranks, Illinois' electoral votes showed
up in the Democratic column for the first time since 1892, and a
Democrat was slated to occupy the state executive mansion for the
first time since 1896.

The Democratic party's success at the local, state, and national
level confronted Rainey with a new problem—the distribution of the
political plums. Prior to this time the principal political pie at
his disposal was the distribution of free garden seeds and appointments to the military academies. In the case of the latter, he
very early devised a system of district-wide competitive examinations
on which to base his nominations for West Point and Annapolis.[43] In
this way a minute fraction of the spoils could be distributed without
alienating any contending faction. His party's success in the
gubernatorial race did not result in patronage plums because he was
frequently at odds with Governor Edward F. Dunne over how best to
proceed with the Illinois waterway. Only in the area of postmaster-
ships did Rainey exert any special influences. There were twenty-four
post offices in his district not subject to civil service. Rainey
moved with agonizing slowness in the view of partisan Democrats when
it came to replacing Republican holdovers with deserving Democrats.
The customary practice was for the editor of the party newspaper
to be postmaster if he desired the position. With but one major
exception, Rainey appears to have been able to placate contending
factions without breach of party harmony. Likewise in the area of
public buildings for the district, the fruit was slow to ripen.
A post office building for Carrollton was initially approved in
1913, but through a series of economic and political vicissitudes
it was not constructed until 1932 as a part of the depression relief
measures.[44] The nineteen-year gestation period for the post office
dramatically illustrates the point that Rainey's political career
was not supported by patronage, public buildings, and other political
plums.

The first one-third of the "Little Giant's" electoral success
was firmly rooted in a local combination involving the issues
presented, the inheritance of Democratic traditions, the involvement of the populace in the electoral process, the immunity of the
district from reapportionment, and the immersion of the candidate
in public service. While this formula for success was never
embraced in a governmental theory like Douglas's "popular

sovereignty," it served Congressman Rainey very well. As the above pages indicate, the political life of a member of the House of Representatives is entwined with local, state, and national concerns. Rainey's initial success emphasized the preponderance of the local situation, although not to the exclusion of the others. His post–1912 career was to place greater emphasis upon state and national considerations as factors in electoral influence and mastery.

NOTES

1. *CR*, 64:1 (April 5, 1916), 5556; HTR to Walter W. Wright [Carrollton], June 3, 1929, RP.

2. Harvey M. Kabaker, "Estimating the Normal Vote in Congressional Elections," 63.

3. Rodney L. Mott, "Reapportionment in Illinois," 598–602.

4. *Illinois Blue Book, 1931–32*, 719–723; Gilbert Y. Steiner and Samuel K. Gove, "The Legislature Redistricts Illinois," 5–32.

5. V. O. Key, Jr., *American State Politics*, 223; Everett G. Smith, Jr., "Twentieth Century Voting Patterns for President in Illinois," 1–8.

6. *Republic*'s analysis cited in *Patriot*, June 29, 1900, 1:2.

7. *Gazette*, Aug. 3, 1900, 1:3 and 1:4; Aug. 10, 1900, 1:3 and 5:4; *Patriot*, Aug. 3, 1900, 1:2–3 and 4:3; Aug. 10, 1900, 1:2.

8. *Journal* analysis reprinted in *Patriot*, Aug. 22, 1902, 1:1.

9. *Courier* editorial reprinted in *Gazette*, Aug. 29, 1902, 4:4.

10. *Gazette*, Oct. 24, 1902, 4:1; Nov. 7, 1902, 1:4–6; *Illinois Blue Book, 1903*, 545. Institutional reforms such as Illinois' adoption of the Australian ballot in 1891 enhanced split-ticket voting and thus increased the electoral advantage of a bipartisan appeal such as the *Gazette* promoted. Consult Jerrold G. Rusk, "The Effect of the Australian Ballot Reform on Split Ticket Voting: 1876–1908," 1220–38.

11. The best single demographic source for Illinois in the first third of the twentieth century is found in *Report of the Illinois State Planning Commission* ([Springfield], n.p., Dec., 1934, and revised July, 1935), esp. pages 23, 29, 30, 31, 32, 43, 47, 48, 59, 60, and 73 for the sources of these generalizations.

12. Hildegard B. Johnson, "The Location of German Immigrants in the Middle West," 7; Carroll J. Schwartz, "Distribution of the Foreign-Born Population of Illinois, 1870–1950" (M.A. thesis), 25–28; *Fourteenth Census of the United States Taken in the Year 1920*, II, 1335–36; map showing southern sources of Illinois Democratic voting strength in Key, *American State Politics*, 224; Harlan H. Barrows, "Geography of the Middle Illinois Valley," 64–68; *Census of Religious Bodies, 1936*, I, 739–744; *Illinois Blue*

Book, 1931-32, 852-853.

    13. Harold F. Gosnell, *Grass Roots Politics*, Chap. 7, "Rural-Urban Conflict: Illinois," 91-105.

    14. Bliss material reproduced in *Gazette*, Jan. 22, 1904, 4:2.

    15. *Gazette*, June 10, 1904, 1:1-2, 5, and 4:2; *Patriot*, June 10, 1904, 1:3, and June 17, 1904, 4:1.

    16. *Illinois Blue Book, 1905*, 615.

    17. Carter H. Harrison, *Growing Up with Chicago*, 227; HTR to Wm. J. Bryan, Washington, Dec. 10, 1920, in Bryan Papers, Box 33.

    18. Williams to the Democracy of the twentieth congressional district, Pittsfield, Feb. 13, 1906, as printed in *Gazette*, Feb. 16, 1906, 1:2; campaign promises in *Gazette*, Aug. 23, 1906, 1:1 and 2:3-4.

    19. Bryan to HTR, Lincoln, Neb., Sept. 8, 1906, RP; *Gazette*, Oct. 18, 1906, 1:1; "Rainey of Illinois," 3:3.

    20. *Illinois Blue Book, 1907*, 632.

    21. GAR resolutions in *Gazette*, March 5, 1908, 4:1 and March 12, 1908, 4:1. Rainey's support for veterans, however, did not reach excess; his name never appeared on the National Voters' League list of congressmen whose private pension bills surpassed the bounds of propriety.

    22. The essence of the charges are printed as an extension of remarks in *CR*, 60:1 (May 30, 1908), Appendix 238-245.

    23. *Ibid.*

    24. *Gazette*, July 16, 1908, 4:3; for Williams's original remark see *CR*, 56:2 (Feb. 8, 1901), 2169.

    25. *Collier's*, XXXIV (March 18, 1905), 9, 11-12; Chicago *Tribune* and *Record-Herald* comments reprinted in *Commoner*, V (March 17, 1905), 2, and (March 24, 1905), 5, respectively; Chicago *Tribune*, Sept. 8, 1906, 1:1 and 4:1; Mark Sullivan, "Comment on Congress," 20.

    26. *The Public* of June 19 quoted in *Gazette*, June 25, 1908, 4:2; *Daily Democrat* of June 26 quoted in *Gazette*, July 2, 1908, 4:2; *News* of June 23 quoted in *Gazette*, July 9, 1908, 4:1. For a consideration of Post's and *The Public*'s parallel crusade against the privileged and plutocratic "interests" consult Dominic Candeloro, "*The Public* of Louis F. Post and Progressivism," 109-123.

    27. *Republican* quoted in *Gazette*, July 2, 1908, 4:2; bureau's operation described in *ibid.*, Aug. 6, 1908, 1:5.

    28. *Ibid.*, Aug. 13, 1908, 4:2, and Aug. 20, 1908, 1:3-5; *Patriot*, Aug. 13, 1908, 1:6, and Aug. 20, 1908, 1:5; Williams to HTR, Pittsfield, Aug. 11, 1908, RP.

    29. *Gazette*, Oct. 29, 1908, 4:2; Charles Boeschenstein

(Chairman, Illinois Democratic State Central Committee) to HTR, Chicago, Sept. 4, 1908, RP; editorial, "Mr. Danskin's Bold Stand," *Patriot*, Sept. 17, 1908, 4:1.

30. *Illinois Blue Book, 1909*, 404. Because of Rainey's strong showing over Bryan, the *Gazette* of Nov. 12, 1908, 4:1-2, suggested HTR as the 1912 presidential nominee.

31. HTR, "The Thirteenth Census and the Sixty-second Congress," 170-171; *Gazette*, July 21, 1910, 4:1, and Oct. 20, 1910, 4:1.

32. *Gazette*, Sept. 29, 1910, 1:2, and 3:1-6. For analysis of the Illinois complexities regarding Prohibition, see John D. Buenker, "The Illinois Legislature and Prohibition, 1907-1919," 363-384.

33. Bowe to HTR, Jacksonville, Ill., Oct. 5, 1910, RP; Danskin to HTR in *Patriot*, Oct. 13, 1910, 4:2; editorial, "Danskin for Congress from the Twentieth Congressional District," *The Illinois Issue*, V (Oct. 28, 1910), 6-7.

34. Circular letter dated from Carrollton, Nov. 2, 1910, as published in *Gazette*, Nov. 3, 1910, 1:1.

35. *CR*, 58:3 (Feb. 17, 1905), 2808-2809.

36. *Illinois Blue Book, 1911*, 368.

37. Peter H. Odegard, *Pressure Politics*, 267-269; *Patriot*, May 6, 1915, 1:1; Dec. 14, 1916, 1:4; July 24, 1919, 4:2. To place Prohibition in the larger context of the progressive movement, see James H. Timberlake, *Prohibition and the Progressive Movement, 1900-1920*, 1-2.

38. HTR to Wheeler, Washington, Dec. 6, 1911, RP. Kenneth W. Hechler, *Insurgency*, 233, calls this a valuable letter in evaluating Bryan's role in the progressive movement, while William R. Gwinn, *Uncle Joe Cannon*, 249, uses these observations to minimize the dictatorial power of Speaker Cannon and to maximize the reformer's dual standard in judging Speakers.

39. William F. McCombs to HTR, New York, Oct. 18, 1911, RP; *CR*, 62:2 (March 7, 1912), 2958; *Patriot*, April 11, 1912, 1:1-2; Rainey's Bryan Memorial Speech, 5867.

40. HTR to Wheeler, Washington, Dec. 6, 1911, RP; Sullivan, "Comments on Congress," 13; Lynn Haines, *Law Making in America*, 88.

41. HTR to Capt. John E. Wright (chairman, Progressive party in twentieth congressional district), Carrollton, Sept. 24, 1912, RP.

42. *Gazette*, Nov. 7, 1912, 1:3; *Illinois Blue Book, 1913-14*, 593.

43. HTR's first appointment to Annapolis was Mark C. Bowman and to West Point was Leo Dunsworth. See *Patriot*, May 20, 1904, 1:4, and Sept. 22, 1905, 1:3-4.

44. HTR to Gov. Dunne [Washington, D.C.], May 9, 1914, RP; *Patriot*, Nov. 14, 1912, 4:3; Oct. 23, 1913, 1:4; Nov. 29, 1913, 4:1-2; summary of post office history in *Patriot*, June 9, 1932, 1:3-4.

3

A "Gadfly" in State and National Politics

The combination of electoral success and political prominence earned
by Congressman Henry T. Rainey during his first decade of service
enabled him to play an expanded role in matters relating to state and
national politics. Rainey has been likened to a busy gadfly (horse-
fly) whose sting was felt by a reluctant Democratic donkey and a
slow-moving Republican elephant.[1] As gadfly, his role was to agitate,
to aggravate, and to attack. In state politics the downstate
congressman struggled, albeit unsuccessfully, for reform in the
faction-ridden Democratic party. At the national level he served
as the party's liberal conscience during the period of Republican
ascendancy in the 1920s. In both levels of political activity he
strove constantly for change within the established party system
rather than outside of it. As the agrarian unrest intensified in
the late 1920s and early 1930s, Rainey became the spokesman for
farmers attempting to prod both parties into remedial action. The
relative security of Henry T.'s political position within his
congressional district enabled him to enjoy a modicum of independence,
to employ a political conscience, and to embrace practical reforms.
     Some insights into the complexities of Illinois politics during
the first three decades of the twentieth century are revealed by an
examination of Rainey's career. The explanatory cliché "Chicago
versus downstate" fails to consider adequately the factionalism
within the state's dominant political parties. In the case of the
Democratic party at the turn of the century there was a conservative
faction dominated by Roger C. Sullivan, boss of Cook County Democrats,
and a progressive component under the leadership of Carter H.
Harrison, Jr., longtime mayor of Chicago. After 1905 the party
division became a three-cornered affair when Edward F. Dunne wrested
the mayoralty nomination from Harrison. Dunne was identified with
the progressive Harrison forces, but his drive for personal power
was enhanced in 1912 by his election as governor of the state. The
contest among these factions was largely one of power rather than
principle since the three groups took similar stands on statewide
issues.[2] As a downstate Democrat, Rainey became embroiled in this
internecine warfare among the metropolitan antagonists struggling
for control.
     Rainey's close identification with William Jennings Bryan
disposed him to favor the Harrison wing of the state party. When
Bryan declined to be a presidential candidate in 1904, the progressive faction selected William Randolph Hearst as their standard

bearer. In a speech before the Iroquois Club, Chicago's version of
Tammany Hall, Rainey lauded Hearst's presidential qualifications.
At the subsequent state convention, the faction of the party controlled by Sullivan and John P. Hopkins, former mayor of Chicago and
chairman of the state committee, ruled with an iron hand. This
Sullivan-Hopkins crowd rejected enough contested county delegates,
including Harrison, to insure their control of the delegation to
the national convention.

Although the state convention ultimately endorsed Hearst for
President, the Harrison-Hearst wing of the party contested the
delegate selection process at the national convention in St. Louis.
Bryan pleaded unsuccessfully in behalf of the Harrison cause, and
this affront to majority rule stung Rainey deeply. At a Jackson
Day banquet in Chicago he declared: "When the history of political
parties in Illinois is written, high up on the roll of political
infamy will be placed the names of the four or five men in Illinois
who are directly and personally responsible for the outrageous gavel
rule in the Democratic state convention in 1904."[3] A few months
later Rainey joined forces with an anti-Sullivan reform group in
downstate Illinois.

The defeat of Alton B. Parker in 1904 was a severe blow to
Rainey's hopes for the national Democratic party. The election
results confirmed his desire that the party should reflect the
current progressive uprising in many states. In a New York City
address he charged that the Democrats' inattention to reforms led
to a silent protest during which the party's voters stayed home.
Thus, the party lost by default rather than defeat. The remedy
was a militant Democratic party embracing such reforms as the
initiative and referendum, municipal ownership of traction lines,
shorter hours for labor, and protection for the rights of children.
Indicating that the November election results had demonstrated the
insufficiency of two ultra-conservative parties, Rainey demanded a
resurrected party which was radical, aggressive, and progressive.
The significance of Rainey's remarks was not lost on editor Hearst,
for he pledged the support of his newspapers in any campaign which
Rainey might make to attain this ideal in Illinois politics.[4]
Back in the Prairie State the forces for progress began to mobilize
for a campaign against boss rule.

The vehicle through which the state's politics were to be
purified was the Democratic Majority Rule League of Illinois. Among
the prime movers in the establishment of the league was Congressman
Rainey. On May 7, 1905, a group of forty downstate Democrats and
two Chicagoans met to establish a radical force whose purpose was
"to unite all democrats who are opposed to gavel rule and boss
domination into a phalanx to protect the party from a repetition
of the disgraceful and tyrannical methods by which the party was
outraged at the last state convention."[5] Millard Fillmore Dunlap
of Jacksonville, formerly Hearst's campaign manager, was selected
as president and Theodore Nelson of Chicago as secretary-treasurer.
The Majority Rule League was a loose coalition of Bryan Democrats
who opposed the conservative elements in the party, although the
league disavowed support for any one candidate or issue. These

men deplored the incongruity of a party pledged to oppose the "interests" being directed by individuals tainted by the liquor companies and the gas combines. At its zenith in 1906, the league membership included politicos from throughout the downstate area.

Their principal objective was the removal of Roger C. Sullivan from the Democratic national committee because he was the symbol of the unsavory aspect of Illinois politics. In anticipation of the state convention, the Majority Rule League met in March, 1906, and endorsed Rainey as their candidate for temporary chairman on a harmony plea. Bryan complicated the convention agenda by releasing a letter through Judge Owen P. Thompson of Jacksonville, a league organizer, in which Bryan demanded that Sullivan resign his position as national committeeman. Quite naturally Sullivan declined and quickly struck out at the "Jacksonville cabal," as he termed the Majority Rule League. In a letter to the convention delegates, Sullivan defended his stewardship and denounced the outside influence working through the Thompson-Rainey-Dunlap triumvirate. When the convention met in Peoria, the Sullivan contingent was in control. An initial draft of the platform contained a specific plank condemning the mileage grab vote of Congressman Rainey. With this blackmail in hand, Sullivan forced Rainey to retire from the field as a candidate for temporary chairman. The Sullivan forces then swept the convention posts and the platform was amended to remove the mileage grab reference. A league-inspired resolution joining Bryan in requesting Sullivan's resignation was defeated by a 2 to 1 margin. The convention, however, adopted a resolution favoring Bryan as the party nominee two years hence.[6] The Majority Rule League was unsuccessful in its efforts to straighten the tangled morass of Democratic politics in Illinois.

Upon his return from a world tour in September, Bryan resumed his personal attack upon the Sullivan machine. Before the Jefferson Club, an informal alliance of Democrats opposed to the Sullivan-Hopkins political methods, the Great Commoner proceeded to read Sullivan out of the party "on the charge of being a corporation pirate who is in politics for profit only." From New York City Sullivan issued a reply filled with invective at Bryan's rule or ruin disposition. The party boss decried efforts to purify Illinois politics when such men as Henry T. Rainey, "who still impudently claims that he can defend his attempt to collect from the public treasury the mileage he has never spent," were involved.[7] The divisions within Illinois' Democracy were still very much in evidence. If Rainey were to aspire to a statewide elective office such as governor or senator, the continued splits within the party would represent serious obstacles.

Rainey's activities in behalf of the Majority Rule League form a background to the serious party schism erupting in 1914. Generally his participation in state politics was minimal throughout his career. As a member of the federal crowd, his involvement was seldom actively sought by state-oriented politicians. During all but six years of Rainey's national legislative career, Republicans were fully entrenched in the executive mansion in Springfield. This situation undoubtedly placed a damper on any eagerness to play

an active role at the state level since the prospects for success
were dim. An additional restraint was the factionalism within the
Illinois Democratic party. Since Rainey represented the frustrated
reform element within the party, opportunities to change the image
and success of the state's Democratic party were slight.[8] Nevertheless, Rainey's prominence in the tariff reform fight of the Wilson
administration's first year thrust him into a situation laden with
political danger.

The controversy arose over the choice of the party's senatorial
nominee in 1914. The conservative-liberal cliques were unable to
agree upon the selection of a single candidate. The conservative
forces were generally agreed upon Roger C. Sullivan. Sullivan was
favored for the nomination by Joe Tumulty, President Wilson's private
secretary, who felt indebted to Sullivan for swinging the Illinois
delegation to Wilson at a crucial moment in the 1912 Baltimore
convention. The liberal factions were at a loss for a single
candidate upon whom they could unite. One progressive wing was
led by Senator James Hamilton Lewis and Governor Edward F. Dunne.
This splinter had the enthusiastic support of Secretary of State
William Jennings Bryan and Carl Vrooman, Assistant Secretary of
Agriculture, who wished to be a candidate for the nomination. The
second liberal element was led by Mayor Carter H. Harrison, with the
influential backing and favor of William Randolph Hearst.[9] Rainey's
name was frequently mentioned as the best possible candidate upon
whom the liberals might unite in order to oppose Sullivan in the
primary.

The important question was, would Rainey consent to make the
Senate campaign? The plight of the progressive elements demanded
that he be tempted. Bryan believed Rainey would consider making the
race as a party obligation if the other progressive candidates withdrew from the contest. Governor Dunne sought to persuade others to
leave the field clear for Rainey. Dunne thought that all could unite
on Rainey, but then Bryan reported things were going badly because
Rainey absolutely refused to run. Carl Vrooman offered to help
uncomplicate the matter by withdrawing if Rainey would make the
race, but to no avail. Mayor Harrison termed Rainey the only
desirable candidate, yet indicated the congressman distinctly was
not in the running.[10] Rainey steadfastly maintained that he was
only a candidate for renomination and re-election to his seat in
the House. As a practical politician he undoubtedly realized that
the factionalism within the party and the normal Republican pre-
dominance did not portend success for any statewide elective office.

The result was a three-cornered contest among the Democrats
for the primary nomination. Sullivan had the support of the conservative wing of the party; Congressman Lawrence B. Stringer
claimed the adherence of Democratic liberals; Vrooman ran under
the banner of the "Wilson-Bryan League." Each side sought President Wilson's favor, but he wisely would not intervene in the
matter. The primary results indicated a significant victory for
the Sullivan organization. The wounds opened by the split were
not closed after the ballots were counted. Carl Vrooman bolted
the party and supported the Bull Moose senatorial candidate.

Others, like Harrison, Lewis, and Dunne, injured the party's cause by their calculated inactivity.[11]

The Democratic State Central Committee, looking ahead to the state convention, sought a figure who could help seal the party rift. Believing as he did in party responsibility, Rainey was a logical choice. As dean of the second largest Democratic state delegation in Congress, he was asked to deliver the principal address and he agreed. At the state convention in Springfield, he opened his speech with a plea for party harmony behind the candidacy of Roger Sullivan, but most of his remarks were in praise of the national administration. Rainey extolled those policies which brought peace, happiness, and prosperity while Europe engaged in war. He acclaimed the wise and patriotic guidance of the greatest President in half a century and the marvelous record of performance achieved in Congress. There followed an elaborate discussion of eighteen Democratic campaign promises which were kept. Rainey also praised the firm, uncompromising, unyielding, inexpensive foreign policy conducted by the administration. Under the Democrats' auspices, he claimed, the starry banner of the republic "stood, not for war and human misery, but for the progress, happiness, comfort, and prosperity of all the people."[12] These were legitimate and laudable Democratic issues based on the national party record, but they did not bring together the feuding Democrats of Illinois.

In the months that followed, Roger Sullivan's senatorial candidacy attracted considerable attention and provided a political dilemma for President Wilson. Sullivan was portrayed as "either a peril to the nation or a long suffering patriot in search of a delayed reward." His progressiveness, or lack of it, was the question at issue. Proponents argued that he was progressive because he had supported Wilson at Baltimore. Opponents claimed Sullivan was as progressive as a pyramid and that he would back up President Wilson with the same enthusiasm displayed by Italy in backing up Austria at the outset of World War I. Democrats dissatisfied with Sullivan pointed out that only the hopelessness of Champ Clark's cause and the earnest pleading of the delegation had brought him into the Wilson camp. His critics had likewise chafed under his boss rule of the state for the past decade.[13] Wilson was faced with this decision. Should he make a friendly gesture to the Democratic Old Guard by endorsing Sullivan at the risk of alienating the progressive wing, or should he remain aloof from the contest entirely?

In the interest of party loyalty, Rainey endeavored to prod Wilson in the direction of an endorsement of Sullivan. Several Democrats who were prominent businessmen in Chicago supplemented Rainey's plea by urging Tumulty to procure an unequivocal endorsement from the President. Rainey urged Wilson's support in the interest of harmony, solidarity, and success in Illinois. He was sure the President could not fail to comply because the party's strength in the Senate was marginal. At first Wilson agreed to an exchange of letters between himself and Rainey. The congressman drafted a letter endorsing Sullivan which the President was to sign. In the meantime Wilson changed his mind. Apparently he

yielded to pressure from Illinois liberals and prohibitionists who
implored him to give no hint of assistance to Sullivan because of
his conservatism, his open affiliation with the liquor interests,
and his questionable reputation. Bryan brought direct pressure
upon the President by threatening to resign as Secretary of State
and go to Illinois to speak against Sullivan.[14]

Meanwhile, the draft of Wilson's proposed letter went through
two revisions. The intent of the letter was to caution Democrats
against abandoning the principle that party men were bound by the
free choice of the people at the polls. The President wished it to
be known that he always stood by the primary results and he thought
it the duty of every Democrat who cared for the success and sincerity
of his party to do likewise. Draft three differed from draft two in
that it added this unequivocal statement: "Mr. Sullivan has been
selected in a fair primary and therefore he is entitled to the
support of the party." But the letter was never published or used
in any form in the campaign. The only outward indication of
presidential favor came later in an address by Postmaster General
Albert Sidney Burleson at Peoria. As a passing remark, Burleson
announced that the President favored Sullivan's election.[15]

In spite of the Bryan-Wilson impasse, Rainey personally worked
for Sullivan's election. Almost simultaneously with the Wilson
negotiations, Rainey devoted the last two weeks in October to a
concentrated campaign in behalf of the state Democratic ticket,
especially Sullivan. Rainey justified his action on the ground that
the next Senate would find a close division and every Democratic
vote would be needed. Years later Rainey wrote Ray Stannard Baker
to the effect that if the President's letter had been used in the
campaign, Sullivan would have been elected.[16] The possible truth
in that statement would be difficult to determine, but it seems
unlikely. Rainey's campaign for party harmony and the state boss
did not go unnoticed, however. Two years later Sullivan helped
secure Rainey's election as delegate-at-large to the national
convention.

Rainey's lack of success in the role as party peacemaker dis-
couraged him from vigorous participation in state politics until
1924 when Judge Norman L. Jones, his one-time law partner, became a
Democratic candidate for governor against four other aspirants.
He was successful in the primary, but faced a formidable opponent
in the Republican incumbent, Governor Len Small. During the fall
campaign, Rainey participated in a virtual three-ring political
circus—congressional, gubernatorial, and presidential. The theme
of his speeches was honesty in government. The Democratic faith,
Rainey is reported to have said, started with the commandment "Thou
shalt not steal." At each level of the election contest, he detected
scandals which should prevent Republicans obtaining a public trust.
He attempted to associate Calvin Coolidge with the infamies of the
Harding administration. Governor Len Small's first term was
criticized for its looseness with the taxpayer's money. At the
district level, Rainey questioned the personal financial conduct
of Guy Shaw, his Republican opponent. The congressman stumped
his district and the state exploiting this strategy, but to little

avail—the sovereign people decided in favor of Rainey but against
Jones and John W. Davis, the Democratic presidential candidate.[17]
The Jones campaign represented Rainey's last major venture into
state politics.

Another avenue in which Rainey could endeavor to influence
party fortunes was formal participation in the national conventions.
As a result of his conciliatory role in the Sullivan candidacy, he
became persona grata to all Democratic factions and a viable candidate for the quadrennial party meeting. He sought the opportunity
to attend the 1916 convention in St. Louis as an official delegate
and was endorsed by the state central committee. In repayment of
his political debt, Roger Sullivan assured Rainey that he would run
as well in Cook County as any other candidate on the primary ticket.
Rainey pledged himself as a Wilson delegate and let his views be
known in a speech placed in the *Congressional Record*. In his
remarks he compared Lincoln and Wilson in their second election
efforts. Both faced times of crisis and both found their strength
in the people. The Illinois congressman concluded that it was not
best then or now to swap horses while crossing streams.[18] Rainey
and only one other downstate candidate were selected as delegates-
at-large.

During the convention he served as the Illinois member on the
platform committee and as a member of the subcommittee to draft the
final document. On all foreign policy issues and most domestic
issues, the Wilson administration had provided the resolutions
committee with a preferred draft of planks. The only issue over
which there was a serious division was women's suffrage. Rainey
joined Senators Thomas J. Walsh of Montana and Henry F. Hollis of
New Hampshire in advocating a strongly worded recognition that women
be given the same voting rights as men. Of the twelve states then
granting suffrage to women, all except Illinois were west of the
Mississippi. In deference to a strong minority viewpoint, the tone
was softened so that the plank recommended women's suffrage for
favorable action by the states. It did not advocate congressional
enactment of a suffrage amendment as Rainey and others had hoped.
This single plank was the only one voted on independently by the
convention. A minority report watering the plank even further was
rejected.[19] Rainey could take considerable pride in his constructive contribution at his first national convention representing
Illinois' Democratic party.

In 1920 Rainey sought participation in the San Francisco
convention and was selected again as delegate-at-large. The
biggest topic of conversation was the presidential nomination.
Although Bryan had written Rainey suggesting that he become a
candidate for the party's top post, the Illinoisan declined to have
his name considered. Rainey's personal preference was A. Mitchell
Palmer of Pennsylvania, Wilson's Attorney General. At the convention, George Brennan, successor to Roger Sullivan as state
Democratic boss, introduced Rainey as the man to speak for the
majority of the Illinois delegates in seconding Palmer's nomination.
The other leading contenders were William Gibbs McAdoo, Wilson's
Secretary of the Treasury, and Governor James M. Cox of Ohio.

According to the recollection of Carter H. Harrison, Illinois' convention votes were, for a time, pledged to Palmer as a result of a deal
with Rainey. Brennan led the anti-McAdoo forces at the convention
presumably because McAdoo was an avowed dry whereas Chicago was
decidedly wet in its sentiments. In addition, Brennan was peeved
that McAdoo had refused to recognize the Sullivan machine in the
distribution of federal patronage. Rainey's seconding speech was an
innocuous recital of Palmer's personal appeal and record stressing
Americanism and law and order. When it became apparent that Palmer
could not secure the nomination, the Illinois delegation shifted to
Cox. The Ohio governor ultimately emerged as the winner, and as his
running mate the convention selected Franklin D. Roosevelt, Assistant
Secretary of the Navy. Even though his personal choice failed to
attain the honor, Rainey loyally offered his services to the national
ticket and they were gratefully received.[20]

Although the Cox-Roosevelt ticket (and Rainey, too) lost their
election bids in the postwar return to normalcy, the persistent
gadfly remained optimistic. Immediately following the 1920 landslide, Rainey wrote McAdoo predicting that the Californian would be
the party's nominee in 1924. As that convention approached, the
congressman gave no indication that his preference had changed.
C. M. Brown, an influential Democratic politician in California,
urged Rainey to be a McAdoo booster at the convention since the
nomination could be secured with little friction and the election
won easily. After McAdoo was besmirched in the Teapot Dome investigation as a result of his association with Edward L. Doheny, Brown
minimized the revelations and urged Rainey to use his influence to
counteract the Republican propaganda. McAdoo and Rainey were very
anxious to talk things over before the New York convention, but
there is no record of what may have happened between them.[21] As a
delegate to the convention from the twentieth congressional district,
Rainey was a firm McAdoo supporter.

As a representative of progressive Democracy, Rainey went to
the convention with a prepared set of personal views which he wished
to suggest as planks in the party platform. The two most important
proposals called for a popular referendum on the League of Nations
and an anti-Ku Klux Klan statement opposing "any organization or
sect denying religious freedom." Other proposals called for downward
revision of the tariff, measures for the relief of agriculture, and
a generous pension policy for all war veterans. Rainey's role
at the convention is obscure, but he himself recalled associating
with Bryan and witnessing his vain attempts to bring order out of
chaos.[22] The 1924 Democratic marathon left the party weakened,
divided, and ultimately defeated.

Postmortems of the 1924 national election were numerous.
Franklin D. Roosevelt elicited from all the convention delegates
their analysis of the party's defeat. Pessimistically, Rainey
wrote that the Democrats could not win until Republican policies
led to economic disaster. He theorized that the party had underestimated the strength of the Klan issue. The deliberate injection
of the religious issue into the political scene, he thought, was
a crime which should eliminate its perpetrators from future active

participation in party leadership. According to Rainey, there was too much urban domination and contesting for spoils in local contests to the disregard of state and national political fortunes. In an address before the National Democratic Club, Rainey additionally placed the blame on Republican control of the press. In the off-years, he said, the Democrats gained but in the presidential years they lost. He attributed this to a stupendous advertising program conducted by the Republicans. By alleging that the Democrats were enemies of successful business, the votes of businessmen and laborers were swayed to the Republicans in presidential years.[23]

Rainey's pessimism was so great that he declined to be a candidate as delegate to the 1928 convention in Houston. However, when Illinois' former Governor Frank Lowden withdrew from Republican contention and that party's convention refused to endorse a strong farm plank, Rainey concluded that Governor Al Smith could not lose if the Democrats adopted an unequivocal agricultural policy statement. He urged that it read: "We are in favor of making the tariff effective as to farm products by the equalization fee method of farm relief." As a lobbyist, the Illinois congressman addressed the platform and resolutions committee in behalf of his farm plank, urging the party to meet the agricultural issue courageously and squarely since it could elect any candidate and sweep any political party out of office.[24] The party accepted his plea for redress of agrarian grievances, but Rainey overvalued the efficacy of the farm problem at this time.

In contrast to his despair four years earlier, Rainey's comments on the 1928 election exhibited hope that the party of Jefferson and Jackson would rebound successfully. He communicated to Governor-elect Roosevelt of New York his belief that the Hoover administration would provide inadequate farm relief and thus supply a major campaign issue. Rainey specifically indicated that the party's "leadership will devolve upon yourself as the Democratic governor of our leading state." The prospects for a presidential victory improved after the 1930 off-year elections gave the Democrats a majority in the House of Representatives. As majority leader he was in a position to develop issues which would contribute to his party's subsequent success. As the convention approached, Rainey crystallized his own thinking on the issues by preparing a contribution for a New York *Times* symposium on Democratic leaders' suggestions for the 1932 platform. His frequent contacts with candidate Roosevelt enhanced the opportunity to expound his views. Whenever Roosevelt stopped in Washington on trips between New York and Warm Springs, Rainey was among those present for consultations. A brainstorming committee composed of Cordell Hull, A. Mitchell Palmer, and Rainey combined to draft planks for recommendation to the convention when it convened in Chicago. Although the majority leader was elected as a delegate-at-large from Illinois, he did not attend the convention due to the pressure of legislative business. Rainey announced that his alternate would cast his vote for Roosevelt and predicted that the two-thirds rule for nominating candidates would be changed to a simple majority.[25] While Rainey's influence on this last convention of his lifetime was indirect, he was pleased with the party

platform and the selection of the standard bearer. His final venture into national policy determination was an unqualified success
in contrast to some of his earlier endeavors. Even though Rainey
was busily engaged in the state and national political arenas, he
also had to direct appropriate attention to the third ring of the
congressional circus, his own district.

Each year members of the House of Representatives must keep one
eye on the legislative calendar and another on the political barom-
eter in their home region. Representing a district that seldom made
any trouble about continuing his services, Rainey could allocate
much of his time to other endeavors. He had been unopposed in the
1914 primary, but had been unable to attend the district convention
because Congress remained in session. He protected his interests
by explaining to each delegate that as a result of the two Wilson
years the Democratic party had "already become the constructive,
conservative party of progress in the United States." The ratification of the primary results by the convention was merely ceremony.
While most of the progressives returned to the Republican fold,
there was still a three-cornered contest. The Rainey machine worked
its magic with a 7,455 vote plurality.[26]

The renomination and re-election campaign of 1916 was largely
a matter of routine for Rainey. In the Republican camp there was
the unusual occurrence of a primary contest to determine the honor
of opposing the Democratic incumbent. Walter B. Sayler outstripped
W. B. Strang by a vote of 3,971 to 3,640. In an effort to find a
winning argument, candidate Sayler made Rainey's labor record an
issue in the campaign. In response, Samuel Gompers, president of
the American Federation of Labor, had written John F. Walker,
president of the Illinois State Federation of Labor, defending
Rainey's service on the Labor Committee (his first important
congressional committee assignment). Gompers noted that Rainey was
an advocate of the eight-hour day and concluded that he was "kindly,
helpful and influential toward all measures affecting the interests
of labor and beneficial to the people as a whole." The National
Voters' League provided an independent assessment of the Rainey
record. While 90 percent of the congressmen were classed as "mawsh
members" (might as well stay home), Rainey was included among those
10 percent who controlled legislative activities. He was categorized
as strongly partisan with a fair record and deserving re-election.
Since Rainey was devoting substantial electioneering time away from
the district, President Wilson expressed his appreciation and voiced
the hope that Rainey was not neglecting local interests. "It would
be," Wilson noted, "a very serious disappointment to us all if you
were not yourself returned to Congress. I take it for granted,
however, that your constituents know and value you too much to make
that possible." The region's returns were characteristically
Democratic, with Wilson carrying the district on Rainey's coattails.[27]
The President failed to carry Illinois statewide, but was returned
to the White House by a narrow margin in the electoral college. Until
1976 this was the only time in the twentieth century when the Prairie
State's electoral votes had not gone to the national winner.

The "Khaki Election" of 1918 provided the populace with a

unique opportunity to review directly the record of their congressmen
and indirectly the accomplishments of their President. Amidst the
myriad of activities competing for time and attention at the height
of the Great War, an off-year election was held. The pressure of
congressional duties kept Rainey from making a personal canvass of
the district. His public appeal for voter support was phrased in
this manner: "I submit my non-partisan war record . . . to the
voters of all parties . . . and it is for them to determine . . .
whether they can be better represented by a new man, inexperienced
and not familiar with legislation, than by myself." The congressman
openly sought bipartisan support for re-election in stark contrast
with the President's partisan request for the return of a Democratic
Congress. Late in the campaign Wilson issued this statement: "If
you have approved of my leadership and wish me to continue to be
your unembarrassed spokesman in affairs at home and abroad, I
earnestly beg that you will express yourselves unmistakably to that
effect by returning a Democratic majority to both the Senate and
the House of Representatives." The extraordinary circumstances
which justified such a request in Wilson's mind did not impress
Carrollton's Republican newspaper editor. The *Patriot* advised its
readers that Wilson's partisan appeal would undoubtedly have the
opposite result because he had earlier asked that politics be
adjourned for the duration of the war. It was noted that a person
did not have to vote Democratic in order to prove one's patriotism.[28]
Significantly, the Democratic *Gazette* did not reprint or call
attention to the President's October 25 statement.

Subsequent historical investigations have revealed that the
issues in the 1918 contest were not limited to a candidate's loyalty
to presidential policies. Also significant were sectional
animosities arising from personal and economic issues. Both were
noted by the opposition press in the twentieth congressional district.
The issue was personal in that the North and West resented southern
domination of Congress. This was doubly infuriating since two
influential Democrats, Speaker Champ Clark of Missouri and Ways and
Means Chairman Claude Kitchin of North Carolina, had been noteworthy
opponents of much of Wilson's program. The division was economic
in that there was disparity in governmental policies toward such
sectional agricultural commodities as wheat and cotton. The
Patriot's assessment of the situation indicated that Rainey tended
to favor southern cotton instead of Illinois wheat in the matter of
price fixing, but no fault could be found with his patriotism in
contrast to Clark and Kitchin. When the election results were
tallied, Rainey's margin of victory was down appreciably to 3,171
votes, the narrowest margin since 1904.[29] While his race does not
provide any clear-cut indication of the efficacy of Wilson's
loyalty plea or of the effectiveness of sectional divisions along
personal or economic lines, Rainey, along with other Democrats,
suffered in the general trend. The twentieth district was the
only one left in the Democratic column in downstate Illinois.

The state's Republicans were heartened by their congressional
election successes. It became evident that a determined bid would
be made to unseat Rainey. Early in January, 1920, Guy L. Shaw of

Beardstown announced his candidacy for the GOP nomination. Shaw
had been born at Summer Hill in Pike County on May 16, 1881. After
attending local public schools, he graduated from the College of
Agriculture at the University of Illinois. He then engaged in
agricultural pursuits and the development of overflow lands along
the Illinois River bottom. He presented himself as the farmers'
candidate. In addition to being an aspirant for Congress, Shaw
was a delegate to the Illinois consitutional convention which began
meeting on June 6, 1920, and continued until October 10, 1922.
Neither candidate was opposed in the primary, but the 12,211
Democratic votes and 11,416 Republican ballots did not forecast well
for the incumbent.[30]   Indeed, 1920 was an election year which would
bear watching.

At the national and district levels, Rainey endeavored to set
the tone of the campaign by stressing Wilson's successes and his own
country connections. In Congress he flayed the Republican majority's
inability to control the high cost of living during this "reconstruction period," a failure which vindicated Wilson's demand for
the return of a Democratic Congress. As the election neared, he
focused upon the broken campaign promises and the extravagance of
the Republicans. This contrasted sharply, according to Rainey,
with a Democratic record of successes. He strengthened the campaign
material by enumerating and discussing eighteen Democratic achievements of the recent past and then contrasting these with a list of
seven Republican miscues. At the local level, Rainey emphasized his
rural record. At a farm bureau picnic in White Hall, he declared
himself to be "a farmer by birth, a farmer by education, a farmer
by environment, a farmer by preference, and a farmer in fact." As
illustrations of his legislative accomplishments in these areas,
he cited the repeal of the daylight saving law—"a contest between
the golf sticks of the city bred and the hoes and harrows of the
farmer"—and the passage of federal hardroads appropriations. During
this campaign, he utilized a brochure prepared by an unidentified
friend to promote his candidacy. This election pamphlet was aimed
particularly at Democratic critics of the Wilson administration, and
suggested to Wilson detractors that a fight against the President
was a fight against Henry T. as well.[31]   The Rainey campaign was
irrevocably tied to the Wilson record.

To stimulate interest in an otherwise lackluster campaign, a
group of forty Carrolltonians prepared a set of questions for
candidates Shaw and Rainey to answer. The questions and the
responses provide some insight into the campaign issues as perceived locally. The first three questions concerned the League of
Nations—perhaps reflective of Wilson's call for a "solemn referendum" on this subject. Shaw announced himself as against any
league with or without reservations. Rainey favored the immediate
ratification of the treaty as drawn, but would not object to
reservations which did not impair its essential integrity. On a
question concerning compulsory military training, both candidates
recorded their opposition. Shaw indicated he favored the immediate
return of American soldiers from Europe, whereas Rainey argued they
should be maintained there to safeguard the ideals for which so

many sacrifices had been made. On a question about whether the
people should have a direct vote on a declaration of war, neither
candidate favored such a proposition, although Rainey expressed
sympathy for the concept of popular participation whenever practical.[32]   The major difference between the two candidates was on
the League of Nations. Rainey was decidedly more internationalist
in his political outlook than his Republican opponent.

Apart from the league issue, the 1920 general election held
another uncertainty—the soldier vote. Following the Armistice,
there was considerable speculation that doughboys returning from
the battlefields would be a political force to be considered at
the ballot boxes. Political analysts were uncertain about a
pro- or antimilitary vote. The GOP guessed that the soldier vote
was isolationist and bought a full-page advertisement in *The
Legion Weekly* to proclaim that if Harding were elected "American
affairs will be discussed by American public servants in the City
of Washington, not in some foreign capitol [*sic*]." Just before
the election, the *Patriot* made a general appeal in behalf of ex-
doughboys on the Republican county ticket. Voters were reminded
that it was the Republican party which had taken the lead in
recognizing the serviceman and rewarding his patriotism.[33]   It
is now impossible to determine the positive or negative impact of
such a claim, but it deserves more consideration than election
accounts have accorded it.

The 1920 election was supposed to be a "solemn referendum"
on the League of Nations, but it proved instead to be a popular
rejection of the party in the presidency. The voters decided it
was time for a change in national administrations and in congressional representation. In the twentieth district, Guy Shaw
possessed a majority of 3,909 votes. Rainey outpolled the general
party ticket by over 7,000 votes in the district, but this consola-
tion did not change the outcome. The general dissatisfaction was
demonstrated by the fact that he carried only two of the ten
counties.and thus became a lame-duck congressman.[34]

There were many imponderables about the forces at work in the
1920 election. One consideration concerns the newly enfranchised
women who were voting for the first time in all races. The state
of Illinois offers a unique opportunity to study this question
since a separate record of the votes of men and women was kept.
Studies of this influence by women indicate that they did not
exercise the privilege to the same extent as men, that they leaned
toward the moral and good government side of public issues, and
that they reacted against radical economic proposals. The slightly
greater support given by women to Harding over Cox is attributed
to the widespread opinion that Cox was the more wet and the more
radical of the two candidates. The men favored Harding by 70
percent and the women by 75 percent. At the local level in Illinois,
the Cox candidacy carried only three counties, one of them Greene.[35]
The combination of the landslide proportions among the male voters,
plus the Republican inclinations of the female members of the
electorate, made it nearly impossible to overcome such a handicap.
Rainey's fate was shared by nearly every Democratic congressional

candidate north of the Ohio River.

With the passage of time, Rainey found a number of ways to explain his defeat. Immediately after the election, the reason most frequently suggested was the existence of too many stay-at-home Democrats. Rainey indicated that some 15,000 Democrats in his district had not gone to the polls. A month after the election, he rationalized that he had fully realized the danger of Democratic apathy but was unable to stir the voters to action. Two years later he humorously quipped that every congressman ought to be defeated at least once every eighteen years. Fourteen years after the event, he blamed the defeat on the advice of friends who thought there was no opposition.[36] In retrospect, it seems that he misjudged the times, failed to take necessary precautions, and indeed faced well nigh impossible odds.

Rainey could have rationalized his political retirement at the age of sixty years, but instead he immediately began mending his political fences. Although he expressed to McAdoo the thought that the defeat was absolutely unimportant to him personally, he dispatched a circular letter to all the newspapers in the district. By this means he thanked his constituents for their support during the past eighteen years. He said that the greatest compliment he had ever received was the 7,000 votes by which he led the party ticket, and reminded them that his term did not end until March 4, 1921. In the meantime he would be at his post every hour of every day to render the best possible public service.[37] His actions were not those of a politician contentedly retiring from the scene with past laurels to remember.

Rainey was soon making necessary legal arrangements to contest the election of his Republican opponent. The election contest which Rainey brought against Shaw was based more on aspiration than on expectation. In the notice of contest filed against Shaw, Rainey asserted that Shaw had not filed the necessary papers following the general election with the clerk of the House of Representatives. He also charged that his Republican opponent had not properly accounted for $1,000 donated to the campaign by the Republican national committee, and further asserted that this money was diverted to Shaw's own personal use. The case which Rainey presented to support his brief was extremely weak. The testimony given before the House Elections Committee concerning the misuse of funds was hearsay and circumstantial. The reports required of Shaw were apparently submitted but not in time to meet the deadlines. The Rainey election challenge was based on the most technical violations of the then existing corrupt practices law. The committee found that no action of Shaw's thwarted the statute or infringed upon the best interests of the people in the district. A resolution was passed declaring that neither the dignity nor the honor of the House required Shaw's exclusion by that body.[38] This election contest does not particularly reflect credit upon Rainey because of the spuriousness of the charges. It nevertheless furnished the desired result because by tarnishing the record of his successful opponent, it contributed to the reversal in the subsequent election.

There was little doubt in 1922 that Rainey would be a candidate

for renomination; however, the primary was enlivened by his first
contest since 1908. Supposing that the Rainey spell over the party
members had been broken, Allen T. Lucas of Chandlerville and Loren
H. Wittner of Rockport entered their names on the ballot. As an
aid to renomination, Rainey obtained strong endorsements from labor.
The Conference for Progressive Political Action, a railroad union
organization whose purpose was to promote election of progressives
regardless of political affiliation, supported Rainey. A full-page
ad displayed a pro-labor voting record on thirty-eight of the
thirty-nine issues selected by the railroad brotherhoods. Samuel
Gompers of the AFL again provided a favorable evaluation of the
Rainey labor record. The decision of the Democratic electorate was
overwhelmingly pro-Rainey; he carried every precinct in the entire
district except the two in which his opponents resided. Meanwhile
Guy Shaw was unopposed in the Republican primary.[39] Overconfidence
was not characteristic of the subsequent Rainey campaign.

No stone was left unturned in an effort to get out the vote and
secure re-election in this off-year. Rainey offered to engage in a
series of debates with Shaw across the district, but the incumbent
declined. In the absence of debates, the ex-congressman prepared a
series of criticisms released to the press of the district in an
effort to keep Shaw off-balance answering charges and defending his
record. In an effort to show Rainey's bandwagon appeal, numerous
testimonials from individuals and newspapers were circulated to
district editors. Just before the November election date, Rainey
sent a brief brochure to his friends of both parties in the district.
In the communication he noted that after the 1920 election he had
received hundreds of letters from Republican well-wishers who assured
him that his defeat was not intended. Similarly, the brochure said,
an equal number of letters came from Democrats who did not vote at
all and who were unaware that his re-election was in jeopardy. Since
the district was too large for personal contact, the note appealed
to its recipients to see their friends and neighbors in behalf of
Rainey and to be sure and vote on election day. The strategy was
completely successful. Rainey carried each of the ten counties
with an overall majority of 5,000 votes.[40] Following this return
to Congress for a second career, Rainey was never seriously challenged in either party primary or general election.

Throughout the remainder of the 1920s and the early 1930s, the
principal feature of the twentieth district's campaigns was the farm
problem. In the 1924 campaign against Shaw (an original member of
the House farm bloc organized by L. J. Dickinson of Iowa), Rainey's
record on agricultural relief was the principal issue. The Illinois
Agricultural Association supplied farmers with an evaluation of the
voting records of incumbents seeking re-election. Rainey was
listed among those who had made formal expression to the American
Council of Agriculture that they were willing "to vote for and
support legislation that will afford agriculture equality with
industry and labor." On the negative side of the ledger, he was
prominent in that list of candidates who had voted against the
first McNary-Haugen farm relief bill. Yet, on the credit side was
his support of Henry Ford's Muscle Shoals power-fertilizer project

as endorsed by the Farm Bureau. The *Prairie Farmer* rated the Rainey-
Shaw contest as anybody's guess. The article noted that Shaw's farm
voting record was uniformly good during his first term, while Rainey
had disappointed many by his active role against the principles of
McNary-Haugen. Rural reaction to the Rainey record was favorable as
he survived the Coolidge cyclone.[41]

The good times enjoyed by many in the 1920s were woefully
lacking in farm communities. In 1926 the question of farm relief was
again the principal issue. Although unopposed in the primary, the
local farm bureau publication made quite an issue of Rainey's
supposedly poor farm voting record. Of the five issues presented
as a basis for judgment, Rainey was recorded as absent on four and
as against the first McNary-Haugen bill. A lengthy letter to the
Greene County farm adviser, R. J. Laible, disclosed that the four
measures on which he was recorded as absent came before Congress
while Guy Shaw represented the district. Rainey explained that his
vote against McNary-Haugen was in deference to his own version of
price equality for agriculture. The farm adviser, who was new to the
county, admitted that the record was strikingly inaccurate and
presented the readers of his circular with revised information. Once
the record was clarified, there was no question of Rainey's renomination, but the defeat of the second McNary-Haugen bill created a sea
of agrarian discontent. A record of support for farm measures was
essential to electoral success in his district. In an address on
"Equality for Agriculture" at the White Hall Farm Bureau picnic,
Rainey stated the farmer required "a better price for the things
he has to sell, not larger interest installments to meet [the
administration's plan]." The farmer, he said, "must be given the
advantage that the tariff gives to industry, whether that tariff
be a high protective tariff or a low tariff." In the meantime,
the only course for farmers was an expression of their opinions at
the ballot box. With an unequivocal endorsement from the *Prairie
Farmer* and implicit approval from the Illinois Agricultural Association, Rainey was presented in a favorable light. His position was
resoundingly endorsed at the polls with a landslide majority of
8,000 votes. He carried all counties in the district except Morgan,
the home of his Republican opponent, Horace H. Bancroft.[42] The
farmers' friend gained another two-year term in his congressional
seat.

Each turn of the legislative electoral cycle brought increased
attention to the farmers' plight. As already noted, Rainey's national
reputation as spokesman for farmers enabled him to carry their concern to the Democratic convention in 1928. His own district was
conceded to be safe since his Republican opponent gained the honor
by strength of 426 write-in votes. The magnitude of the farmers'
plight locally transcended party lines as bipartisan support recorded
another exceptional 8,000-plus majority. Similarly, in 1930 the
advent of the general depression augmented Rainey's claim as the
best hope for legislative attention to rural problems. The majority
of 17,275 votes represented an unprecedented endorsement of his
service. He carried all but five of the approximately 300 precincts
in his constituency.[43] His personal triumph was accompanied by

Democratic congressional gains throughout the nation.

His party's rise to majority status and his own ascendancy
enabled Rainey to become majority leader. From this position,
he became a principal critic of the Hoover administration, especially its farm policy. Since his renomination was uncontested
and his re-election seemed secure, the "Democratic gadfly" concentrated upon criticizing the Republican record while saying little
about alternative programs which victorious Democrats would substitute. Typical of the Rainey stings was a vituperative speech on the
subject of "Four Years of Hoover in the Twentieth Congressional
District of Illinois and Especially in Greene County." The vaunted
Hoover promises had dissolved into deplored Hoover problems without
benefit of executive direction to correct the situation. If Rainey
had little respect for Republican leadership, the feeling was
reciprocal. In Hoover's campaign speeches, there are derogatory
references to Rainey's sabotage tactics in Congress and in campaigning. In his memoirs, the President described Rainey as holding
"honorary degrees from all the schools of demagoguery." Hoover's
congressional intermediary, Willis C. Hawley, attributed Rainey's
lack of legislative cooperation to his intention to beat Hoover at
the polls. The strategy of criticism plus the worsened economic
conditions contributed to an overwhelming electoral defeat. The
district election returns showed a staggering majority of 21,072
over Republican William J. Thornton.[44]

Now that the Democrats controlled the legislative and executive
machinery, they could be held accountable for the conduct of affairs.
As Speaker of the House of Representatives, Rainey became closely
identified with New Deal policies, including the first Agricultural
Adjustment Act for farm relief. The 1934 off-year election was the
nation's initial opportunity to pass judgment on the new administration. Rather surprisingly Rainey was opposed for renomination by
James H. Kirby, one-time Illinois legislator, but he did not present
formidable opposition. The primary, however, took on added significance when it became a bellwether of public sentiment toward the
New Deal recovery program. Just prior to the April 10 primary,
Rainey released a statement to the press charging that Wall Street
interests were pouring money into his district as a lesson to
President Roosevelt. It was supposed that the stock market regulation bill, the agricultural adjustment legislation, and other
recovery acts had earned the enmity of the New York financial
interests. According to Rainey's informants, a special effort was
being made to embarrass the administration by securing his defeat
in the nation's earliest congressional primary. The 5 to 1 margin
of victory for Rainey indicated no substantial dissatisfaction with
him, the President, or New Deal policies.[45] For the seventeenth
consecutive time, he secured his party's endorsement for Congress.
His death in August precluded a final judgment at the general
election. Scott W. Lucas of Havanna, running on the Rainey-
Roosevelt record, secured election to the congressional seat with
a normal majority over Republican challenger, Warren W. Wright.

During Rainey's thirty years of legislative service, there
were occasions when his name was mentioned seriously for other

political offices. In 1914 he resisted major entreaties to become
a candidate for the United States Senate. On other occasions he
was suggested as a possible gubernatorial or vice-presidential
candidate. In a few instances he was touted as a presidential
"dark horse." He disregarded these political bees in favor of his
role as gadfly. Rainey made a conscious decision to build a career
of professional legislative service in the House of Representatives.[46]
He was eminently successful in this chosen profession, as constituent
satisfaction demonstrated.

This examination of the last two-thirds of the Rainey career
reveals his ability to maintain and extend his local base of support
and to exercise a considerable influence in state and national
politics. A combination of forces determined that his role would
be in the minority faction of state reformers prior to World War I.
During the decade following his re-election in 1922, his concentration upon farm relief as the primary issue enabled him to transcend
partisan politics in presenting his record to the people. Within
this context, Rainey's stable and safe political constituency made
it possible for him to become both a political conscience and a
party critic. His longevity in this role make it possible for him
to become majority leader and then Speaker. A more detailed examination of the issues in which Rainey was interested will provide a
topical cross section of one congressman's approach to the nation's
problems in the early twentieth century. The preceding description
of his electoral approach has revealed the constancy of Rainey's
attention to constituent needs—local, state, and national. Foremost among these was the development of an Illinois waterway connecting Lake Michigan with the Gulf of Mexico. Its accomplishment
encompasses his entire career.

NOTES

1. Marvin W. Block, "Henry Thomas Rainey: Some Major Aspects
of His Legislative Career" (M.S. thesis), Chap. 3, "Democratic
Gadfly," 34-53; Lee Uhle, "Gadfly Rainey," 187.

2. John D. Buenker, "Edward F. Dunne," 5-6; Paolo E. Coletta,
"Secretary of State William Jennings Bryan," 92, n. 78; Thomas B.
Littlewood, *Horner of Illinois*, 31. The best compendium for
biographical sketches of Illinois Democrats during this period is
Walter A. Townsend, *Illinois Democracy*, Vol. 2-4.

3. Chicago *American*'s report of the speech reprinted in
Gazette, March 20, 1903, 4:1-2; Harrison, *Stormy Years*, 233-235;
Townsend, *Illinois Democracy*, I, 265-267; speech printed in *Gazette*,
Jan. 13, 1905, 4:2-4.

4. New York speech in *Gazette*, April 21, 1905, 4:2-3, and
May 12, 1905, 1:5; John B. Wiseman, "Dilemmas of a Party Out of
Power: The Democracy, 1904-1912" (Ph.D. thesis), 61; Hearst to
HTR, New York, May 1, 1905, RP.

5. *Illinois State Register*, May 9, 1905, 4:2.

6. *Daily Illinois Courier*, March 12, 1906, 1:4–5; Chicago *Tribune*, Aug. 1, 1906, 1:3 and 3:2–4; Aug. 16, 3:1; Aug. 21, 1:3 and 4:4–5; Aug. 22, 1:8, 2:1–8, and 4:4; Paolo E. Coletta, *William Jennings Bryan*, Vol. II, 380.

7. Chicago *Tribune*, Sept. 5, 1906, 1:3 and 3:1–2; Sept. 8, 1906, 1:1 and 4:1–2; "The Sullivan Case," 14. Interestingly President Roosevelt encountered similar divisions among Illinois Republicans. Consult Joel A. Tarr, "President Theodore Roosevelt and Illinois Politics, 1901–1904," 245–264.

8. For a general treatment of Illinois politics during this period, see Theodore C. Pease, *The Story of Illinois*, and Robert P. Howard, *Illinois: A History of the Prairie State*.

9. John M. Blum, *Joe Tumulty and the Wilson Era*, 83.

10. Dunne to Bryan, Springfield, May 25 and June 12, 1914; Vrooman to Bryan, Bloomington, June 14, 1914; Harrison to Bryan, Chicago, June 15, 1914, Bryan Papers, Box 30.

11. Blum, *Joe Tumulty*, 82–83; Chicago *Tribune*, Sept. 8, 1914, 11:3–4 and Sept. 9, 1:1.

12. Speech printed in *CR*, 63:2 (Sept. 25, 1914), Appendix 1023–25.

13. George Fitch, "Politics in Illinois," 21–22.

14. Blum, *Joe Tumulty*, 83; for Bryan's role see J. O. McMath to George Brennan, Indianapolis, Aug. 20, 1923, copy in RP under date of Sept. 9, 1923.

15. For the intricacies of these draft letters see Blum, *Joe Tumulty*, 286, ns. 56 and 57; carbon copy of second draft of Wilson to HTR, [Washington], Oct. 12, 1914, in Wilson Papers, Series II. The second draft is reproduced in Ray S. Baker (ed.), *Woodrow Wilson: Life and Letters*, 90–91. The third draft is printed in Joseph P. Tumulty, *Woodrow Wilson as I Know Him*, 102.

16. HTR to Baker, [Washington], Aug. 5, 1932, as paraphrased in Baker, *Woodrow Wilson*, V, 91, n. 4, and in Blum, *Joe Tumulty*, 286, n. 57.

17. Carlinville *Enquirer* analysis of tactics reproduced in *Gazette*, Sept. 3, 1924, 4:3; *Illinois Blue Book, 1925–26*, 846, 911–912, 930.

18. Sullivan to HTR, Chicago, March 25, 1916, RP; *CR*, 64:1 (April 12, 1916), Appendix 748–750.

19. New York *Times*, June 15, 1916, 3:3; June 16, 3:6; and June 17, 1:1 and 2:4–7. For insights into the Illinois campaign for statewide women's suffrage in 1913 and adoption of the Nineteenth Amendment in 1919, consult the reminiscences of Grace Wilbur Trout, "Sidelights on Illinois Suffrage History," 145–179. Wilson's reluctance on the women's suffrage issue is summarized by C. K. McFarland and Nevin E. Neel, "The Reluctant Reformer," 33–43.

20. HTR to Bryan, Washington, Nov. 15, 1919, Bryan Papers, Box 32; *Official Report of the Proceedings of the Democratic National Convention . . . 1920*, 119-121; New York *Times*, July 1, 1920, 2:2, and July 3, 1920, 2:6; Harrison, *Growing Up with Chicago*, 316; George White (chairman, National Democratic Committee) to HTR, New York, Aug. 13, 1920, RP.

21. HTR to McAdoo, Carrollton, Nov. 8, 1920, McAdoo Papers, Box 243; Brown to HTR, Redlands, Calif., Dec. 15, 1923, and March 26, 1924, RP; McAdoo to HTR, Los Angeles, Calif., May 26, 1924, RP (copy in McAdoo Papers, Box 304); HTR to McAdoo, Washington, June 2, 1924, and McAdoo to HTR, [Los Angeles], June 9, 1924, McAdoo Papers, Box 305.

22. New York *Times*, June 22, 1924, 9:3; Rainey's Bryan Memorial Speech, 5867. For general activities of the Illinois delegation see Gerald L. Gutek, "George Brennan and the Illinois Delegation in the Democratic Convention of 1924" (M.A. thesis).

23. Five-page letter of HTR to FDR, Washington, Dec. 30, 1924, Roosevelt Papers, Group II Replies to FDR's Circular Letter, Dec., 1924, Illinois—1924-25; speech of Feb. 17, 1925, printed in *CR*, 68:2 (March 4, 1925), 5557-59.

24. New York *Times*, June 24, 1928, 2:4.

25. HTR to Roosevelt, [Washington], Dec. 15, 1928, as quoted by Earland I. Carlson, "Franklin D. Roosevelt's Post-Mortem of the 1928 Election," 302-303; New York *Times*, May 29, 1932, IX, 3:4-5; Cordell Hull, *The Memoirs of Cordell Hull*, I, 131-132, 150-151; New York *Times*, June 27, 1932, 11:2.

26. HTR to participants in Democratic congressional convention, [Washington], undated, as printed in *Gazette*, Sept. 23, 1914, 2:2-3; *Illinois Blue Book, 1915-16*, 671, 711.

27. *Illinois Blue Book, 1917-18*, 548; Gompers to Walker, Washington, Oct. 16, 1916, as printed in *Gazette*, Nov. 1, 1916, 1:6; "Mawsh Members," 1, 8; Wilson to HTR, Shadow Lawn, N.J., Oct. 23, 1916, as printed in *Gazette*, Nov. 1, 1916, 1:2; *Illinois Blue Book, 1917-18*, 601.

28. HTR to district convention, Washington, undated, as printed in *Gazette*, Sept. 25, 1918, 1:4-6; Ray S. Baker and William E. Dodd (eds.), *Public Papers of Woodrow Wilson*, V, 286-288; editorial, "How 'Politics Adjourned,'" *Patriot*, Oct. 31, 1918, 4:1-2.

29. Selig Adler, "The Congressional Election of 1918," 447-465; Seward W. Livermore, "The Sectional Issue in the 1918 Congressional Elections," 29-60; editorial, "Politics and the War," *Patriot*, Oct. 3, 1918, 4:1; *Illinois Blue Book, 1919-20*, 610, 653.

30. *Biographical Directory of the American Congress, 1774-1961*, 1588; *Illinois Blue Book, 1921-22*, 714.

31. *CR*, 66:1 (July 28, 1919), 3262; HTR telegram to chairman of Democratic congressional convention, Washington, May 4, 1920, as

reproduced in *Gazette*, May 12, 1920, 1:2; *CR*, 66:2 (June 3, 1920), 8395–96, and (June 5, 1920), 9201–9202; *Patriot*, Sept. 2, 1920, 1:1–3; a copy of the 1920 brochure is affixed to a typescript prepared by Hugh A. Morrison and Robert T. Patterson, "Hon. Henry Thomas Rainey, 1860–1934 . . . record of services . . . as given in the indexes of the *Congressional Record* (available only in the Rare Book Room of the Library of Congress, presumably prepared in 1934).

32. For the questions see *Patriot*, Aug. 26, 1920, 4:1–2; Shaw's brief yes and no responses in *ibid.*, Sept. 30, 1920, 4:1; and HTR's detailed reply in *ibid.*, Oct. 7, 1920, 1:3–4.

33. Samuel G. Blythe, "The Soldier in Politics," 16–17, 79, 82; Philip Von Blon, "The Soldier Vote," 32–33, 37–38; Legion ad in Dixon Wecter, *When Johnny Comes Marching Home*, 373; editorial, "Over the Top for Them," *Patriot*, Oct. 28, 1920, 4:1.

34. *Illinois Blue Book, 1921-22*, 800.

35. Stuart A. Rice and Malcolm M. Willey, "American Women's Ineffective Use of the Vote," 641–647; Willey and Rice, "A Sex Cleavage in the Presidential Election of 1920," 519–520; David Burner, *The Politics of Provincialism*, 70, n. 4. For another study of state factors see Herbert F. Margulies, "The Election of 1920 in Wisconsin," 15–22.

36. HTR to Claude Kitchin, Carrollton, Nov. 8, 1920, Kitchin Papers, Reel 32; HTR to Keith Vawter, Carrollton, Nov. 18, 1920, RP; HTR to Bryan, Washington, Dec. 10, 1920, Bryan Papers, Box 33; excerpt from HTR letter printed as a biographical note accompanying an article in *Prairie Farmer*, XCV (Aug. 25, 1923), 6; HTR to Merrill H. Johnston, [Washington], March 13, 1934, RP.

37. HTR to McAdoo, Carrollton, Nov. 8, 1920, McAdoo Papers, Box 243 (copy in RP); "Mr. Rainey Thanks His Constituents," *Gazette*, Nov. 10, 1920, 1:3, and *Patriot*, Nov. 11, 1920, 4:1.

38. Rainey brief in *Contested-Election Case of Henry T. Rainey v. Guy L. Shaw*; U.S. Congress, House, Committee on Elections No. 2, *Contested-Election Case of Rainey v. Shaw*, Hearings, 67 Cong., 1 Sess.

39. Clark to Conductor R. McD. Smith of Roodhouse, Washington, March 4, 1922, and Gompers to Smith, unknown, March 11, 1922, as reproduced in ad appearing in *Gazette*, March 29, 1922, 7:1–2; *Illinois Blue Book, 1923-24*, 809.

40. The 1922 election brochure dated Carrollton, Oct. 31, 1922, RP, "Correspondence" file for June, 1923, another copy in "Newspaper clippings—Miscellany" file; *Illinois Blue Book, 1923-24*, 777.

41. "How Illinois Congressional Candidates Stand," 4; "Records the Best Guide for Voting," 7; *Illinois Blue Book, 1925-26*, 846.

42. *Greene County Farm Bureau Bulletin*, April 10, 1926, 5;

HTR to R. J. Laible, Washington, April 15, 1926, and Laible to Members of the Greene County Farm Bureau, Carrollton, April 20, 1926, as printed in the *Bulletin*, April [20], 1926, unpaged; excerpts of speech in *Gazette*, Aug. 25, 1926, 1:5-6 and 5:4; "Candidates for Congress," 4; "Know Your Friends When You Go to the Polls, Vote Accordingly," 3; *Illinois Blue Book, 1927-28*, 914.

43. *Illinois Blue Book, 1929-30*, 883, and *1931-32*, 861.

44. Speech reproduced in *Gazette*, Nov. 3, 1932, 1:6 and 7:2-3; Herbert Hoover, *The Memoirs of Herbert Hoover*, III, 101-104, 262-263, 276; *Illinois Blue Book, 1933-34*, 701-702, 736.

45. *Newsweek*, III (Aug. 25, 1934), 29; New York *Times*, April 1, 1934, I, 26:6-7, and Chicago *Tribune*, April 1, 1934, 11:4-5; *Illinois Blue Book, 1935-36*, 923, 961.

46. For elaboration of this career view consult Nelson W. Polsby, "The Institutionalization of the U.S. House of Representatives," 166, 168.

4
Promoter of the Illinois Waterway

The most pervasive problems dominating the interests of the
citizenry in Illinois' twentieth congressional district concern
the Illinois River. The constituency of this bottomland district
is affected by the river in terms of its navigability, flood control,
purity, and commercial value. The advancement of local internal
improvements has long been an avenue for success in a political
career, and Congressman Rainey's experience reinforces the generalization. Before entering Congress, he had decided upon improvement
of the Illinois River as his cardinal objective. Calhoun County,
nestled between the Illinois and Mississippi rivers, was especially
interested in his propositions. The Calhoun *Republican* quipped
that Rainey would receive triple the amount of praise for removing
the dams from the Illinois River as he would if he were content to
follow party policy and damn the tariffs.[1] Rainey's concern for
the development of inland waterways in general, and the Illinois
basin in particular, embraces a major component of his congressional career.

From the earliest days of man's exploration of the Illinois
country, he has dreamed of an all-water connection between the
Great Lakes and the Mississippi River system. In 1673 the explorers Louis Joliet and Father Jacques Marquette noted that a canal
cut through a short distance of prairie would connect Lake Michigan
to an Illinois River tributary. Development of such a link did not
begin until 150 years later, when improved transportation became
necessary as an aid to settlement. In 1822 Congress approved
legislation which inaugurated the canal-building era for Illinois.
In 1848 the Illinois and Michigan Canal was opened to traffic, and
for a time the dream of a lakes-to-gulf waterway was a reality.
The significant growth in the population of Chicago in the latter
half of the nineteenth century demanded that this aid to navigation also become a means of sanitation. In 1900 the upper end of
the canal was replaced by the Chicago Sanitary and Ship Canal,
which served this dual function. With the passage of time, the
lower portion of the Illinois and Michigan Canal became outmoded
and was virtually abandoned as an aid to navigation. At the turn
of the twentieth century, there was a renewed interest in the
expansion of water routes in the Middle West, especially a demand
for a lakes-to-gulf deep waterway. This movement found historical
antecedents in nearly a century of agitation for a continuous
water transportation system extending from New York to New Orleans

by way of the Great Lakes and the Mississippi River.

The Prairie State's contribution to such a development became known as the Illinois waterway. Initially this term was used to denote an improvement paralleling the lower portion of the Illinois and Michigan Canal from Lockport to LaSalle (see accompanying map). This link in the lakes-to-gulf concept was located wholly within the state and entirely financed by a bond issue approved in 1908. Because of the inadequacy of state finances, the federal government provided support beginning in 1931. After this date, the expression "Illinois waterway" includes the entire Illinois River from Grafton at the southern extremity to Lake Street in Chicago on the Chicago River and to the Twining Basin Number Five on the Calumet River (see accompanying map). The Illinois waterway may be likened to the waist of an hourglass connecting the Great Lakes-St. Lawrence system with the Mississippi-Panama Canal outlets. In addition, it may be described as a bottleneck, because it was twenty-five years from the constitutional authorization for construction to the work's completion. The history of the Illinois segment of the lakes-to-gulf waterway reveals an entanglement of political, constitutional, economic, legal, and international issues which defy easy comprehension.[2] Since Representative Rainey of the Illinois River bottomlands was the only major political figure involved whose career embraces the generation of time from inauguration to implementation, an examination of his interest in the matter provides insight for an understanding of the waterway issues.

As congressman-elect, Rainey had stated that the lock and dam system permitting slack water navigation was antiquated and should be removed from the river. He favored the development of a deeper waterway by dredging the river where necessary and then dumping the diggings along the bank to deepen the channel and aid in building a levee. Rainey advocated federal government assistance for this improvement because current programs were aiding the lower Mississippi Valley in reclaiming floodlands through the use of levees and were assisting western areas in the redemption of arid lands through irrigation projects. Apart from making the Illinois River an important commercial outlet, he believed this scheme would afford effective competition for monopolistic railroads. When Congress was called into special session beginning on November 9, 1903, he took advantage of the opportunity to introduce bills relating to his Illinois River projects. The two most significant items were resolutions favoring the removal of the federal government's dams from the Illinois River at Kampsville and LaGrange and urging an investigation of the flow of water through the Chicago Sanitary and Ship Canal into the Illinois River. Rainey maintained that the rise in the river level due to the obstructions and the increased flow from Chicago had inundated and rendered useless between 250,000 and 300,000 acres of Illinois farm land.[3] Both of these matters came to have an integral relationship to subsequent activity on behalf of a lakes-to-gulf deep waterway.

Initially, however, only that portion of the Rainey program relating to the federal dams was implemented. Rainey's proposal had called upon the War Department to remove the dams entirely,

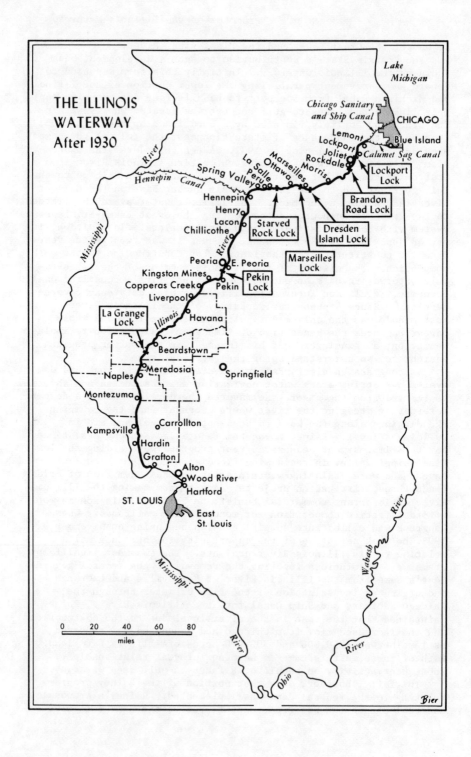

THE ILLINOIS
WATERWAY
After 1930

Lake
Michigan

Chicago Sanitary
and Ship Canal

CHICAGO

Lemont
Lockport
Joliet
Rockdale

Blue Island
Calumet Sag Canal

Lockport
Lock

Brandon
Road Lock

Marseilles
Ottawa
Morris

La Salle
Peru
Spring Valley

Hennepin Canal

River

Mississippi

Hennepin

Henry
Lacon
Chillicothe

Starved
Rock Lock

Dresden
Island Lock

Marseilles
Lock

Peoria
E. Peoria

Kingston Mines
Copperas Creek
Liverpool

Pekin

Pekin
Lock

River

La Grange
Lock

Illinois

Havana

Beardstown

Naples

Meredosia

Springfield

Montezuma

Carrollton

Kampsville

Hardin
Grafton
Alton
Wood River
Hartford

ST. LOUIS

East
St. Louis

Wabash
River

Mississippi

River

River

Ohio

0   20   40   60   80
miles

Bier

but the chief engineer objected and that resolution was withdrawn.
A substitute measure, which the chief engineer approved, called
for lowering the dams two feet instead of removing them. The
Chicago Sanitary District was made responsible for the lowering
and the expense involved since the increased diversion had raised
the river's normal depth and contributed to the flooding. This
resolution had the approval of Isham Randolph, chief engineer of
the Chicago Sanitary District. After House and Senate approval of
the bill, Randolph indicated that the work would begin presumably
in late August or early September. Seemingly the first step had
been taken toward deepening the channel, but the freshman congressman had much to learn about the operations of government bureaucracy.
Before the dams could be removed or even lowered, it would be
necessary for a government survey to be made. It was not anticipated that this survey could be completed before June, 1905.[4]
Congressman Rainey and his constituents were soon to learn that
patience and perseverance were necessary virtues if the waterway
situation were to be improved.

The pervasiveness of the waterway issue is illustrated by the
focus given Rainey's maiden speech before the House of Representatives. His remarks contain a number of thoughts centering upon
the idea of waterway development. The concept itself was not new,
but his speech does represent a renewal of agitation aimed at
securing congressional approval of federal support for inland
waterways. As the next chapter will demonstrate, this revival of
interest in waterways was closely associated with the movement for
the conservation of natural resources. In his remarks, Rainey
proposed to consider the building of the Panama Canal in its
relation to a deep waterway from the Great Lakes to the Gulf of
Mexico. There was an irresistible logic of events, he said,
which led him to conclude that the natural direction for commerce
was in north-south avenues and that this was about to commence.
Since the building of the Isthmian Canal was but an extension of
the Mississippi River, it was only natural that work begin to
make the Father of Waters and its tributaries ready for the
expanded commerce. The immediate results of such an investment,
he concluded, would be to double the nation's coastline and to
compete with the east-west—oriented railroads.[5] The fledgling
congressman's initial speech was favorably received in the
district and among the Chicago and St. Louis dailies. Rainey had
struck upon an issue which was nonpartisan and popular in its
appeal and also national in its impact.

As he launched his personal campaign for waterway improvements,
the most pressing problem was the mobilization of the favorable
response his plea had received. As early as 1860, the people of
the nation's interior had seized upon the association/convention
system as the best means of promoting desired internal improvements. In waterway matters, such organizations stressed the
commercial importance of the rivers, the impossibility of concerted action by the several states, and thus the necessity for
national action. Agricultural interests also promoted water
improvements as a means of regulating railroad rates. By the turn

of the century, two new elements—a series of great floods in the Mississippi watershed and the scientific study of the problems associated with the conservation of natural resources—had added new urgency to programs for waterway improvement.[6] The times were propitious for a Lakes-to-Gulf Deep Waterway Association such as Rainey envisioned.

Another leading congressional supporter of such an organization was Chicagoan William Lorimer, a member of the House Committee on Rivers and Harbors. At Lorimer's invitation, Rainey accompanied him in November, 1905, on a 1,700-mile, thirty-day inspection of the all-water route from Lake Michigan to the Gulf of Mexico. The Rainey speech on the lakes-to-gulf waterway had attracted considerable attention to this goal. With this impetus, the voyage was not intended so much to create sentiment in favor of such a project, but rather to organize that which already existed. The party traveled only in the daytime, stopping at every hamlet, village, town, and city. At the major population centers they organized local lakes-to-gulf deep waterway societies. At St. Louis they received an especially warm welcome because this was one of the hotbeds of sentiment in favor of such a project. There, a day and a half was devoted to discussing with the leaders of various commercial clubs the successes achieved thus far and the possibilities of a convention for all these newly formed associations. In the journey from St. Louis to New Orleans, the launch was visited by other interested congressmen, but only Lorimer and Rainey lasted throughout the entire journey. Rainey made forty-one speeches in behalf of the deep waterway, stressing the commercial and conservation aspects. As a direct result of the Lorimer-Rainey effort, forty-five associations were formed then and countless others were created as an indirect result of their trip.[7]

Following the successful conclusion of this journey, the next step was to coordinate the individual efforts of the local associations. With the assistance of the St. Louis organizations, the first convention of the Lakes-to-Gulf Deep Waterway Association was called for November 15-16, 1906. Lorimer served as temporary chairman and Rainey as acting secretary until the permanent organization of the association could be effected. When delivering one of the major addresses at the convention, Rainey expressed the dominant theme that the "only way to regulate railroad rates is to improve these sixteen thousand miles of navigable rivers."[8] Henry T. Rainey had materially assisted as midwife in the birth of this pressure group.

The declared purpose of the association was development of a deep waterway trunk line from Chicago to the Gulf of Mexico by way of the Des Plaines, Illinois, and Mississippi rivers and cooperation in the expansion of the collateral feeders. The policy established at that first meeting was for a deep waterway with a minimum depth of fourteen feet and an ultimate depth of twenty-four feet. The membership of the association consisted of delegates appointed each year by governors of the states, mayors of cities, and heads of commercial and civic improvement associations. To that end, Rainey had helped in chartering a social and commercial club in Carrollton. He attended each of the annual conventions as a delegate from the Carrollton Commercial Club. Financial support of the organization came largely through popular contributions from interested groups in the Mississippi Valley. Presidential leadership in the organization was provided by William K. Kavanaugh, president of the Wiggins Ferry Company. As a practical riverman, Kavanaugh served as an effective advocate and lobbyist for the improvement of the Mississippi River. The establishment of this association in 1906 marks the first real impetus for the Mississippi route as opposed to the St. Lawrence passage for unlocking the inland lakes. From its headquarters in St. Louis, the association carried on educational and publicity campaigns by means of lectures and publications. For a time the Lakes-to-Gulf Deep Waterway Association proved to be a useful supplement to congressional pressure for federal action.[9] This association marked one approach to the ever pressing urge for development of the water transportation resources of the nation.

The logical place to promote federal support of internal improvements was in the halls of Congress. To achieve that purpose, Lorimer became president and Rainey secretary of an informal lobby of Mississippi Valley congressmen. During the early portion of Theodore Roosevelt's second administration, the national legislature was concerned principally with the other side of the transportation coin—the railroads. Rainey used interest in railroad rate regulation to promote the waterway proposal. He called the regulation and control of railroad rates the greatest economic question presenting itself for solution in the United States. Initially he favored the granting of additional powers to the Interstate Commerce Commission so that it could not only declare a rate unreasonable, but also could decide what was a reasonable rate and place it in effect within a fair period of time. Illinois' lone Democratic congressman was not enthusiastic about the Hepburn bill for railroad rate regulation because legal regulation would prove impossible and impractical. Rainey argued the position that competition from waterways was the only solution short of government ownership of railroads, as the Populists had demanded.[10]

In Rainey's view, the land and water transportation issues merged into one central problem—should the federal government intervene in the public interest? Rainey's answer was a decided yes. During the next session of the Fifty-ninth Congress, he and his waterway cohorts attempted to produce the answer in the national legislature. They hoped to amend the rivers and harbors appropriations bill so that it would provide $31,000,000 for the lakes-to-gulf project. Rainey made a lengthy speech in behalf of this waterway scheme. He repeated his argument that only through internal waterway improvements could competition be provided for the railroads and thus insure adequate regulation of railroad rates because mere laws, such as the Hepburn Act, would prove a failure. He urged his fellow congressmen to become a part of the "new era—the water-controlling period of the world—a

time when men quit talking about what can be done with rivers
and canals, and a time when men commence to do something." This
line of thought indicates that Rainey was influenced by Alfred
Thayer Mahan's ideas. Rainey coupled waterway improvements with
pleas for national defense. He resorted to ridicule by naming
some of the insignificant rivers included in the bill while the
Illinois and Mississippi rivers and the Chicago ship canal had
been neglected. To substantiate the need for this north-south
transportation net, Rainey offered a sequel to the Turner frontier
thesis. Rainey argued that in the settlement stages a country's
population followed east-west lines. Once a great section is
filled up, a north-south movement commences. As an example he
showed how men living along the fortieth parallel in New York,
Illinois, and California are engaged in similar occupations
producing kindred products. For a time the artificial east-
west movement is maintained as the raw material of the west must
be exchanged for the manufactured goods of the east. With the
spread of industrialization, this artificial movement stops.
Then a north-south movement commences in order that the products
of two different climates may be exchanged. This north and south
exchange, he maintained, had been and always would be the natural
movement of commerce. On these foundations he based his case for
the development of the lakes-to-gulf waterway.[11] Rainey and his
colleagues were unsuccessful in their endeavors to overcome
Chairman Theodore Burton's opposition to such an expenditure.
The fight for this inland waterway would have to be renewed at a
later date.

The locus of the waterway struggle now shifted from the
national to the state surroundings. Various schemes which would
permit the development of a deep waterway within the confines of
Illinois were suggested. The most important of these proposals was
a plan presented to the General Assembly by the Chicago Sanitary
District. The district was created in 1889 in an effort to relieve
the municipality of Chicago of the menace to public health created
by the flow of sewage into Lake Michigan, the source of the city's
water supply. A specially designed drainage canal reversed the
flow of the Chicago River in order to carry the city's refuse
through the divide and down into the Illinois and Michigan Canal.
At a cost of $50,000,000, this drainage canal was completed in
1900; it served the dual object of a sewerage outlet and a deep
waterway connecting Lake Michigan with the Illinois and Michigan
Canal. In 1907 the sanitary district sought legislation which would
allow it to connect the Chicago drainage canal with the Illinois
River system rather than the Illinois and Michigan Canal as a waterway in exchange for all the revenues that might be derived from
the development of waterpower sites along the route. This would
have meant the extension of the existing drainage canal by a few
miles and it would have provided limitless revenues for the developers of the power sites and the sanitary district. Rainey thought
the suggestion was fraught with too many disadvantages, and
especially believed it would prevent the development of a deep
waterway with federal government support.[12] The Illinois legislature

was convened in special session in the autumn of 1907 to consider
the matter. Rainey endeavored to defeat the sanitary district's
proposition when it came before the state legislators.

The Rainey resistance is best summarized in a circular letter
sent to all national congressmen, the Illinois state legislators,
and the press of Illinois. He argued that the state of Illinois
could not *"be benefitted in the least by a deep waterway which will
terminate in the woods three miles south of Joliet."* He described
the proposal as a subterfuge for private concerns to control the
only major waterpower-producing section in the state. Rainey
predicted that the success of this scheme would force the abandonment of a real deep waterway from Chicago to the Gulf of Mexico.
In addition to the waterpower leeches, Rainey implied there was a
plot by the railroads to thwart the use of any waterway which might
result. Since the sanitary district trustees proposed to sell the
right-of-way along the Illinois and Michigan Canal, Rainey foresaw
that such a proposal would allow the railroad interests to acquire
the land, thus preventing the building of terminals and warehouses
along the probable waterway route. He summarized his objections by
declaring that the sanitary district's proposal was "absolutely
illogical and untenable."[13]

As principal critic of the sanitary district's proposal, Rainey
lobbied against the proposition when the General Assembly convened
in special session to consider waterway policy. He succeeded in
defeating that proposal and substituting an amendment to the Illinois Constitution which would permit an alternate scheme. Rainey
and Lyman E. Cooley, noted waterway engineer and secretary of the
Illinois Internal Improvement Commission, drafted a resolution which
would permit the state of Illinois to construct a channel connecting
the Chicago Sanitary and Ship Canal with the Illinois River near
LaSalle. Up to $20,000,000 in bonds could be issued for this pur-
pose, with the bonds to be repaid out of revenues derived from the
sale of waterpower.[14] This allocation of funds was designed so that
Illinois could cooperate with the national government in the construction of a deep waterway.

At the regular election in 1908, the citizens of Illinois were
called upon to register their approval of this amendment. Together
with Lorimer and others, Rainey carried on a vigorous campaign for
the proposal. Traveling at his own expense, he canvassed the entire
state in behalf of his pet project, making 200 speeches in behalf of
the amendment. Using a stereopticon to present an illustrated
lecture, Rainey verbally and visually carried his audiences over the
proposed route. These stump speeches played a significant role in
acquainting the people of Illinois with the waterway issue. This
seventh amendment to the Illinois Constitution, approved in all
counties except four, committed the state of Illinois to a means of
fostering the deep waterway project within her boundaries.[15] The
exact program for spending the authorized sum became a matter of
conflict between Rainey and subsequent state administrations.

While the state government had been committed to a portion of
the lakes-to-gulf deep waterway, the national government remained
unconvinced. The annual meetings of the association endeavored to

provide stimulation. The second convention was held in Memphis,
Tennessee, on October 4-5, 1907. President Roosevelt, accompanied
by a group of Cabinet officers, governors, congressmen, and other
dignitaries, traveled by steamboat from Keokuk, Iowa, down the
Mississippi to the convention city. In a speech before the convention, Rainey noted that "we are today in this middle ground to bind
together the corn fields of the North and the cane fields of the
South." As the theme for the second convention, the association had
adopted the expression from Rainey's St. Louis address that "river
regulation is rate regulation." President Roosevelt in his address
noted the desirability of navigable streams providing a measuring
stick for railroad rates.[16] Even though the President had honored
the convention with his presence, a tour of inspection, and an
enthusiastic speech, there were still innumerable obstacles to
federal support of the waterway idea.

The campaign of the waterway associations was undaunted by the
lack of success at the national level. At the 1908 Chicago meeting
of the deep waterway association, the idea that the waterway's
future was as a helper rather than a competitor of the railroads
began to permeate the thinking of numerous waterway advocates. In
the absence of James J. Hill, chairman of the board of the Great
Northern Railway, Rainey was asked to read Hill's speech entitled
"The Future of Rail and Water Transportation." Hill described the
relation between water and rail transportation as one "of harmony,
of helpfulness and of co-operation" because the two carriers were
"supplementary instead of mutually destructive." Although Rainey
read the speech, there is no indication that he accepted the shift
in emphasis which was overtaking the association. On a more harmonious note, the Chicago conventioneers endorsed the Illinois
constitutional amendment as they envisioned "Fourteen feet through
the Valley," a depth which would accommodate lake vessels.[17] The
implication for federal-state cooperation in internal improvements
was favorable if the constitutional amendment was successful.

While the lakes-to-gulf waterway idea was spreading, the federal government was still not moved to favorable action. In fact,
the Corps of Engineers issued a report certifying the feasibility of
a fourteen-foot channel from the lakes to the gulf *but* recommending
that the project not be pursued. The report claimed that the
estimated expense of $158,000,000 was not justified by the commerce
involved. The engineers were favorably disposed toward a waterway
of eight- or nine-foot depth throughout. The *Engineering News*
noted that this report will squelch "the shouters for '14 ft.
through the Valley' [who] must perceive the folly of trying to
promote great engineering schemes with hot air alone." Nevertheless, Rainey adamantly did his best to minimize the unfavorable
aspects of the corps' report. In an interview released in the St.
Louis *Republic*, he juggled the figures in such a manner that the
estimated real cost was only $30,000,000 to $40,000,000; he thought
the expenditure of such an amount justifiable.[18] Henry T. knew well
that what technicians may propose, politicians can, and do, dispose.

The fulcrum for Rainey's national interest in internal improvements continued to be the Lakes-to-Gulf Deep Waterway Association.

His contribution to the 1909 meeting was enlisting the navy's aid in dramatizing the occasion. A torpedo boat flotilla accompanied President William Howard Taft as he journeyed down the Mississippi from St. Louis to the convention site; an armored cruiser squadron and the battleship "Mississippi" came by sea to the New Orleans meeting site. In spite of presidential approbation, the association entered its fifth year without favorable national action. The motto of the association now read "River regulation is rate regulation. River improvement is railroad improvement." In a brief address before the fifth convention, Rainey chastised the membership for succumbing to the railroad propaganda which de-emphasized the competition between water and rail carriers. Specifically he decried the loss of organizational militancy in upholding competition as the best means of regulating transportation rates. At the close of the conference, Rainey became involved in a heated resolutions' controversy when he attempted to censure President Taft for failure to promote the deep waterway project fully. Ultimately he acquiesced to the majority, and the section critical of the President was stricken from the resolutions.[19] Although the association scheduled its next annual assembly for Chicago in 1911, it failed to meet and ceased to be a pressure group on the waterway issue. For the next several years the struggle for a deep waterway was conducted at the state level.

As the Democratic gadfly, Rainey would be an irritant to both Republican and Democratic state administrations as plans were presented for developing the Illinois connection in a deep waterway extending from Chicago to New Orleans. Even before approval of the constitutional amendment, there had been fear that the project was susceptible to political influence. The Chicago Association of Commerce urged the appointment of a nonpartisan commission of businessmen to supervise the undertaking in order to assure its proper administration and economical completion. Following the official word of the amendment's acceptance, the Chicago *Record-Herald* urged the progressives of both parties in the General Assembly to resist any attempts at political jobbery in executing the plans immediately.[20] The businesslike approach to the development of the Illinois waterway typified the Progressive era's concern for efficiency and economy in the execution of public projects. As various programs for construction were presented, Congressman Rainey served as a watchdog to assure satisfactory adherence to the deep waterway concept as he perceived it.

During the 1909 regular session of the General Assembly, waterway proposals revealed certain philosophic and political differences among the advocates within the Republican party. One faction was headed by Governor Charles S. Deneen, who was supported by Isham Randolph, chief engineer of the Chicago Sanitary District, and by Frank P. Schmitt of Chicago, leader of the administration's measure in the Senate. The governor's proposal called for a fourteen-foot waterway with construction by the state to begin immediately and with major attention to the development of the waterpower sites in the sixty-one mile project.[21] Republican party stalwarts presenting an alternate plan were led by United States Senator—designate

William Lorimer, assisted by Lyman E. Cooley, engineer and secretary of the Illinois Internal Improvement Commission, and by Thomas H. Riley of Joliet and Edward J. Smejkal of Chicago in the House of Representatives. The Lorimer scheme proposed a twenty-four-foot canal to accommodate naval ships desiring to reach the Great Lakes; the state was to await federal government assistance in the remainder of the waterway and to show minimal concern for the development of hydro-electric power.[22]   The two factions remained at loggerheads and were unable to arrange a satisfactory compromise during the regular session. A subsequent special session devoted to waterway legislation also failed to reach agreement, so no action was taken toward the execution of the Illinois waterway during Governor Deneen's administration.

The factionalism previously noted in the Democratic party is also characteristic of Republican circles in Illinois. The waterway appropriation provided a center for the struggle of rival political groups. The differences in the Deneen-Lorimer approaches are best explained in terms of control over any patronage which might result incidental to the project. Presumably, the governor's position would be strengthened if the state took the initiative in this endeavor. If the United States government provided a liberal finan- cial contribution, certain advantages of a political nature would devolve upon the Senator.[23]   Each sought to foster his own political advantage to the detriment of the popular mandate expressed in the constitutional amendment.

As the stalemate between Deneen and Lorimer was extended, Rainey began to take issue with their proposals. On balance, his sympa- thies lay with the Lorimer deep waterway approach, yet he urged immediate action rather than await federal assistance. After a respectful silence during which the contending factions continued to stall the undertaking, Rainey could contain himself no longer. In political speeches around Chicago, the downstater lambasted Governor Deneen's handling of the waterway matter. He accused the governor of advocating a waterway bill which would create an army of political leeches who would drain the state's funds without produc- ing a satisfactory waterway. Most significantly the congressman charged that the governor had sold out to the waterpower interests who wished to exploit that feature of the project. In order to effect a compromise, Rainey subsequently proposed a three-point scheme for immediate attention. He suggested state and national cooperation in the construction, the formation of a special state commission to supervise the project, and the levying of tolls for the use of waterpower sites. His compromise received the endorsement of the 1911 Democratic state convention, but this attempt at media- tion came to naught.[24]   The best that could be expected was that a change in administrations following the gubernatorial elections would break the impasse.

At the 1912 general election, Illinois Democrats secured con- trol of the governor's mansion for the first time since before the turn of the century in the days of John Peter Altgeld. The prospect for federal-state cooperation dimmed considerably because it soon became apparent that Governor Edward F. Dunne and Congressman Rainey did not agree on a number of matters. Conflicts between them arose over the handling of a foot-and-mouth-disease control program, the administration of local patronage, the policy of water conservation, and the development of the Illinois portion of the deep waterway. The latter was the area of most severe disagreement between them.

By the time the Dunne administration was inaugurated, the concept of internal waterway improvements was being buffeted with pro and con arguments. The stillborn Illinois waterway was the subject of increasing attention since a policy remained to be established. The railroad interests continued to maintain that waterway development was not antagonistic to their business. Railroad entrepreneur James J. Hill emphasized the need for *deep* waterways and urged a second priority for the Illinois waterway after the lower Mississippi from New Orleans to St. Louis was made navigable. The Corps of Engineers had re-examined the Illinois River in 1910 and reaffirmed commercial justification for a channel only eight to nine feet in depth. Some outspoken critics were more severe in their denunciations. Economics professor Harold G. Moulton concluded after lengthy study "that the project is visionary in the extreme, and that the dream of one day beholding the flags of all nations unfurled before Chicago breezes will never be realized." William Arthur Shelton, another political economist, deduced that "it would be a pure economic waste to construct a Lakes-to-the-Gulf Deep Waterway."[25] While the realists were having their say, the dreamers continued to see visions of success, albeit by different methods of accomplishment.

From the congressman's perspective, matters reached a serious stage when Governor Dunne publicly supported a proposal for an eight-foot waterway. In a Chicago speech on October 10, 1914, the state's chief executive unqualifiedly endorsed an eight-foot project since it would cost only $3,075,000 and it could eventually be deepened to fourteen or twenty-four feet. Dunne asserted that such a project was "not a pork barrel proposition, but a fine utilitarian project." In a subsequent press release, he backed the proposal as supplemental to and not antagonistic toward railroad transportation. A biennial message to the Forty-ninth Illinois General Assembly placed special emphasis upon the passage of a bill to effect such a waterway. The Illinois House of Representatives approved such a measure on May 25, 1915. The governor was especially pleased at Republican support of the measure since this was "a pure, clean business proposition without an element of politics in it."[26] Illinois action was fast moving to a climax.

At this critical time, Congressman Rainey began to show publicly his disapproval of the Dunne waterway proposal. He received permission to address the Illinois Senate on the matter. In an allotted half-hour, he opposed the bill as a too shallow waterway. He contended that an eight-foot project would forever doom a deeper waterway because assistance from the federal government would not be forthcoming. Rainey also opposed surrendering complete control of the development of electrical power to the waterway parasites, Samuel Insull and the North American Water Power group at Marseilles. He quoted letters from Lyman E. Cooley as being opposed to the measure. To counteract the argument that a depth greater than eight feet was not possible in the Mississippi River, Rainey argued that the amount of commerce between Chicago and St. Louis alone justified the increased depth in Illinois. He concluded by hoping that the senators would throw a monkey wrench at a bill, which he called "the worst piece of legislation ever conceived by any Legislature in any State in this Union."[27] In spite of his fervent plea, the Senate voted to approve the bill by a 3 to 1 margin. The legislature was overwhelmingly opposed to the Rainey stand, but he did not give up the fight.

Governor Dunne was elated over the bill's passage and made numerous speeches in support of his waterway. In a statement to the press on the day of passage he said the law would enable the state of Illinois, "unless some unforeseen and unrecognized legal difficulties intervene," to open up the commerce of the lakes to an unobstructed passage to the gulf and to take advantage of the commercial revolution resulting from the opening of the Panama Canal. In a Chicago speech, Dunne deplored the delay of the past years and stated that further procrastination in opening the channel would be a commercial, financial, and political blunder. In October Rainey reiterated his criticisms and added that graft was inherent in the plan. Dunne immediately replied that Rainey's statements were full of assertions of reckless facts and that his charges of graft were so wildly absurd as to be grotesque. At Davenport, Iowa, Dunne praised the project as of incalculable value and of tremendous importance to the people of the Mississippi and Illinois rivers region. In its broadest perspective, the Dunne project represented a public works program for the state's unemployed, a proposal with far-reaching social, humanitarian, political, and economic implications.[28] While the governor was attempting to maintain enthusiasm for his eight-foot project, Congressman Rainey was quietly working behind the scenes to oppose him.

Governor Dunne had hinted that some unforeseen and unrecognized legal difficulties might intervene. The opposition focused upon a two-pronged campaign. One thrust would have the measure declared unconstitutional because it did not fulfill the conditions approved by the people in the 1908 referendum. State Senator William A. Hubbard of Carrollton spearheaded this attack, first in the General Assembly and then in the courts. Judge Norman L. Jones ultimately decided that "the tadpole ditch," as Hubbard labeled the eight-foot barge canal, was not a deep waterway within the context of the 1908 campaign.[29] This decision was not appealed to the Illinois Supreme Court since the Dunne waterway received a death blow from the federal government. As a second line of approach, Rainey sought to get the War Department, which controlled all such projects on navigable streams, to disapprove the plan. This course of action was successful. The War Department found that an eight-foot project was not a worthy deep waterway expenditure. Secretary of War Newton D. Baker refused to grant a new hearing on the proposal. By mid-1916 the "Dunne sewer ditch," as it was derisively called, was dead.[30] The Dunne river development plan had been successfully blocked. The next state administration, that of Frank O. Lowden, would make another attempt to redeem the pledge of 1908. Promoter Rainey would again assume suzerainty over the project.

The transportation crisis brought on by World War I reawakened interest in rivers and canals as avenues of commerce. By the spring of 1918 the nation's railroads were staggering under the massive burdens produced by the wartime emergency. Millions of tons of foodstuff, armament, machinery, and military supplies were piled at freight terminals awaiting movement to ports of embarkation. To assist in alleviating the traffic snarls, the War Department turned to the rivers for assistance. The government formed a Federal Barge Line to maximize the use of existing and new tonnage in the allevia-tion of the transportation difficulties.[31] In the Midwest the incapacity of the railroads was such that there was a renewed demand for waterway improvements. Among the leading advocates was Henry T. Rainey, who persuaded President Wilson to endorse the dredging of the old Illinois and Michigan Canal in order to reconnect the Chicago Sanitary and Ship Canal with the Illinois River. At a cost of $150,000, it was alleged that the revitalized canal would release 20,000 freight cars for other needs. Rainey estimated that ninety days would be needed for the work and believed that his proposal would relieve the transportation congestion expected when fall crops were harvested. With the endorsement of the Corps of Engineers, funds were made available through the War Department so that Illi-nois could overcome the constitutional restriction on internal improvements and accomplish the desired work. Rainey was deeply appreciative of the President's assistance in this matter.[32] The dredging of the Illinois and Michigan Canal was a small measure when contrasted with the imposing lakes-to-gulf deep waterway, but it was a constructive step in the direction of an improved internal water-way system.

The nation's river systems had been rediscovered by the war; following the war they continued to be employed. A combination of circumstances now renewed attention to the fulfillment of the Illi-nois waterway proposition. The enlargement of the Erie Canal to permit an uninterrupted passage of freight from Chicago to New York provided impetus for a similar improvement of the waterway from the lakes to the gulf. Also, the opening of the Panama Canal had added importance to the commerce of the Mississippi River valley and to the water routes. The wartime revival of the Illinois and Michigan Canal stimulated interest in the historical antecedents of the lakes-to-gulf deep waterway.[33] These factors contributed to reopen-ing the question of the Illinois segment of the deep waterway in 1918.

Since the passage of the constitutional amendment a decade earlier, development had been deterred by the divided counsels of the waterway advocates. The 1916 Republican party platform, silent on the deep waterway issue, was a source of embarrassment to candidate Frank O. Lowden because it might be said the railroad interests dominated him. He had favored the project for years and proposed to review the matter if elected governor. Once in office in 1917, he appointed Mortimer G. Barnes, a graduate of the University of Michi-gan and a renowned engineer with pronounced achievements in the construction and improvement of waterways, as chief engineer in the Department of Public Works and Buildings, Division of Waterways.

Barnes reviewed the data available and concluded that the Deneen plan
of a ship canal had been too grandiose and that the Dunne proposal
of a barge canal had been too puny.[34] The waterway division set to
work to upgrade the barge concept so that it would meet federal
specifications and accommodate the actual and future commercial
needs of the state.

During the war period, Lowden sketched his version of the linkage
between the sanitary district channel and the Illinois River at
LaSalle. He envisioned a barge canal whose system of locks would
enable whole fleets to pass through without breaking formation. The
governor also saw this public works project as an antirecession
device in the period of slump anticipated after World War I. Following his lead, the division of waterways recommended a channel
whose minimum depth was eight feet in earth and ten feet in rock at
extreme low water. The miter sills of the locks were to be made
deep enough to afford a draft of fourteen feet in case the channel
should be deepened at some future time. The locks themselves were
to be 110 feet in width and 600 feet in usable length so that a
barge fleet carrying 7,500 tons, the equivalent of several train
loads, would pass without separation in its journey. While the principal purpose of the improvement was navigation, the series of five
dams would provide valuable waterpower sources. Significantly, these
plans were made in conjunction with federal engineers and in conformity to national specifications so that the secretary of war could
not find fault with the Lowden plan. In a message to the General
Assembly on January 8, 1919, the governor presented his recommendations, and the proposal became law on the following July 1.[35]

The Illinois waterway, a subject for discussion for years as an
essential part of a lakes-to-gulf water route, seemed near realiza-
tion. The secretary of war gave initial approval on January 6, 1920,
and final approval on March 6. Even though the project had received
all the necessary official endorsements, it was not without criticism.
In a lengthy series of articles for the *Engineering News-Record*,
Charles W. Baker presented the arguments against any government
investment in inland waterways. He offered the Hennepin Canal in
Illinois as an excellent illustration of a canal project which had
proven to be a failure. Baker warned that investment in waterways
was the chief source of waste in the public's business. A copy of
the Baker series was sent to Governor Lowden for his information.
Chief Engineer Barnes responded with a fifty-eight-page defense of
the state's project. On November 6, 1920, the first earth was turned
at a point west of Marseilles, and the actual construction of the
Illinois waterway was begun. As a result of the Rainey cooperation
with the Lowden administration in the revival of the Illinois and
Michigan Canal, he became reconciled to the abandonment of the cry
"fourteen feet through the Valley." Before leaving office, Governor
Lowden expressed his appreciation for Rainey's services in connection
with the waterway.[36] While the governor believed the construction
work would be completed in three years, this view was too optimistic.
It had taken a dozen years for Rainey's effort in behalf of the 1908
amendment to reach the productive stage; it would be an equal length
of time before the project was completed.

The planning and construction initiated by Lowden were continued during the subsequent administration of Governor Len Small. While business interests were concerned about seemingly needless delays, the development continued through the decade of the 1920s. Governor Small promised to proceed with such rapidity as was consistent with economical operation. While the initial construction timetable called for a three-year schedule, a combination of high costs, litigation over right-of-way, and negotiations over waterpower delayed normal progress on the work. During Small's eight years in office, construction of locks and dams proceeded at five locations—Lockport, Brandon Road, Dresden Island, Marseilles, and Starved Rock. The waterway system overcame a fall of 140 feet in the sixty-five-mile stretch of the Des Plaines and Illinois rivers between the end of the Chicago drainage canal and the Illinois River near Utica. By 1929 the project was 75 percent completed, but the state's $20,000,000 fund was nearly depleted.[37] The exhaustion of state revenues reawakened Henry T. Rainey's interest in the construction phase of the project.

During most of the 1920s, Rainey concentrated upon the conservation aspects of waterway development. The following chapter traces his concern in the areas of flood control, water pollution, hydroelectric production, and water diversion. In order to foster the fruition of the lakes-to-gulf goal, he became involved with two aspects of the construction problem. First, there was the need to convince the federal government to deepen the Illinois River channel from Utica to the mouth at Grafton. Second, a means had to be found to supplement state resources so that the Lockport to Utica section could be finished. Rainey was instrumental in securing solutions to both of these problems.

At the turn of the century, the pressure groups demanding a lakes-to-gulf deep waterway had concentrated upon assistance from the federal government. The support given by Illinois citizens in the 1908 bond approval had temporarily lulled concern for the lower reaches of the Illinois River. Now that construction was underway, this anxiety recurred. The Illinois River below Starved Rock is very sluggish, having a fall of only twenty-eight feet in 225 miles. In 1880 Congress had accepted a report authorizing a seven-foot channel in the lower Illinois. There were two federally owned dams and two state-owned dams built to raise the water level to seven feet. The size of the locks and the depth of the channel were now inconsistent with the design of the Illinois waterway. In 1926 concerned Illinois congressmen (including Rainey) successfully lobbied for an item in the rivers and harbors bill authorizing a nine-foot stream and the removal of the outmoded dams. The Senate concurred in early 1927. Because of the time intervening for surveys and contracts, the actual improvement of the lower Illinois did not begin until May, 1930. It was estimated that it would take three years to dredge a nine-foot depth and to widen the channel to a minimum of 200 feet.[38] Subsequent events demonstrated that the completion of this aspect of a deep waterway would coincide with consummation of the upper river activities.

Very early in the administration of Governor Louis L. Emmerson,

who took office in 1929, it was perceived that the state could not
complete its commitments to the Illinois waterway because funds were
nearly exhausted. As a solution, Rainey suggested that the entire
project be turned over to the national government which could appropriate additional funds. Following a two-day inspection tour of the
Illinois River sponsored by the Illinois Manufacturers' Association
for state and national politicians, Rainey was appointed chairman of
a committee whose responsibility was to determine the powers of the
state to finish financing the stretch of waterway from Lockport to
Utica and to examine the details, obligations, and commitments if
the state turned the project over to the federal government. Ultimately, the committee urged federal absorption of the entire project.
Under the terms of the agreement, the remaining state funds would be
used to provide bridges and maintenance; the federal government
would provide $7,500,000 for completion of the dams, locks, and
machinery. These recommendations were incorporated in the Rivers
and Harbors Act of 1930, and President Hoover signed the measure on
July 5. Federal funds for the Illinois waterway embracing Chicago
to Grafton became available on February 23, 1931, as a rider to the
Army Appropriations Act. It was anticipated that the construction
would be completed by April, 1933. The improvement of waterways
received an additional impetus under the New Deal when Congress
authorized the Public Works Administration to stimulate relief and
recovery through such activities.[39] The Illinois barge system as
part of the lakes-to-gulf waterway profited from this federal largess.

As the completion date for the Illinois waterway neared, it was
especially fitting that Speaker Rainey was elected chairman of a
congressional committee to arrange the program for the official opening of the waterway. Initial proposals for a flotilla of vessels to
proceed from Chicago down the Mississippi to the Gulf of Mexico were
abandoned because of the severity of the Great Depression. The committee settled for a ceremony at New Orleans on May 31, 1933, when
a bottle of Lake Michigan water was used to christen two barges
about to begin the upstream journey. More elaborate festivities
were planned for Chicago on June 22. Secretary of War George H. Dern
represented President Franklin D. Roosevelt on this occasion. In his
dedicatory remarks, Secretary Dern praised the waterway's contribution to economic recovery and conservation of the nation's resources.
Mayor Edward J. Kelly of Chicago warmly praised the economic benefits
to be derived by the metropolitan area as a result of the project's
completion. Speaker Rainey, an ardent advocate of the project for
thirty years, climaxed the ceremony by dwelling on the history of
the movement to link Lake Michigan with the Gulf of Mexico.[40] A
generation had elapsed between conception of the Illinois waterway
component and its completion. Congressman Henry T. Rainey was the
only major political figure whose active involvement spanned these
years.

Even as the lakes-to-gulf waterway was being dedicated, it was
threatened by an international transportation improvement in the St.
Lawrence River. Canada and various states along the Great Lakes,
including power interests in Canada and New York, were especially
desirous of securing their own avenue to the sea. Agitation for

such an undertaking reached one climax when President Hoover negotiated a treaty with Canada for building a St. Lawrence waterway.
This diplomatic action was subject to approval by the United States
Senate. Proponents of the Illinois waterway generally opposed this
undertaking because they feared the drain in funds and water from
their project. Just as the Chicago *Tribune*'s boat, the "Sea King,"
was making an unofficial trip over the Illinois waterway in March,
1933, there was considerable fear that it would be a waterless
waterway if the St. Lawrence Seaway Treaty were approved. Both of
Illinois' senators and most of the state's congressional delegation,
including Speaker Rainey, opposed the treaty. In an effort to placate the Mississippi Valley, the engineers in the War Department
proposed the expenditure of an additional $15,530,000 on the Illinois
waterway. The proposal included the removal of the ancient and
decrepit lock-and-dam systems at Kampsville and LaGrange. In order
to insure a navigable nine-foot channel, the Illinois River would
be widened to 300 feet and new locks and dams installed just below
Peoria and at LaGrange, nine miles downstream from Beardstown. This
engineer's report assured a navigable waterway with a minimum diversion of water through Chicago as specified in the proposed St.
Lawrence Seaway Treaty. The inducement of the War Department became
more attractive in the light of an engineering report which indicated
that improvements would have to be made in the Illinois waterway if
the water supply were limited severely. Ultimately, the dam at
Peoria was started in 1935 and the one at LaGrange in 1936.[41] With
the completion of these two projects, the system was finished from
Chicago to Grafton. The suspicions of the St. Lawrence seaway were
unfounded because subsequent events proved the two systems were
complementary rather than competitive.

To this day the Illinois waterway remains an active component in
the state's and the nation's economic life. Rainey could take considerable pride in the fruition of this dream of pioneer explorers.
He had assisted mightily in the inauguration of the campaign for a
deep waterway and had served intermittently in the developmental
years. In recognition of this deep interest in the nation's internal waterways, the Congress directed that the lock and dam at Alton,
Illinois, be named in his honor.[42] While the Illinois waterway
itself bears no reminder of his role as instigator, developer, manipulator, and critic, that barge network today stands as a constant
reminder of his service to district, state, and nation. With considerable justification, Henry T. Rainey deserves recognition as
promoter of the Illinois waterway. Coequal with the waterway's commercial development but less tangible are the congressman's efforts
in behalf of the valley's environment, revealed in the subsequent
chapter.

NOTES

1. *Republican* quoted in *Gazette*, Feb. 6, 1903, 4:2.

2. An excellent legislative history may be found in Mildred C.
Werner, "The History of the Deep Waterway in the State of Illinois"

(M.A. thesis), esp. 57-84; see also Robert A. Waller, "The Illinois Waterway from Conception to Completion, 1908-1933," 124-141.

3. HTR remarks on his bills in Chicago *Chronicle* news story reproduced in *Gazette*, Nov. 13, 1903, 4:2; for the legislation consult *CR*, 58:1 (Nov. 19, 1903), 390-391.

4. Randolph to HTR, Chicago, Aug. 23, 1904, reproduced in *Gazette*, Sept. 2, 1904, 4:4; Brig. Gen. A. Mackinzie (Chief of Engineers) to HTR, [Washington], March 3, 1905, reproduced in *Gazette*, March 17, 1905, 1:2.

5. *CR*, 58:2 (Dec. 15, 1903), 266-268.

6. Issac Lippincott, "A History of River Improvement," 633, 637, 649. For a consideration of the regional impulse which such lobbying groups represent, consult Burton I. Kaufman, "Organization for Trade Expansion in the Mississippi Valley, 1900-1920," 444-465.

7. For discussion of Lorimer's role on the waterway questions see Joel A. Tarr, *A Study in Boss Politics*, 163-171, 200, 208-216, 221, 230-232, 240, 262, 315.

8. *Minutes of the Deep Waterway Convention* [1906], 5, 27-36, 56, 83-84.

9. "Personalities: The Mississippi's Greatest Riverman [Kavanaugh]," 272-273; William R. Willoughby, *The St. Lawrence Waterway*, 74-75.

10. *CR*, 58:3 (Feb. 7, 1905), 2012-16.

11. *Ibid.*, 59:2 (Feb. 1, 1907), 2098-2106.

12. Alexander J. Jones, "The Chicago Drainage Canal," 158-159; W. Frank McClure, "The Chicago-St. Louis Waterway," 209-210; HTR views in *CR*, 60:1 (May 30, 1908), Appendix 238.

13. The letter dated Carrollton, Sept. 27, 1907, is printed in double columns in *Gazette*, Oct. 3, 1907, 1:3 and 4 and 2:1 and 2.

14. For the legislative maneuvering see *Illinois State Register* for Oct. 10, 1907, 12:3, and Oct. 17, 1907, 3:1; and *Illinois State Journal* for Oct. 15, 1907, 3:3, and Oct. 16, 1907, 10:1.

15. HTR to Wm. F. Mulvehill (Chief, Division of Waterways), Carrollton, Sept. 22, 1927, RP; "Election Returns, State Officers 1882 [on] Secretary's Office, Illinois," page 117 for 1908 amendment vote by counties. Records housed in the state archives in Springfield.

16. Lakes-to-the-Gulf Deep Waterway Association, *Report of the Second Annual Convention*, 1907, 142-143; Theodore Roosevelt, "Our National Inland Waterways Policy," 3.

17. Lakes-to-the-Gulf Deep Waterway Association, *Third Annual Convention*, 1908, 61-76, 172.

18. R. B. Way, "Mississippi Improvements and Traffic Prospects," 152-153; "The Report upon the Proposed 14-ft. Deep Waterway from Chicago to New Orleans," 686-692; editorial "Why a 14-ft. Deep

Waterway through the Mississippi Valley Is Not Worth While,"
694-695; *Republic* interview as paraphrased in *Gazette*, June 17,
1909, 4:2.

19. Beekman Winthrop (Acting Secretary of the Navy) to HTR,
Washington, Aug. 30, 1909, as printed in *Gazette*, Sept. 9, 1909,
4:2; Lakes-to-the-Gulf Deep Waterway Association, *Fourth Annual Convention*, 101-105, 157-169.

20. Chicago *Record-Herald*, Nov. 10, 1908, 3:6; editorial, "The
Deep Waterway," *Record-Herald*, Nov. 13, 1908, 8:2.

21. Chicago *Record-Herald*, Jan. 29, 1909, 2:5; April 29, 1909,
4:4; and May 19, 1909, 2:4; "The Administration of Charles S.
Deneen, 1905-1912" ([Chicago]: Charles S. Deneen Campaign Committee, [1912]), 31-39.

22. Chicago *Record-Herald*, Feb. 5, 1909, 5:1; Feb. 18, 1909,
5:5; March 20, 1909, 8:2; March 26, 1909, 7:1; April 27, 1909,
10:2; May 13, 1909, 2:4; and June 4, 1909, 1:7.

23. Harold G. Moulton, *Waterways Versus Railways*, 451-452;
Royal J. Schmidt, "*The Chicago Daily News* and Illinois Politics,
1876-1920" (Ph.D. thesis), 332-334.

24. Rainey speeches reported in Chicago *Record-Herald*, Nov. 5,
1910, 4:6; resolution paraphrased in *Gazette*, July 6, 1911, 1:1;
Patriot, Oct. 26, 1911, 4:2.

25. Hill, "Highways of Progress: The Future of Our Waterways,"
12779-91; "The Report of a Board of Engineers on the Illinois Section
of the Lakes-to-the-Gulf Waterway," 269; Moulton, *Waterways Versus
Railways*, 352; William A. Shelton, *The Lakes-to-the-Gulf Deep
Waterway*, 100.

26. Chicago address in William L. Sullivan (ed.), *Dunne: Judge,
Mayor, Governor*, 598-599; also: press release, 603; biennial message, 660-661; statement to Chicago *Tribune*, 720. Economist Shelton
was vigorously opposed to the Dunne proposal also. See his "A
Waterway between Chicago and St. Louis: A Study in Freight Rates,"
64-78.

27. *Journal* of the Illinois Senate, 49 General Assembly (May 27,
1915), 1040-66.

28. Press release in Sullivan (ed.), *Dunne*, 721; also: Chicago
speech, 723-725; reply to HTR, 770-772; Davenport address, 775-778.
See also Buenker, "Edward F. Dunne," 13.

29. *Patriot*, April 15, 1915, 3:3; Dec. 9, 1915, 1:4; Dec. 16,
1915, II, 2:1-3; Feb. 3, 1916, 4:3-4; and Aug. 3, 1916, 1:6.

30. *Patriot*, Oct. 28, 1915, 1:1; telegram of HTR to Editor James
McNabb, Washington, Feb. 27, 1916, as printed in *Gazette*, March 1,
1916, 1:1; Henry M. Pindell to HTR, Peoria, March 2, 1916, RP;
Gazette, May 24, 1916, 1:2.

31. Walter Havighurst, *Voices on the River*, 259.

32. HTR to Wilson, Washington, April 4, 1918; Wilson to HTR, [Washington], April 12, 1918; HTR to Wilson, Washington, April 13, 1918; White House Files, Memorandum of HTR letter of May 2, 1918; Wilson to Baker, [Washington], May 6, 1918; Wilson to HTR, [Washington], May 13, 1918, all of preceding in Wilson Papers, File VI-B, Folio 357 A; HTR to Wilson, Washington, May 17, 1918, Wilson Papers, File VI, Folio 357.

33. James W. Putnam, *The Illinois and Michigan Canal*, 156-158.

34. William T. Hutchinson, *Lowden of Illinois*, I, 286; Robert H. Jones, "The Administration of Governor Frank O. Lowden of Illinois, 1917-1921" (M.A. thesis), 57-60; Alvin G. Mathews, "How Illinois Will Feed Her New Waterway" (M.A. thesis), 10-11.

35. Frank O. Lowden, "Illinois: The New Keystone of the Union," 272; William L. Sackett, "The Lowden Plan for the Illinois Waterway," *Illinois Blue Book, 1919-20*, 134-138; Werner, "History of the Deep Waterway," 70-71.

36. Bessie L. Ashton, "The Geonomic Aspects of the Illinois Waterway," preface; Charles W. Baker, "What Is the Future of Inland Water Transportation?," 19-28, 85-89, 137-144, 184-191, 234-242; Mortimer G. Barnes, *Inland Waterways: Their Necessity, Importance and Value in Handling the Commerce of the United States, and Reducing Transportation Costs*; Lowden to HTR, Springfield, Dec. 31, 1920, RP.

37. Hugh L. Maxwell, "Illinois Waterway Delayed Needlessly," 16; Small to Col. C. R. Miller reproduced in "Illinois River Project," 19; William L. Sackett, "The Illinois Waterway and Its Benefits," *Illinois Blue Book, 1921-22*, 337-342; *Illinois-Progress, 1921-1928*, 260-280.

38. *Illinois-Progress, 1921-1928*, 283; *Division of Waterways, Ninth Annual Report, July 1, 1925 to June 30, 1926*, 47-50; *Gazette*, June 16, 1926, 1:2; *CR*, 69:2 (Feb. 23, 1927), 4631; *Patriot*, May 30, 1929, 1:5.

39. *Gazette*, April 17, 1929, 1:1; *Illinois State Register* for Aug. 24, 1929, 1:4, and Aug. 29, 1929, 3:1; *Division of Waterways, Thirteenth Annual Report, July 1, 1929 to June 30, 1929*, 22-39; "Program for Completion of Lakes-to-the-Gulf Waterway," Hoover Papers, Box 165; *Division of Waterways, Fourteenth Annual Report, July 1, 1930 to June 30, 1931*, 10; Leahmae Brown, "The Development of National Policy with Respect to Water Resources" (Ph.D. thesis), 36-37; J. Edwin Becht, "Commodity Origins, Traffic and Markets Accessible to Chicago Via the Illinois Waterway" (Ph.D. thesis), 3-5.

40. Chicago *Tribune*, April 30, 1933, I, 8:3; *Prairie Farmer*, CV (June 10, 1933), 3; Chicago *Tribune*, June 21, 1933, 10:2-3; June 22, 1933, 1:8 and 2:1; and June 23, 1933, 1:1 and 10:1-4; *Illinois Blue Book, 1933-1934*, 571-574.

41. Chicago *Tribune*, March 1, 1933, 2:3-8; Dec. 28, 1933, 6:1-3; and Jan. 3, 1934, 1:1 and 2:2-4; *Division of Waterways, Twenty-first Annual Report, July 1, 1937 to June 30, 1938*, 20. For the intricacies

of the St. Lawrence situation see Willoughby, *The St. Lawrence Waterway*.

42. *Gazette*, June 3, 1938, 1:2 and 8:3; *CR*, 76:3 (May 20, 1940), 6432.

5

Champion of Water Conservation

Throughout history man has endeavored to utilize nature's resources
for his advantage. Only in the twentieth century Americans have
given thought to the conservation of their bounty for posterity's
use. Among these exploitable resources are the nation's natural
waterways. The preceding chapter has demonstrated the distinct
economic service which waterways provide as a transportation
medium. Two additional economic uses enhance the importance of
water resources to mankind. Man may concentrate a river's natural
fall in one place and through a waterwheel or generator derive
power for his machines. He may also reclaim the river bottomlands
and utilize the fertile soil for agricultural pursuits. These two
enterprises received increasing attention in the twentieth century
as a part of the broad concern for the preservation of the nation's
resources.

During Henry Thomas Rainey's three decades of public service
he was an ardent champion of conservation measures, especially
those relating to public power, pollution, and flood control.
Then as now, interest in the nation's environment was for some
leaders an unending struggle. At the apex of his career Speaker
Rainey urged that conservation be promoted more rigorously than
ever before. He defined conservation as the effort to "preserve
for future generations all those things adapted to the physical
well-being and the comfort and the happiness of the people who
will live on this earth and within the boundaries of the continen-
tal United States long after we are gone." While Rainey's
legislative interest centered upon water, he included trees,
grasslands, coal, oil, and wildlife among the subjects for wise
use. He took the view that it was the "people" versus the "interests." His criticisms of the alleged waterpower trust centered
upon a concern for economic justice, and he felt no compunction
about urging federal participation in the regulatory process.
While he was not adverse to pleas for efficiency, this purpose in
conservation was subordinate.[1]

The origin of the expression "conservation" to denote activities in behalf of resource preservation is clouded by time. Among
the claimants for originating the concept is W J McGee, St. Louis
geologist and campaigner for multiple-purpose river development.
McGee was among those in attendance at the initial meeting of the
Lakes-to-Gulf Deep Waterway Association inspired by the Lorimer-
Rainey activities. He was disappointed in the single focus of

the convention upon the navigational possibilities of the Father
of Waters while neglecting comprehensive water management programs.
In a subsequent article he urged that a cooperative state and
national effort be made to coordinate all projects relating to
river improvement. Among the concerns he listed were preserving
forests, saving soil, purifying water, developing waterpower,
promoting irrigation, protecting bottomlands, and constructing
canals. The magnitude of these endeavors taken collectively would
require technical competence, central planning, and efficient
management. Many conservationists came to see efficient resource
development in these terms. While Gifford Pinchot may deserve
credit for first using the term "conservation" in February, 1907,
W J McGee looms especially significant for directing attention to
the need for a coordinated approach to internal improvements.[2]
As befitted the conditions of the Illinois valley, Congressman
Rainey embraced some of the McGee concerns, but always with
special attention to thwarting predatory interests.

Water concerns naturally dominated Henry T.'s conservation
interests. Prior to his departure for congressional duty, he
endeavored to acquaint himself with his river district's needs.
The most pressing local problem resulted from damaging Illinois
River floods. According to one estimate, 400,000 acres of bottomland were subject to overflow between Peoria and Grafton. The
local citizens blamed the flooding in part upon the system of
slack water dams in the river. There were two federal dams at
Kampsville and LaGrange and two state dams at Henry and Copperas
Creek. As a preliminary fact-finding endeavor, Rainey requested
that the federal agricultural department make available an expert
to examine the land drainage problems of the Illinois valley. The
issuance of this report in 1906 marks the first study by the
national government of Illinois River drainage problems.[3] Rainey
repeatedly introduced measures calling for the lowering or removal
of these dams, but the obstructions remained in the river until
the mid-1930s. Finally, as a part of the expanded Illinois waterway, these dams were removed and replaced by modern structures.

Rainey's early interest in conservation matters and his earned
reputation as investigator thrust him for a time into the middle
of the bitterest conservation controversy of the twentieth century.
The eruption of the Gifford Pinchot-Richard Ballinger dispute was
the occasion for a congressional investigation of the operations
of the Bureau of Forestry and the Department of Interior. The
selection of the membership of that committee of inquiry proved to
be a controversial issue in its own right. Normally it would have
been the prerogative of Speaker Joseph G. Cannon to select the
committee members, but a coalition of Democrats and insurgent
Republicans passed a resolution presented by Representative
George W. Norris denying him that authority. Now that the House
itself could select the members of the investigating committee,
each party met in caucus to determine its nominees. As a member
of the Committee on Irrigation of Arid Lands and an outspoken
critic of the Taft administration, Rainey was a logical choice as
one of the inquisitors. The Democratic caucus also selected

Ollie James of Kentucky. An editorial in the *National Monthly*
characterized Rainey's selection as about as welcome to President
Taft "as a shower on a new bonnet." The President and his party
sought means by which to remove these Democratic nominees from the
investigating committee. Amidst editorial allegations that the
committee was being prepared for a whitewash investigation, the
Republican caucus agreed upon the strategy that their party would
nominate the investigating committee members of both parties.
Ultimately, they accepted James but rejected Rainey and substituted
James T. Lloyd of Missouri. Muckraking journalist Samuel Hopkins
Adams described the pressures used by Taft to keep Rainey off the
committee as a violent stretch of executive power. The ploy,
nevertheless, proved effective, for the Republican majority maintained its insistence that their party should nominate all members
of the special committee. However, the implications of the initial
union of Democrats and insurgent Republicans was noted by the
leadership of all factions during the ensuing fight against Cannonism.[4] Rainey had inadvertently precipitated the parliamentary
crisis which contributed to the subsequent overthrow of Speaker
Cannon.

The publicity accompanying Rainey's nonselection on the investigating committee brought him to the attention of the archetype
of conservation, Gifford Pinchot. As president of the National
Conservation Association, Pinchot invited Rainey to become a
director in the organization so that they might work together "for
the advancement of conservation, and especially for a constructive
national policy on water power." He was enthusiastic about Rainey's
service as a champion of water conservation in Illinois and attributed to Henry T. the principal credit for preserving successfully
the few waterpower sites remaining in the nation.[5] While Rainey
served as a director of the association, his greatest single
contribution to the conservation movement lies in connection with
activities climaxing in the national Water Power Act of 1920.

In the House of Representatives, Rainey played a significant
role in first harassing and then harnessing the exploiters of
public power. Until 1908 it had been the practice of Congress to
grant unrestricted authority to private companies for utilization
of power sites. These bills were passed without debate under
unanimous consent arrangements. Rainey should be credited with
commencing the congressional fight against the waterpower trust
because he made it a practice to be present when these bills were
brought up for passage and to offer objection to unanimous consent.
His obstructionist tactics ultimately caused him to be assigned to
an informal group within the Wilson administration who were
charged with drafting a federal waterpower bill.[6]

Public attention to the waterpower problem began innocently
over a question of unanimous consent for permission to print material in the *Congressional Record*. Richard Austin of Tennessee
objected to such a request by Rainey. In the exchange, Rainey
ended by saying "I have no objection to the objection of a man who
is in favor of the Water-Power Trust." The next day Representative Austin gained the floor to refute the accusation. Rainey

retaliated with a carefully prepared speech on the principles of
government concern for waterways and their development. He
asserted that the national government had no valuable right in
these navigable rivers except the right to develop the waterpower
therein. Nevertheless, the federal government was being asked to
give this asset away and at the same time to expend money in
maintaining river channels and banks. Rainey claimed to have personally blocked six private waterpower bills, thereby saving
$25,000,000 for the United States. As a policy, he advocated that
one-sixth of the proceeds from power sites be paid into the
Treasury and earmarked for developing rivers, preserving their
channels, and protecting the land on either side of the stream.
A parallel policy, he said, was the earmarking of all the money
derived from the public domain for the purpose of reclaiming arid
western lands. He asked, "Is it any stretch of the constitutional
powers of this Government to extend that same principle of conservation to our rivers and to stop this practice of giving them
away?"[7] This was the initial statement of the Rainey solution to
the granting of waterpower franchises.

Three days after this exchange, a dramatic effort was made to
secure special privilege for a series of power projects. On
July 22, 1912, the Committee on Interstate and Foreign Commerce
presented a waterpower bill of the omnibus type. Seventeen projects were grouped in a single measure in order to secure the favor
of the greatest number of interested parties. It was drawn on the
pork-barrel principle with no provision for charges or regulation.
In a bitter fight that lasted several weeks, Rainey offered the
principal Democratic opposition to the measure. Initially, he
urged delay until there was more information available about proposed projects. He then suggested the possibility of a hydroelectric commission like Canada's to regulate rates, although he
doubted that the United States was ready to go that far. After
marshaling the evidence prepared by Harry A. Slattery, secretary
of the National Conservation Association, Rainey presented an
hour-long speech against the omnibus bill. He said: "No king or
emperor in feudal days ever gave away as much of the resources as
this committee seems to be willing to do." Noting that these
bills contained no adequate safeguards, he hoped that an awakened
public conscience would make it impossible to grant gifts of this
character unless there was a provision for protection to consumers
against exorbitant charges and for tolls to the national government. A large part of his speech was devoted to examining the
merits of each of the dam proposals and to establishing that the
chief proponent, Republican Richard Austin, was a member of the
waterpower interests.[8] As a result of this public scrutiny, the
omnibus bill was doomed.

The dispute over a proper waterpower policy was not ended,
however, because one of the projects in the omnibus bill reappeared
as a separate measure. This was an authorization for a dam across
the Coosa River in Alabama. Prime mover of this bill in the Senate
was Democrat William Bankhead of Alabama, states' rights champion
of an unregulated power industry. It was equally well received by

the Democratic majority in the House led by Alabaman Oscar W.
Underwood, chairman of the Ways and Means Committee. In spite of
the position of these Democratic leaders, Rainey continued his
opposition to the measure. In addition to his previous objections
to the omnibus bill, Rainey pointed out that the states could not
prevent waterpower monopolies and thus the public needed a program
of federal regulation. He urged that "the policy of conservation
which is being so widely discussed and so widely favored throughout the country" begin at this point. While advocating river
improvements, he was not anxious to give away valuable franchises
to exploiters. He forecast a popular demand that the House discharge its full duty and extend to all resources "that character
of conservation which is consistent with the advanced ideas of the
present century." In concluding, he stated that no national asset
was so valuable and so important as the power in our rivers. It
belonged not to those who might desire to exploit it and reap
tremendous profits, but to the whole people who had a right to
demand reasonable prices and a fair share of the proceeds for the
national government.[9] Even though the Coosa River bill ultimately
passed both houses, it was vetoed by President Taft.

Rainey's conservationist stand on the waterpower issue evoked
much favorable comment, but there was some question whether his
political party could be entrusted with the advancement of conservation policy. Pinchot had great praise for the few Democrats,
like Rainey, who had supported publicly controlled power, but he
concluded that these men were too few and that it was not safe to
trust the Democratic party with the conservation interests of the
nation in the 1912 election. Mark Sullivan examined the same
issue and lauded Rainey's intelligence for comprehending that
"water-power grabs are today just what the big railroad land grabs
were a generation ago." After the success of the Democrats in the
presidential and congressional elections, Sullivan hoped that
forward-looking men like Rainey who had embraced "modern thought
and doctrines of government, including conservation" could lead
their party in constructive gains for conservation.[10] Up until this
time, the conservation program had been identified primarily with
the Republicans. Rainey did all in his power to make the Democratic party function in behalf of conservation.

For the first time in the twentieth century, a Democratic
administration was confronted with the problems relating to conservation. The congressional conflict began on June 24, 1914, when
William C. Adamson of Georgia, chairman of the House Committee on
Interstate and Foreign Commerce, introduced a bill which would
amend the General Dam Acts of 1906 and 1910 governing leases on
waterpower sites outside the public domain. Supposedly the bill
had President Wilson's approval, but conservationists were
convinced that their "must" provisions had been rendered innocuous or omitted entirely. Rainey was among those leading the
effort to improve the bill before passage. According to Rainey,
the conservationists' demands were tolls for the government,
adequate price regulation for the consumer, and a definite period
within which these companies were to operate. Leases were to be

made for definite terms and "recapture at fair value" was not to
be made so difficult as to constitute a permanent lease. Rainey
favored a commission to perform these regulatory operations, as
Canada had done. He argued that capital, investors, consumers,
and taxpayers would benefit under such a system. The following
day, he continued his presentation by countering some of the objections offered by the conservationists' critics. The tolls would
not be unconstitutional because no firm was required to enter into
these relations with the government. Nor would such tolls increase
the cost to the consumer, he said, because the companies would
have to absorb the expense in order to compete favorably with
steam-produced electricity. To vote for the bill without amendments, Rainey asserted, would be to vote in the interest of the
consolidation of waterpower groups and against the interest of the
general public. The final bill as amended from the floor was
considered to be "a fairly good conservation measure."[11] The
amended version passed the House but not the Senate, and thus modification of the national waterpower policy was still in the future.

Rainey's tactics prompted President Wilson to invite him to a
private conference on the matter. The President reportedly
explained that considerable private capital was ready to go into
these developments, but Rainey's objections were delaying economic
advancement. The congressman countered with the conservationists'
viewpoint and, according to him, converted the President to the
need for adequate safeguards. Later Wilson asked Rainey to serve
as a member of an informal group which would frame a proper bill.
Also active in the group was Secretary of the Interior Franklin K.
Lane, Gifford Pinchot, and O. C. Merrill of the Forest Service.[12]
The product of their efforts was delivered to the respective chairmen of the committees having jurisdiction in the House and Senate.

The next session of Congress encountered the waterpower issue
in a new guise: the power development possible at Niagara Falls.
Democratic Senator John K. Shields of Tennessee, an advocate of
immediate development, was promoting new legislation on the subject.
In presenting his case to the public, Shields emphasized that each
additional horsepower developed in the streams meant preserving
thirteen tons of coal a year. The conservationists, however,
looked upon the measure as further exploitation of the Falls.
Congressman Rainey resumed his fight for government compensation
for the use of this national asset. He expounded upon the
association of the Aluminum Company of America and General Electric
Company as being the trusts which would profit from the authorization. In a subsequent speech, he reiterated the philosophy of the
water conservationists concerning these projects. He admitted
favoring government ownership and distribution, but he realized
that at this time he would have to settle for compensation to the
government and a workable recapture clause. Rainey hoped that the
passage of the Niagara Falls bill with these safeguards would serve
as a model for future legislation of this character. In his final
speech in favor of the modified bill, he emphasized the revenue
possibilities in such a proposal. In the face of growing government expenditures, he said, the old policy of gratuitously giving

away this national asset was indefensible.[13]   The House accepted
the bill with the conservationists' principles incorporated.   At
President Wilson's request, Rainey met with interested senators to
facilitate passage of the bill by that body.   The measure failed
to pass the Senate, but the principles of waterpower conservation
were nevertheless gaining wider acceptance.

The principal arguments on the measure had been advanced by
each side.   The subsequent maneuvering for waterpower legislation
was conducted in the cloakrooms rather than on the floor of Congress.   As a part of a revision in 1917, the informal committee
proposed that a federal waterpower commission composed of the
secretaries of War, Interior, and Agriculture be appointed to
administer such general guidelines as Congress thought advisable.
This measure was known as the "Three Secretaries' Bill."   The
President suggested that a special waterpower committee in the
House consider the proposal as an administration bill.   In slightly
modified form, this bill passed the House, but the Senate adjourned
without taking action on it.   In the next session, a similar bill
passed the House and the Senate, and President Wilson signed it
into law on June 11, 1920.[14]   After a decade of debate and dicker-
ing, the Water Power Act of 1920 had come into being.

The passage of the Water Power Act inaugurated a new policy
of continuing public ownership and federal trusteeship of waterpower sites.   The legislation did not provide for multiple-purpose
river development, as some conservationists had demanded.   Its
focus was restricted to hydroelectric development on both public
lands and navigable streams.   It did not provide for flood control,
as Rainey desired, nor for pollution regulations, which he also
preferred.   Still, it did prevent speculative holding of power
sites by requiring prompt construction.   The legislation imposed
a fifty-year lease with definite recapture opportunities.   It also
imposed a charge for the privilege of using public waters.   While
the measure was a compromise, most conservationists greeted it as
the culmination of a successful progressive reform.[15]   Congressman
Rainey had provided substantial public and private input into
legislation which contained necessary restraints and yet fostered
appropriate economic opportunity.   He had assisted in moving the
concept of conservation of waterpower from the theoretical to the
practical by means of political action.

Rainey's struggles with the waterpower interests were not
limited to the national scene.   Within his district and his state
he had two electrical octopuses with which to contend.   The Keokuk
and Hamilton Power Company located at Keokuk, Iowa, supplied electricity for much of his district.   The Economy Light and Power
Company with a site under development at Dresden Island stood in
the path of the Illinois waterway.   In his speeches on waterpower
regulation, Rainey frequently drew upon the local situation for
examples.   The activities of the Economy Power and Light Company
represented the more serious challenge to cherished Rainey objectives.   The Illinois constitutional amendment of 1908 had provided
for the construction of a deep waterway and the development of any
waterpower which might result.   The attainment of this second

objective was even longer in gestation than the completion of the waterway itself. As early as 1905, Governor Charles S. Deneen had appointed an Internal Improvements Commission to investigate these twin projects in behalf of the state. The report issued in 1907 supported a fourteen-foot channel and state control of the water-power. The commissioners believed that the entire cost of the waterway might be repaid in fourteen to seventeen years by the revenue obtained from the sale of waterpower. The governor then urged the legislature to take the steps necessary to authorize such a combined development.[16]

The potential of waterpower development in the Illinois River had not been lost upon private developers. Commercial enterprises, including a hydroelectric plant, had already grown up in the rapids at Marseilles. The Economy Light and Power Company under the presidency of Samuel Insull was endeavoring to secure similar concessions at Dresden Heights. Through a secret gentleman's agreement with the commissioners of the Illinois and Michigan Canal, the Insull company was to control the power potential at this site in the Illinois River system. For a consideration of $2,200, the firm gained a "perpetual" lease of the flowage rights in the Des Plaines River. Also procurred was an easement for the stringing of electric wires, and for $500 a small tract of land on which to build the powerhouse. For a total consideration of $2,700, the Insull enterprise had secured rights variously valued at $5,000,000 to $15,000,000. News of this arrangement began to leak in the summer of 1907. Coincidental with this power "grab," the Chicago Sanitary District sought legislative approval to extend its terminus at Lockport another six miles southward through Joliet in order to develop additional waterpower.[17] This combination of private and public waterpower developments served to impede the potential construction of a deep waterway connecting the lakes to the gulf.

As a result of his interest in the navigational aspects of a deep waterway, Rainey was cognizant of the impediment posed by private developers of waterpower. As noted in the previous chapter, he vigorously opposed the sanitary district proposal because it would not result in a deep waterway beyond the woods south of Joliet. The Marseilles facilities represented no serious threat since they could be bypassed with a short canal. In order to frustrate the designs of the Economy Light and Power Company, the Illinoisan proposed that the General Assembly pass an act author-izing the federal government to collect and retain all revenues arising from the sale of electrical power created by building the waterway. After the national government had been reimbursed for the construction costs, the surplus revenues would revert to the state for public use. This proposal, thought Rainey, would commit the federal government to the completion of the waterway from Chicago to New Orleans, and it would ultimately provide an immense revenue for the state.[18] Neither the General Assembly nor the Congress acted upon the proposition.

The Illinois General Assembly concentrated on the question-able leases granted to the Economy Light and Power Company. On

November 6, 1907, the legislature adopted a resolution urging an
investigation of the situation because the proposed dam would be
detrimental to the deep waterway project. As a result of the
subsequent inquiry, the legislature approved a law voiding the
contract and an injunction was obtained to stop construction. A
flash flood in December, 1907, destroyed the physical construction
at Dresden Heights, but the court litigation dragged on for years.
In a series of cases before the state Supreme Court, the Economy
Light and Power Company won its contentions. The only victory
for the state was the stipulation that the leases were not perpetual
but limited to twenty years, of which eight years had already
elapsed.[19]   The state had little recourse but to delay any construction there, pending the expiration of the lease at Dresden
Heights.

In the meantime, the General Assembly had approved the
submission of a constitutional amendment on the question of a state-
financed waterway development. The voters were asked to approve
a $20,000,000 bond issue whose twin objectives were a deep waterway
and public power. In presenting the issue to the voters, proponents were prone to stress the negligible cost involved since
waterpower revenues would ultimately pay for the project. Governor
Deneen urged voter support of the proposition because the waterpower by-product would enable the people of Illinois to provide
the waterway without cost. Rainey was equally exuberant when
claiming that an anticipated $3,000,000 or $4,000,000 annual revenue
would make the project self-liquidating. State development of
hydroelectric energy was also presented as a means of frustrating
the waterpower grabbers.[20]   In addition to the general sentiment
favoring waterways, the appeal of an inexpensive internal improvement undoubtedly fascinated the electorate.

Because of the difficulties previously recounted, the Democratic administration of Governor Dunne made no progress in
redeeming the pledge of a waterway for power as well as for
navigation. The Lowden administration began efforts in both
directions. Simultaneously the division of waterways was presenting plans to the War Department for approval of the navigational
features of the waterway and was preparing proposals for the
development of waterpower subject to the approval of the Rainey-
promoted Federal Power Commission. The navigational plans avoided
conflict with the existing power project and industry at Marseilles
by proposing a 12,000-foot canal to bypass this industrial complex.
The initial request for authority to develop hydroelectric power
under the national Water Power Act of 1920 did not include the
Dresden Heights site since the Economy Light and Power Company
lease was still in operation.[21]

The development of the hydroelectric potential in the Illinois
waterway was stalled for a score of years due to court litigation
and administrative review. The application for a preliminary
permit was made to the Federal Power Commission on November 20,
1920. Designated as Project No. 48-Illinois, the preliminary
permit was granted on January 14, 1922, for a period of three
years. On January 5, 1925, the state made formal application for

a license authorizing development, but no action was taken by the commission pending the outcome of a suit before the United States Supreme Court regarding the diversion of water from Lake Michigan at Chicago. A final decision on this matter was rendered on April 1, 1930. The state subsequently amended the application on February 4, 1932, to request permission to proceed with immediate power construction at Brandon Road, Dresden Island, Marseilles, and Starved Rock. The request for all sites except Marseilles was approved by the commission on November 18, 1932, and then rescinded on July 29, 1933, because Michigan, Minnesota, Ohio, and Wisconsin had filed a protest on December 22, 1932, which the commission wished to consider. Because of economic conditions, the matter was not reviewed until January 25, 1938, at which time Illinois was ordered to show cause why the license should not be terminated. In a report filed on March 22, 1939, the state defended its case by stressing the prior investment in the undertaking. It was not until the 1940s that the state began to realize a benefit from the hydroelectric potential inherent in the Illinois waterway.[22]   In that intervening score of years, the only power utilized was that at Marseilles where a previously existing private utility company had a plant. Public development of hydroelectric potential seems inherently beset by various difficulties.

The intricacies of conservationists' demands for the public regulation of hydroelectric power are minimal when compared to the complex issues surrounding the use of rivers for purposes of sanitation. In Illinois, the controversy centered upon the "Chicago water diversion," that is, the practice of allowing the metropolitan area to dispose of its untreated sewage by releasing it into the Mississippi River system. As an expanding Chicago population outgrew the capacity of Lake Michigan to absorb the city's refuse without contaminating the drinking water, engineers devised an alternate scheme of purification. In the late nineteenth century, an accepted theory held that any stream would cleanse itself after a few miles of flow if the refuse were properly diluted by an adequate supply of water. The plan called for cutting a channel connecting the Chicago River with the Des Plaines River and reversing the flow of the former. In this way Chicago's sewage, greatly diluted by lake water, could flow inoffensively down the Illinois River. This practice of diverting a portion of Lake Michigan's water to serve as a diluting agent had the effect of altering the water levels in the Great Lakes area.[23]   An innocent practice begun at the turn of the century was to have state, national, and international repercussions. For three-quarters of a century, the ecological questions arising from the amount of diversion at Chicago plagued such varied groups as shippers and diplomats, conservationists and politicians, downstream city dwellers and jurists, lowland farm owners and manufacturers, water-power developers and propagandists.

The early history of the Chicago River diversion reveals the nature of the controversy that was to develop. Originally the city utilized the Illinois and Michigan Canal as its channel for the solution of the sewage disposal problem. As the metropolitan

area grew and the waste problems became more acute, Chicago author-
ities decided to build a new and greatly enlarged canal to divert
completely the Chicago River from Lake Michigan. The Illinois
General Assembly in 1889 authorized the creation of the Chicago
Sanitary District, with power to construct and maintain a channel
of sufficient dimensions to dispose of the sewage and to serve as
a link in a lakes-to-gulf waterway system. In 1894 the Chicago
Sanitary District began constructing such a canal, with a minimum
depth of fourteen feet, at a cost of $50,000,000. On January 16,
1900, Lake Michigan water began its journey to the Gulf of Mexico.
Within minutes of the marriage of waters, Missouri filed suit
objecting to the potential pollution. Within a year Ohio, Pennsylvania, and New York also began efforts to stop or restrict the
amount of diversion. In 1899 the Secretary of War had issued a
permit authorizing a diversion from Lake Michigan into the drainage canal of 5,000 cubic feet per second. A subsequent order two
years later reduced this amount to 4,167 cubic feet. Nevertheless,
the sanitary district claimed the right under Illinois statute to
divert 10,000 cubic feet if conditions required it.[24] Thus, there
began a lengthy dispute over which governmental agency had control
over the amount of flowage from Lake Michigan into the Chicago
Sanitary and Ship Canal.

The diversion activities of the Chicago Sanitary District did
not excite significant concern until the decade of the 1920s.
When the canal was initially opened, the lake levels were on the
upgrade due to an abnormally high rainfall, and thus there was no
occasion for alarm from the transportation standpoint. In 1908
the International Waterways Commission, composed of American and
Canadian representatives, urged that the diversion be limited to
10,000 cubic feet in order not to destroy the scenic beauty of
Niagara Falls, to impede the production of hydroelectric power, or
to interfere with navigation in harbors bordering on the Great
Lakes. The Supreme Court of the United States found on February 19,
1906, that the Missouri allegations of pollution resulting in the
increase of typhoid fever were unproven. For the time being at
least, the nation's highest court through Justice Oliver Wendell
Holmes held that the dilution system was working satisfactorily.
Nevertheless, the federal government in 1907 requested an injunction which would restrain the sanitary district from reversing
the flow of the Calumet River in order to increase the dilution
through the proposed Calumet-Sag Canal. A second suit was instituted in 1913 when Secretary of War Henry L. Stimson refused to
grant any additional diversion through the existing channel. By
mutual agreement of both parties, these two suits were tried as a
unit. A decision was not rendered, however, until 1925 when the
Supreme Court delivered an opinion against the sanitary district.
The court held that the district had no inherent right to divert
water for sanitary or navigational purposes, and that the Secretary
of War had sole authority to control this matter. The War Department subsequently issued a temporary permit authorizing a diversion
of 8,500 cubic feet on the condition that Chicago immediately
undertake the construction of adequate sewage treatment plants.[25]

By 1920 the aspect of the Chicago diversion which most concerned downstaters was the pollution allegedly emanating from
Chicago. While the dilution system had worked for a time, it
was evident to everyone's nose that contamination was present.
Among the pressure groups organized to protest this growing menace
was the Illinois Valley Protective Association. At an early
meeting in Carrollton, Rainey vowed his support in urging Chicago
into immediate action. During the fall of 1923, a Senate committee
headed by Medill McCormick of Illinois began studying the lower
Illinois River's waterway possibilities. In testifying before the
committee, Rainey threatened to oppose all waterway schemes which
did not make adequate arrangements for the safe disposition of
Chicago sewage. Especially he deplored the lack of protection
afforded the drainage districts, the loss of the fish, clam shell,
and pearl industries in the Illinois River, and the amount of
pollution Chicago poured into the waterway. He vowed to oppose,
on its merits and by every parliamentary tactic known, any bill
which did not protect valley property owners from the ravages of
Chicago's diversion. As another facet of his opposition, Rainey
enlisted the aid of the state's administrative agencies. His
principal success was the reduction of contamination in the Illinois River due to factory wastes. Because of his efforts, the
Illinois Department of Public Works and Buildings investigated
the discharge of acids, chemicals, and other poisonous industrial
wastes which were polluting the river. The guilty parties were
meat-packing companies and a corn-products firm; not all the
river's pollution came from Chicago sewers.[26]

The subject of the diversion of water from the Great Lakes
became of increasing concern to Congress. Rainey introduced a
bill which he believed would adequately safeguard the interests of
his downstream constituents. His bill did not attempt to restrict
the amount of diversion because he felt Congress would probably
legalize the current practice anyway. It did provide for financial
protection to the property owners injured by the diversion, and
it did endeavor to reduce flooding by requiring a level maintenance
of the water supply. Rainey wanted the Chicago diversion to be as
small as possible and yet maintain navigation and provide sewage
disposal until Chicago could make other arrangements. As a
minority member, Rainey had no illusions that his bill would be
reported out by the committee, but he hoped the committee would
incorporate the suggestions protecting the people of the Illinois
valley. The features of the Rainey bill were merged with the waterway bill of Congressman William E. Hull of Peoria. As a Republican
and a member of the House Committee on Rivers and Harbors, Hull's
measure stood a better change of passage. Rainey presented a
major speech in behalf of the merged bills at a Peoria meeting.
He deplored the fact that "the Illinois River, with all of its
romance and its beauty gone, has now become the greatest and the
most offensive open sewer to be found anywhere on the face of the
earth." He insisted that the water flowing down the valley had to
be pure and expressed no patience with the Corps of Engineers'
proposition to give Chicago twenty or twenty-five years in which

to remedy its sewage difficulties. Rainey maintained that the
amount of the diversion did not matter so long as the federal government would support levee protection, remove the dams obstructing
the flow of water, and assure the purity of the water. He concluded
by urging unified support throughout the state on "one of the
greatest questions involving at the same time transportation by
water, sanitation, water power, and the preservation of Lakes that
have ever been submitted to the American Congress since the adoption
of the Constitution."[27] Acting jointly, Rainey and Hull hoped to
stimulate public support for a maximum effort in the next Congress.
Their efforts were to be aided by Supreme Court action on the
question of legislative right to control the diversion and by
severe flood conditions along the Illinois River.

The principal arbiter of the Chicago diversion question
proved to be the judicial chamber rather than the legislative halls.
In 1925 the Supreme Court had ruled that the Secretary of War was
empowered to regulate the amount of diversion, if any, at Chicago.
This decision was challenged almost immediately by the states
bordering on the Great Lakes. The complainants charged that the
Chicago diversion had reduced the lake levels substantially and
that no authority could grant a permit which allowed any diversion.
Illinois denied the charges and asserted that it was taking water
from Lake Michigan under a legal permit authorized by the Secretary
of War. The states of the lower Mississippi valley joined the case
as defendants, contending the Chicago diversion raised their river
level and thus aided navigation. Former Justice Charles Evans
Hughes was appointed special master in the case to determine the
facts for the court. In his report, he held that the complaining
states had established that the diversion through the drainage
canal had inflicted considerable damage to their navigational,
commercial, and other interests. Hughes did not find any demon-
strable improvement in the navigation of the Mississippi. The
Supreme Court then decided that since the purpose of the diversion
was for sanitation rather than navigation, the Secretary of War
had no power to issue permits. The court justified temporary
permits until such time as sewage disposal plants were completed.
The case was then referred to the special master for determination
of a practical solution to the sewage problem. On April 21, 1930,
the Supreme Court presented its decision in the lake levels case
by mandating a gradual reduction in the diversion subject to a
review in 1965. A final decree with an effective date of March 1,
1970, was entered on June 12, 1966. It ordered a maximum withdrawal
of 3,200 cubic feet, including the waters in the Chicago and
Calumet rivers which ordinarily would have entered the lake. By
previous court orders, the city of Chicago had been required to
accelerate the construction of sewage treatment plants.[28]

Whereas the judicial branch of government came to carry the
greatest influence in the resolution of waterway questions relating
to sanitation, the legislative and executive branches were predom-
inant in flood-control matters. Another problem arising in part
from the Chicago dilution and diversion system was excessive
flooding in the Illinois River valley. The gentle slope of the

Illinois plain had made flood damage a concern for generations.
A combination of successive seasons in which there was an abnormally high rainfall and an increased flowage resulting from the
Chicago diversion increased the demand for appropriate protection
in the lowlands downstream from Chicago. In the 1910s, conservationists had sought flood control as one of the elements in a
multifaceted program of river development. The chief congressional exponent of conservation measures which had flood-control
components was Democratic Senator Francis G. Newlands of Nevada.
He was joined in the House of Representatives by Robert F.
Broussard, Democrat of Louisiana. When Broussard moved to the
Senate in 1915, Rainey took over the House sponsorship of the
Newlands proposal. The purpose of this multifaceted legislation
was to prevent flood damage in the rivers of the Mississippi
watershed and to provide public development of waterpower. The
bill included an appropriation of $60,000,000 covering ten years.
It asked that one-third of the amount be granted immediately in
order to set the machinery in motion.[29] While the Newlands-Rainey
proposal for the coordinated development of the Mississippi
waterway had the endorsement of President Wilson's Cabinet, the
Congress was unwilling to approve such a gigantic step, but the
concept was revived in the 1920s.

In 1922, the Illinois River valley experienced the first of
a series of floods which were to mark that decade as among the
worst in the state's history. The plight of Rainey's constituents
dramatically reminded him of the multipurpose river development
system which included levees, reservoirs, reforestation, spillways, irrigation, and a proper development of waterpower. In
subsequent testimony before the House committee holding hearings
on Illinois River matters, Rainey listed the problems confronting
the Illinois River basin as the destruction of marketable fish,
the curtailment of navigation, and the dangers of unnecessary
flooding. He supported his bill providing for federal government
aid for levees along the Illinois River. This bill, which provided
the same aid for landowners along the Illinois as was given those
on the Mississippi, was unanimously approved by the Committee on
Rivers and Harbors, and was incorporated in an omnibus rivers and
harbors bill. When Representative Theodore E. Burton of Ohio
proposed elimination of the $36,000,000 appropriation for levee
protection and a nine-foot channel between Utica and the mouth of
the Illinois River, Rainey ably defended the two provisions, and
the motion to strike out the Illinois portion of the omnibus bill
was defeated.[30] The Senate version, however, retained only the
authorization of federal government endorsement for a nine-foot
channel from Chicago to New Orleans. The dream of federal
support for a Great Lakes-to-Gulf of Mexico deep waterway was
finally realized after a score of years. This bill, however, made
no provision for levee assistance from the national government.
Mother Nature helped to further that part of the Rainey program.

The whole Mississippi River valley was subjected to severe
flooding during the fall of 1926 and the spring of 1927. The fall
floods left 7,750 homeless, inundated 200,000 acres, and destroyed

$200,000,000 worth of property in the Illinois valley, principally
from Peoria to Grafton. The depth of water on drainage and levee
districts was as great as fifteen feet in some cases. In the city
of Beardstown, 80 percent of the city was submerged to a maximum
of twelve feet. This appalling calamity clearly demonstrated to
Frank R. Reid of Illinois, chairman of the House Committee on
Flood Control, that Rainey's advice on federal government aid for
levee districts should be heeded. Reid promised to do everything
in his power to effect the principles for which Rainey stood.[31]
The crisis was accentuated when spring floods added to the
disaster. Throughout the whole Mississippi valley, the property
damage was estimated at $400,000,000, and 700,000 persons were
made homeless. The whole nation's attention was directed toward
the problem; Rainey endeavored to contribute to the solution.

Part of Rainey's efforts were directed toward interesting
the executive branch of government in the Illinois valley's flood
problems. He wrote to President Coolidge, calling attention to the
deplorable situation due to flooding in the Illinois River lowlands. Since Coolidge was sending Secretary of Commerce Hoover as
his personal representative to investigate the lower Mississippi
River, Rainey hoped the President would also find it possible to
send Hoover to the Illinois valley to study conditions and make a
personal report. The President's private secretary replied that
the army engineers and the members of the specially formed Mississippi River Commission would make a very careful study of the whole
situation before reporting to the President. Rainey subsequently
telegraphed the President, urging that he call a special session
of Congress to deal with the situation, but to no avail. On
previous occasions, Rainey had been successful in enlisting the aid
of the Secretary of War. In directing Secretary Dwight F. Davis's
attention to the calamity, he pointed out that people in Beardstown were compelled like Venetians to use boats in the streets
from October, 1926, until June, 1927. The United States government,
Rainey charged, was responsible for this unfortunate condition.
Rainey enlisted the aid of Republican Carl R. Chindblom of Illinois
in promoting a survey of the situation by the Secretary of War,
but the latter was uncooperative.[32] Rainey was unable to move the
executive branch of government to his line of thinking; it remained
for Congress to take the necessary action.

A major item on the agenda of the Seventieth Congress was
water conservation legislation. Rainey placed in the hopper a
number of bills to accomplish flood control. His ideas were reminiscent of the comprehensive programs advocated by Senator Newlands.
The most important bill called for the appropriation of $210,000,000
for flood control throughout the Mississippi watershed. Rainey
proposed the formation of a National Waterways Council and a Water
Control Board to cooperate with the states in securing the greatest
possible development of the waterways and water resources of the
United States. The measure finally passed by Congress, the Jones-
Reid Act of May, 1928, appropriated $300,000,000 for the erection
of levees, drainage basins, and spillways in troublesome parts of
the river. In contrast to the Rainey proposal, this legislation

provided immediate relief for the flood situation but neglected
comprehensive planning for the future. Rainey was not sure that
the bill would be adequate for his district's relief, but it was a
step in the right direction.

Once the principle of federal assistance for levee building
was established, it became relatively easy to secure state aid as
well. During the Great Depression, levee construction became a
major factor in the Hoover administration's relief activities.
While local levee and drainage districts were required to provide
a portion of the necessary funds, the principal burden was assumed
by the federal government in cooperation with the states. During
the New Deal years, the Reconstruction Finance Corporation absorbed
the responsibility for activities in behalf of drainage and irrigation districts. To assist with this task in 1933, Rainey secured
the employment of Emil Schram, a constituent and chairman of the
board of directors of the National Drainage Association, as
reorganizer for the RFC.[33] In a generation of time, Speaker Rainey
had witnessed considerable strides in the remediation of flood
conditions throughout the nation. While the programs fell short
of the comprehensive developments which he and others envisioned,
his efforts had contributed to constructive gains.

As the natural forces of the river came under control,
conservationists directed their attention to the private developers profiting by these systematic improvements. Special concern
was focused upon the electrical power industry which was mushrooming
in the 1920s. By 1929, Gifford Pinchot and Rainey had agreed to
begin a fight against the power monopolies. The Federal Power
Commission's regulatory authority was being challenged through
propaganda and court actions. To Vincent Y. Dallman of the *Illinois
State Register*, Henry T. observed that Illinois was more firmly in
the grasp of the power trust due to the Insull pyramid of holding
companies than any other state in the Union. As lobbying agents,
he noted that the power trust controlled chambers of commerce,
lecturers, country newspapers, women's clubs, college textbooks,
and professors. Rainey urged a campaign of public information to
dispel the falsehoods and to urge the continuance of public
regulation. In a radio interview, he noted that the iron age was
being replaced by the electrical age, a new era when men of great
wealth were organizing into corporations seeking to control the
declivities in the rivers for their own private benefit. As an aid
to public information on the subject, he supported the activities
of the National Popular Government League, which urged the public
operation of Muscle Shoals, the enforcement of the federal Water
Power Act, and the appointment of sympathetic administrators to
regulatory commissions. This group endeavored to popularize the
issue as part of the 1932 election campaign. While this concern
did not rival the depression in its political impact, Rainey
continued to present himself as a strong public power man. He
maintained his position in spite of opposition from the *Illinois
State Journal*, a Republican newspaper in Springfield allegedly in
the control of Ira Copley (power-trust spokesman) through Insull
money. Among Rainey's last legislative acts was an endorsement of

additional funds to continue an investigation of public utility corporations.[34] The struggle for public regulation of utilities would be carried on by others following his death.

A concern for conservation typified Rainey's activities throughout his career. A parochial interest arising in his district grew to a cosmopolitan interest in resource use for the state and the nation. The navigational advantages of waterway development were equalled in importance by the allied benefits relating to conservation—development of waterpower, prevention of floods, reclamation of riparian lands, purification of water, and regulation of electric rates. In recognition of his many services to the conservation cause, the Civilian Conservation Corps facility near Carrollton was named the Henry T. Rainey camp. The CCC was one of the most valued of the New Deal alphabet agencies. During a three-year period, this group of young men planted 571,565 trees on the farms of seventy-four cooperators and on public grounds.[35]

This history of the Illinois waterway in both its transportation and allied features illustrates the interrelationship of resource problems. The undertaking had begun in 1908 principally as a transportation medium and electric-power source. By dint of circumstances, if not foresight, policymakers were forced to take other elements into consideration. This combination of conditions included the question of water supply and waste disposal for the city of Chicago and surrounding suburbs, the problem of lake levels and their effect on commerce, the relative value of waterpower developed in Illinois or at Niagara, and the degree of flooding and pollution permissible in the Illinois River valley. The coordinated solution to all these problems as envisioned by many conservationists was not realized. Yet, over time the elements of piecemeal activity meshed into a systematic whole which permitted efficient use of available water resources.[36] The principles of conservation include the practice of democracy in resource use. The process is slow but successful, as the Rainey activities indicate. Rainey also maintained this same type of vigilance for the public interest in matters relating to such domestic concerns as tariffs, taxes, and trusts.

NOTES

1. HTR radio address on April 8, 1934, reprinted in *CR*, 73:2 (April 17, 1932), 6778. For contrasting interpretations of conservation see J. Leonard Bates, "Fulfilling American Democracy," 29–57, and Samuel P. Hays, *Conservation and the Gospel of Efficiency*, esp. 261, 265–266.

2. Whitney R. Cross, "W J McGee and the Idea of Conservation," 159–160; W J McGee, "Our Great River," 8576–84; Gifford Pinchot, "How Conservation Began," 262–263.

3. *Gazette*, Jan. 16, 1903, 4:4; exchange of correspondence between HTR and Dr. A. C. True (Director of the Agricultural Experiment Stations) reprinted in *Gazette*, Oct. 16, 1903, 4:4; and Feb. 9, 1906, 4:1.

4. *CR*, 61:2 (Jan. 7, 1910), 404; editorial, "Rainey and James," *Gazette*, Jan. 20, 1910, 4:2; "Ballinger Whitewash Is Upset," 164; New York *Times*, Jan. 20, 1910, 1:3; Adams, "The Joke's on You," 54; *CR*, 61:2 (Jan. 20, 1910), 837–841; New York *Times*, Jan. 21, 1910, 2:2–3; Rose M. Stahl, "The Ballinger-Pinchot Controversy," 124; Charles R. Atkinson, *The Committee on Rules and the Overthrow of Speaker Cannon*, 99; Geoffrey Morrison, "Champ Clark and the Rules Revolution of 1910," 52. John D. Baker, "The Character of the Congressional Revolution of 1910," 679–691, places the fight against Cannonism outside the progressive pale.

5. Pinchot to HTR, Washington, Feb. 23, 1917, RP; Pinchot to HTR, Washington, March 10, 1917, as printed in *Gazette*, April 4, 1917, 1:2; HTR to Pinchot, Washington, March 12, 1917, Pinchot Papers, Box 204.

6. HTR summarized his conservationist activities in a speech before the Cosmos Club in Washington on June 25, 1932. Printed in *CR*, 72:1 (July 15, 1932), 15458.

7. *CR*, 62:2 (July 18, 1912), 9249, (July 19), 9349–50 for Austin's remarks, and 9350–51 for Rainey's statement.

8. *CR*, 62:2 (July 25, 1912), 9656–58 and (Aug. 20), 11369–75, 11378–80; Jerome K. Kerwin, *Federal Water Power Legislation*, 130–135.

9. *CR*, 62:2 (Aug. 22, 1912), 11587–89; Kerwin, *Federal Water Power Legislation*, 135–140.

10. Pinchot, "The Democrats and Conservation," in "The Story of the Democratic House of Representatives," a condensed chapter appearing in Haines, *Law Making in America*, 31; Mark Sullivan, "Comments on Congress," 13; and his "The Most Important Thing," 15.

11. *CR*, 63:2 (July 24, 1914), 12678–83; (July 25, 1914), 12777–78; evaluation is that of Judson King, *The Conservation Fight from Theodore Roosevelt to the Tennessee Valley Authority*, 45–46.

12. Banquet address in honor of Harry Slattery as printed in *CR*, 72:1 (July 15, 1932), 15458; Doris B. Whitney, "Highlights in the Career of the Late Speaker of the House, Henry T. Rainey" (carbon copy of typescript, 1951), 3; Lester V. Plum, "The Federal Power Commission" (Ph.D. thesis), 32–33.

13. New York *Times*, Nov. 12, 1916, V, 10; *CR*, 64:2 (Dec. 22, 1916), 698–702; (Jan. 24, 1917), 1922–23; and (Feb. 7, 1917), 2789.

14. Plum, "The Federal Power Commission," 33.

15. Bates, "Fulfilling American Democracy," 53; Hays, *Conservation and the Gospel of Efficiency*, 239–240.

16. "The Administration of Charles S. Deneen, 1905–1912" ([Chicago]: Charles S. Deneen Campaign Committee, [1912]), 31 *passim; Illinois State Register*, Jan. 10, 1907, 11:3.

17. Putnam, *The Illinois and Michigan Canal*, 89–90; *Patriot*,

Aug. 29, 1907, 3:4-6.

18. Circular letter sent by HTR to members of Congress, members of the Illinois legislature, and the press of Illinois, Carrollton, Sept. 27, 1907, reprinted in *Gazette*, Oct. 3, 1907, 1:3-4 and 2:1-6.

19. *Illinois State Register*, Nov. 6, 1907, 10:1-4; Chicago *Record-Herald*, Nov. 7, 1907, 1:3 and 3:3; Nov. 20, 1:7; Nov. 22, 1:5 and 7 and 5:5-7; Dec. 7, 3:1; and Dec. 31, 1:3; Peoria *Herald-Transcript*, June 27, 1908, 3:3 and 4:2; "The Administration of Charles S. Deneen," 32.

20. Charles S. Deneen, "Vast Wealth for the State," 123, 129; HTR in *CR*, 60:1 (May 30, 1908), Appendix 238; John L. Mathews, "Water Power and the 'Pork Barrel,'" 456.

21. Mathews, "How Illinois Will Feed Her New Waterway," 12, 14; "The Illinois Waterway," 409.

22. *Division of Waterways, Twenty-first Annual Report, July 1, 1937 to June 30, 1938*, 21; *Twenty-second Annual Report, July 1, 1938 to December 31, 1939*, 31, 34.

23. F. Darvin Davenport, "The Sanitation Revolution in Illinois, 1870-1900," 306-326; John Clayton, "How They Tinkered with a River," 32-46; Maurice O. Graff, "The Lake Michigan Water Diversion Controversy," 453-471; William R. Willoughby, *The St. Lawrence Seaway*, 100-101.

24. C. Arch Williams, *The Sanitary District of Chicago*; William B. Philip, "Chicago and the Downstate: A Study of Their Conflicts, 1870-1934" (Ph.D. thesis), 200-231.

25. Peoria *Herald-Transcript*, June 6, 1908, 1:5; Williams, *Sanitary District of Chicago*, 39-42, 199; *Illinois State Register*, March 27, 1908, 2:5; Daniel Whiting, "The St. Lawrence Seaway Power Project," 78.

26. *Patriot*, Oct. 7, 1920, 1:1-2; *Gazette*, Oct. 24, 1923, 1:1 and Nov. 21, 1:5-6; *Division of Waterways, Eighth Annual Report, July 1, 1924 to June 30, 1925*, 54, 56.

27. H.R. 6822 in *CR*, 68:1 (Feb. 9, 1924), 2221; U.S. Congress, House, Committee on Rivers and Harbors, *Hearings on the Improvement of the Illinois and Mississippi Rivers*, 79-84, 222-225, 756-806, 930-933; Peoria speech of Jan. 24, 1925, as printed in *CR*, 68:2 (Feb. 13, 1925), 3648-54.

28. Cornelius Lynde, "The Controversy Concerning the Diversion of Water from Lake Michigan by the Sanitary District of Chicago," 243-260; Clayton, "How They Tinkered with a River," 46.

29. Francis G. Newlands, "The Use and Development of American Waterways," 48-66; Arthur B. Darling (ed.), *The Public Papers of Francis G. Newlands*, II, 290.

30. U.S. Congress, House, Committee on Rivers and Harbors, *Hearings on the Improvement of the Illinois River, Ill. and the*

Abstraction of Water from Lake Michigan, 143–162; *CR*, 69:1 (June 3, 1926), 10667–71, 10675; *Gazette*, June 16, 1926, 1:2.

31. *Illinois-Progress, 1921–1928*, 286; Reid to HTR, Aurora, Oct. 20, 1926, RP. For an overview of the flood problem consult Bruce A. Lohof, "Herbert Hoover, Spokesman of Humane Efficiency," 690–700.

32. HTR to Coolidge, Carrollton, May 2, 1927, RP; Everett Sanders to HTR, Washington, May 5, 1927, as published in *Gazette*, May 11, 1927, 1:1; Sanders to HTR, Washington, May 13, 1927, RP; HTR to Davis, Carrollton, May 11 and June 10, 1927, RP; Chindblom to HTR, Washington, June 21, 1927, RP.

33. Leahmae Brown, "The Development of National Policy," 74–75; Jesse H. Jones, *Fifty Billion Dollars*, 172, 529.

34. HTR to Pinchot, Washington, Feb. 2, 1929, Pinchot Papers, Box 2144; Pinchot to HTR, Washington, Feb. 9, 1929, RP; HTR to Dallman, [Washington], Jan. 13, 1931, RP; HTR interview with NBC's Wm. Hard on Jan. 4, 1932, in *CR*, 72:1 (Jan. 5, 1932), 1298–1300; "Power Records of the Presidential Candidates," *Bulletin* No. 153 of the National Popular Government League for March 18, 1932, 1–2; King, *Conservation Fight*, 252–253; Dallman to HTR, Springfield, Feb. 24, 1934, RP (see especially Mrs. Rainey's notations added in Jan., 1935, and her personal interview observations reported by Helen E. Graff, "Henry T. Rainey—An American Statesman" (M.A. thesis), 58; Edwin L. Davis (Commissioner of FTC) to HTR, Washington, March 12, 1934, RP.

35. *Patriot*, Nov. 15, 1934, 1:5; *Greene County Farm Bureau News Letter*, VII (April, 1936), 2, and (July, 1936), 6.

36. The best overview of conservation policy respecting waterways, flood control, and waterpower may be found in Donald C. Swain, *Federal Conservation Policy, 1921–1933*, 96–122.

6

Opponent of the "Interests"

In the view of progressive reformers early in the twentieth
century, the most vexatious problem facing the nation was control
by the "interests," a euphemism for big business operating counter
to the public's welfare. In economic terms, the concern focused
upon control of trusts, reduction of tariffs, and reform of taxes.
An examination of Henry T. Rainey's legislative career provides an
opportunity for a longitudinal study of his approach to these
pervasive issues. During his congressional tenure, Rainey was a
bitter opponent of monopoly, high protective tariffs, and regressive taxes. In the first decade of this service, he established
a record on these domestic issues which endeared him to most of
his Democratic colleagues. His verbal attacks upon monopoly and
his opposition to protective tariffs fitted nicely with the dogma
of Democracy. His activities resulted in considerable campaign
material which the party exploited. His notoriety and partisanship
were admirable qualities when seeking loyal Democrats to entrust
with major committee responsibilities. These considerations, plus
a genial personality and a northern constituency, made him a logical
choice for membership on the influential Ways and Means Committee.
His attitude in matters relating to waterways and conservation had
been essentially bipartisan throughout in spite of delays and frus-
tration. In contrast, his demeanor on economic policies was
extremely partisan almost without exception. His single most
important legislative accomplishment was the adoption of the commission concept in tariff making.
     In Congress any individual's success and influence upon the
legislative process is determined in part by committee assignments.
The Rivers and Harbors Committee would have been a logical appointment for a new legislator with a constituency and interests such
as Rainey's. The retirement of Walter Reeves, an Illinois Republican, had created a vacancy on that committee in 1903, but it was
supposed correctly that the place would more likely go to some
Illinois Republican. The Fifty-eighth Congress was the first in
which "Uncle Joe" Cannon of Illinois assumed the Speakership.
Cannon decided to break precedent and allow the minority leader,
John Sharp Williams of Mississippi, to appoint the Democratic
members to committees.[1] Because of the spoils associated with the
Rivers and Harbors Committee, it then ranked fourth among the
House committees in power and prestige. As an added complication
in organizing the new House, its total membership had been increased

from 357 to 386 because of the reapportionment based on the 1900
census. As an additional entanglement, there were 120 members
elected for the first time. When party leaders coupled the importance of the committee, the influx of new members, and the one-term
tradition in Illinois' twentieth district, the result was ample
justification for overlooking Rainey's preference. His only assignment was to the inconsequential Committee on Pacific Railroads.
His return to the next Congress in spite of the Theodore Roosevelt
landslide in 1904 merited him further consideration. He was reas-
signed to Pacific Railroads and in addition was given committee
assignments with Labor, Irrigation of Arid Lands, and Enrolled Bills.
With the exception of being dropped from Pacific Railroads in 1909,
Rainey retained these assignments until 1911. As a minority
member, his voice was rarely influential whenever these committees
deliberated. Rainey's chief legislative interests were separate
from his committee responsibilities. He would have to earn a
prestigious position by his activities in the legislative chamber.

During his first years in Congress, Rainey was one of those
Democrats who tried to demonstrate the need for a reform outlook
within the party. The principal object of his attention was tariff
reform. Although Congress was debating ship subsidy legislation,
the land-locked congressman utilized the opportunity for opening
an indirect attack upon the protective tariff as well. According
to Rainey, ship subsidies had failed miserably over the last fifty
years. It was the protective tariff which was largely responsible
for the inability of the United States to compete with the British
merchant marine. The navigation laws, he charged, prohibited
buying ships in foreign markets and the tariff laws prevented
building them. The two combined to produce depressing and disastrous effects on the American shipping industry. The solution he
presented was to pay no subsidies to any shipping line, to repeal
the navigation laws forbidding purchase of foreign-made vessels,
and to reduce the protective tariff so that there could be free
material for shipbuilding. As an indication of the topic's
importance, this criticism was Rainey's second major address before
the Congress. A leading national journal of the shipping industry
suggested that the utterances of the Illinoisan were especially
valuable because he saw the problem in perspective and without the
distortions caused by close association with the industry. In
1907 Rainey renewed his attack upon the philosophy of ship subsidies. The importance of the issue as a political weapon was not
lost upon William Jennings Bryan.[2] While Rainey's pleas did not
meet with congressional approval, the significance of the issue
lay in the national political stature which he was earning. He
had found a problem whose importance transcended his district's
boundaries.

The most remembered congressional action in Rainey's fledgling
years was a spectacular attack upon the tariff schedules. His
entering wedge was a scathing denunciation of the watch trust.
Before beginning his speech, he displayed on an easel in front of
the Speaker's rostrum a large photograph of a New York City store.
Across the front of the store was a sign covering an entire story

which was inscribed as follows: "Great protection sale. Waltham
and Elgin watches bought in England cheaper than in America and
brought back to undersell this market." Rainey must have startled
Speaker Cannon when he referred to the presence of the picture and
averred that he was going to conduct "a kindergarten for 'standpat'
Republicans." Using the photograph as his entry, he demonstrated
that on one side of the tariff wall one price was made to an American consumer and on the other side, where competition was free,
another and a lower price was charged to foreign consumers of
American goods. Such a practice he described as "a nefarious,
outrageous business." Resuming his "kindergarten class" the next
day, Rainey, magician-like, successively drew from his large
person three Elgin and three Waltham watches. To substantiate
his point about a two-price system, he gave the case history of
each of the watches. He concluded that such a practice was not
in the interest of domestic consumers. Avowing that he was
honestly and conscientiously trying to represent the interests
of the people, he charged that the Republican members were
bought "body, soul, boots and breeches" by the trusts and that
they served merely as decoys placed on the pond by the big business
interests.[3] These charges and the tangible evidence he presented began to awaken Americans to the efficacy of lower tariff
rates. Though his attack was aimed at a specific trust, he
intended the conclusion drawn to be given the widest possible
application.

The speech was a sensation. A wire service story noted
the completeness of the research presented, the strength of the
indictment rendered, and the spectacular interest produced by the
display of watches. The American Press Association distributed
a cartoon caricature of Rainey lampooning the watch trust. The
St. Louis *Republic* succinctly stated that Rainey had "lucidly shown
Illinois voters who cultivate the virtue of punctuality how
they are mulcted in the purchase of time pieces by the highly
protected Watch Trust." The *Commoner* noted that "republican
members were whipped into silence by the powerful showing he
made." In a weekly Washington newsletter, Missourian Champ
Clark observed that the speech was one "likely to set men to
examining their chronometers to count the hours till the day
when we shall have a Democratic house."[4] Rainey's watch trust
speeches were a thrust at a weak point in President Theodore
Roosevelt's armor because he desired to avoid any element of
tariff controversy during his administration.

The stand taken by Rainey against trusts represented a survival from the days of Populism. Farmers of the Midwest had
been imbued with a fear of corporate wealth and monopoly.
Their suffering at the hands of railroads, banks, middlemen, and
manufacturers had made them antimonopolists. This vestige
of agrarian discontent was continued after 1900 as one of the
components of the progressive movement. Rainey's role during
these years was as reporter-reformer producing muckrake evidence
for the exposure of trusts. In addition to his criticism of
the watch trust, he, along with many others, focused upon the

Standard Oil Company as the embodiment of the trust evil. His
special concern was the close connection between privilege and
politics. He charged that the trusts had contributed to a
$16,000,000 Republican slush fund in order to defeat the Demo-
crats in the 1896 election. During this speech, he reserved the
greatest amount of invective for Roosevelt's attitude and policy
toward the trusts. He minimized the effectiveness of the "ear-
splitting detonations from the White House" as a sham fight
between the administration and the Standard Oil Company. He
charged that the presidential messages were a bluff because a
sincere attack upon the company would include the complete
removal of the high tariff on petroleum.[5] Rainey subscribed to
the view that the protective tariff was the mother of trusts.
At various times he had introduced separate bills calling for
tariff reductions on agricultural implements, serums, coal,
lumber, watches, white paper, wood pulp, and crude oil. These
measures were dutifully assigned to the Ways and Means Committee
and there they were allowed to die. This shotgun approach to
tariff revision was supplanted by a thorough re-examination
during the early Taft administration.

In 1908 William Howard Taft had been elected President on
a campaign plank which promised revision of the tariff rates.
The Congress was called into special session on March 15, 1909,
to redeem that commitment. Since Rainey was not a member of the
Ways and Means Committee, he had no hand in drawing the Payne-
Aldrich bill. When it came to be debated on the floor of the
House, he was among the outspoken critics and delivered one
major speech in the House against the proposal. He labeled the
Payne bill "the most infamous measure of tariff oppression ever
conceived by tariff beneficiaries and their representatives."
Capitalizing on his acquired knowledge of watches, he attacked
that part of the schedule with a seven-point objection and a
display of seven Swiss watches that would be denied importation
under the schedule. The low tariff advocate was especially
incensed because the Republicans were only pretending to reduce
tariff rates. After the bill reached final form, he found
another disquieting feature. The bill granted to the President
authority to lower rates toward those nations which did not
discriminate against American trade. Rainey insisted that this
was a grant of legislative authority and was thus unconstitutional. If the President were to be granted such a discretionary
power, he thought it best for Congress to provide low rates and
then allow the Chief Executive to raise them against nations
discriminating against the United States.[6] His suggestion of
this alternate scheme to accomplish the same objective was
unheeded. Rainey was not very satisfied with this first tariff
legislation in which he had been a participant. The members of
the minority party would strive to make political capital of
the increased rates.

Congressman Rainey did his personal best to make the tariff
and trust combination an effective political issue. One source
of embarrassment for the Taft administration would be congressional

investigations in this area. Rainey concentrated his strongest
protestations upon the tariff-inspired monopoly known as the
sugar trust, which he described as "the most corrupt and rotten
trust ever created by the protective tariff system." Rainey
addressed the House in favor of his resolution requesting an
investigation of the handling of the sugar trust frauds. He
pointed out that four or five resolutions to this effect "sleep
the sleep that knows no waking" in the Rules Committee, that
"graveyard of those meritorious measures which might . . .
prove detrimental to the progress of the Republican party."
Rainey noted that the Justice Department had instituted proceedings only against the "little fellows." The reason, Rainey
said, lay in the fact that Attorney-General George W. Wickersham
was "a sugar trust attorney." Since the President's brother,
Charles P. Taft, also represented that interest, there was a
natural disinclination to prosecute, according to Rainey. His
accusations were so blatantly political that he only succeeded
in getting himself blacklisted from White House social functions.[7]
Such social ostracism did not deter Rainey; he continued to
exploit issues which would discomfort the Republicans and
contribute to Democratic election gains.

Democratic control of the lower chamber following the 1910
elections confronted Rainey and his colleagues with a new problem. It was one thing to be a member of the minority party
constantly criticizing the opposition's activities. It was
another set of problems to become a member of the majority
party with responsibility for leadership. The organization of
the new House could contribute to the success or failure of the
party's presidential fortunes two years hence. Initially there
was no hint that Rainey would be elevated from his previous
responsibilities. It was believed that labor interests would be
in good hands because of his presence on the Labor Committee.
In fact, there was a possibility he might be chairman. A party
caucus was called for January 19, 1911, to determine tentative
organization for the next Congress. It was decided to select
the members of Ways and Means so that they could begin preparing tariff legislation immediately. The caucus also decided to
make the Democrats on the Ways and Means group the Democratic
Committee on Committees. The Speaker was thus deprived of the
influential power of making committee appointments. Participation on the Ways and Means Committee was so time-consuming that
the members held no other standing committee assignments.
Because of his low tariff views, midwestern location, and seniority (for a northern Democrat), the caucus placed Rainey on Ways
and Means.[8] He had earned a position of influence from which
he could design party fiscal policy, and he retained this
assignment until 1933 when he became Speaker.

Rainey's selection to the Ways and Means Committee represents a watershed in his career. The Democratic caucus had
selected fourteen members as their component of the committee;
among them were Oscar W. Underwood of Alabama (chairman), Claude
Kitchin of North Carolina, Cordell Hull of Tennessee, and

A. Mitchell Palmer of Pennsylvania. William Gordon Brantly of
Georgia was the only member who did not advocate a tariff for
revenue only. The contemporary observer, Mark Sullivan, was very
hopeful about the prospects for this committee. Because of the
committee's responsibility to raise revenue, to act as a policy
committee for the Democrats, and to function as their Committee
on Committees, he described it as the most powerful congressional
committee in the history of the United States. Sullivan observed
that it was the best committee since 1845 to undertake major
tariff revision in the interests of the people. In a subsequent
article, the youthfulness of the committee's members was noted.
At age fifty, Rainey was the oldest. Thus, Sullivan wrote, if
they conducted themselves to the satisfaction of the public
there were many good years and great honors in store for all of
them. Rainey was now among the party leaders who could test his
capabilities in the Sixty-second Congress.[9]

The party leadership endeavored to make a record in the
House which would commend the national ticket to the people in
1912. It was generally conceded that tariff reform would be a
key component to the party's future electoral success. In
approaching tariff revision the party had the choice of writing
an entirely new tariff (this had been the customary practice) or
of changing it schedule by schedule (the popgun or shotgun
approach). Prior to his selection on the committee, Rainey
emphatically favored a complete revision of the Payne-Aldrich law
in one bill. Speaker-designate Champ Clark, however, expressed
a preference for separate tariff bills, and this was the tactic
ultimately adopted. As the Democrats began their task, George
Harvey, proponent of Wilson's presidential candidacy, warned
them that they could turn a feast into a funeral if the tariff
issue were mismanaged. During the spring and fall, the newly
constituted committee held hearings on various facets of the
tariff. Rainey was designated as head of a subcommittee preparing the cotton schedule. It was anticipated that a 50 percent
reduction might be possible.[10] In all, the Congress presented
three tariff bills covering five schedules for President Taft's
signature. Each was vetoed, but the party had introduced a
significant issue for Woodrow Wilson's successful campaign.

Beginning on March 4, 1913, the Democratic party assumed
complete control over the executive and legislative branches of
government. For the first time in Rainey's ten congressional
years, his party had the opportunity and the responsibility to
enact its legislative program. The leadership capability which
was demonstrated and the domestic issues which were developed
during the preceding Congress under Taft were now utilized. Ray
Stannard Baker observed that President Wilson was fortunate in
having an unusually able group of Democratic congressmen (Rainey
mentioned among them) with whom to deal. There was much speculation about the exact nature of the tariff restructuring to be
performed by the Democrats as a result of their 1911 to 1912
activities. This issue was the first to be considered by the
"New Freedom" legislators. Rainey's role in the actual

preparation of the Underwood tariff bill is largely obscured by
the passage of time. He was placed in charge of the subcommittee
which drafted the agricultural schedules. The most controversial
feature of this subcommittee's work was the wool schedule.
Underwood, chairman of the Ways and Means Committee and also
majority floor leader, was committed to a tariff on raw wool. He
won all the Democrats on the committee to his view, except Rainey
and Francis Burton Harrison of New York. As an alternative to a
floor fight which Harrison and Rainey threatened, Underwood
suggested leaving the decision up to the President. In separate
interviews, each of the three men presented their views to Wilson.
At a subsequent session of the committee, Underwood announced
that the bill would be drawn on a free-wool basis. When the
bill came before the House for debate, Rainey maintained that a
tariff on raw wool was the "keystone in the arch of protection."
In this bill, he declared, we recognize that fact and "with all
the force of a mighty party, with all the impact made possible by
20 years or more of waiting, we have kicked the keystone from the
arch, and the arch is already commencing to crumble."[11] By the
time Congress convened in special session on April 8, the bill
was nearly ready for consideration.

Rainey took an active part in the debates on the bill since
he was most anxious to redeem the Democratic promise of tariff
reduction. His first major speech in the bill's defense came
after Republican Sereno Payne of New York had prophesied disaster
to industry, to foreign trade, to wages, and to productivity if
the bill became law. Rainey replied that the people wanted this
tariff revised downward; they wanted competitive conditions
re-established; they wanted a rate made lowest upon the necessi-
ties of life and highest upon the luxuries. The inclusion of an
income tax, he said, represented the dawn of a new era in the
fiscal policy of the government; it was a scientific revision of
the tax structure carrying out Democratic theories. Rainey's
argument was a plea that steps be taken to remove the artificial
tariff barriers because advanced methods of transportation and
communication made natural barriers between nations less formidable. The exchange of goods, he said, should be "unaffected and
unhampered by unnatural trade conditions and restrictions." He
also defended placing numerous foodstuffs on the free list.
Rainey argued that the farmers of the nation were courageous
enough to support a cheaper breakfast table and a cheaper market
basket for the people of the great cities. In a speech extended
in the *Record*, Rainey joined President Wilson in criticizing the
propaganda of the life insurance companies in their misrepresen-
tation of the income tax features of the bill. This intentionally
misleading information, he said, was merely the device by which
the vested wealth of the country attempted to create a popular
swell of opposition to a proposal which would finally cause the
very wealthy to pay their fair share of the tax burden. Using a
folksy approach in a St. Louis *Post Dispatch* interview, Rainey
listed the benefits to be received by the average consumer. He
argued that a man and woman's "homebuilding efforts are as much

entitled to protection as any other industry in the country."[12]
As Rainey explained this measure, it took on the appearance of
a "protective tariff," but the protection was afforded the
common man, not industry. As a high-ranking Democrat on the Ways
and Means Committee, he was appointed to the conference committee
which ironed out the differences between the House and Senate
versions of the bill. The resulting Underwood-Simmons bill
reduced rates generally and added a considerable number of items
to the free list. Rainey could be justly proud of his strenuous
efforts in behalf of tariff reform. His role in the fulfillment
of the progressive demand for the scientific consideration of
subsequent tariff revision was even more significant.

The concept of a nonpartisan, independent agency to advise
on tariff policy antedated the twentieth century. President
Chester A. Arthur had appointed a Tariff Commission which
recommended an average reduction of about 20 percent, but Congress had responded with an average increase of 10 percent. The
idea then lay dormant until the twentieth century when reformers
revived this approach in order to take the vexatious problem
out of the hands of politicians and place it in the hands of
experts. This idea gained supporters, especially among Republican adherents. Rainey was suspicious, however, and feared that
the Republican idea of a tariff expert was a man "either in favor
of maintaining schedules just as they are or revising them
upward." He suspected that anyone advocating a different theory
would be considered a visionary dreamer. President Taft, nevertheless, had found authority under a minor provision of the
Payne-Aldrich Act and appointed an advisory body on September 14,
1909. The activities of this board became part of the intense
partisan struggle over tariff schedules in 1910 to 1912. The
Democratic party was unsympathetic to the usefulness of such a
board. In echoing these sentiments, Congressman Rainey charged
that the Republican theory of a tariff board appointed by and
responsible to the Executive relieved Congress of its constitutional burden and responsibility in revising tariffs. He warned
that Congress would be relieved of all its functions except to
distribute farmers' bulletins and vegetable seeds. Congress
voted to abolish the Taft board in 1912.[13]

Still, the advocates of a "scientific" tariff maintained
their campaign. The question of a Tariff Commission became one
of the issues in the 1912 presidential election. Theodore
Roosevelt and the Progressive party firmly advocated such a
policy; Wilson and the Democrats were steadfastly opposed.
Shortly after attaining office, Postmaster General Albert S.
Burleson submitted a lengthy report on the subject for the President's consideration. Burleson made this observation: "While
a permanent commission would not solve the tariff question,
take the tariff out of politics, make a purely scientific tariff,
or do other impossible things, it could be very serviceable."
During the fashioning of the Underwood bill, Mark Sullivan
suggested that now that the Democrats had "made some essential
reductions, a tariff commission, or some body like it, can take

up the work of necessary adjustments." No serious legislative
move ensued until the United States Chamber of Commerce began to
stimulate discussion among business groups. In August, 1915, a
group of influential businessmen formed the National Tariff
Commission League, with Howard H. Gross as principal lobbyist.
By the end of 1915, the chamber of commerce and the league
claimed that 700 business organizations had endorsed their stand
for a Tariff Commission.[14]   The focal point of their pressure
was an attempt to get Woodrow Wilson to reverse his position.

Evidence of an official change in administration policy was
soon forthcoming. In a published letter, the President let it
be known that he would favor "some such instrumentality as would
be supplied by a Tariff Board." In a second letter, the President justified his reversal of position on the basis of changed
world economic conditions. He quickly indicated, however, that
he had given "no thought whatever of a change of attitude toward
the so-called protective question." There was new leadership on
the Ways and Means Committee which could be expected to implement
the President's wishes. Former chairman Oscar W. Underwood had
been elected to the Senate, and Claude Kitchin of North Carolina
succeeded him as chairman of Ways and Means and as majority
leader. Kitchin was the logical leader to superintend the
administration's suggestion, but in this instance, as in so many
others, Kitchin found himself out of step with the President.
He refused to sponsor such a bill because it represented a
radical departure from traditional Democratic policies. He did
give assurances to Wilson and Secretary of the Treasury William
Gibbs McAdoo that he would not actively oppose the bill and
might even vote for it eventually.[15]   The mantle of leadership
for this measure fell to the second ranking Democrat on the Ways
and Means Committee, Henry Thomas Rainey.

On the day the President's letters appeared in print, Rainey
launched his campaign in behalf of a Tariff Commission. In a
lengthy letter to Secretary McAdoo, he outlined the conditions
which made this commission absolutely necessary. He explained
that his conversion to the idea had come during the Sixty-second
Congress when the new Democratic majority had begun working on
tariff proposals. The tariff board, he wrote, had provided the
most reliable sources of information available when studying
tariff revisions. After conferring with Kitchin on the matter,
Rainey indicated to McAdoo his willingness to make the fight
for the bill in the committee and on the floor of the House.
That same day Rainey addressed the Congress in advocacy of a
Tariff Commission. He defended the President's shift in position,
cited the threat of future German competition as the compelling
need for such a board, and promised the Republicans a chance to
redeem their campaign pledge to favor the adoption of a Tariff
Commission plan.[16]   Rainey's personal campaign in behalf of the
President's proposal was initiated.

On February 1, 1916, Rainey presented a preliminary tariff
commission bill. The introduction of the bill followed a visit
of Secretary McAdoo to the Capitol, during which he consulted

several of the Democratic members of the Ways and Means Committee. At the suggestion of Secretary of Agriculture David F. Houston, the board was to be called the United States Tariff Commission. This was especially necessary, Houston wrote, in view of the fact that the commission might wish to make investigations in foreign countries. Representative Kitchin and lobbyist Howard Gross also made suggestions as to the bill's initial form. The bill provided a commission comprised of five members, not more than three from the same political party. Former senators and representatives were ineligible for appointment so that it would not become a lame-duck body. In a statement to the press, Rainey stressed that Congress was not asked to delegate any legislative powers but the commission would be given the widest possible investigative powers. He was quoted as saying that the collection of data by this nonpartisan board would make possible an intelligent revision of tariff rates after the war.[17] The initial proposal was in the legislative hopper.

There was considerable maneuvering as interested persons offered suggestions for changes in the bill. It was proposed that there be an even number of members on the commission, with the major parties equally represented. Objection was made to the restriction forbidding the appointment of former congressmen. Still others thought that appointments should be made with due regard for the interests of agriculture, labor, manufacture, and commerce. Appointments for a twelve-year term were advocated. Another suggestion was that the commission report to the whole House rather than just to the Ways and Means Committee. Slight changes in wording were recommended as a means of emphasizing the nonpartisan character of the body and thereby encouraging wider acceptance of the idea. President Wilson let it be known most emphatically that he would oppose the suggestion of Democratic Representative Henry A. Barnhart of Indiana that Congress have a part in naming the members of any proposed commission. Nevertheless, Rainey was of the opinion that some revisions would have to be made in order for the bill to gain complete acceptance among Democratic members.[18] The result of this divergence of opinion was the redrafting of the bill and its reintroduction.

On March 27 Rainey introduced what was clearly identified as the administration bill for a Tariff Commission. The revised bill contained two major changes. The membership of the commission was increased from five to six, so it became bipartisan rather than nonpartisan. Also the bill stipulated that it be a permanent body with an annual appropriation of $300,000. Salaries for members were set at $10,000, a relatively high figure in those days. In a statement accompanying the introduction of the bill, Rainey said this bill would "come as near removing from the tariff unfair and unreasonable partisan action . . . as any measure yet conceived."[19]

General enthusiasm for a Tariff Commission continued to be evidenced in leading journals. The wartime situation, it was argued, demanded such a body to arrive at the facts affecting world trade. The main support for the Tariff Commission was on the principle of scientific inquiry rather than the details of administrative organization. The specifics were left to Congress to provide, but the lawmakers let the Rainey proposal languish in committee for the next three months. The President reminded Rainey of his very deep and intense interest in the measure as he was exceedingly anxious that nothing should hamper its passage.[20] The proposal had not been forgotten; it was waiting to be advanced along with other features of the 1916 revenue legislation.

When the measure came to the floor of the House for debate, Rainey made a forty-minute speech in its behalf. He paid special tribute to all the numerous groups that had contributed to the drafting of the measure. In answer to the criticism of Republican Joseph Fordney of Michigan that the bill excluded congressmen and businessmen from the commission, Rainey pointed out that this provision was included at the insistence of the United States Chamber of Commerce. As to the shift in his and the Democratic party's stand, he averred that a "wise man, of course [,] changes his mind." The two principal industries of the United States, he said, were raising corn and revising the tariff. Since 1860 the United States had had eleven complete tariff revisions and two attempted revisions—a tariff convulsion on an average of once every four years. By contrast, Germany had revised her tariff once in thirty-seven years and France once in twenty-eight years. The United States, he concluded, needed such an agency in order to promote business stability and to minimize these economic upheavals.[21]

The most critical stage for the bill was in the consideration of amendments proposed from the floor of the House. Rainey successfully turned back a proposal by Ohioan Nicholas Longworth that would reduce the term from twelve to six years and require the appointment of a Democrat and a Republican at each two-year opportunity. Rainey failed, however, when Republican Longworth submitted a motion to strike the feature preventing congressmen from serving on the commission. The eligibility of lame ducks had an important ramification in Rainey's later career. New York Congressman John J. Fitzgerald, chairman of the Appropriations Committee, successfully threatened the permanency of the body by requiring annual appropriations for its work. In an economy move, Republican Representative William Green of Iowa succeeded in reducing the salaries from $10,000 to $7,500.[22] In the final version of the measure as passed by the House, the only serious modification was the limitation on permanency.

The struggle for a Tariff Commission was drawing to a successful conclusion. The President was evidently pleased with the House product because he proposed an early use of the powers which the Rainey bill authorized to the Chief Executive. The bill subsequently passed the Senate unchanged and was signed into law by the President on September 8, 1916. The United States Tariff Commission proved to be so significant that the enabling legislation might have been known to posterity as the Rainey Act, but the fates decreed otherwise. In order to systematize the series of revenue proposals and to assure passage of the Tariff Commission, all such legislation was presented as one measure. The Tariff Commission was embodied as section 7 of the Revenue Act of 1916. The President made the appointments on March 21, 1917, and the commission began to function on March 30.[23]

The adoption of the concept of a scientifically regulated tariff was widely acclaimed as one of the successes of the Wilson administration. As its principal proponent in Congress, Rainey greeted the signing of his bill as the dawn of a new tariff era when political manipulation would be gone from the scene. President Wilson viewed the commission as the means whereby United States industries could be prepared for the industrial competition and tariff adjustments following the conclusion of the Great War. The passage of the Tariff Commission legislation deprived Republican presidential candidate Charles Evans Hughes of an issue to exploit. This legislation was an important component of the Democratic campaign promises of peace, prosperity, progressivism, and preparedness. Following Wilson's re-election victory, it was suggested that this commission would be severely tested in ensuing months because of the rapidly changing nature of the European competition.[24] Without a doubt the Tariff Commission should rank with the Underwood tariff as an embodiment of the evolving ideas inherent in the New Freedom of the Wilson era.

Subsequent historical treatments of this legislation note the importance of the Tariff Commission in understanding the metamorphosis of Wilson's progressivism. This measure appealed to former supporters of Roosevelt's Progressive party, to western farmers, to organized labor, and to nonfinancial elements of the business community. Each of these groups believed there was advantage for them in placing tariff legislation on a businesslike foundation. This move on Wilson's part antagonized southern agrarians and free-trade advocates who feared protectionism in a new guise. The employment of technical experts at the expense of politicians was a signal victory for progressive concepts. Significantly the Democratic party had modified its low tariff stance slightly in favor of modified protection when scientific evidence warranted such action. While still a party advocating a tariff for revenue only, some slight concession to selected protectionism was evident.[25] As promoter of the legislation, Rainey exhibited some of the same transformation as Wilson.

The Tariff Commission figured prominently twice more in Rainey's career. The first occasion arose after his defeat in 1920. As a lame-duck congressman, he endeavored to feather his political nest with an appropriate government appointment. In a lengthy letter to McAdoo, Rainey suggested himself as a candidate for the Democratic vacancy on the United States Tariff Commission. He hoped McAdoo would bring the matter to the President's attention. Such a position would have enabled Rainey to assist the Democratic members of the Ways and Means Committee on the approaching tariff revision, a task for which he was well suited. Rainey thought that the Senate would confirm the appointment because of a long-standing tradition of favoring former members of Congress and because of the legal requirement that a minority party member be appointed. In addition to McAdoo, numerous other confidants around the President's

sickbed supported Rainey's candidacy. On March 1, 1921, Rainey's
nomination was forwarded by Wilson to the Senate for confirmation.
Democrat Furnifold M. Simmons of North Carolina made a speech in
Rainey's behalf and then asked unanimous consent for consideration
of the appointment. Republican Senator George H. Moses of New
Hampshire objected and there the matter rested in the waning hours
of the Wilson administration. Rainey was optimistic that the
appointment might be renewed by incoming President Warren G. Harding.
He indicated to McAdoo and Kitchin that some Republican senators
had held out such a hope; however, there is little evidence that
Harding ever gave Rainey's appointment serious consideration.[26]
Political factors had kept the "father" of the Tariff Commission
off that body. Ironically, it had been Rainey's original desire to
prohibit ex-congressmen from membership on the tariff board.

Following Rainey's return to Congress in 1923, he was able to
aid the maintenance of the Tariff Commission concept. During the
1920s, the federal regulatory agencies such as the Federal Trade
Commission and the national fact-finding boards such as the Tariff
Commission were beset with difficulties. By judicious use of the
appointive power, President Calvin Coolidge was solidifying conservative control of these bodies. In the case of the Tariff
Commission, low-tariff advocates had no chance of reappointment.
Replacements were found whose protectionist principles were in
accord with the prevailing business climate.[27] Rainey was power-
less to alter the appointment policy, but he did protect the
financial independence of this body from critics in both parties.
Many Democrats as well as Republicans were disenchanted with the
commission concept of a public agency due to its pro-business bias.

In 1925 the House was considering an appropriation of
$712,000 for the continuance of the Tariff Commission. The Demo-
cratic leadership endeavored to embarrass the Republicans by
removing the money from the commission's allocation. John Nance
Garner, Democrat of Texas, moved an amendment which would prevent
the expenditure of funds. Rainey was incensed at this tactic. The
Garner amendment was approved during the deliberations in the
Committee of the Whole. At the first opportunity, the Illinoisan
gained the floor to defend the commission's operation. He said
emphatically that he would decline to follow the "unfortunate
leadership" which would trample on the grave of Woodrow Wilson.
This incident, Rainey asserted, proved that the original bill
calling for a permanent annual appropriation was correct. In his
view, the Garner leadership "did not lick the stuffing out of the
Republican Party; it licked it out of the Democratic Party."
Rainey urged Democrats to reject this leadership and to sustain
this feature of the appropriation bill at a roll call vote. In
this instance his advice was heeded, and the Tariff Commission's
operating funds were approved by a 3 to 1 margin.[28] The principle
of a scientific revision of the tariff was reaffirmed even though
it was somewhat tarnished by misuse of the appointive power. The
incident is also noteworthy as an illustration of Rainey's extreme
loyalty to Wilson and his disillusionment with the Democratic
party's leadership in the 1920s.

Before experiencing the legislative disappointments and frustrations of the 1920s, Rainey had several years of constructive service during the wartime emergency. An unusual set of circumstances thrust him into a position of unofficial leadership during the period from 1916 to 1919. Many of the legislative responsibilities normally incurred by Speaker Champ Clark and Majority Leader Claude Kitchin were shoved aside because of philosophical disagreements with President Wilson's foreign policy. There was understandable coolness between Clark and Wilson dating to 1912 when they were rivals for the Democratic presidential nomination. Clark's opposition to preparedness programs, conscription, and the declaration of war in 1917 accentuated the differences between the legislative and executive heads of government. On these three issues Kitchin was also more in accord with Clark than Wilson. Thus in revenue matters significant legislative responsibilities devolved upon Rainey as second-ranking Democrat on the Ways and Means Committee. In addition, Kitchin's extended illness in mid-1918 reinforced the delegation of responsibilities to Rainey. There was never any formal abdication of leadership positions by either Clark or Kitchin, yet it was understood that on certain matters cooperation between the White House and the Hill would be secured through Representative Rainey.[29] The legislative record he had earned during the Tariff Commission struggle had highlighted his importance as a Wilson lieutenant. This role was extended during the war Congresses.

Rainey directed almost all his energies to harnessing the nation's finances in such a way as to assure adherence to principles of progressive taxation, that is, to assess the largest tax burden against those with the greatest ability to pay. The special session of Congress which was called to declare war in April, 1917, turned to securing the means of financing that undertaking. The first measure toward that end was a bond bill authorizing an expenditure of seven billion dollars in prosecuting the war against Germany, including a loan of five billion to the Allies. Rainey referred to the bond issue as "the first battle in the great world conflict in which we are entering." The House unanimously endorsed the bond measure and directed its attention to war revenue measures. As a member of the drafting subcommittee, Rainey was reported as being in favor of practically confiscatory taxes on all annual incomes above $100,000 in order to prevent war profiteering. On May 10, the Ways and Means Committee reported a hastily drawn revenue bill quintupling previous annual tax yields by relying heavily upon income, war profits, and excise taxes. As floor leader for the war revenue bill, Rainey confined himself to one major speech in the bill's behalf and numerous short replies to criticisms made on the floor. He expressed the view that half the war's cost ought to be financed by direct taxes. The people needed to realize that "every man's life, every man's fortune, every man's income" would be pledged to the successful prosecution of the war. In phrases sounding like John F. Kennedy, Rainey said the public needed to be reminded that "the Government has been doing things for them" and now they "must do something for this Government." He

stood squarely behind the policy of conscripting the incomes of
those men able to pay. As a concluding thought in defense of this
massive tax program, Rainey argued that a man "has not discharged
his duty to his country when he has simply placed a flag in front
of his home"; he must contribute his revenues toward the successful
conclusion of the war.[30]

The measure passed the House essentially in the form recommended by the committee. The Senate was more deliberate in its
consideration. A final bill was agreed upon on October 3, 1917.
This legislation was especially noteworthy in its application of
fiscal justice as conceived by the prewar progressives. The law
imposed the heaviest burden of taxation on wealth and luxurious
consumption rather than upon the expenditures of the great mass of
people. In the view of Edwin Seligman it was "an appreciable
forward step in the direction of realizing the principle of ability
to pay."[31]   The Revenue Act of 1917 offers strong illustration of
the retention of progressive ideals in spite of the war's intrusion
upon democratic institutions. Within the limits of his capability,
Rainey was anxious to maintain this feature of economic justice.

The haste with which the House acted in the preparation of
the 1917 Revenue Act was not repeated in the legislation for the
1918 to 1919 fiscal year. It had been decided that the taxes could
be made retroactive, so there was plenty of time for investigation
and deliberation. Chairman Kitchin was ill a great portion of
this time and Rainey served as acting chairman of the Ways and
Means Committee in his absence. Unfortunately there is little
information about Rainey's influence on the formulation of the bill,
although it can be demonstrated he continued to favor war profits
taxes based on the English system of soaking the rich and an excess
profits tax. When the measure came to be debated on the House
floor, Rainey handled the arguments over constitutionality. One of
the controversial features of the bill was a provision which made
the salaries of the President, federal judges, and all state
officials liable to a tax. The objection raised was that making
tax laws applicable to salaries of all public servants at all governmental levels would be contrary to the Constitution. Rainey
said he had "little sympathy with these hair splitting decisions
as to questions of constitutionality on this floor when the Nation's
life is in peril." He pointed out that the Constitution's friends
were those who believed it was flexible enough to permit the
government to levy the necessary taxes. Those who raised objections were unpatriotic, in his view.[32]   He was perfectly willing
to employ an elastic interpretation of the Constitution if it
assured the financial solvency of the nation.

The revenue bill of 1918 became inextricably connected with
problems relating to prohibition and drug addiction. Under the
guise of the wartime emergency, the prohibition forces had successfully amassed legislative strength to foster temperance within
the nation. The proposed revenue legislation contained a clause
vastly increasing the internal taxes on beer and whisky. In his
only unequivocal public statement expressing approval of prohibition, Rainey said: "I have voted always for antisaloon measures,

in obedience to the sentiment in my congressional district and to
the dictates of my own conscience. I have not been a professional
prohibitionist, proclaiming for the purpose of obtaining votes my
attitudes on these questions."[33] While treatments of prohibition
abound, the equally significant concern for drug abuse has been
generally neglected.

While no lexicon of reform laws includes antinarcotics legislation, it falls within the purview of the progressive movement.
Rainey contributed significantly to legislation regulating the
traffic in narcotics. The principal law in this area was the
Harrison Narcotics Act approved on December 17, 1914. Rainey had
participated behind the scenes in the legislative drafting of this
measure. When the Supreme Court rendered the initial legislation
largely inoperative, he assisted Congressman Francis Burton
Harrison of New York in redrafting it to meet judicial objections.
The Carrollton *Patriot* described the revamped law as "one of the
best upward movements inaugurated since the abolition of human
slavery." Essentially the law required the registration of all
persons engaged in drug transactions with the district director of
internal revenue. The sale, exchange, or transportation of drugs
was regulated and penalties were provided for violators.[34]

In 1918 to 1919, Rainey was called upon to take an even more
active role in the examination of the nation's drug policy.
Shortly after the perfection of the original legislation, pressure
began mounting for additional federal solutions to the habit-
forming drug problem. In January, 1917, Charles B. Towns, drug
authority in New York, had circulated a twenty-page pamphlet in
Congress urging a legislative, medical, and sociological investigation into the subject. In March, 1918, Secretary of the Treasury
McAdoo responded by appointing Rainey as chairman of a select
committee to study the situation. He subsequently revealed to
Congress that the committee's preliminary findings showed the
strict enforcement of prohibition to be accompanied by an increase
in the rate of drug addiction. In dry territories, the increased
consumption of patent medicine remedies, which were merely whiskey
mixed with opium and similar preparations, had resulted in an
alarming increase in the number of addicts. The Ways and Means
Committee incorporated into the revenue bill Rainey's amendment to
the Harrison Anti-Narcotic Law. This amendment forbade the sale
of narcotics, except for medicinal purposes under prescription,
anywhere in the United States. The select committee's final
report contains multifaceted recommendations in the alleviation of
social problems resulting from drug addiction.[35] Rainey had
performed a valuable service in highlighting the connection between
alcoholism and drug addiction. The Anti-Saloon League heartily
joined in the campaign against the twin evils, but the battle was
not yet won.

The dual aspect of the 1918 revenue proposal was subjected to
careful scrutiny by legislators. In closing the debate on the bill,
Rainey devoted most of his time to justifying the inclusion of such
legislation in a revenue measure. He pointed out that the proposal
had the sanction of the Surgeon General and of the Secretary of

the Treasury. He further justified the inclusion of the narcotics
law revisions because the Supreme Court had held that only through
a revenue feature could the moral objectives of the law be upheld.[36]
The narcotics rider remained a part of the bill. The House version
of the bill passed on September 18. The Senate later approved
this feature of the bill and it was signed into law.

In the interval between the Sixty-sixth Congress (November,
1919) and the Seventy-second Congress (December, 1931), the Wilson
lieutenant again experienced the exasperations of being a member
of the minority party. Rainey's own defeat in the 1920 general
election ended one career in opposition to pernicious trusts, high
tariffs, and inequitable taxes. Another career, with similar
principles but different impact, began with Rainey's re-election
to Congress in 1922. This interruption in his seniority of service
had a debilitating effect upon his legislative influence. In 1920
Chairman Claude Kitchin had confided to Rainey that he planned to
accept only the minority leadership if offered and relinquish his
position on Ways and Means. As number two Democrat on the committee, Rainey was his logical successor; however, the defeat of
Rainey and of Cordell Hull elevated John Nance Garner to the first
position on the minority side. Representative Adolph J. Sabath,
Rainey's intimate friend from Chicago, endeavored to hold Rainey's
rank on the committee until he should be returned to Congress, but
such a practice would shatter long-established precedents. It is
doubtful that the ambitions of Representative Garner would tolerate
such a move. The Democratic leadership did decide to do something
nearly as unprecedented by keeping a vacancy on the committee in
anticipation of Rainey's return two years hence. The Democratic
caucus in 1923 confirmed Henry T.'s return to Ways and Means, but
near the bottom of the committee ladder. His prior service enabled
him to be the number eight Democrat of the eleven-member Democratic
delegation.[37] A decade would pass before Rainey would be able to
work his way to the number one rank on the committee. In 1933 he
relinquished the potential chairmanship to accept the Speakership
of the House.

The struggle between conservatives and liberals in the 1920s
is typified by their varying approaches to fiscal policy. The
then staggering debt of twenty-six billion dollars incurred by the
United States during World War I became a political as well as an
economic problem. The Harding and Coolidge administrations maintained that the amount ought to be reduced; at the same time they
sought to decrease the wartime tax burden on the public. The
conservatives desired the burden to be lifted most quickly from
the wealthy, who could then use the amount hitherto marked for
taxes to develop national industry and therefore national income
and general prosperity. Suggestions to implement this philosophy
were embraced in the various tax recommendations made by Secretary
of the Treasury Andrew Mellon. The liberals, on the other hand,
believed that the taxes on excess profits, estates, inheritances,
and incomes should be continued at high rates, with the primary
alleviation granted to those in the lower income brackets. This
group of Democrats and insurgent Republicans rallied around no

single proposal. As the decade unfolded, the bourgeois business trend became pervasive and the conservative view predominated by 1929.[38] Among the few holdouts was Congressman Rainey, whose minority reports and public outcrys were ineffectual against the rising tide of prosperity. Thus, his second political career against the "interests" is devoid of the constructive attainments which marked the middle decade of his thirty years' service.

The Rainey record on trust, tariff, and tax legislation indicates a general adherence to progressive philosophies in the legislative deliberations. His agrarian background made him suspicious of big business, especially exemplified by the watch, sugar, and power trusts. He did not consider such monopolies as inevitable, but rather the result of special favors frequently conferred by high protective tariffs. His campaign against these evils helped restore his party to political control in 1912. During the Wilson administration, he contributed to the downward revision of the tariff in the Underwood bill. His most significant accomplishment came in the tariff commission legislation of 1916. In the wartime revenue legislation, he endeavored to promote progressive principles of taxation within a broad framework of fiscal responsibility. Rainey's legislative experience with this triumvirate of concerns helped plot his course when he assumed positions of leadership first as majority leader and then as Speaker. This survey of the economic issues confronting the nation emphasizes the perseverance of the problems and the progressive performance of one of the participants.

NOTES

1. *Gazette*, Nov. 13, 1903, 4:2; George R. Mayhill, "Speaker Cannon under the Roosevelt Administration, 1903-1907" (Ph.D. thesis), 54-55.

2. *CR*, 58:2 (April 5, 1904), 4310-20; editorial, "'On Watch,'" *The American Syren and "Shipping" Illustrated*, May 28, 1904, 174-175; *CR*, 59:2 (Feb. 26, 1907), 4028-29 and 4033-37; "Light on the Ship Subsidy Proposition," 4-5.

3. *CR*, 59:1 (April 5, 1906), 4823-26, and (April 6), 4858-62.

4. *Gazette*, April 12, 1906, 4:3-4; cartoon in *Patriot*, July 20, 1906, 1:4; *Republic* comment reproduced in *Gazette*, May 17, 1906, 4:1; "Mr. Rainey's Kindergarten for Standpatters," 6; Clark release in *Gazette*, April 26, 1906, 4:2.

5. *CR*, 60:1 (Feb. 13, 1908), 2004-2008.

6. *CR*, 61:1 (April 3, 1909), 1016-24, and (July 31), Appendix 132-134; HTR, "The Legal Effect of the Maximum Provision of the Aldrich-Payne Tariff Law," 414-416.

7. *CR*, 61:2 (April 14, 1910), 4694-4706; Archie Butt (Taft's presidential aide) to Clara (his sister-in-law, Mrs. Lewis F. Butt), Washington, June 10, 1910, as published in Archie Butt, *Taft and Roosevelt: The Intimate Letters of Archie Butt, Military Aide*,

I, 379. Apparently Mr. and Mrs. Rainey gained a reprieve in April, 1911, but they did not attend the concert or send regrets. Butt to Clara, Washington, April 23, 1911, as published in *Intimate Letters*, II, 621.

8. Frank B. Lord, "The Next Senate and House," 255; New York *Times*, Jan. 20, 1911, 1:5; Edward G. Lowry, "The Tariff Revisers," 8.

9. Sullivan, "Comment on Congress," 20, and his "Looking Forward," 14; Elston E. Roady, "Party Regularity in the Sixty-third Congress" (Ph.D. thesis), 12.

10. Sullivan, "Comment on Congress," 12; Champ Clark, "What the Democrats in Congress Will Do," 205–206; George Harvey, "Will the Democratic Party Commit Suicide?," 1–8; *Gazette*, June 8, 1911, 1:1; "The National Capital," 6.

11. Baker, *Woodrow Wilson: Life and Letters*, IV, 111; Henry C. Emery, "The Democrats and the Tariff," 193–214; HTR address before Wilson day luncheon in Pittsburg, Pa., on Dec. 27, 1924, *CR*, 68:2 (March 4, 1925), 5571–72; *CR*, 63:1 (April 28, 1913), 650.

12. *CR*, 63:1 (April 28, 1913), 646–50, (May 1, 1913), 925–26, (May 2), 971–972, and (May 8, 1913), Appendix 131–135; *Post Dispatch* interview reprinted in *Gazette*, May 22, 1913, 1:2–3.

13. Joseph F. Kenkel, "The Tariff Commission Movement" (Ph.D. thesis), 1–97; *CR*, 60:1 (Feb. 13, 1908), 2004–2008; James E. Watson (comp.), *Federal Commissions, Committees and Boards*, 31; *CR*, 62:2 (June 7, 1912), 7814–16.

14. Copy of "Memorandum—Tariff Commission," about April, 1913, in Burleson Papers, Vol. 7; Sullivan, "Comment on Congress," 9; Robert H. Wiebe, *Businessmen and Reform*, 148–149; "Do We Want a Tariff Commission?," 14.

15. Wilson to Kitchin, [Washington], Jan. 24 and 26, 1916, as printed in New York *Times*, Jan. 27, 1916, 4:5–6; New York *Times*, Feb. 2, 1916, 4:6, and Feb. 13, 1916, 1:8; Thomas F. Logan, "Watching the Nation's Business," 223; Arthur S. Link, *Woodrow Wilson and the Progressive Era*, 228, n. 14.

16. HTR to McAdoo, Washington, Jan. 27, 1916, McAdoo Papers, Box 153; *CR*, 64:1 (Jan. 27, 1916), 1648–50.

17. Houston to McAdoo, [Washington], Jan. 31, 1916; McAdoo to Kitchin, [Washington], Feb. 1, 1916; Gross to McAdoo, Chicago, Feb. 1, 1916, McAdoo Papers, Box 154; H.R. 10585, *CR*, 64:1 (Feb. 1, 1916), 1983; New York *Times*, Feb. 2, 1916, 4:5–6.

18. McAdoo to HTR, [Washington], Feb. 3, 1916; Houston to McAdoo, Washington, Feb. 5, 1916; Gross to McAdoo, Washington, Feb. 7, 1916; Gross to McAdoo, Chicago, Feb. 9, 1916, McAdoo Papers, Box 154; William Kent (R., Calif.) to Wilson, Washington, Feb. 23, 1916; Wilson to Kent, [Washington], Feb. 28, 1916, Wilson Papers, File VI, Folio 180; New York *Times*, Feb. 22, 1916, 3:7; recollection of HTR, *CR*, 68:2 (March 4, 1925), 5573.

19. H.R. 13767, *CR*, 64:1 (March 27, 1916), 4980; New York *Times*, March 28, 1916, 7:5-6.

20. "The Tariff Board," 273; Logan, "Watching the Nation's Business," 257; Wilson to HTR, [Washington], May 10, 1916, Wilson Papers, File VI, Folio 180.

21. *CR*, 64:1 (July 7, 1916), 10588-92; New York *Times*, July 8, 1916, 4:4-5.

22. *CR*, 64:1 (July 10, 1916), 10753-57, 10763-64; New York *Times*, July 11, 1916, 1:4.

23. Wilson to Samuel M. Hastings (President of Illinois Manufacturers' Association), Washington, July 28, 1916, as printed in Baker and Dodds (eds.), *The Public Papers of Woodrow Wilson*, IV, 258; Kenkel, "The Tariff Commission Movement," 119-125; Watson, *Federal Commissions*, 62; Roy G. and Gladys C. Blakey, *The Federal Income Tax*, 112-113.

24. New York *Times*, Sept. 11, 1916, 12:4-5; L. 'Ames Brown, "Preparedness for Peace: An Authorized Statement of President Wilson's Plans," 12-13; Charles W. Eliot, "The Achievements of the Democratic Party and Its Leader since March 4, 1913," 434; "Comment on Congress—Changing Tariffs Quickly," 9.

25. Richard M. Abrams, "Woodrow Wilson and the Southern Congressmen, 1913-1916," 434-435; Arthur S. Link, *Wilson: Confusions and Crises, 1915-1916*, 344-345.

26. HTR to McAdoo, Washington, Dec. 30, 1920, McAdoo Papers, Box 246; David F. Houston to Joseph Tumulty, [Washington], Jan. 13, 1921, a copy in RP; McAdoo to Admiral Cary T. Grayson, Beverly Hills, Calif., Jan. 18, 1921, McAdoo Papers, Box 247; HTR to Tumulty, Washington, Jan. 25 and Feb. 14, 1921, Wilson Papers, File VI, Folio 180 A; McAdoo to HTR, [Washington], March 1, 1921, McAdoo Papers, Box 249; HTR to Wilson, Washington, March 2, 1921, Wilson Papers, File II; *CR*, 66:3 (March 3, 1921), 4404; HTR to McAdoo, Washington, March 4, 1921, McAdoo Papers, Box 249; Claude Kitchin to President [Harding], [Washington], March 17, 1921, and HTR to Kitchin, Washington, March 18, 1921, Kitchin Papers, Reel 33.

27. G. Cullom Davis, "The Transformation of the Federal Trade Commission, 1914-1929," 437-455; J. Richard Snyder, "Coolidge, Costigan and the Tariff Commission," 131-148.

28. *CR*, 68:2 (Jan. 31, 1925), 2821-22, (Feb. 2), 2888-91, and (Feb. 5, 1925), 3078.

29. Champ Clark, *My Quarter Century of American Politics*, II, *passim*; Alex M. Arnett, *Claude Kitchin and the Wilson War Policies*, *passim*; Richard Bolling, *Power in the House: A History of the Leadership of the House of Representatives*, 97-99.

30. *CR*, 65:1 (April 13, 1917), 667-671; New York *Times*, April 28, 1917, 4:3 and May 2, 1917, 1:2; Blakey and Blakey, *The*

Federal Income Tax, 132–133; *CR*, 65:1 (May 17, 1917), 2468–69, and (May 19), 2612.

31. Edwin R. A. Seligman, "The War Revenue Act," 31.

32. New York *Times*, July 30, 1918, 1:1 and 6:2–3; *CR*, 65:2 (Sept. 16, 1918), 10364, 10374.

33. *CR*, 65:2 (May 23, 1918), Appendix 414–415.

34. Winfield Downs (ed.), *Encyclopedia of American Biography*, XI, 34; editorial, "Doctors and Dope," *Patriot*, April 15, 1915, 4:1; Arnold H. Taylor, *American Diplomacy and the Narcotics Traffic, 1900–1939*, 130–131.

35. New York *Times*, Jan. 3, 1917, 4:3; HTR to Daniel C. Roper (Commissioner of Internal Revenue), [Washington], Aug. 27, 1918, Kitchin Papers, Reel 26; *CR*, 65:2 (Sept. 23, 1918), 10674–75; Taylor, *American Diplomacy and the Narcotics Traffic*, 124–125; Treasury Dept., U.S. Department of Internal Revenue, *Traffic in Narcotic Drugs*.

36. *CR*, 65:2 (Sept. 18, 1918), 10466–69; HTR to C. D. V. McKinley, Carrollton, Aug. 16, 1920, RP.

37. Kitchin to HTR, Washington, Nov. 18, 1920, RP; Sabath in *Memorial Services . . . Henry T. Rainey*, 74–75; Field, "The Amherst Illustrious," 22.

38. Burner, *The Politics of Provincialism*, 162ff.; Benjamin G. Rader, "Federal Taxation in the 1920's," 415–435.

7
Participant in Foreign Affairs

In the careers of most congressmen, domestic affairs, such as
election campaigns, internal improvements, conservation programs,
and revenue bills, become entwined with an interest in foreign
policy. By constitutional provision the United States senator may
become more directly involved due to the necessity for approving
nominations and treaties. Nevertheless, a member of the House of
Representatives may become interested through that body's control
of the purse strings or via diplomatic ramifications found in a
domestic problem. During the career of Henry Thomas Rainey, he
occasionally became engaged in significant episodes relating to
foreign affairs. Early in his career, he was engrossed in matters
pertaining to the Panama Canal. As with all Americans, he became
embroiled in the swirl of diplomatic activities surrounding World
War I. During the postwar years, he was concerned about war debts'
settlements and the world situation, especially diplomatic recognition of the Soviet Union in 1933. While Rainey's primary
interest was domestic issues, he could also poke an inquisitive
and intelligent nose into foreign affairs.
    Much has been written about the nature of midwestern concern
for overseas commitments in the twentieth century. Cogent arguments may be marshaled to indicate that the Midwest was isolationist
in its principal attitude toward foreign affairs. An opposing view
holds that this generalization has been overdrawn, while still
another approach supports a vacillating picture of involvement or
noninvolvement, as interior interests seemed to dictate.[1] An
examination of the Rainey diplomatic involvements reveals that he
was neither an isolationist nor an internationalist; rather, he
may be characterized as a participationist. His view of the United
States' role in world affairs embraced selective participation in
diplomatic concerns where national advantage could be gained. This
consideration largely dictated his response to various diplomatic
engagements.
    Upon his arrival in Washington in 1903, one of Rainey's first
official acts was to introduce a resolution authorizing the return
of Revolutionary War hero John Paul Jones's remains to the United
States. He assisted in the passage of the necessary legislation
authorizing the location of Jones's burial site in France and the
return of his body. He also supported the erection of a suitable
monument for Jones's reinternment at Annapolis.[2] After a century
of neglect, Rainey's efforts contributed to the position of honor

which Captain John Paul Jones has regained in American naval lore.

A significant diplomatic issue early in the twentieth century was the independence of Panama and the construction of the Panama Canal. Following a revolution in the Colombian isthmus in November, 1903, the United States extended *de facto* recognition to the new government in Panama. The Democratic party took an aggressive stance against President Theodore Roosevelt's action on the Panama question. Initially Rainey disputed his party's position and supported the President's policy of immediate recognition. In brief remarks before the House, he plainly indicated that he could not take a stand against progress. He reasoned that the completion of the Panama Canal under American auspices would contribute to the advancement of a great waterway from the lakes to the gulf.[3] While his later concern for the details of construction and recognition would antagonize Roosevelt, Rainey remained an enthusiastic supporter for this aspect of "big stick" diplomacy because of implicit benefit to section and country.

As a result of Rainey's penchant for facts, he made a private and unannounced trip to the Panama Canal Zone for a personal inspection in March, 1907. He purposely made the trip alone, avoiding the typical congressional junket in order to become fully advised of the situation there. As a result of an eight-day investigation, he was enthusiastic over the progress made with the canal but most unfavorably impressed with the management of the commissary department. A careful investigation of the commissariat, he believed, "would bring to light a scandal 'second only to the meat scandal of the Spanish-American War.'" Beyond a poorly organized commissary, he found nothing to criticize. In the muck-raker tradition, Rainey was of a journalistic mind, a reporter-reformer. In a series of eight weekly articles published in the Carrollton *Gazette*, traveler Rainey provided further insight into what he observed in Panama. His initial charges of graft in the commissary and of fraudulent purchases of supplies had resulted in an investigation, but he was not called to present any testimony. He surmised that the investigators had "either found enough evidence to sustain my charges or they don't propose to find any evidence."[4] Rainey's visit to Panama and his published observations had several important results. For one, his stereopticon lecture on the Panama Canal became a popular item on the Chautauqua circuit. For another, his firsthand knowledge of the Panama Canal and his hundreds of pictures served him well as he argued for the deep waterway. Finally, this background became useful as various features of the Panama Canal matter became politically controversial.

Congressman Rainey contributed to the political explosiveness of this topic. He made exposure of the Panama Canal acquisition an overriding issue for himself in the second session of the Sixtieth Congress. On the opening day (December 7, 1908), he introduced a resolution which called for the appointment of a committee to investigate the purchase of the Panama Canal property. According to the Indianapolis *News*, Rainey announced that all he wanted to do was to prove or disprove any evidences of fraud in the acquisition of the isthmus. After listening to President

Roosevelt's special message to Congress on the subject, Rainey was
willing to admit the validity of the transfer; however, he was
quoted as saying that the message did not clear up the question of
whether the government had been "the victim of Wall Street jobbing
operations."[5] Rainey feared that predatory interests sought
personal gain resulting from the Panamanian revolution and subsequent American involvement. Various newspapers, principally the
Indianapolis *News* and the New York *World*, thought similarly and
clamored for a congressional investigation.

The question of the propriety of the Panama Canal procurement
is complicated by two main streams of action, one judicial and the
other legislative. To counteract the insinuations and allegedly
libelous editorials of the *News* and the *World*, President Roosevelt
instituted a libel suit against the two offending newspapers.
Rainey felt that such an action on the part of the government was
unconstitutional.[6] However, he was only tangentially involved
with this aspect of the affair. His concern was to amass the
evidence and foster the legislative side of the controversy through
a congressional investigation.

By the end of January, 1909, Rainey was ready to validate the
need for a searching inquiry into affairs at Panama. In an hour
and forty minute speech, he impressed upon his fellow congressmen
the need to avoid the graft which felled the French companies.
He declared it was not sound statesmanship and true patriotism to
wish away evidence of any questionable transactions. The first
alleged instance of graft was in an appropriation, which was
instituted at Henry Cabot Lodge's insistence, for two ships for
the Panama Railroad Company. The specifications on these vessels
were so drawn that only two ships unwanted by a Massachusetts
firm would fill the bill. In addition, an expenditure would be
necessary to make these vessels serviceable, and the Colon Harbor
facilities in Panama would have to be dredged to accommodate them.
Such unwarranted extravagance was to be condemned, thought Rainey.
Muckraking specialist Samuel Hopkins Adams described the exposure
of the Lodge ship purchase as "full of jagged edges and acid."[7]
The reputation Rainey earned for biting oratory in the watch
trust attack was being re-enforced by his assertions that this
action also was not in the public interest.

Circumstances in Panama seemed even more suspicious to the
inquisitive. There Rainey detected twin schemes to divest the
Republic of Panama of its revenues and to steal the forests and
public lands. The chief vultures in the first scheme, he charged,
were Senor Don José Domingo de Obaldia, President of Panama, and
William Nelson Cromwell, New York lawyer extraordinary. He
identified the men behind the infamous and outrageous scheme to
secure Panama's timber as Cromwell, Roger L. Farnham, W. S. Harvey,
and Charles P. Taft, brother of the President-elect. Rainey argued
that since the United States guaranteed Panama's independence from
foreign nations, we ought "to guarantee their independence against
the outrageous demands of these modern buccaneers of finance." An
investigation was necessary, he asserted, because all these patriotic gentlemen had had the complete cooperation and the active

assistance of the administration and its hand-picked successor.[8]
At this point he rested his case.

Repercussions were soon evident in both Panama and the United
States. According to Rainey's Panama informant, Sam B. Dannis,
his remarks caused a great stir there. William Cromwell issued a
denial of the charges and the Panama Assembly passed a resolution
calling the speech slanderous. An official telegram labeled it a
disrespectful official speech, and the Panamanian minister lodged
a formal diplomatic complaint against Rainey's "wholly baseless
and highly offensive statements."[9]

Rainey's remarks had stirred an international controversy
and released a flood of activity on the domestic scene. There
was a stream of denials from the parties whom Rainey implicated,
and he dutifully placed these in the *Congressional Record*. He
also clarified that the investigation was done at his own expense
by contradicting in the most emphatic manner all assertions that
he received the assistance of the New York *World*. In matters of
legislation, Rainey vigorously opposed the bill providing for the
government of the Panama Canal because it delegated too much
authority to the Chief Executive. It was, he said, an absolute
surrender by the legislature to executive authority; soon congressmen would be left with nothing to do but draw salaries. His
efforts to restrict the presidential discretionary powers by amending the bill met with little success.[10] The majority was unwilling
to consider his reservations because the political motives seemed
so apparent.

By mid-February the administration forces were prepared to
deliver their counterattack. Congressman William Lovering of
Massachusetts opened the defense. The essence of Lovering's
remarks was that the *World* did indeed provide the material and thus
it was to be discounted, that blackmailers and ex-convicts were the
sources of information and thus it should be disregarded, and that
Rainey had abused the privileges of the House, "a shameless prosti-
tution of the rights of free speech." Using material supplied by
Cromwell, Representative Jacob Olcott of New York chose to defend
the character and actions of the accused persons. In a private
letter, President Roosevelt referred to Rainey as a "scoundrel"
and in public he nominated him for the Ananias Club, that select
group of personalities whom Roosevelt singled out as especially
noteworthy deliberate liars. In speeches in the South, President-
elect Taft urged his listeners not to be "led astray by buncombe
speeches on the floor of the House of Representatives."[11] In this
fashion, the administration marshaled its efforts to refute the
Rainey claims.

Opposition only intensified Rainey's desire to make good on
his charges of spoliation on the isthmus. In an interview he
asserted that no administration official had made a real answer to
his charges; he also reaffirmed his support for the canal but his
opposition to graft. A few days later Rainey launched into his
second major speech on the canal episode. He began this indictment
by lecturing his fellow public servants on a legislator's role.
Rainey adduced that there were two methods of procedure to follow.

On one course a congressman must remember not to attack wrongdoing
in high places, he must not antagonize great corporations or men of
great wealth except in general terms, and he must "absolutely fail
to see evidence of individual guilt in public matters, or if you
do see it, you must keep still about it." Pursuing this course
would mean a pleasant and lucrative stay in Washington. On the
other hand, if a congressman came with a more serious motive and
endeavored to discharge his oath of office by discovering and
denouncing gross improprieties, then he could expect to be vilified,
abused, and misrepresented by newspapers friendly to the administration and by congressmen representing the interests under attack.
Though the second course was the harder and more difficult, Rainey
vowed he did not wish to represent "the winter colony of million-
aires."[12] It was in this context that Rainey persisted in going
to the root of any mishandling of affairs in Panama. He failed,
however, to dislodge his resolution from the Rules Committee, and
general interest in the subject waned. A new President and new
issues presented themselves for attention. The Panama Canal acquisition was forgotten—for a time.

Popular and personal interest in Panamanian affairs subsided
for a period of two years, and then the issue resumed political
significance. When President Taft called the Sixty-second Congress
into special session on April 4, 1911, the Democrats were especially
anxious to create advantageous issues so that they might secure
control of the presidency and of the Senate in the 1912 elections.
One means of embarrassing the administration was to launch a series
of investigations. Ex-President Roosevelt assisted the Democratic
cause by his famous statement at the University of California on
March 23, 1911, when he said, "I took the Canal Zone and let
Congress debate, and while the debate goes on the Canal does also."
Soon thereafter Rainey reintroduced his request for an inquiry into
the purchase of the Panama Canal. The resolution was referred to
the Committee on Foreign Affairs, where it remained for a time.
The Chicago *Record-Herald* speculated that the Democrats were hesi-
tant to bring the matter into prominence because it might savor of
a political persecution to go after Roosevelt when he was out of
office. Further, there was the thought that to the country at
large it was inconsequential how the United States got the isthmus
so long as it was obtained and the canal was being built.[13] Nevertheless, the matter would be revived when the Democrats thought
it propitious.

The Rainey resolution concerning the acquisition of Panama
was still pending before the Foreign Affairs Committee in December,
1911. Preliminary to launching the investigation, Congressman
and Mrs. Rainey had spent about four weeks in a personal recon-
naissance of the Canal Zone. In contrast to the broad range of
accusations Rainey had made, the resolution was framed to limit
severely the area of investigation by the committee. The resolution purported to arise from the statement of a former President
that he "took" Panama from the Republic of Colombia without
consulting Congress. (It has been shown that the resolution's
true origin antedated that impetuous and outspoken statement.) The

resolution further cited the incessant petitioning of Colombia
requesting that the matter be submitted to the Hague tribunal for
adjudication. It next stated the inconsistency of the United
States professing to submit all international controversies to
arbitration except this one. It was resolved that the Committee
on Foreign Affairs investigate this subject and report with convenient speed.[14] The legal and international ramifications crowded
out such teasers as what became of the $40,000,000 paid by the
United States for the property and archives of the New Panama
Canal Company, or of the $10,000,000 paid to the Republic of
Panama; whether there was or was not a syndicate of Americans
interested in the sale of the Panama Canal to the United States
and who the members of that syndicate were; and how the infant
Republic of Panama had been protected or exploited by those responsible for its creation.

The Foreign Affairs Committee heard testimony on the resolution
principally during January and February, 1912. Before the hearings
began, press reports indicated a likely attack upon former President Roosevelt. When the hearings opened on January 26, Rainey
asserted that "representatives of this Government made possible the
revolution on the isthmus of Panama." It was his contention that
Panama's declaration of independence was prepared in the office of
William Nelson Cromwell and that the State Department was cognizant
of the fact that a revolution was to occur on November 3, 1903.
That date, Rainey contended, was deliberately selected for the
reason that American papers would be filled with election news and
thus would not give much attention to news from the isthmus of
Panama. He concluded that the part the United States had played
for months prior to the revolution was a stain upon the history of
the government. Rainey did not desire that the isthmus be returned
to Colombia. Such a move would have been impossible since most of
the countries of the world had recognized the Republic of Panama.
The intent of the resolution, as expressed by Rainey, was to make
it possible for the United States to once again become a gentleman
among the nations by submitting the matter to arbitration. If it
should be determined that the actions of the United States had been
in violation of international law and Colombia had been wronged,
then appropriate remuneration should be provided by the United
States government.[15]

The villain of the story was not Theodore Roosevelt, as many
had hoped, but rather William Nelson Cromwell. In Rainey's
testimony before the committee, he described Cromwell as "the most
dangerous man this country has produced since the days of Aaron
Burr, a professional revolutionist--and . . . one of the most
accomplished lobbyists this country has ever produced." The most
sensational part of this line of testimony was Rainey's assertion
that the Republican platform plank in 1900 favoring an isthmian
canal was induced by a $60,000 campaign fund donated by Cromwell.
In Rainey's estimation, this was the only factor which accounted
for the sudden shift in Republican sentiment. The 1896 Republican
platform had favored the Nicaraguan route, and as late as May 16,
1900, Senator Mark Hanna's Committee on Interoceanic Canals had

issued a report severely criticizing the methods of Cromwell and
his Washington lobby favoring the Panama route. The subsequent
donation by Cromwell allegedly was charged to the Panama Canal
Company in Paris as a part of his necessary expenses.[16] This series
of ideas represents a digest of the Rainey views on the Panama
affair.

An interested bystander in these proceedings was that "former
President of the United States," Theodore Roosevelt. In a private
letter, Roosevelt appeared pleased with the course of events. He
wrote that the more they investigated him and the taking of the
canal, the sooner people should understand that it would be non-
sensical to approve of the canal then and not approve of his doing
"the only possible thing" that could give the United States the
canal.[17] The Rainey testimony and evidence were not so severe an
indictment of Roosevelt's policies as his congressional charges
had indicated would be forthcoming. Essentially the hearings
revealed a close relationship between Roosevelt and the archvillain,
William Nelson Cromwell. The implication supplied Democrats and
conservative Republicans with potential grist for the 1912 campaign.

Historical assessment of the investigation runs the length of
the continuum from severest condemnation to highest praise. In a
Roosevelt biography, Lord Charnwood contemptuously dismissed the
results as "totally worthless" and suggested that the report never
be referred to as an authority for anything. More charitably,
Gerstle Mack minimized Charnwood's overstatement but, nevertheless,
stated the opinion that it certainly added little of value to the
stock of public information. At the opposite extreme, Tyler Dennett
assigned to the *Story of Panama* a position as the most complete
and authentic record yet available about one of the most remarkable
propaganda campaigns ever undertaken to influence legislation in
the United States. Roosevelt specialist Elting E. Morison described
the inquiry as the "most useful politically" of the investigations
initiated by the first Democratic House since 1895.[18] Amidst this
diversity of opinion, what objective conclusions can be drawn?

It seems clear that the impelling motivation behind this
investigation was political, an attempt to embarrass the incumbent
administration. Undoubtedly Rainey's initial interest had been a
genuine concern for conditions in the commissary at Panama, for the
elimination of all graft in the building operation, for an equita-
ble legal system safeguarding civil rights, and for the minimization
of executive usurpation of legislative responsibilities. These
laudable motives became submerged in the zealous search for damaging
political evidence against the party in power. In the testimony,
some presumptions of a scandalous nature are raised but not proved.
No subsequent court action follows the recitation of evidence.[19]
As a political weapon, it apparently proved to be a dud, for there
is little indication of this issue being used effectively in the
1912 presidential campaign.

The investigation's most potent force was long range. As
Rainey's careful phrasing of the resolution indicates, it probably
was intended partly as an educational device to stimulate public
support favoring arbitration of the controversy with Colombia. In

the Sixty-third Congress, Rainey introduced a resolution con-
templating the referral of the American dispute with Colombia
to the Hague for adjudication. His move was supported by
Democratic Senator Gilbert M. Hitchcock of Nebraska. A change
in administrations prompted the Colombian government to again
seek redress of its grievances. President Wilson and Secretary
of State Bryan were amenable to some adequate monetary atonement,
and Rainey was constrained by the administration not to press his
resolution pending the outcome of these negotiations. A treaty
was arranged in 1914 whereby the United States expressed sincere
regret for the 1903 incident and promised to pay Colombia
$25,000,000. The Senate rejected the treaty because Roosevelt's
friends opposed any acknowledgment of American guilt. In 1922,
after Roosevelt's death and Wilson's retirement from the White
House, a similar treaty without the expression of regret was
ratified by both countries. Rainey was not in Congress during
this term, and there is no ascertainable record as to how he
felt about the settlement of this question. Ironically, the
Republicans claimed the whole credit for this amelioration of
Latin American relations. It is difficult to assign the specific
influence which the Congressional report, Story of Panama, may
have wielded in bringing about public sentiment favorable to this
settlement, but it was probably slight. The discovery of vast
oil deposits in Colombia weighs far more heavily.[20]

The Panama Canal figures briefly in the Rainey career in one
other connection, the Panama Canal tolls' controversy. In August,
1912, Congress approved an exemption for American ships engaged in
coastal trade from the payment of tolls for use of the Panama
Canal after its completion. The British government objected that
this was a violation of the Hay-Pauncefote Treaty of 1901.
Although the Democratic platform of 1912 had endorsed the exemption,
President Wilson later concluded that such a practice would be in
violation of treaty obligations. In a congressional address of
March 5, 1914, he urged repeal of this exemption. Among the party
regulars supporting the President in this reversal was Henry T.
Rainey. In summarizing his view of the controversy, the Illinoisan
appealed to a set of time-honored Democratic precedents favoring
justice and equality which transcended any platform promises. In
addition to the implied promise of the party's unwritten constitution, Rainey stressed the practical advantage of rapprochement
with Great Britain. He feared toll retaliation and he stressed
that one chapter of dishonor at Panama was sufficient.[21] On the
following day, the House approved the President's recommendation
and the Senate concurred in mid-June. Rainey exhibited a special
sense of party regularity and a sympathy for national integrity in
these diplomatic dealings.

Rainey's involvement in the Panama episode represents his
major foreign policy concern prior to World War I. He gave
sporadic attention to matters involving naval appropriations. When
Theodore Roosevelt sent the Great White Fleet on its world cruise
in 1907 to 1909, Rainey initially endorsed the idea. He expressed
the belief that there would be an "inevitable conflict" between the

white and yellow races. This "peace-compelling squadron" would
demonstrate United States military capability. Yet, when the navy
sought an appropriation to provide funds for the repair of these
same ships, he offered an amendment which would exclude monies for
such a purpose. Although his amendment was defeated, it illustrates
the Bryanite Democrat's basic distrust of a large military establishment.[22] Rainey frequently endeavored to curtail expenses and reduce
extravagance in the military appropriation bills.

As unofficial watchdog of the Treasury, he presented himself as
an opponent of the "big navy" concept. When President Roosevelt
proposed the building of the first American dreadnought, Rainey was
among those who spoke in opposition to a naval building program.
His interest was the unwholesome impact of the steel trust upon the
nation's defense posture. Rainey sponsored an investigation into
the Bethlehem Steel Company's contracts with the Navy Department.
As a result of this inquiry, he later succeeded in amending the
naval appropriations bill so that foreign as well as domestic
producers of steel could bid on the contracts. Rainey assured
Congress that this practice would guarantee better and cheaper
steel. He settled for this concession to economy since he could
not stem the popular enthusiasm for four new battleships. Nevertheless, Rainey was a continentalist and saw no need for such weaponry.
During the debate on the naval appropriations bill in 1911, he
declared: "Our splendid isolation is our best defense. Our
extensive preparations for war are as absurd, as foolish, and as
criminal as was the children's crusade for the recovery of the Holy
Land." He was especialy irked at the inconsistency of steel
magnate Andrew Carnegie's representing himself as an advocate of
international peace, yet promoting extensive national investments
in armaments.[23] The Rainey worry over possible profiteering in the
military preparedness program was in keeping with the progressive
tradition. He reflected the progressive's disinclination to trust
large corporations and their attitude toward war because he
believed there was a connection between monopolies and militarism.

During the years preceding 1917, Henry T. Rainey, like the
American people generally, took little cognizance of the outbreak
of war in Europe. After the initial revulsion at European
barbarity, the nation complacently settled into the belief that it
could not involve the United States. During the summer of 1915,
Rainey consistently expressed support of President Wilson's
diplomatic policy toward Germany. The loss of American lives
occasioned by the sinking of the liner "Lusitania" on May 7, 1915,
inaugurated a series of diplomatic exchanges. In occasional
telegraphic dispatches to the New York *Times*, Rainey uniformly
supported Wilson's efforts to resolve the diplomatic impasse in
an amicable fashion. In a commencement address, the congressman
praised Secretary of State William Jennings Bryan's conciliation
treaties as the pattern for peace. By use of such diplomatic
devices, Rainey hoped to divert revenues ordinarily marked for
war to such domestic pursuits as internal improvements and conservation activities. On still another occasion, he defended the
presidential policy of significant loans to the Allies. Mindful

of his German constituency, he was quick to point out that such loans were available to the Central Powers also.[24]   Henry T. was hopeful that the administration through normal diplomatic channels would be able to preserve the nation's neutrality.

On the subject of preparedness, Rainey declined to follow the President's lead. This midwestern congressman was unwilling to consider the consequences of a serious breach in diplomatic relations. In 1915 he admitted that conditions might warrant appropriations for coastal defenses, but not for an improved navy. He hoped there would be a general disarmament following the war; then such expenditures would be unnecessary. Though unwilling to countenance preparedness himself, he ably defended before the House the right of the Illinois Manufacturers' Association to advocate national preparedness. Rainey stoutly denied they were doing so in their own self-interest.[25]   National preparedness was not a part of the Rainey solution to the crisis in foreign relations, but a free discussion of the issue was.

In 1916 President Wilson carried on a concerted campaign to awaken America to the need for preparedness. Rainey accurately reflected the wishes of his district by refusing to budge from his own position. The Chicago *Tribune*, at this time a persistent champion of a foreign policy based on national self-interest, severely criticized Rainey and his fellow Illinois congressmen for their failure to follow the President's lead. Rainey and his colleagues had voted against an army provision which called for a military force of 250,000 men. The *Tribune* editorial charged the men with extraordinary lunacy in the obstruction of plans for national defense. The editorial concluded that they were unfit to represent the state in the national legislature. In sharp contrast, newspaper sentiment within the twentieth congressional district was decidedly pro-Rainey and anti-*Tribune*. Editor James McNabb of the Carrollton *Gazette* found only one newspaper in the district favorable to the *Tribune*'s position. The concensus of area news-papers found that the congressman represented the sentiment of the district in particular and the state in general. Typical was the assertion of the Carrollton *Patriot* that the *Tribune* was "plumb daffy" on the preparedness question and that Rainey deserved re-election because of his stand against militarism.[26]   At least the southwestern section of Illinois appeared to be decidedly isolationist and noninterventionist at this time.

Rainey seldom committed himself on the possible threat of war. When he did, it was to express support of the President and to advocate a minimum of involvement. After the diplomatic break with Germany in February, 1917, he loyally stood by the President. Rainey deplored the rupture but believed the President could not do otherwise. He expressed the belief that if war should be declared, it would not be long in duration nor would any troops be called from the United States. The United States' participation, he believed, would be limited to the use of the fleet to aid the Allies in choking off supplies to Germany.[27]   Rainey minimized the gravity of the situation and was not cognizant of the commit-ments which the United States would be called upon to make.

Rainey was among those who actively participated in the
House debate following the President's request of April 2, 1917, for
a declaration of war. He warned against underestimating the
importance of the step about to be undertaken. As justification
for entrance into the war, he listed the heinousness of German
warfare, the tyranny of the Hohenzollerns, the audacity of
Zimmerman's note, the unrestricted submarine warfare, and the
natural sympathy for France. "This night," he said on April 5,
"we throw aside the grave clothes of our isolation and take our
proper place among the nations of the world." Wilsonian idealism
permeated his closing remarks. Rainey concluded with the following
peroration:

> We fight for our rights upon the seas. We fight the
> battle for civilization, for humanity, for free govern-
> ments in Central Europe and against the tyranny of the
> Hohenzollerns. . . . We do not enter this war for
> territorial aggrandizement or for money indemnities.
> We enter this war for the purpose of keeping the lights
> of civilization burning brightly on the ocean highways
> of the world, for the purpose of keeping the nations of
> the world from slipping back into the darkness of the
> Middle Ages. We fight for the flag upon whose starry
> folds the sun never sets. We fight for the flag which
> brings freedom wherever it goes.

Although Rainey initially opposed preparedness, he became
reconciled to a declaration of war for these idealistic purposes.
In voting on the war resolution, Rainey was among the 373 representatives to follow the President. Among the fifty who voted nay was
Claude Kitchin, House majority leader and chairman of the Ways and
Means Committee.[28] It has already been noted how Kitchin's
reluctance to support the war necessitated Rainey's leadership in
war revenue measures.

Immediately after the declaration of war, the President was
beset by offers of congressmen to resign their seats in order to
serve in some capacity in the armed forces. Although fifty-seven
years of age, Rainey requested a presidential executive order
permitting him to enlist. The President's reply received wide
circulation in an effort to show the need for civil as well as
military personnel. Wilson wrote that in these circumstances "it
is just as much a man's duty to stay at a post such as you have
been assigned by your constituents as it is for a man to volunteer
for an army."[29] Rainey's contributions to the war effort were to
be on the home front. He would best serve his country's needs by
diligent performance of his legislative responsibilities.

In addition to his contributions to legislation financing the
war, Rainey was a staunch defender of the administration's domestic
policies which were aimed at a successful prosecution of the war on
the home front. In March, 1918, he provided the administration's
defense of Harry A. Garfield's efforts to relieve transportation
tie-ups because of a coal shortage by ordering heatless Mondays.
Certain senators whom Rainey called "knockers" thought the Garfield

edict unheralded, unnecessary, and arbitrary, but Rainey
justified the action as essential to a successful war effort.
Another administrative agency which received Rainey's support
was the Committee on Public Information headed by George Creel.
The Illinoisan defended press censorship and justified the wartime
mania for conformity. He warned the House that while "making the
world safe for democracy we must not make it safe for socialism."
According to Rainey, "the little amenities, the tolerance extended
in times of peace to the disturbers of the peace and to disloyal
elements . . . [should] no longer prevail in time of war." At
the same time, Rainey's altruistic interests caused him to work
closely with war food administrator Herbert Hoover. In the postwar period, the farm-belt congressman urged the Republican
majority to favor relief appropriations for Europeans. He argued
that from the standpoint of humanitarianism, material self-interest,
and national honor, the United States could do no less than provide
assistance to those suffering the ravages of war. Some Republicans
had criticized the relief program, especially the part Herbert
Hoover played in it. Rainey absolved Hoover of any association
with the program's difficulties. In opposing Republican hecklers,
the partisan Democrat praised Hoover's constructive ability, and he
cited the Hoover war record as superior to that of any current
Republican statesman. Hoover's honors and achievements, according
to Rainey, were greater than those earned by any general in the war.[30]

Throughout the war and reconstruction years, Illinois' senior
Democratic congressman was a dependable champion of the President's
program and his administrative lieutenants. He praised the time-
liness of Wilson's Fourteen Points speech because it encouraged the
Russians to stay in the war and the nonmilitary party in Germany to
oppose the war from within that nation. In the further evolution of
peace aims, the President delivered a speech on February 11, 1918,
establishing "four principles" of a just peace. The President's
statement elicited from Rainey the observation that it brought
peace nearer by splitting the Central Powers. He did not, however,
consider the four principles an adequate basis for future
negotiations, as German Chancellor Hertling suggested. Rainey was
eager to prosecute the war until the Allied flags flew from the
castles of Hapsburg and Hohenzollern, and he heartily endorsed the
Fourth Liberty Loan speech in which Woodrow Wilson further outlined his League of Nations concept. He expressed the hope that,
if a League of Nations to enforce the peace of the future were
attained, the war would not have been fought in vain. He also
defended Wilson's rejection of the German peace note of October, 1918,
evidently agreeing that an armistice could not be considered with the
existing German government and that there could not be peace while
enemy troops occupied Allied territory.[31]

Once the peace treaty was negotiated, Rainey's public support
of the President continued. He warmly endorsed Wilson's western tour
to explain the Treaty of Versailles and the League of Nations to the
people. As the controversy lingered, he predicted that the treaty
would be taken out of the 1920 campaign as an issue because it
would be ratified before Congress recessed for the conventions. He

said: "The Senate won't dare to do otherwise. Everybody will get together on some harmless reservations and all will be satisfied." Rainey joined Bryan in opposing Wilson's desire to make the League the chief issue in the 1920 campaign. Each seriously underestimated the intransigence of both the Senate Irreconcilables and the President. In a subsequent statement before the House, Rainey deplored the peace treaty's being delayed for purely partisan purposes. He attributed the unfortunate conditions found everywhere in the world to this delay. As a member of the House of Representatives, Rainey was not directly concerned with ratification of the peace treaty. However, by his opposition to a resolution to declare the end of war with Germany, he was able to sustain the President's position. He also voted to uphold the presidential veto. The measure lacked the necessary two-thirds for overriding a veto. When the issue became important in his personal campaign for re-election in 1920, Rainey's stand placed him in the camp of the mild reservationists.[32] Illinois' leading downstate congressman could be counted upon to support the President's position on matters of diplomatic importance relating to the war's conclusion.

In the postwar years, no major element of foreign policy attracted Rainey's attention until the war debts issue of the mid-1920s. At the same time that he was resisting the inducements of the Mellon revenue measures, he was waging an equally ambitious and determined fight against some of the proposed war debt settlements, especially those involving Italy and France. The Ways and Means Committee held brief hearings on the proposed debt agreements. The January 5, 1926, hearing was described as a stormy one because Rainey objected to a favorable report on these compacts. He requested and received permission for a day's delay in the committee report so that he might voice his opposition, particularly to the Italian agreement. In a prepared statement, Rainey criticized the insufficiency of evidence upon which the World War Debt Funding Commission based its recommendations. He urged delay because the American people would not wish to be a party "to the perpetuation in Italy of a tyranny as dominant and as outrageous" as that of Mussolini. Cordell Hull of Tennessee joined Rainey in expressing the belief that a dictatorship was not a sufficiently stable form of government to guarantee a contract extending over a half-century period. Hull and Rainey were the only committee members signing the minority report.[33]

Rainey continued his vigorous opposition to the Italian war debt settlement on the floor of the House. He was assisted in his campaign by materials provided by Charles Edward Russell, a journalist and special diplomatic representative under Wilson. The debt agreement stipulated that Italy should repay 2.1 billion dollars over a period of sixty-two years at an interest rate of 0.4 percent. It was Rainey's contention that this did not represent Italy's capacity to pay. He submitted that this virtual cancellation of the debt was neither fair nor honest to the American people who bought the war bonds and to the taxpayers compelled to pay for them. Rainey endeavored to prove his point about capacity to pay by an extensive survey of the policies of the Italian government. During

the course of his two and one-half hour presentation, he accused
the debt commission and the Ways and Means Committee of relying
too heavily upon Italian sources of information for their conclusions. These, he said, were unreliable because of severe press
censorship and arbitrariness of the regime. Theodore Burton of
Ohio, a member of the debt commission and sponsor of the bill,
offered the principal reply. The rebuttal centered upon the
belief that the internal affairs of that nation had no bearing
upon the best possible refunding arrangement. While some foreign
policy analyses have imputed partisan political motives to his
opposition, Rainey's position was in keeping with the Wilsonian
view of moral diplomacy.[34] He was making value judgments about
the suitability of an agreement with the Mussolini dictatorship.

Rainey subsequently conducted an equally ineffective but
less extensive campaign against a similar agreement proposed for
France. The arrangement provided that 4.1 billion dollars be
repaid over a period of sixty-two years at an interest rate of 1.6
percent. Only Rainey's name was attached to the minority report
which deplored the settlement being railroaded through Congress
without the slightest evidence of France's inability to repay. He
criticized Congress for refusing to grant relief for the American
farmers but granting it to the farmers of France by canceling half
their debt. Experience with the Italian debt question indicated a
new danger in such negotiations. Rainey asserted that American
commercial interests were profiting by the settlement of the debt
problem. He rejected a policy of revenue losses in which "a
hundred million people shall bow reverently and in suppliance to
the invisible arm of steel which reaches out from Wall Street."
As an alternative suggestion, he proposed the little known Wilson
scheme that an American commission periodically determine how much
these debtor nations could and ought to pay. The specter of a money
trust fired Rainey's Populist inclinations, and he repeated his
opposition in the next Congress when further reductions were
proposed for France. It was his argument that when the loans were
granted, there was the expectation that they would be fully repaid.
Rainey's position on the war debts was in the "Uncle Shylock"
school of thought and contrary to much opinion which favored outright cancellation of the total indebtedness.[35] For reasons of
fiscal responsibility, he continued to be an outspoken critic of
any reduction or cancellation of the war debts owed the United
States by European nations. Later he acquiesced to a position of
revision if there were compensatory tariff reductions made abroad.

In the early 1930s, Rainey was intimately involved with the
nation's most controversial diplomatic problem, the recognition of
Soviet Russia. During the summer of 1931, the congressman made a
self-appointed, privately financed trip to Russia. He expressed
the belief that a conscientious legislator ought to become fully
acquainted with the exact facts regarding Russia's five-year program.
He particularly wished to study the communal farms. On June 15 he
departed on his journey, and by mid-July he was traveling inside
Russia, spending about a month covering 7,000 miles. In a lengthy
interview covering his initial impressions, Rainey observed that

Americans were provincial because they did not have enough diplomatic
sense to realize the penalty now being paid for a foolish policy of
isolationism. The congressman was much impressed with Russia's
progress and potential, and according to the New York *Times*, deplored
particularly the fact that the United States refused to grant
diplomatic recognition to Russia. In the Rainey viewpoint, the
huge potential market for American goods in Russia should have
prompted the United States to follow the customary diplomatic
niceties. His favorable opinions were elaborated in a series of
dispatches appearing in the *Illinois State Register*.[36] As a result
of this trip, he became one of the leading proponents of Russian
recognition.

Rainey insisted that recognition of Russia would serve as a
means of stimulating economic recovery for businessmen and farmers.
He referred to nonrecognition as "an economic crime" resulting from
shortsighted statesmanship. The *Nation* quoted him as saying it was
foolish to sit back and allow American factories to stop running
and people to stay idle when this vast potential market was undevel-
oped. He always urged farm groups to support recognition because
Russia had not erected tariff barriers and thus would become an
immediate outlet for the nation's farm surplus. On November 16,
1933, the President formally announced the official resumption of
diplomatic relations between the nations. Russian sources gave
special mention to Speaker Rainey's support in achieving that goal.
Rainey expressed his gratification that this avenue of recovery was
now open.[37] The promise of economic stimulation did not meet
expectations, but the goal of a restoration of normal diplomatic
relations with Russia was fulfilled.

During the decade of the 1920s, Rainey could not be characterized as wholly isolationist or internationalist, although the
balance of the scales was inclined toward the latter. As an
internationalist, he favored American participation in the Permanent
Court of International Justice, commonly known as the World Court.
He described the Republican policy of noninvolvement as shortsighted because American interests were being sacrificed by a
refusal to participate in the "councils of the nations." As
majority leader of the Democrats in 1932, Rainey blamed Republican
isolationist policies for contributing to the worldwide depression.
It was his view that the League of Nations was rendering "a
valuable service" in behalf of world peace. Although the United
States was not a member, he stressed America's constant contact in
unofficial capacities. The isolationist bent in Rainey's outlook
may be characterizdd by his narrow view of the war debt situation
vis-à-vis the role of the United States as a creditor rather than
a debtor nation. On balance, the years of Rainey's service
minimize the myth of midwestern continentalism and the legend of
isolationism in the 1920s.[38] Within the limited purview of a
member of the House of Representatives, Rainey's inclination was
toward involvement in world affairs.

The congressman's overriding interest in economic matters
compelled him to embrace the broader perspective of foreign policy.
As the worsening economic conditions of the 1930s engulfed the

the world, Rainey became even more attuned to the interdependence of nations for survival, as evidenced by his support for Russian recognition. On the domestic scene, the agricultural problem with its glut of surplus commodities necessitated an exploration of the world market as a solution. The following chapter's examination of Rainey's perspective on the farm situation will illustrate the importance of a cosmopolitan rather than a parochial outlook. Thus it may be generalized that the midwesterner's career may be placed on the continuum of foreign involvement as participationist, inclined toward internationalism, and definitely not isolationist.

NOTES

1. For representative examples see Ray A. Billington, "The Origins of Middle Western Isolationism," 44-64; William G. Carleton, "Isolationism and the Middle West," 377-390; Selig Adler, "Isolationism since 1914," 335-344.

2. Interview with Mrs. Rainey reported by Helen E. Graff, "Henry T. Rainey—An American Statesman," 66-67; H. J. Res. 42, *CR*, 58:1 (Nov. 19, 1903), 391; *Patriot*, Aug. 18, 1905, 1:5; *CR*, 59:1 (June 4, 1906), 7808-12.

3. *CR*, 58:2 (Dec. 15, 1903), 266-268; *Patriot*, Dec. 25, 1903, 1:1-2 and 4:1. In this and subsequent stances HTR epitomized the analysis presented by Gerold E. Markowitz, "Progressivism and Imperialism," 257-275.

4. Chicago *Record-Herald*, April 3, 1907, 10:1; *Commoner*, VII (April 12, 1907), 14; series begins in the *Gazette* of April 18, 1907, and ends in the issue of June 6. The quotation appears in the issue of May 16, 1907, 2:1.

5. H. Res. 443, *CR*, 60:2 (Dec. 7, 1908), 8; *News* of Dec. 16, 1908, as cited in Clyde Peirce, *The Roosevelt Panama Libel Cases*, 79.

6. Rainey quoted by St. Louis *Republic* of Jan. 19, 1909, as cited by Peirce, *Roosevelt Panama Libel Cases*, 86. For a most detailed and heavily documented study of the judicial aspect of the Panama situation see Peirce's work.

7. *CR*, 60:2 (Jan. 26, 1909), 1424-26; Adams, "The Joke's on You," 55.

8. *CR*, 60:2 (Jan. 26, 1909), 1426-31, documentation accompanying the speech on 1431-41; for HTR's evidence involving Charles P. Taft in the timber intrigue see three-page letter of Sam B. Dannis to HTR, Ancon, Canal Zone, Dec. 31, 1908, RP.

9. Sam B. Dannis to HTR enclosing newspaper clippings containing Cromwell denial and Assembly resolution, Ancon, Canal Zone, Feb. 5, 1909, RP; copy of telegram of Panama Secretary of Foreign Affairs to Panama Consul in New York City, Feb. 1, 1909, RP; C. C. Arosemena (Panamanian Minister) to Secretary of State, Washington, Feb. 8, 1909, as printed in *Papers Relating to the Foreign Relations of the United States*, 1909, 470-471.

10. For the denials see *CR*, 60:2 (Jan. 29, 1909), 1590-92, and New York *Times*, Feb. 2, 1909, 1:5; for HTR's efforts to change the bill see *CR*, 60:2 (Feb. 5, 1909), 2102-03, 2107-08, 2113-14.

11. For Lovering's remarks and then Olcott's see *CR*, 60:2 (Feb. 12, 1909), 2270-82, 2285-90; Roosevelt to Cromwell, Washington, Feb. 13, 1909, as printed in Elting E. Morison (ed.), *The Letters of Theodore Roosevelt*, VI, 1518; New York *Times*, Feb. 14, 1909, 1:8 and 2:1.

12. New York *Times*, Feb. 15, 1909, 2:1; *CR*, 60:2 (Feb. 22, 1909), 2884-85.

13. H. Res. 32, *CR*, 62:1 (April 6, 1911), 113; Chicago *Record-Herald*, April 10, 1911, 9:2.

14. U.S. Congress, House, Committee on Foreign Affairs, *The Story of Panama*, 47, for the resolution.

15. Chicago *Record-Herald*, Jan. 24, 1912, 2:2; U.S. Congress, *Story of Panama*, 52-53.

16. U.S. Congress, *Story of Panama*, 61-62, 70-72. Cromwell is described as "shrewd, energetic, resourceful, experienced, and generally amiable though he sometimes exasperated those who disagreed with him" by Gerstle Mack, *The Land Divided*, 417. For a defense of Cromwell see Dwight C. Miner, *The Fight for the Panama Route*, 76, 102, 152. Miner says the Rainey description is "exaggerated."

17. Roosevelt to Joseph Bucklin Bishop, New York, Jan. 29, 1912, in Morison (ed.), *Letters of Theodore Roosevelt*, VIII, 492. For an appraisal of Roosevelt and Panama see Robert A. Friedlander, "A Reassessment of Roosevelt's Role in the Panamanian Revolution of 1903," 535-543.

18. Lord Charnwood, *Theodore Roosevelt*, 144; Mack, *The Land Divided*, 478; Dennett, *John Hay: From Poetry to Politics*, 365; Morison (ed.), *The Letters of Theodore Roosevelt*, VIII, 275, n. 2.

19. The libel suits instituted by the United States government in February, 1909, against the *World* and the *News* were quashed by October. Peirce, *Roosevelt Panama Libel Cases*, 104-122.

20. H. Res. 74, *CR*, 63:1 (April 23, 1913), 357; E. Taylor Parks, *Columbia and the United States, 1765-1934*, 440-457; Paolo Coletta, "William Jennings Bryan and the United States-Colombia Impasse, 1903-1921," 486-501.

21. *CR*, 63:2 (March 30, 1914), 5868-71; Roady, "Party Regularity in the Sixty-third Congress," 207; Edward S. Kaplan, "William Jennings Bryan and the Panama Canal Tolls Controversy," 100-108.

22. *Patriot*, July 25, 1907, 1:2; *CR*, 61:3 (Feb. 20, 1911), 3024; John Milton Cooper, Jr., "Progressivism and American Foreign

Policy," 265.

23. *CR*, 60:1 (April 15, 1908), 4780–81; H. Res. 498, *CR*, 61:2 (March 12, 1910), 3122, 3418; *CR*, 61:3 (Feb. 21, 1911), 3094–3100.

24. Cedric Cummins, "Indiana Looks at the World War–1914," 307–344; HTR to New York *Times* Editor, Carrollton, appearing in the *Times* of May 15, 1915, 5:4; June 1, 1915, 5:5; and July 11, 1915, II, 4:2; *Patriot*, June 3, 1915, 1:5–6; editorial, "Rainey Approves Big Loan," *Patriot*, Oct. 21, 1915, 4:1.

25. HTR to New York *Times* Editor, Carrollton, July 24, 1915, appearing in *Times*, July 25, 1915, II, 5:2; *CR* 64:1 (April 27, 1916), 6934–36.

26. Editorial, "Illinois in Congress," Chicago *Tribune*, May 10, 1916, 8:2; editorial, "The Tribune's Diatribe," *Gazette*, May 24, 1916, 1:1–2; editorial, "Rainey and the *Tribune*," *Patriot*, May 11, 1916, 4:1.

27. Paraphrase of HTR views in Jersey County *Democrat* as reprinted in *Gazette*, Feb. 14, 1917, 1:1.

28. *CR*, 65:1 (April 5, 1917), 387–388, 413. For a sympathetic portrayal of Kitchin in these years see Arnett, *Claude Kitchin*.

29. HTR remembrance in *CR*, 68:2 (March 4, 1925), 5572–73; Wilson to HTR, Washington, April 12, 1917, New York *Times*, April 13, 1917, 5:1.

30. *CR*, 65:2 (March 1), 2868–71; (Jan. 11, 1918), 860–862; (Feb. 8, 1918), 1872–73; *CR*, 66:2 (March 15, 1920), 4359–61.

31. New York *Times*, Jan. 9, 1918, 2:4; Feb. 12, 1918, 2:2; Feb. 27, 1918, 2:4; Sept. 17, 1918, 2:4; Sept. 29, 1918, I, 12:4; Oct. 9, 1918, 3:4.

32. *CR*, 66:1 (Sept. 2, 1919), 4637; New York *Times*, Jan. 10, 1920, 1:8 and 2:2; *CR*, 66:2 (March 15, 1920), 4360; votes on H. J. Res. 327 in *CR*, 66:2 (April 9, 1920), 5480–81 and (May 28), 7808–7809; *Patriot*, Oct. 7, 1920, 1:3.

33. New York *Times*, Jan. 6, 1926, 5:1, and Jan. 7, 1926, 41:2; testimony of HTR before committee printed in *CR*, 69:1 (Jan. 13, 1926), 1994–98.

34. HTR to Russell, Washington, Jan. 9, 14, 1926, in Russell Papers, Vol. 14; *CR*, 69:1 (Jan. 13, 1926), 1976–90; Forrest Crissey, *Theodore E. Burton: American Statesman*, 287–288; George L. Grassmuck, *Sectional Biases in Congress on Foreign Policy*, 91, 93–94.

35. *CR*, 69:1 (May 29, 1926), 10370–71, and (June 1, 1926), 10438–43; *CR*, 71:2 (Dec. 12, 1929), 554–556, 561, 565; Benjamin D. Rhodes, "Reassessing 'Uncle Shylock': The United States and the French War Debt, 1917–1929," 787–803.

36. HTR to Earl Smith, [Washington], April 4, 1931, RP; New

York *Times*, Sept. 6, 1931, 5:3-4; interview information from Mrs. Rainey appearing in Graff, "Henry T. Rainey," 67-73; dispatches appearing in the *Register* between August 2 and November 15, 1931. For an interesting discussion of the impact of such visits see Lewis Feuer, "American Travellers to the Soviet Union, 1917-1932," 119-149.

37. New York *Times*, April 26, 1932, 7:1; *Nation*, CXXXIV (May 18, 1932), 567; *IAA Record*, XI (Sept. 1933), 9, and *Prairie Farmer*, CV (Nov. 11, 1933), 20; summary of "ZA Industrializatsiiu" for Nov. 20, 1933, appearing in Robert P. Browder, *The Origins of Soviet-American Diplomacy*, 161; New York *Times*, Nov. 21, 1933, 33:3. For further discussion of the American interest in recognition see Edward M. Bennett, *Recognition of Russia*; also Paul F. Boller, Jr., "The 'Great Conspiracy' of 1933," 97-112.

38. *CR*, 68:2 (March 3, 1925), 5413; *CR*, 69:2 (Dec. 16, 1926), 612; radio address of Jan. 4, *CR*, 72:1 (Jan. 5, 1932), 1299; HTR to J. Harry Faulkner, [Washington], May 14, 1934, RP; William A. Williams, "The Legend of Isolationism in the Twenties," 1-20; Robert James Maddox, "Another Look at the Legend of Isolationism in the 1920's," 35-43.

8
Friend of the Farmer

During the decade of the 1920s, there was almost continual agitation
for agricultural relief. The leaders of the farm population sought
two objectives: the control of agricultural policy by themselves
rather than representatives of the industrial community and the
commitment of national policy to equalize agriculture with manufacturing. As representative of the largest agricultural district in
the state, Rainey became embroiled in the farmers' struggle for
political power and prosperity. The controversy centered upon the
McNary-Haugen proposal for farm legislation. During the Coolidge
administration, McNary-Haugenism became the same rallying symbol for
twentieth-century agrarians as free silver had been for nineteenth-
century Populists. From Congressman Rainey's return to Congress in
1923 until his death he was intimately concerned with the plight of
the farmer. In this rural versus urban struggle, he was personally
as well as professionally involved.

Rainey's second career was that of a gentleman farmer. He
devoted spare time and energy to the growth and development of his
rural estate. In 1909 he had indulged his agrarian instincts by the
purchase of a 200-acre farm a mile east of Carrollton for the then
record price of $150 per acre. The farming arrangement was a
partnership with first David R. Reynolds and then A. D. Bower
supplying year-round management and labor. By 1933 the farm had
increased to 485 acres and was considered a demonstration mecca for
those interested in scientific agriculture.[1] The improvement of
this farm was the congressman's chief nonpolitical interest.

By the early 1920s, the Rainey-Reynolds farm operation had
become a showplace of modern agriculture. As a scientific dirt
farmer, Rainey was an enthusiastic supporter of purebred livestock
and of improved farming techniques. Originally the farm had involved
a stockfeeder operation including both cattle and hogs, but during
World War I the emphasis was switched to a dairy herd as more
profitable. By example, Rainey hoped to encourage agricultural
diversification in an area dominated by wheat, corn, and fruit
growing. His milk cows were all registered Holstein-Friesian, and
the physical facilities provided a model of ideal dairying conditions.
The chief crops were corn, alfalfa, and legumes. As an interesting
sideline, the congressman raised Japanese deer commercially. The
Rainey farm was frequently used by the University of Illinois College
of Agriculture as a demonstration center for scientific agriculture.[2]

As an advocate of scientific farming, Rainey was instrumental
in fostering local farm improvements. The original impetus for a
farm bureau-like organization came in November, 1913, at an annual

meeting of the Greene County Fair Association, over which Henry T.
presided. The resultant Greene County Farm Improvement Association
did not survive because of lack of funds, but the advent of
federal aid under the Smith-Lever Act helped alleviate that
problem. Beginning on September 20, 1917, the Carrollton *Patriot*
launched another campaign for such an organization as an aid to
the war effort. By January 3, 1918, the local farm bureau was
officially instituted.[3] Rainey was consistently a member of this
organization. The bureau's bulletin is replete with references
to his activities in behalf of local agricultural advancement.

The Rainey farm endeavored by example and inducement to
foster self-help programs among farmers. Walnut Hall regularly had
a tent display at the Greene County Fair. Such an exhibit
certainly did him no harm politically, and it served to demonstrate
results by practical example. In order to encourage the use of
purebred animals for breeding purposes, Rainey-Reynolds, under farm
bureau auspices, donated their young bulls to groups of farmers who
would organize into clubs to use and care for these animals.
Although dairying was a minor industry in the county, they hoped to
enable farmers to improve the profitableness of their herds.[4]
Henry T. justly deserved his local reputation as a progressive
farmer, but his early legislative record was exceedingly spotty for
a representative with such a predominantly rural constituency.

Prior to his defeat in the 1920 election, Rainey gave only
passing legislative attention to matters relating to agriculture.
During the Theodore Roosevelt and William Howard Taft administrations, Rainey demonstrated only incidental attention to matters
specifically affecting farmers. He barely improved on that image
in the Wilson years. Although the New Freedom was marked by such
significant farm measures as the Smith-Lever Agricultural Extension
Act, the Federal Farm Loan Act, and the Smith-Hughes Vocational
Education Act, Rainey's only espousal of these bills was his vote
in the House chamber. His contribution to farm policy was limited
to the suggestion that Carl Schurz Vrooman of nearby Bloomington be
induced to serve as Assistant Secretary of Agriculture under
David F. Houston. Vrooman became the principal exponent of the new
agriculture which emphasized cooperation in the attainment of
agriculture's goals.[5] It was at the state level that Rainey first
began to develop a keener appreciation of his constituency's needs
on bread and butter issues.

Among the controversies which developed between Rainey and
Democratic Governor Edward F. Dunne was the latter's handling of an
epidemic of foot and mouth disease among Illinois cattle. The
farmers of Greene County had been experiencing difficulties with
drought, cinch bugs, army worms, corn stalk disease, and hog cholera.
To these natural difficulties was added bureaucratic incompetence
when foot and mouth disease was introduced from Indiana and
Michigan. As a precaution, Dr. O. E. Dyson, state veterinarian,
imposed a quarantine on the entire state. On behalf of Greene
County stock growers, Rainey argued that there was not a case of the
disease within 100 miles. In a strongly worded letter to the
governor, Rainey presented a six-point indictment of Dyson's conduct

and demanded his resignation, which Dunne refused to request.
The congressman ultimately was successful in getting the order
modified in those portions of the state where the danger did
not exist. The incident is important for understanding part of
the estrangement between Dunne and Rainey. Of equal significance
is the demand on the part of both local newspaper editors that the
congressman take a greater interest in affairs nearer to home,
leaving such issues as the Panama Canal to others.[6] The advice
was not completely wasted, for Rainey began to perfect his role as
friend of the farmer.

In the national legislature, Walnut Hall's proprietor busied
himself with a number of minor agricultural interests. These
included the campaign of the Chicago *Drovers' Journal* to require
the installation of automatic warning bells and/or gates to reduce
the number of accidents at railroad crossings in rural areas, the
demand to authorize the use of mixed flour (the dilution of wheat
flour with other cereal grains), the repeal of the daylight saving
law, and the request for truth-in-fabric legislation. None of
these endeavors were successful. The record clearly indicates the
meager nature of Rainey's congressional credentials as representative of a rural electorate. In the 1920 election campaign, his
Republican opponent, Guy L. Shaw, made an issue of his own farm
interests while denigrating Rainey's sparse legislative activities
in this area. In combination with the other factors at work in
the 1920 election, the lack of a strong performance in agricultural matters contributed to Rainey's only defeat in a general
election. While available records do not reveal that he personally
gave this factor much, if any, consideration, it is noteworthy
that his subsequent congressional activities were more relevant to
the problems of the twentieth district. Rainey continued to perform
the role of statesman in matters relating to foreign policy, tariffs,
and taxes, but he was more conscious of the impact upon his rural
constituency.

The defeated congressman lost little time in mending his local
fences. While he concerned himself with such parochial interests as
lowered rural telephone rates and improved "hard" road connections,
his principal contribution was service on a statewide committee
dealing with agricultural problems. In March, 1922, Dr. Eugene
Davenport, Dean of the College of Agriculture at the University of
Illinois, invited Rainey to join a committee studying the farm
situation in Illinois in order to determine policy directions for
the next twenty-five years. The committee on Illinois agricultural
policy, more commonly known as the Committee of Fifteen, studied
such topics as soil and climate, transportation, manufactures, waterpower, and drainage. Rainey served as chairman of a subcommittee on
farm financing and as a member of the subcommittee on rural life.
The committee developed a platform for organized agriculture in
Illinois which sought to preserve and perpetuate farm prosperity in
cooperation rather than competition with industry and labor. The
committee warned that "if the American people do not accept the
challenge to establish equality for agriculture and prosperity for all
its essential groups, they [will] have met the first great defeat in

our country's history."[7]   These activities, plus the growing
importance of Walnut Hall in providing agricultural leadership,
enabled Rainey to present an improved farm record in the 1922
election.

When the "freshman" congressman returned to the legislative
halls in 1923, he had a new perspective on the problem of farm
prosperity.   It was generally recognized that the agricultural
community was not enjoying the relative prosperity of other elements
in the American economy.   There were numerous legislative proposals
aimed at remedying this situation.   Chief among these was a bill
sponsored by Senator Charles L. McNary of Oregon and Representative
Gilbert N. Haugen of Iowa.   As part of the bill's provisions, eight
basic farm commodities—wheat, flour, corn, cotton, wool, cattle,
sheep, and swine (together with any foodstuff derived from the last
three)—were to be subject to a two-price system.   There would be
a higher American price for the domestically consumed portion of
the crop, while the remainder would be sold in foreign markets at
the world price.   To cover the loss involved, farmers would be
charged an equalization fee, or tax, on each unit of the farm
commodity sold.   It was assumed that this fee would be far less
than the benefits derived from the higher domestic prices.   The
American or parity price was based on the relative ratio of prices
farmers received to the prices they paid.   The years 1905 to 1914
were selected as the base period most accurately reflecting farm
prosperity vis-à-vis industry.   This proposal received the
enthusiastic endorsement of the American Farm Bureau Federation.[8]

On March 12, 1924, Henry T. Rainey was catapulted into the
national spotlight on this question of farm relief.   On March 10
he had received a demand from President Sam Thompson of the Illinois
Agriculture Association that he actively support and vote for the
McNary-Haugen bill as the soundest legislation of all the proposed
farm relief measures.   Rainey immediately drafted a reply in which
he outlined twenty-five questions about the proposal which he
thought needed further discussion.   He indicated that he had
started out with the intention of supporting the bill since the
farm organizations were endorsing it, but on closer study he found
features which were exceedingly objectionable.   He further stated:
"It would be much easier for me in an agricultural district like
mine, so far as the next election goes, to accept your suggestions
and avoid the implied threat which goes with them, than to oppose
this bill."   Nevertheless he believed "the passage of a measure . . .
so revolutionary as this measure, so destructive of all our present
systems of exchange and marketing, involving the possible destruction
of the present primary markets for farmers is fraught with grave
possibilities, and may result in untold injury to an industry which
is now almost prostrate."[9]   Rainey invited Thompson's early and
complete reply to his reservations about the bill.   Opponents of
farm relief measures gave Rainey's letter wide publicity.

The specific allegations in the twenty-five item indictment are
not as important as the controversy which their publication fostered.
Rainey believed most farmers agreed that the bill was unworkable and
dangerous.   He had not intended, he wrote, that his letter to

Thompson should receive so much attention, but the publicity
might "contribute something toward solving these difficult
problems." Rainey confided to Upton Sinclair that his objections
to Thompson had served to inject some "needed sanity in our public
affairs." Rainey was of the opinion that before his letter there
would not have been ten votes against the bill, and yet nearly
everyone in Congress believed this particular legislation was
undesirable. According to Rainey, the legislators were cowed by
the implied threats of the Farm Bureau.[10] Rainey's initial motives
seem legitimately aimed at discussing the bill in order to improve
it by removing objectionable features. The publicity accorded his
stance, however, shoved him into a position as a hard-core
opponent of the first McNary-Haugen bill.

Indicative of this transformation was the further exchange of
correspondence between Rainey and Thompson. The letters were filled
with epithets of character assassination. A full three weeks
elapsed before Thompson replied; the rebuttal appeared in print
before it reached Rainey. Thompson's reply accused Rainey of
"consorting more with the special interests opposed to the bill
than with the basic, underlying interests of American agriculture."
After a categorical reply to each of the Rainey points of discussion,
the letter implied that Rainey's mind was no longer open to objective
consideration of the bill. Argument was wasted, said the reply,
because the opposition was "mired in a morass of evasions, sophis-
tries and deceits." Rainey replied in a like manner because he
considered the letter "a slanderous personal attack." He asserted
that Thompson did not write the letter but had permitted himself
"to become a sewer through which some wild-eyed Bolshevik" poured
out personal vilification. Rainey charged that no other statement
of similar length had "so much personal abuse, so many scandalous
statements, so many direct falsehoods, so many statements of
economic untruths." He concluded that enacting the McNary-Haugen
bill into law "would be like administering poison to a dying man."[11]
Rainey offered to debate the question throughout Illinois, but no
one accepted the challenge. The participants in this exchange
succeeded in generating more heat than light on the situation.

The important role that George N. Peek, president of the Moline
Plow Company, played in formulating and propagandizing the McNary-
Haugen plan was at first unrealized. There was considerable
speculation about the author of Thompson's reply. More than a month
passed before Rainey ascertained that it was Peek. The congressman
later made an issue of Peek's participation in the farm question
because Peek had been most prominently engaged in "farming the
farmers" due to high farm machinery costs.[12] Rainey objected most
strenuously to the overt propaganda activities of the farm bureau
in behalf of the bill. Apparently this triggered his publicly
proclaimed opposition to the proposal. A more normal course would
have been for him to raise his objections in committee hearings. If
the bill were not sufficiently modified, then he could seek redress
from the floor of the House. The sensational way in which his
position was publicized made him the darling of the opponents of all
farm relief and a devil to certain agrarian interests.

Editorial and personal reaction to Rainey's opposition ranged from enthusiastic endorsement to caustic condemnation. The majority of opinion favoring his opposition to the McNary-Haugen bill came from those with business affiliations. Typical was the editorial comment, appearing in the *Modern Miller*, rabidly opposed to McNary-Haugenism and the first to mention his stand. The *Miller* editorial said Rainey had sandbagged the proposition in a masterful way. Never, in the opinion of the editor, had so "vicious [a] piece of legislation had the blow-holes pointed out [so] fully." Individual opinion from Illinois farmers generally held that he was a Judas Iscariot to his class. A farmer from the western part of the state characterized this sentiment by giving this advice: "Get behind the McNary-Haugen Bill, propose a better [one], or for God's sake go way back and sit down."[13] At this time, the numerous farm journals and country papers were not united in their support of a single farm plan; therefore, Rainey escaped the scathing denunciations which similar opposition would later receive. In terms of material preserved in the Rainey papers, the editorials favoring his position outnumber those opposed, while personal letters criticizing his viewpoint exceed those supporting it. Unorganized grass-roots sentiment appeared to favor the adoption of the McNary-Haugen plan for farm relief.

The principal organized opposition to the Rainey stand stemmed from the Illinois Agricultural Association, the state-level farm bureau affiliate. Under this organization's sponsorship, representatives of the nine county farm bureaus in the twentieth congressional district met in Jacksonville to draft a letter to Rainey. In the letter they denied any dictation from President Thompson and reaffirmed their belief in the McNary-Haugen bill as "a long step in the right direction toward relieving the present distressful state of agriculture." The delegates expressed disappointment in Rainey because he played a very leading part in opposition and neglected to offer any friendly or constructive amendments. The letter urged their congressman not to hinder the bill's coming to the floor for discussion and roll call. Farm bureau representatives of the seventeenth congressional district took similar action.[14] The Illinois branch of the American Farm Bureau Federation was the most active of the state associations in supporting the McNary-Haugen proposal. The organization was unrelenting in its efforts to convert Congressman Rainey.

An extremely sensitive point among critics of farmer Rainey was his relationship with the local farm bureau. E. M. Phillips, Greene County's farm adviser, reported to Rainey that there had been some letters and telegrams from various parts of the state inquiring about his status with the farm organization. Phillips indicated that he had reported Greene County as holding Rainey in very high regard and that the congressman was of great service to farm bureau members in numerous ways.[15] Thus it was established that Rainey's aversion to the farm bureau—sponsored bill did not arise from any prejudice against the organization, but rather a sincere conviction that a price-fixing measure was not the answer to the farmers' plight.

Rainey was not unmindful of the need to support an alternative to the McNary-Haugen measure. Initially he favored the Curtis-Aswell bill which would assist farm marketing cooperatives on a national scale. He described it as a perfectly sane and workable bill for farm relief. Democratic Congressman James. B. Aswell of Louisiana saw some prospects that President Coolidge might favor this bill since the others were too paternalistic and socialistic, but this support never materialized. Rainey attributed the farmers' plight to the unfortunate leadership of recent years which had pursued policies of isolation and a high protective tariff. These were the areas where reverse procedures were needed, he wrote to Clifford V. Gregory, editor of *Prairie Farmer*. Rainey's suggestion of tariff reductions as the solution met with rebuff from Brown County's farm adviser, Walter P. Miller. Miller argued that tariff revision was not a panacea because the commercial and labor interests would oppose such a move and because it was a long-term proposition, while the need was immediate.[16] Nevertheless, Rainey placed two bills in the congressional hopper which would promote agricultural equality through tariff reductions. Henceforth he placed great emphasis upon his tariff reduction suggestions which allegedly would reopen foreign markets that had been closed to farm surpluses.

All this furor had taken place before the McNary-Haugen bill was reported out of committee for debate in the House during late May and early June, 1924. Rainey helped draft the minority report and was one of the leading critics in the debate on the bill. He told fellow congressmen that he was unable to convince himself that this measure would accomplish "the miraculous results claimed for it." Rather, he said, it would produce the very overproduction which it sought to avoid. Rainey asserted that the high-salaried American Farm Bureau Federation officials were just "swivel-chair farmers" whose views could be disregarded. As an appendix to his speech, he printed his farm relief proposal with supporting evidence and supplementary statements. The following day he lost a parliamentary move to substitute his measure for the McNary-Haugen bill. On May 30 he delivered a short speech in which blame for the farmers' present difficulty was laid squarely upon the protective tariff. The next day he closed his opposition by citing a January, 1920, farm resolution which had "vigorously opposed all efforts at governmental price fixing." Six major farm organizations, including the Farm Bureau, had endorsed that stand.[17] Rainey's activities supplemented the objections of the Democratic members of the Agriculture Committee.

The Rainey substitute measure deserves additional attention as a precursor of subsequent farm relief proposals. His idea was to create a commission composed ex officio of the secretaries of Agriculture and Commerce, the chairman of the Tariff Commission, and an administrative commissioner to be selected by the President. Whenever the commission found a surplus existed for export in wheat, flour, or the food products of swine, it could request the President to declare an emergency. Then the commission would estimate the cost of production, add a 10 percent profit, and declare this to be the market price. For those selling in the world market at a deficiency price, the commission would be empowered to issue customs scrip which would be only negotiable in paying tariff duties. It was hoped the revenue loss to the government would be offset by an increased quantity of imports and by farm income rising to the tax-paying brackets. This Rainey proposal antedates by two years the export-debenture plan of Professor Charles L. Stewart of the University of Illinois. Rainey sought to convince Clifford V. Gregory of the proposal's strengths, and the *Prairie Farmer* editor subsequently called attention to its possibilities.[18] This idea becomes significant in subsequent solutions proposed for the farm problem.

The time for argument was over and the vote was at hand. In a preliminary poll of the twenty-six-member Illinois congressional delegation by the *Prairie Farmer*, Rainey was the only downstater definitely against it. In the roll call vote on June 3, the House defeated the McNary-Haugen bill by a vote of 223 to 155. The Illinois Agricultural Association was pleased that, with the exception of Rainey, every Illinois representative from an agricultural district had voted aye. The association printed a two-page, three-color map showing how the McNary-Haugen bill was defeated. Illinois' twentieth congressional district stands out amidst a sea of western and midwestern support for the measure. In assaying the impact of the Rainey opposition, one extensive study concludes that he delivered some of the "most telling blows" at the first McNary-Haugen bill and that he supplied "irreparable damage" to the passage of the measure.[19]

Rainey's conduct during this heated controversy illustrates the dilemma faced by a representative's choice between conscience and constituency. His aggressive opposition to a measure with considerable grass-roots support was a calculated risk. The Carrollton *Patriot*'s editor noted that this was "an example of unusual political candor at this particular time [the Harding scandals]" and classified him as a statesman rather than politician. A member of the Illinois General Assembly stated the other side of the coin in urging Rainey's support of the bill. Representative Ben L. Smith argued that it was consistent with his idea of representative government to favor the legislation if one were convinced that a majority of his constituents supported it even though personal conscience dictated otherwise.[20] As a veteran legislator, Rainey had decided to represent what he believed to be his constituency's interest but not its will. At the general election in 1924, he was able to convince his corn-belt constituents that his stand against McNary-Haugen was in their best interest.

The struggle for the principles of McNary-Haugenism was more fundamental than the legislation itself. In essence it was agriculture's stand against the domination of its affairs and the concerns of the nation by commercial and industrial interests. The rural share of population, voting strength, political influence, economic status, and social well being were in noticeable decline. With characteristic pungency, Mark Sullivan observed that the farmer was on his way to becoming "gardener to an immense manufac- turing and business community."[21] With the usual Bryanite distrust

of things urban, Rainey could be counted upon to resist city
encroachments into rural problems.

After the defeat of the first McNary-Haugen bill, Rainey
had hoped Congress would remain in session until a farm relief
measure was passed. Instead, there was an early adjournment for
the national political conventions. During the lame-duck session
of the Sixty-eighth Congress (December 1, 1924, to March 4, 1925),
the controversial measure did not get beyond the committee stage.
In the subsequent Congress, the original proposal was changed
considerably and came to a vote three more times. Rainey's
position on the measure was now completely reversed, and he
became a staunch supporter of McNary-Haugenism. He attributed
the conversion to the vast changes in the bill and to the need
for getting some farm relief measure approved. The voice of his
constituents and election prospects may have been factors also
because the agrarian sections of the nation were becoming increasingly militant in their support of this type of legislation.[22] In
1926 three farm relief bills were reported for consideration by
the House Agriculture Committee. Rainey actively supported the
McNary-Haugen version of equality for agriculture.

During floor debate on the farm problem, Rainey defended the
revamped Peek bill as the best of the three measures presented.
He objected to the Capper-Tincher bill, the administration-
sponsored measure, because it would merely permit further farm
indebtedness through liberalization of credit facilities. He cast
aside the Aswell bill for an improved cooperative marketing system
as insufficient because it did not adequately improve the status
quo. In contrast, he argued, the Haugen bill would furnish
"immediate relief," provide a system for world distribution of
farm surpluses, and give the farmer the benefit of the tariff
protection now enjoyed by industry. He personally expressed a
preference for tariff reduction in order to increase the purchasing
power of farm products, but he realized this was not possible under
the Coolidge administration. The urgency of the farmers' plight,
he said, commanded that he help the Republicans keep their promises
and make their tariff achieve farm protection.[23]

The shift in Rainey's position became an issue in the floor
debate. Democrat Claude Hudspeth of Texas contrasted the change in
models from 1924 to 1926 regarding the Haugen bill. The Texan
failed to see how "this distinguished low tariff advocate" could
swallow the bill's 100 percent tariff "without grease or wry face."
A few days later, Rainey defended his new position on the basis of
expediency. He asserted that the prospect of downward tariff
revision three years hence, when the Democrats could control the
legislature and the executive, was too distant from the farmers'
immediate need. According to Rainey, the objectionable features in
the bill of two years before had been removed from the legislation
now under consideration. In closing debate on the measure, Rainey
portrayed the bleakness of the farmers' future unless this first
step in the direction of a logical and efficient world marketing
procedure was adopted. He concluded with a plea to urban representatives that they have a vision sufficient to grasp the farmers'

problem as their difficulty to. Rainey voted aye on the passage
of the bill, but it was rejected 212 to 167. The *Prairie Farmer*
report of the proceedings noted Rainey's "especially effective work"
in behalf of the second Haugen bill.[24] Unquestionably Rainey's new
allegiance to McNary-Haugenism contributed to an 8,000-vote majority
in his 1926 re-election.

Given the importance of the issue, it is understandable why a
second defeat for the McNary proposal did not stifle support for the
measure. Renewed efforts were made in the second session of the
Sixty-ninth Congress to pass another version of the bill. Early in
the session, Rainey wrote that the opposition was comprised of "the
great financial interests, the metropolitan newspapers and the
industrial east, a formidable combination indeed." Rainey did his
part to break down this resistance. He urged George E. Brennan,
Democratic party boss in Illinois, to use his influence with New
York's Governor Alfred E. Smith to get the Tammany delegation to
support the bill and to get a united Chicago Democratic delegation
for the bill. Rainey was sure Brennan could appreciate the
advantages of such a move for the 1928 election campaign. If
Coolidge vetoed the bill, he wrote, "God help the Republican party
in 1928." The representative of the twentieth Illinois district
again provided vocal support of the bill during the floor debate.
In the time allotted to him on the final day of debate, Rainey
criticized the substitute bills as being "drafted, supported, and
suggested by the recognized enemies of real farm relief." In
defending the equalization fee, he pointed out that a saving clause
would keep the other features of the bill intact if the fee were
declared unconstitutional. Rainey voted with the majority in
passing the bill. The roll call showed 214 yea and 178 nay.[25] The
elation upon the bill's passage was short-lived because President
Coolidge administered a veto after the Senate had agreed upon the
House version of a general relief bill for agriculture.

In the aftermath of the bill's rejection, Rainey continued to
be among those interested in the economic plight of agriculture.
In behalf of the Executive Committee of Twenty-two of the North
Central States Agricultural Conference, George N. Peek expressed
appreciation for Rainey's support and offered his assistance if
Rainey's agricultural record were ever questioned. He also sought
advice on the course the McNary-Haugen proponents should now follow.
Since there were insufficient votes to pass the bill over the veto,
the only recourse seemed to be to try again next session. Also, the
Rainey bill employing a customs scrip was still available. Charles L.
Stewart, chief of agricultural economics at the University of Illinois,
was the author of a farm relief scheme known as an export debenture.
He corresponded with Rainey about the similarity of the tariff rebate
system provided in their two proposals. The legal technicalities
and constitutionality of such a scheme were also discussed.[26] The
farm problem remained the single most important legislative issue
facing the lawmakers.

During the Seventieth Congress another effort was made to pass
a McNary-Haugen bill. During the summer preceding that Congress,
Rainey delivered a series of lectures on the bill to farm bureau

gatherings in Indiana. The chief subject of criticism was the
President's veto. When Congress convened in December, 1927, the
Peek plan was again before Congress, and with a minimum of debate,
the measure was approved in both Houses. Again President Coolidge
vetoed it, using much the same argument. While the principles of
McNary-Haugen were never enacted, the campaign may have helped
prepare the business community for the New Deal legislation of
the 1930s.[27]   For the time being the doctrine of laissez-faire
was once more triumphant and the farm problem remained unsolved.

Presidential candidate Herbert Hoover had made it known that
McNary-Haugenism did not represent his solution to the farm problem.
During the 1928 campaign, he had promised to call Congress into
special session to develop a sane program of farm relief.   The
legislature responded with the administration-drawn Agricultural
Marketing Act of June 15, 1929, which provided for a nonpartisan
federal farm board and created a revolving fund to be made
available to agricultural marketing cooperatives. Participation in
the program was voluntary, and thus Hoover believed it would not
undermine the initiative of the individual farmer. The government
was not to become involved in any scheme of price control, but it
would assist in the stabilization of farm prices through the
application of business principles.[28]   Congressman Rainey took no
part in the activities surrounding the formation of the federal
farm board, although he later became a frequent critic of its
practices. During the special session of 1929, he devoted his
energies to the tariff legislation then under consideration.

As a twin attack upon low farm income, candidate Hoover had
also promised relief through an upward revision of the tariff
rates on agricultural products. Congress was called into special
session to redeem this promise as well. Once assembled, the
national legislature did not restrict its tariff tampering to basic
farm commodities. In writing to Governor-elect Franklin D.
Roosevelt about the approaching tariff revision, Rainey predicted
that it would be a stiff revision upward. It would thus provide
Democrats with an excellent issue in 1930, he wrote, because the
results would be disastrous to American foreign and domestic
interests. In a press statement just before the convening of
Congress, Rainey pointed out that because of the Constitutional
provision "a representative [rather than a Senator] speaks first,
and most emphatically, whenever taxation is the discussion's theme."
Since 1924 the general Democratic opposition to protective tariffs
had lessened considerably. In 1928 the platform statement had been
similar in its ambiguity to the Republican pronouncement.[29]   Not to
be counted among the backsliders, Rainey let it be known that he
intended to capitalize on the issue.

Through the press and the *Congressional Record*, the Illinoisan
voiced his opposition to what became known as the Hawley-Smoot or
Grundy tariff. During the legislative hearings, Rainey was
unsympathetic to the entreaties of industry for greater protection.
Once the bill was shaped, the minority member held two press
interviews on the same day in order to set forth his opposition.
This low tariff advocate believed it would cost the farmers of the

nation more than $400,000,000, provide no relief whatever for the
basic farm products, and only increase the cost of living to the
farmer as well as the general consumer. A few days later during
House debate, Rainey charged that this measure was the worst of the
more than thirty tariff bills formulated since 1787. He described
it as "a monstrosity without parallel, indefensible in nearly every
paragraph." True Democrats, he said, were opposed to the iniquities
and outrages which were committed in this bill for the special
interests. Governor Roosevelt was pleased with Rainey's attack and
suggested that the tariff would become a major issue in the 1930
off-year elections.[30] In an hour and forty-five minute address,
Rainey had set the pattern for the opposition.

Rainey and Cordell Hull of Tennessee comprised the principal
challenge to the measure. In the limited time available for debate,
Rainey purported to speak for the consumers of the United States.
Farm relief, he told the House, was merely "a subterfuge in order
to make it possible to impose this tremendous burden upon the
consumers of this country in the interest of manufacturing firms
who distribute these large dividends." The following day he
concluded his opposition in this fashion: "If they [the Senate]
make it [the bill] any worse than it is, God help the country: and
if they leave it like it is, God help the Republican Party." In
extended remarks, Rainey added the watch schedule to the list of
damnable increases and expressed the fear that the bill would induce
tariff retaliation. In the final roll call, Rainey was among the
minority of 147 who voted nay. So far as Rainey was concerned, the
major issue against the Republicans was established. He had a
controversy with which he felt comfortable when presenting it to
his constituents. Technically Congress remained in session until
November 22, 1929, while the Senate considered the tariff proposal.
For House members there were lengthy recesses, and Rainey virtually
abandoned the legislative halls in favor of carrying the fight
against the tariff into his district. In a typical interview for
the *Illinois State Register*, he ridiculed the tariff bill as a farm
relief measure. It would, he said, only relieve the farmer of his
profits if there were any. He castigated the Hoover administration
for its failure to aid the farm population. The tariff bill under
consideration, he declared, would "push the farmers along the road
to the economic condition of the peasant farmers of Europe."[31] After
this type of precampaign rhetoric, it was time to return to legislative duties at the regular December session.

During the second session of the Seventieth Congress, Rainey
continued his opposition to the Hawley-Smoot bill. He complied with
a request from the editor of *Prairie Farmer* for a short statement on
why the pending bill would not be beneficial. In the article he
wrote that the bill should be vetoed because Congress had violated
its instructions and exceeded the advice of the President. The end
product, Rainey indicated, was "the most unconscionable tariff bill
any nation ever even contemplated." It certainly would not be in
the interests of farmers generally because representatives of every
farm organization signed a statement condemning the bill. When the
Senate completed action on its version of the legislation, it

differed from that of the House in two important respects. A
Democratic-Insurgent Republican coalition succeeded in adding
amendments which incorporated the previously defeated export
debenture plan for farm relief and which changed the procedure
so that Congress rather than the President could act upon
recommendations of the Tariff Commission. These features were
unacceptable to the administration, and Hoover succeeded in having
both provisions eliminated during the conference committee's
deliberations. The only matter left was disagreement over
schedules. In House debate over the conference report, Rainey
argued against it because the conferees had gone through both
bills and had picked the higher rate whenever there was disagreement. If business organizations had prospered under the previous
legislation, he argued, why help them further "by this artificial
method in their effort to weld the shackles of slavery upon the
consumers of the country?" During consideration of individual
amendments, Rainey urged that from the standpoint of the conservation of natural resources (forests in this case) the tariff bill
ought not to hamper certain imports unnecessarily. He was
successful in getting the House to recede from its position and
concur in Senate amendments providing free wood pulp, free lumber,
and duty reductions on other wood products.[32] At final passage
Rainey voted with the Democratic minority in opposing the bill.
By mid-June, 1930, President Hoover signed into law the second
component of his farm relief package, a tariff act calling for
the highest rates in the nation's history.

With each passing month, Rainey became more disillusioned
with the administration's marketing and tariff legislation as
solutions to agriculture's plight, and he began pressing for
expanded credit facilities for farmers. From the House floor,
he endeavored to alert his colleagues to the need for relief for
farm mortgages. Failing in this effort, he enlisted the aid of
Henry B. Steagall of Alabama, now chairman of the House Committee
on Banking following Democratic organization of the lower chamber.
The Rainey suggestions received a sympathetic hearing and were
merged with the administration's omnibus proposals for relieving
credit stringencies on the international as well as the domestic
scene. On January 23, 1932, President Hoover signed into law a
measure adding $125,000,000 to the capital of the federal land
bank program.[33] While another component of farm relief had been
enacted, farm representatives in general and Rainey in particular
were still dissatisfied with the administration's attack upon the
farm problem.

By 1932 it was evident that the inability of the major farm
organizations to agree upon a single plan for agricultural relief
had delayed successful legislation. The Farm Bureau sought parity
through the McNary-Haugen program. The Grange favored the export-
debenture plan of Charles L. Stewart. The Farmers' Union meanwhile
supported the cost of production scheme of its president, John
Simpson. In a desperate effort to provide some assistance, the
features of each of these programs were combined in the McNary-
Fulmer bill. It provided that the Federal Farm Board could

implement any of these relief schemes with a particular commodity
if the conditions warranted. This omnibus collection of diverse
relief concepts was known as the "three-headed monster." By early
summer it became obvious that this conglomerate could not receive
legislative approval.[34] Agricultural supporters began searching
for an emergency measure which could be enacted as a temporary
stopgap until long-range legislation could be developed.

Now majority leader of the Democrats in the House, Rainey
provided the legislative outlet for this emergency proposal. In
June, 1932, he introduced a farm bill with provisions limited to
wheat, hogs, and cotton. The legislation had been prepared at the
request of Earl Smith, president of the Illinois Agricultural
Association, and had been drafted by Fred Lee, legislative
consultant for the McNary-Haugen bills. Such agriculturalists as
George N. Peek, Chester Davis, Alexander Legge, Clifford Gregory,
and Milburn L. Wilson were consulted. The measure instructed the
Secretary of Agriculture to determine the percentage of the 1933
crop needed for home consumption, and provided bonus payments on
wheat, hogs, and cotton. These amounts were to be paid on the
domestic percentage of each producer's crop, with the money secured
by an excise tax of like amount on the commodities when processed.
There were no production controls in the bill. The proposal received
enthusiastic Farm Bureau support, that organization's first support
of an excise tax and benefit payments instead of the equalization fee
plan.[35] The intent of the Rainey bill was to provide one-year
assistance until a permanent measure could be adopted for agricultural relief.

The bill was referred to the House Committee on Agriculture.
In its deliberations, the committee was practically unanimous in
asserting that the plan would be effective in raising the prices of
wheat, hogs, and cotton. Committee members thought it advisable to
add numerous other farm commodities to the bill. Rainey realized
the impossibility of the bill's being recommended without its
workability being seriously impaired by amendments. He induced
Republican Senator Peter Norbeck of South Dakota to introduce a
companion bill in the Senate where it might avoid the debasing
amendments. The bill was reported from the Senate Committee on
Agriculture and Forestry with only minor amendments, and approved
in the Senate by voice vote almost without debate. The bill's
supporters pressed for immediate action in the House. The
Agriculture Committee, by a 9 to 4 vote, reported the bill unchanged
and recommended passage. Under House rules, no bill could be
brought up for immediate action without a special order from the
Rules Committee. Rainey, with the backing of the downstate Illinois
delegation, tried to get approval for a special order, but without
success. In the meantime, the life of the bill was threatened in
the Senate. Republican Senator Hiram Bingham of Connecticut, an
administration supporter, indicated a desire to obtain the Senate
floor in order to recall the Norbeck bill from the House and move
for a reconsideration. This effort was temporarily blocked by
Senator George W. Norris, who was filibustering against the waterpower trust. The House farm bloc was unable to convince Speaker

Garner and the Rules Committee to allow immediate consideration
of the bill. In the Senate, since no House action was forthcoming,
Norris relinquished the floor. Bingham made his motion to reconsider, and by a roll call vote of 30 to 25, it prevailed.[36]   All
farm relief bills were effectively killed for this session.

The assessment of responsibility for the defeat of the first
Rainey-Norbeck farm relief bill had political implications. For
some, the blame lay primarily on the President because it was
generally understood that Bingham's move to reconsider was taken
at the request of the White House. Reportedly, it was "one more
big, black mark against President Hoover in the minds of farm
leaders." Clifford Gregory attributed the defeat to the refusal
of the Speaker, John Nance Garner, to permit a special rule
bringing the bill to a vote. In Farm Bureau circles, Garner's
refusal was attributed to a desire to postpone agricultural
legislation until the incoming Democratic administration could
obtain credit for it. In assessing responsibility, Rainey
assigned the defeat to Senate Republicans and charged Garner only
with delay.[37]   Adherents of both parties could place the blame on
the other. It seems evident that the bill was eventually doomed
to failure somewhere along the line. Both Republican and Democratic elements contributed to its defeat.

The congressman who initiated the legislative turmoil was
heralded as a hero and his legislation served as a foundation
stone for later measures. In an address at the Greene County Farm
Bureau's annual meeting, Earl Smith complimented Rainey for his
wise and able leadership in advancing the cause of agriculture.
George N. Peek praised the majority leader for putting country
above party by striving for a practical solution rather than
allowing farmers to suffer with resultant political benefits to
the Democratic party. It is undetermined whether the Rainey-
Norbeck bill was actually developed for use in the Roosevelt
campaign, but it is certain that the bill became the basis for
future farm legislation. The Rainey measure represents a transition in farm legislation to the ideas embodied in the first New
Deal agricultural program.[38]   The leaders of many farm organizations supported Franklin D. Roosevelt in the November election
because they believed that he favored similar agricultural relief.

The resounding Democratic election victory seemed to augur
well for farm relief legislation. During summer and fall, 1932,
unrest among farmers was exhibited in milk strikes and farm
holiday movements. Something had to be done to alleviate the
situation. In the domestic allotment plan, as advanced in the
Rainey-Norbeck bill, *Business Week* saw the best opportunity to
resolve the agrarian unrest in the Midwest, the best program to
enlist the support of business and industrial interests, and the
best fulfillment of Roosevelt's campaign specifications for farm
relief. Subsequent national farm meetings used the Rainey bill as
a point of departure for recommending programs of agricultural
relief. The *Prairie Farmer* was sure a perfected Rainey-Norbeck
measure would pass Congress during the short session. Hopefully
it would be a significant step toward equalizing farm and industrial

prices. Rainey assured the Farm Bureau organizations that an
emergency farm relief bill would be introduced the first day of
the session and would be called up for floor debate at the
earliest opportunity under a special rule. He did not expect
Hoover to veto the bill. He also indicated that Roosevelt would
lend his support to the allotment plan.[39] Rainey preferred not
to delay until the next session, even though Hoover and the
Republicans might get some credit for the passage of the measure.

The emergency farm relief bill was placed on the agenda for
the lame-duck session. The first Rainey-Norbeck bill underwent
considerable metamorphosis. A news story commenting on the new
proposal credited Rainey and Chairman Marvin Jones from Texas of
the House Agriculture Committee with putting the bill into final
shape after consulting with farm leaders and the President-elect.
At Roosevelt's suggestion, the commodity list was expanded to
include tobacco. Jones contributed the concept of county and
community participation in the program's administration. In
addition to these modifications, the revised bill went beyond the
original in two important respects. It incorporated the parity
price idea, with 1900 to 1914 as the base period, in an attempt
to determine fair exchange value rather than cost of production.
It also included acreage and production controls. Such an effort
to control surplus agricultural production had heretofore been
anathema to the major farm organizations and their legislative
supporters. George Peek extended his support to the emergency
measure, although he warned against inclusion of too many farm
commodities and the imposition of acreage restrictions and
production controls.[40] The revamped measure passed the House of
Representatives by a sizable majority—203 to 151. Despite the
speed in the House, the bill languished in the Senate and never
came to a vote, but a program of farm relief based along these
lines carried over to the special session of Congress convened in
March, 1933.

For the remainder of his career, Rainey would view the plight
of agriculture from the perspective of the Speaker's chair. Thus
the Illinoisan's role was changed from proponent and proposer to
expediter and explainer. In order to thwart the possibility of
another farm strike, the Department of Agriculture, various farm
organization representatives, and assorted "brain trusters" were
working on a redraft of the farm bill. Their proposal sought to
achieve agricultural equality by working toward the restoration
of parity prices. This was to be done by limiting production and
eliminating surpluses, by making direct payments to farmers who
participated in the production control programs, and by working out
voluntary agreements with processors and distributors of farm
commodities in order to get higher prices for farmers and eliminate
marketing abuses. The program was to be financed by processing
taxes. The proposal left wide discretionary powers to the
Secretary of Agriculture. While the new suggestions retained
vestiges of the second Rainey-Norbeck bill, it is difficult to
determine precise lineage. On March 16, 1933, President Roosevelt
recommended this proposal to Congress. Under the aegis of Illinois'

leading farmer-political figure, the farm bill had smooth sailing
in the House under a rigorous gag rule which limited debate to
four hours and forbade amendments. It passed on March 22 by a vote
of 315 to 98. After the Senate passage of the measure by an
equally lopsided margin, Rainey conferred with Secretary of Agriculture Henry A. Wallace about the appointment of the conferees
who would comprise the conference committee. Certain Senate
features were deleted from the measure, and the result was a
domestic allotment program with controlled inflationary provisions.
It was a cautious and temperate response to the needs of agriculture.[41] In mid-May, the President signed the first Agriculture
Adjustment Act (AAA), the husbandman's Magna Charta.

During summer and fall, 1933, Speaker Rainey especially
interested himself in the effective operation of the New Deal program as it related to farmers. The staunch administration supporter
embarked on a personal campaign to uphold and explain the entire
Roosevelt program to farmers throughout the nation. In order to
deliver his message at the grass roots, he completed a 12,000-mile
airplane tour of the country. At the conclusion of this extensive
crusade, he emphatically denied Republican assertions that there
was formidable unrest in the farm belt. Independent analyses
confirmed his judgment. *Time* noted that the arrival of the first
AAA checks in the corn belt was like "a gentle, pervasive rain,
damping the prairie fire of farmers' anger," while *Fortune* observed
that "Bryans [those demanding silver inflation] are not bred by
benefits."[42] The effect of the first AAA was to supply a soothing
sedative to agrarian discontent.

The second session of the Seventy-third Congress (January 3
to June 18, 1934) was not especially noteworthy for new agricultural laws. Most remarkable of the proposals offered was the
Frazier-Lemke farm mortgage bill. It provided that the federal
government buy all farm mortgages and issue noninterest-bearing
Treasury notes in exchange. Critics of the proposal argued that it
was highly inflationary. President Roosevelt let Speaker Rainey
know that "if this type of legislation passes, the responsibility
for wrecking recovery will be squarely on the Congress." Administration forces were able to thwart a discharge petition which would
have brought the bill to the House floor, and it died on the House
calendar in the closing days of the session. Rainey, as well as
the President, was content to let the Agricultural Adjustment
Administration do its work. In a nationwide radio broadcast after
one year of AAA, he especially praised its efficiency in bringing
relief to drought stricken areas.[43]

During the course of Rainey's involvement with the farm problem, his attention covered the whole spectrum of concerns, including
economic interest, policy formulation, enabling legislation, and
bureaucratic administration. The complexities of the agrarian
difficulties in the 1920s and 1930s constituted a school of hard
knocks for an experienced politician. As Rainey earned positions
of leadership within the party and the Congress, the responsibility
for providing guidance and direction became very burdensome.
Overall, his contributions were twofold—bringing the farmers'

plight into political focus and providing a clear understanding of the congressional legislative process. Although occasionally frustrated in these areas, there was a constant push for constructive reform which climaxed in the first Agricultural Adjustment Act. His contributions were welcomed by his local and national constituencies. Greene County's farmers appreciated his friendship and support, while the agriculturalists of Illinois and the nation enjoyed an outstanding champion in the highest councils of the nation.[44] Rainey's experiences with the farmers' problems provide a microcosm of the additional perplexities he endured—first as majority leader of the Democrats and then as Speaker of the House of Representatives.

NOTES

1. *Patriot*, March 25, 1909, 1:4; HTR to Bower, [Washington], Jan. 18, 1930, RP; Hardy, "'Mr. Speaker' as the Country Squire," 1.

2. *Patriot*, July 17, 1919, 1:1, and Oct. 30, 1919, 1:1-2; HTR to Clifford V. Gregory, [Washington], [April 22, 1922], RP, McNary-Haugen file (hereafter cited as RP, McNH).

3. History of the Greene County Farm Bureau on its twenty-fifty anniversary in *Gazette*, Jan. 15, 1943, 3:2.

4. *Gazette*, March 3, 1920, 1:5; *Greene County Farm Bureau [Bulletin]*, Oct. 20, 1924, 1; *Gazette*, Sept. 21, 1927, 1:1 and 1:6.

5. Carl R. Woodward, "Woodrow Wilson's Agricultural Philosophy," 129-142; Vrooman to HTR, Bloomington, Ill., July 31, 1914, RP; Ross E. Paulson, *Radicalism and Reform: The Vrooman Family and American Social Thought, 1837-1937*, 216-227.

6. *Patriot*, Oct. 28, 1914, 1:1-2, and Dec. 24, 1914, 1:6; *Gazette*, Dec. 30, 1914, 1:1, and Oct. 27, 1915, 1:1; Dunne to HTR, Springfield, March (unk.) 1915, RP; editorial, "Investigate It," *Patriot*, Jan. 7, 1915, 4:1; editorial, "Rainey's 'Butting In,'" *Gazette*, Nov. 3, 1915, 1:2.

7. Committee of Fifteen correspondence, reports, and programs may be found in University of Illinois Archives, Agriculture, Dean's Office, Subject File, 1907-64, Committee: Illinois Agricultural Association, Series No. 8/1/2 Box 15, and subcommittee reports in University Archives, Agriculture, Dean's Office, Herbert W. Mumford Papers, 1919-38, Series No. 8/1/22, Box 1, Agricultural Policy, Illinois, 1922-24; Eugene Davenport, "Twenty-Five Years Hence in Illinois," 15, 20.

8. Gilbert C. Fite, *George N. Peek and the Fight for Farm Parity*, 38-94; Orville M. Kile, *The Farm Bureau through Three Decades*, 126-135.

9. HTR to Thompson, Washington, March 12, 1924, RP, McNH file.

10. HTR to George H. Smith, [Washington], March 28, 1924, RP, McNH; HTR to Sinclair, [Washington], March 28, 1924, RP, McNH.

11. Thompson to HTR, Chicago, March 31, 1924, and HTR to Thompson, Washington, April 9, 1924. Both letters may conveniently be seen in *CR*, 68:1 (April 9, 1924), 5982-86, 5988-92.

12. See RP, McNH, for April, 1924; Fite, *George N. Peek*, 87.

13. Editorial clipping, "Congressman Rainey Sandbags the McNary-Haugen Bill" from *Modern Miller* sent to HTR by Edward H. Causey, Chicago, March 24, 1924; T. E. Burner to HTR, Carthage, March 31, 1924, RP, McNH.

14. *Illinois Agricultural Association Record* (hereafter *IAA Record*), II (April 21, 1924), 3; (May 5), 8.

15. Phillips to HTR, Carrollton, April 24, 1924, RP, McNH.

16. HTR to J. E. Edwards, [Washington], April 12, 1924; Aswell to HTR, Washington, April 17, 1924; HTR to Gregory, [Washington], April 22, 1924; Miller to HTR, Mt. Sterling, April 29, 1924, all in RP, McNH.

17. "Suggested Paragraphs for the Minority Report," RP, McNH-IAA; *CR*, 68:1 (March 23, 1924), 9331-38; (May 24), 9442-46; (May 30), 9958-59; (May 31), 10022-24.

18. Sources for HTR's bill have been previously cited; Stewart to HTR, Urbana, June 22, 1927, RP; HTR to Clifford V. Gregory, [Washington], May 26, 1924, RP, McNH; *Prairie Farmer*, XCVI (May 31, 1924), 7.

19. *Prairie Farmer*, XCVI (May 10, 1924), 8, and (June 14), 8; *IAA Record*, II (June 21, 1924), 2, map on 5-6; Fite, *George N. Peek*, 86-87.

20. Editorial, "Congressman Rainey Has a Backbone," *Patriot*, April 3, 1924, 4:1; Smith to HTR, Pekin, April 7, 1924, RP, McNH. For general discussion of the dilemma consult Lewis A. Dexter, "The Representative and His District," 2-13.

21. Mark Sullivan, "The Waning Influence of the Farmer," 659. The best summary of rural-urban conflict may be found in James H. Shideler, "*Flappers and Philosophers*, and Farmers," 283-299.

22. John D. Black, "The McNary-Haugen Movement," 405-427.

23. *CR*, 69:1 (May 10, 1926), 9126, 9132-34; (May 11), 9223-25.

24. *CR*, 69:1 (May 13, 1926), 9401-9404; (May 18), 9654-55; (May 20), 9761-65; vote on (May 21), 9862-63; *Prairie Farmer*, XCVIII (May 22, 1926), 8.

25. HTR to James McNabb, Washington, Dec. 29, 1926, as printed in *Gazette*, Jan. 5, 1927, 1:4; HTR to Brennan, Washington, Feb. 7, 1927, RP; *CR*, 69:2 (Feb. 17, 1927), 4047-49, vote on 4099.

26. Peek to HTR, Chicago, April 29, 1927; Stewart to HTR, Urbana, June 22, 1927, RP.

27. HTR to W. H. Settle (Indiana Farm Bureau Federation), Carrollton, June 28, 1927, RP; Donald R. McCoy, *Calvin Coolidge:*

The Quiet President, 326-328; John P. Gleason, "The Attitude of the Business Community toward Agriculture during the McNary-Haugen Period," 127-138.

28. Albert U. Romasco, *The Poverty of Abundance*, 21-22, 106-114.

29. HTR to FDR, Washington, Dec. 15, 1928, Roosevelt Papers, Illinois: 1932 Campaign, Pre-Convention; *Gazette*, April 10, 1929, 1:3; Burner, *Politics of Provincialism*, 168.

30. New York *Times*, May 8, 1929, 21:2 and 23:4-5, *CR*, 71:1 (May 11, 1929), 1143-50; FDR to HTR, Warm Springs, Ga., May 20, 1929, RP.

31. *CR*, 71:1 (May 27, 1929), 2018-22; (May 28), 2099-2100; vote on 2106; extended remarks under (May 31), 2215-2216; *Illinois State Register*, Aug. 24, 1929, 2:1-2.

32. Clifford V. Gregory to HTR, Chicago, April 24, 1930, RP; HTR, "Tariff Law Should Be Vetoed," *Prairie Farmer*, CII (May 10, 1930), 5; *CR*, 71:2 (May 1, 1930), 8146-49; (May 2), 8222, 8236-39.

33. *CR*, 71:2 (June 21, 1930), 11443-47; HTR to Steagall, [Washington], Dec. 22, 1931, RP, "Federal Reserve Land Banks" file; Romasco, *Poverty of Abundance*, 190.

34. Christiana McFadyen Campbell, *The Farm Bureau and the New Deal*, 49; Kile, *The Farm Bureau*, 182; Columbia Oral History Memoir of Milburn L. Wilson, IV, 651-652.

35. H.R. 12649, *CR*, 72:1 (June 15, 1932), 13118; features of the bill summarized by Clifford V. Gregory, "The American Farm Bureau Federation and the AAA," 155; Kile, *The Farm Bureau*, 182.

36. For the most complete chronicle of the legislative maneuverings, see "Brief Story of the Rainey-Norbeck Bill," *IAA Record*, X (Aug., 1932), 5.

37. Edwin G. Nourse, *et al.*, *Three Years of the Agricultural Adjustment Administration*, 14, n. 8; Kile, *Farm Bureau*, 183; Gregory, "American Farm Bureau Federation," 155; Campbell, *The Farm Bureau and the New Deal*, 49; Wilson Oral Memoir, IV, 692-693; HTR to Dr. Edwin S. Carr, Carrollton, Aug. 22, 1932, RP, "Farm Relief Bill-Earl Smith" file.

38. *Greene County Farm Bureau News Letter*, III (Aug., 1932), 4; George N. Peek, *Why Quit Our Own*, 51; Gertrude Slichter, "Political Backgrounds of New Deal Agricultural Policy" (M.A. thesis), 76; Gregory, "American Farm Bureau Federation," 155; Wilson Oral Memoir, IV, 687, 689.

39. John L. Shover, "The Farmers' Holiday Association Strike of 1932," 196-203; *Business Week*, Sept. 24, 1932, 15-16; *Prairie Farmer*, CIV (Nov. 12, 1932), 6; HTR to Earl Smith, [Washington], Nov. 23, 1932, RP, "Farm Relief Bill-Earl Smith" file.

40. New York *Times*, Nov. 24, 1932, 9:1; "Domestic Allotment

Plan Principles," *IAA Record*, X (Nov., 1932), 6; Columbia Oral
History Memoir of Marvin Jones, III, 465; copy of memo from Peek
to Jones dated Jan. 2, 1933, RP, "Farm Relief in 1933" file.

41. John L. Shover, "Populism in the 1930's: The Battle for
the AAA," 23-24.

42. New York *Times*, Nov. 2, 1933, 22:3-4; "Millions of Bullfrogs," 16; "Bryan! Bryan!! Bryan!!! Bryan!!!!," 126.

43. Radiograms between Stephen Early and Roosevelt in April,
1934, as reproduced by Roosevelt (ed.), *F.D.R.*, 396-398; speech
printed in *CR*, 73:2 (June 9, 1934), 10999-11000.

44. Tribute in *Greene County Farm Bureau News Letter*, V
(Aug., 1934), 1; "Speaker Rainey Mourned," 4.

9
Majority Leader of the Democrats

How quickly political fortunes may change! The congressional
career of Henry Thomas Rainey illustrates the caprice of Dame
Politics in assigning leadership positions to her patrons.
Following Rainey's return to Congress in 1923, the loss of
seniority had relegated him near the bottom rung in congressional
perquisites. In addition, the philosophical conservatism of his
Democratic colleagues had consigned him to the role of maverick
among the rank-and-file members. Newspaper correspondents dubbed
Henry T. "the La Follette of the Democrats" because of his
progressive political independence. By the end of the 1920s,
Rainey's re-election successes had enabled him to reacquire
sufficient seniority so that the leadership potential exhibited
during the Wilson administration was again utilized. His
activities in behalf of agricultural relief gave promise of his
performance level. The Democratic election victory of 1930
catapulted the veteran Illinois legislator into the position of
majority leader. He acted in this capacity from December, 1931,
until March, 1933. His effective service in this leadership role
enabled him to secure the highest position within the gift of his
colleagues, the Speakership of the House of Representatives. In
a sudden about-face, Rainey moved from back-bencher to party
counselor.

The Seventy-second Congress (1931-33) was the first to be
confronted fully with the problems arising from the Great Depression.
In addition to the normal trials and tribulations of leadership, the
Democratic hierarchy in the House was faced with two conflicting
and yet complementary forces. One factor was the urgent need for
bipartisan cooperation in resolving the economic difficulties of
the nation. The other was the partisan advantage to be gained in
the subsequent presidential election by the continuance or
accentuation of the depression. Rainey and his cohorts endeavored
to navigate between the Scylla of national interest and the
Charybdis of party gain.[1] During this period of economic crisis,
Illinois' senior Democratic congressman sought to guide his party
along lines which would mitigate the effects of the depression and
yet assure the party's success in the 1932 presidential election.

Increased legislative responsibilities for Rainey were contingent upon the outcome of the off-year elections in November, 1930.
Political prognosticators were uncertain whether the party in power
would suffer a major setback due to the depression and other issues.

While it was generally conceded that there would be Democratic
gains in the House, it was not certain whether they could capture
the fifty-four seats necessary for majority status. The election
returns in gubernatorial and senatorial races indicated that the
Democrats had made significant gains, but the outcome in the House
of Representatives was still in doubt. Apparently the people had
voted to take legislative power from the Republicans without giving
it to the Democrats because neither major party had clear control.
Representative Paul J. Kvale, Farmer-Laborite from Minnesota, was
thought to hold the key to the organization of the lower chamber.[2]
The lengthy interval between the election and the assumption of
office in December, 1931, could alter the party alignment because
of deaths, resignations, contests, and special elections.

As the party out of power, the Democrats had to proceed under
the presumption that they would assume control. Thus, there was a
distinct possibility that the 1930 election results would ultimately
enhance Rainey's influence within the party. As early as July, 1927,
Rainey had maneuvered to a position to succeed Finis J. Garrett of
Tennessee as minority leader if Garrett resigned to make a bid for
a Senate seat. Although Garrett did not return to the following
Congress, Rainey could not dispute successfully Texan John Nance
Garner's claim to the minority leadership post. Among the
victorious senatorial candidates in 1930, however, was James Hamilton
Lewis (senator from Illinois between 1913 and 1919), who asked
permission to arrange support for Rainey as a candidate for Speaker
in the Seventy-second Congress. J. Ham, as the pink-whiskered
senator was known, stated that it was senseless to rule out Rainey
for that position merely because of one election defeat. The
Illinois senator feared the cry of "the South in the saddle" if the
position went to a southerner. Even worse, he wrote, would be a
revival of the old slogan: Texas—everything for Texas. Lewis
anticipated that all western Democrats and western liberals (the
Republican insurgents from Wisconsin and Minnesota) would support
Rainey for the Speakership. Lewis was also legitimately concerned
about the impact of House organization upon the 1932 elections.[3]

Rainey replied that he greatly appreciated the endorsement for
a higher position and the offer of assistance. In a lengthy letter,
he outlined his appraisal of the situation. He wrote that he would
be delighted if the honor suggested were conferred upon him, but he
would be still more pleased by the fact that it would give him a
wider opportunity for service to the party and to the country.
Rainey suggested that Lewis seek aid from the Tammany organization
since the New Yorkers were not particularly wedded to the South.
Rainey also indicated individual Republicans who might be inclined
to lend support to his candidacy. Rainey feared that the existing
House leadership did not care to control the next session, but he
thought such control essential as a stepping stone to election
success in 1932. Having a chance to put forth a constructive program
would be beneficial, he thought, in securing complete control of
both Houses and the presidency. He hoped to duplicate the 1910 to 1912
pattern in which Champ Clark's success during his first term as
Speaker contributed to the election of Woodrow Wilson. Rainey closed

with the suggestion that it would not be proper for him to
inaugurate a movement for the Speakership, but that Lewis's
organization of support would have a powerful influence in
determining the party's choice.[4] Rainey was thus receptive to
the idea of advancement.

Even though actual control of Congress was still in doubt,
the behind-the-scenes maneuvering within the Democratic party
proceeded. Rainey received a letter from the Texas delegation
urging his endorsement and cooperation in making John N. Garner
the unanimous choice of the caucus for the Speaker's post. There
is no indication of a deal with Garner, but by early March, 1931,
it was generally assumed that Rainey was slated to be the majority
leader of the next House. Rainey confided to editor V. Y. Dallman
of the Springfield *Illinois State Register* that the fact that the
Speakership, as well as all the important committee chairmanships,
would go to the South made it possible for him to be the next
majority leader. He wrote that he readily preferred that position
since it would provide an opportunity to render more service.
Although there were other candidates for the position, Rainey
dismissed their chances—southern candidates would split the votes
from that area, no southerners would support a Tammany candidate,
and most northerners would favor his selection. He reported the
Illinois Democratic delegation united behind his candidacy for
leader. By April, a recount in a Pennsylvania district had
reversed the Republican majority and the two major parties stood
at 217 each. Thus, Rainey wrote Earl Smith of the Illinois
Agricultural Association, the balance of power lay with the Farmer-
Laborite Kvale. However, chances were good that some vacancies
caused by deaths of Republican members would go to Democratic
candidates for the office.[5] Heightened prospects of Democratic
control increased the scheming.

In the months following the 1930 election, the uncertainties
about party control of the lower chamber became clarified. The
division immediately after the election indicated 218 Republicans,
216 Democrats, and 1 Farmer-Laborite. This nominal Republican
control by a paper-thin margin faded in succeeding months. The
count was so close that organization of the chamber eventually
rested with the party suffering the fewer losses by death of its
elected members during the months before the new Congress met.
There were thirteen deaths in a year's time, more Republicans than
Democrats. In the resulting special elections to fill these
vacancies, more Democrats won than Republicans. It appeared that
Congress would convene with 217 Democrats, 216 Republicans, one
Farmer-Laborite, and one vacancy not to be filled until January,
1932.[6] The people had determined a course of action which gave
the Democrats tenuous control.

Thus, the maneuvering for the majority leadership reached its
crucial phases in November, 1931. The leading southern candidate
and favorite of the Garner forces was John McDuffie of Alabama,
Democratic whip during the preceding session. Other southern
candidates with obvious support were John E. Rankin of Mississippi
and Joseph W. Byrns of Tennessee. Northern candidates, besides

Rainey, were John J. O'Connor of New York and William A. Ayres of
Kansas. On November 23, McDuffie announced his withdrawal from the
race in the interest of party harmony. At that point Rainey claimed
he was certain of 133 out of the 217 Democrats and thus was assured
of the post. On November 25, a special election in Texas gave the
Democrats an outright majority in the lower chamber, with two
vacancies still unfilled. At this point, Rankin withdrew in favor
of Rainey so that a northerner could be selected. The contest was
now virtually narrowed to Rainey and O'Connor. At the Democratic
caucus on December 5, the choice went to Rainey. Opposition to
O'Connor was based principally on his Tammany connections and his
wet stance on prohibition.[7] When Congress organized on December 7,
1931, the Democrats were in control for the first time in twelve
years. Rainey was now in the top echelon of the House Democracy.

The Illinoisan's selection for the second post in the House
caused considerable analytic comment. The local newspaper noted
with pardonable pride that Henry T. "might become floor field
marshall and, like Henry of Navarre, call upon his fellow Democrats
to follow where his white plume [a reference to his lustrous crown
of white hair] shows in battle." The Washington correspondent of
the Kansas City *Star* thought Rainey's progression to a leadership
position was very logical since "Northern Democrats with seniority
are about as hard to find as Southern Republicans." *Time* magazine
attributed Rainey's selection to the influence of Speaker-designate
Garner who induced the southerners to withdraw and who squelched
the O'Connor boom. It was noted that Democratic colleagues labeled
Rainey as a "radical" in his political views because he favored a
low tariff, high surtaxes on the wealthy, no foreign debt moratorium,
government operation of Muscle Shoals, and diplomatic recognition of
Russia. The *Prairie Farmer* was especially pleased to see a farm
bloc supporter and a midwesterner in such a position of influence.
Reportedly, one of the objections to Rainey's candidacy was that "he
talked too much on too many subjects, too often." The *New Republic*'s
editorial writer agreed this was a point well taken, but observed
that his claims were so strong and the alternatives so weak that it
was impossible to sidetrack him. In an editorial *Collier's* wondered
if a man who had been a member of the minority party most of his
career and frequently "a minority of one in that minority" could
adjust to being in a position requiring tact, moderation, and public
restraint.[8] The congressman proposed to demonstrate that the
mixture of tenure and geography which contributed to his elevation
had a foundation in merit as well.

In an exclusive interview for the Chicago *Tribune*, Rainey
described his new role in the legislative chamber. He admitted that
he would no longer be able "to give 'em hell" any time he wanted
because his new responsibility would require him to be "a worker of
compromises and a healer of wounds." Rainey regretted leaving his
role as firebrand and assuming the job of party harmonizer, but he
expected to meet the challenge. A short time after the session was
underway, the New York *Times* noted that "the La Follette of the
Democrats" was adjusting to the job. Whereas he had been known as
a picturesque Illinois farmer whose feelings had been aroused in the

past and whose expressions were more in superlatives than measured phrases, Rainey was becoming accustomed to being the Democratic guide.[9]   At the age of seventy-one years, he was embarked upon a new career in the House of Representatives.

At best the team of Garner and Rainey was a marriage of convenience. Garner believed that Rainey had few qualities of leadership and was too often "loose-jawed." Instead of allowing his chief lieutenant to assume partial control, the new Speaker planned to retain most of the authority normally given to the majority leader. There was a fundamental difference in the principles for which the two men stood. Garner's brand of conservative Democracy did not mesh well with Rainey's liberalism. Their relationship had not been completely harmonious since both possessed strong personalities and aspirations for leadership. During the following session of Congress, their differences would be subordinated in the interest of party and country.[10]   The election of 1930 thus established new leadership in the lower chamber. It also inaugurated a new phase of the political and economic struggle which highlighted the decade.

The first issue which Rainey attacked in the Seventy-second Congress was the tariff. The Hawley-Smoot tariff of 1930 was essentially a product of the predepression mania for prosperity. International economic conditions were greatly altered when tariff matters again were given legislative consideration. The Democratic House reopened the tariff question as one facet of the nation's economic ills. In anticipation of Democratic control, Rainey urged that the party present a strong legislative program to counter the Republican policies. Tariff revision through reciprocal arrangements should be part of that program. In early November, 1931, Rainey outlined that part of a legislative program which would free world commerce from "a hardening of the trade arteries" by a downward revision of the tariff on a reciprocal basis. In a later statement, he repeated that the tariff must be lowered substantially, but only through mutual concessions from other countries. Rainey placed the tariff "foremost" among all the important problems facing the new Congress. His signed article in the New York *Times* indicated an additional urgency in the matter because Great Britain was about to retreat behind an imperial trade barrier. This would effectively close America's best and only free market.[11]   According to Rainey, the only answer was tariff reciprocity.

In the new Congress, Rainey was in a position to present his views forcefully. In addition to his leadership position, he was retained on the Ways and Means Committee. He was now third in rank behind Chairman James W. Collier of Mississippi and Charles R. Crisp of Georgia. By early January, 1932, the committee had prepared a resolution endorsing an international economic conference to explore tariff reductions. In a radio interview, Rainey stoutly denied that the Democrats were setting out to destroy the nation's tariff system, but he emphatically asserted that they were seeking to reduce world trade barriers in a sane, safe, and sensible fashion. In a fifty-minute floor speech, Rainey defended the plan against critics who feared too great cooperation with a conference

in which the League of Nations might be involved. He pointed
out how groundless such fears were because under the Republican
regime (March, 1921—June, 1929) there had been fourteen official
conferences with the League by the United States government,
nineteen additional conferences at which America was semi-
officially represented, and eighty-four occasions when semipublic
organizations in the United States had unofficially participated. He argued that one additional conference beside
these 117 would not alter the United States' relation with the
League of Nations. In concluding debate on the proposal, Rainey
urged that this new avenue of approach be used to accomplish the
freeing of world markets.[12] This resolution and its companion
bill never received the combined blessing of the legislative and
executive branches of government. However, the issue was set for
the 1932 campaign when the Democratic platform included a
reciprocity plank and a call for an international economic conference.

The deteriorating international economic condition also
focused attention upon the war debt situation and the Hoover
moratorium. Ordinarily the House does not become involved in
diplomatic matters, but this issue was an exception since the
question of revenue was involved. In mid-1931 Hoover had sought
congressional approval in advance for his proposal to declare a
one-year postponement on all war-debt payments. Congress was not
then in session, and the President sought support by sending
telegrams to various congressional leaders. Rainey received such
a request but, consistent with his previous objections to reducing
the Italian and French debts, he declined to give his support.
When Congress convened in December, a resolution approving the
postponement of foreign debts for fiscal 1932 was approved overwhelmingly. However, Garner and Rainey succeeded in attaching a
rider which declared in emphatic language that no further
executive concessions on debt arrangements would be sanctioned by
Congress. The President's hands were effectively tied. Rainey
correctly predicted that pressure would be applied again in June
when payments were to be resumed.[13] The Illinoisan steadfastly
refused to consider any outright cancellation of the eleven billion
dollars owed to the United States by foreign nations as part of the
World War I debt.

The question of another moratorium arose before the opening of
the second session of this Congress. Republican Senator William E.
Borah of Idaho suggested that an international conference be convened to review the war debts and their impact upon economic
recovery. Rainey immediately reacted in the negative. As the date
for convening Congress drew near, suggestions about debt revision
were rampant. Rainey held a press conference in which he ridiculed
such ideas because Congress was in no mood to approve them. He did
modify his position slightly by indicating that he would consider
"scaling down" the debt in exchange for tariff adjustments.
Preceding a congressional conference with Hoover on the debt question,
Rainey gave advance warning that he would not sanction a revival of
the World War Debt Funding Commission because it would imply a

policy favoring reduction or cancellation. Following the conference, Rainey's position was unchanged--no cancellation, no
reduction, no discussion. The general impression given the
President was that Congress would be unfavorable to any war debt
revision.[14] The Rainey view was in agreement with that of
President-elect Roosevelt. The incoming administration would
inherit the problem because Hoover was stymied by an unyielding
Congress.

The first of the depression-oriented Congresses was more
concerned with domestic rather than foreign problems. Most of the
time of the national legislature was devoted to balancing the
budget and alleviating the nation's internal economic ills. As
majority leader, Rainey readily assisted Hoover's efforts to
balance the national budget, but he differed with the President on
relief programs. Rainey exercised his prerogative as majority
leader to explain his views on the current economic crisis and to
suggest constructive alternatives. During a radio interview,
Rainey expressed the belief that the Democrats favored progressive
income and inheritance taxes as sources of revenue, while the
Republicans opposed them and advocated a regressive sales tax. He
suggested that the federal government would need to enter the relief
field to prevent suffering and starvation after private, municipal,
and state sources for relief were depleted. Rather than a public
works program, he preferred the reopening of closed factories through
tariff reductions.[15] These were Rainey's views on the major domestic
problems at the opening of Congress. The emergency situation and
the responsibilities of leadership would necessitate modification of
these initial views.

The immediate problem faced by congressmen in both parties was
balancing the budget. The nature of the revenue bill which would
cover the expected deficit was a matter of continuing controversy.
In a prepared statement, Rainey expressed regret that the taxpayers
must now be subjected to new and staggering burdens of taxation.
He extended the hope that a progressive program of legislation to
be advanced by the Democrats would compel the very wealthy to pay
their full share of government expenses. Rainey resisted Republican
suggestions that taxes be made retroactive in an effort to make
financial ends meet. The New York *Times* editorially described Rainey
as "a veteran hunter of that mysterious entity known as 'wealth.'"
It was expected that he would turn "a frosty eye on the whole corps
of relievers and nostrum-sellers" who were expected to descend upon
Congress. At the same time, Speaker Garner delivered a figurative
spanking to his lieutenant for doing too much predicting about
Democratic tax proposals. The *New Republic* praised Garner's success
in restraining Rainey from exploding political dynamite which would
destroy the public's faith in the ability of the Democratic party
to handle the reins of government successfully.[16] As part of a
responsible majority, Rainey was not expected to lead too far in the
espousal of equalitarian economic doctrines.

The Democratic leadership had asserted that the new Congress
would not hamper the President in his efforts to deal with the
depression. As an illustration of good faith, Garner and Rainey sent

a letter to all thirty-three chairmen of House committees urging
their vigilance in reducing appropriation requests. Specifically
it was stressed that no bill authorizing additional expenditures
be reported unless there were compelling and urgent reasons for
doing so. Minority Leader Bertram Snell of New York sent an
identical letter to the ranking minority members of the same
committees. Holding the line on expenditures was only part of the
battle, since the Treasury anticipated a sizable deficit. The
House Ways and Means Committee began to investigate the possibilities
for new sources of revenue. In order to proceed more quickly, the
committee was divided into smaller groups to study various aspects
of the tax situation. Rainey became chairman of a seven-member
subcommittee investigating the sales tax. In spite of Rainey's
known aversion to the sales tax and despite the testimony of those
who had studied the Canadian experience, the subcommittee decided
to incorporate this feature into the proposal. The full committee
not only endorsed the recommendation but also determined to make
this facet the main feature of the bill. The committee report
devoted considerable space to justifying the inclusion of a
manufacturer's excise or sales tax. In anticipation of heated
debate, it was argued that: (1) every other conceivable source had
been considered and found wanting because of insufficient funds to
be derived or because of discriminatory features, (2) the tax was
limited to a two-year emergency and exceptions were provided for
food stuff, farm seed, and fertilizer, and (3) the proposal did not
seriously impair the principle of ability to pay since the rate was
so small (2-1/4 percent). The report concluded that no other
source of revenue would yield the necessary funds "with as little
protest, as little annoyance, and as little disturbance to business
as a manufacturers' excise tax."[17] President Hoover gave administration support to the sales tax proposal as the best means of
balancing the budget. The sales tax then became the focal point
for a renewal of the battle between conservatives and liberals over
the distribution of the tax burden.

Rather surprisingly the majority leader was found to be among
the supporters of the sales tax measure. The shift from progressive
tax principles was justified on the basis of a more compelling need
for fiscal responsibility. When the bill was debated on the floor
of the House, the question, Rainey told House members, was whether
the method would be a sales tax, the painless method, or a revival
of wartime excise taxes, the nuisance method. Rainey candidly
admitted that for many years he had strenuously opposed the sales
tax as an incorrect method of taxation; however, the seriousness of
the economic crisis necessitated its use as an emergency measure.
During the speech, he humorously defined the method of levying taxes
as "the science of getting the most feathers with the least
squawking of the goose." He believed the sales tax was that means.
Rainey delivered a major radio broadcast explaining the need for a
balanced budget and the various tax methods. He then encouraged his
listeners to write members of Congress urging government solvency
and expressing a preference for either the sales or excise taxes.[18]
These efforts were not sufficient to stem the tide against a sales

tax measure.

Debate on the sales tax feature of the revenue bill degenerated into a donnybrook against the House leadership. The revolt was led by Fiorello H. La Guardia, independent Republican from New York, and Robert L. Doughton, Democrat from North Carolina. These men led a coalition known as the "allied progressives" against the bipartisan revenue bill. They marshaled the usual arguments against a general sales tax and defended the working class from the iniquities of regressive taxation. As a substitute for the sales tax, the coalition supported a variety of soak-the-rich schemes. In an effort to stem the revolt, Speaker Garner personally took the floor of the House to make an impassioned plea for fiscal solvency. This maneuver, plus several concessions which Acting Chairman Crisp of the Ways and Means Committee offered, was unsuccessful. The skillful tactics of La Guardia and Doughton resulted in the deletion of the sales tax feature by a vote of 223 to 153. Only forty Democrats, of which Rainey was one, supported the sales tax at the crucial vote. Republican Representative Cyrenus Cole of Iowa recalled the defeat of the sales tax as "one of the saddest days in Congress since the declaration of war in 1917."[19] The radicals had gained a hard-fought victory; however, the budget remained to be balanced.

In spite of his setback, Rainey continued to work for fiscal solvency. Immediately after the defeat of the sales tax, he delivered another radio address urging popular support for a balanced budget. The Ways and Means Committee quickly presented substitute excise taxes which would help reduce the deficit. The matter of paramount importance, Rainey reminded the House membership, was balancing the national budget, and these nuisances taxes could help attain that objective. The modified revenue bill for 1932 then passed the House by an overwhelming margin. The House version of the bill with its soak-the-rich features was a decided victory for the progressive forces. Conservatives had the satisfaction of a measure which promised to make revenues equal expenditures. The Senate version of the bill included no sales tax feature, but it did provide an upward revision of some tariff rates in the guise of revenue production. Despite the pleas of Senate leaders, it included import duty increases for oil, lumber, coal, and copper. When the bill went to conference, Rainey was appointed one of the House conferees. He refused to sign the conference report which he charged was a complete surrender to those trusts already enjoying excessive tariff protection. The low tariff advocate criticized Acting Chairman Crisp for surrendering to the Senate conferees on so important a matter because the revenues earned would be negligible. In opposing the tariff features of the conference report, Rainey told the House that "I may be the last Democrat, but I am going to be a Democrat to the last." His objections were unheeded; the conference committee recommendations, including the tariff raises, were approved by voice vote.[20] The Revenue Act of 1932 contained a combination of conservative and progressive features. Through the deliberations, Rainey's role had vacillated between the conflicting schools of thought, but he consistently favored fiscal responsibility.

The congressman's penchant for a balanced budget determined his stance on the soldiers' bonus issue, another perplexing problem confronting the Seventy-second Congress. During the Harding administration, veterans of World War I had succeeded in securing the enactment of legislation which provided a bonus as compensation for their small salaries as compared to those who had stayed in civilian life. Their demand amounted to $3,400,000,000 spread among 3,500,000 veterans. In order to amortize the payment, the bonus would be redeemable in twenty-five years (1945). In the meantime, the veteran would be issued a bonus certificate and the federal Treasury would contribute $112,000,000 annually toward the redemption fund. As the depression worsened, groups of veterans began demanding the immediate payment in full of these bonus certificates. Congress responded to these pressures in 1931 by approving legislation which enabled veterans to borrow up to 50 percent of the face value of their certificate as an advance. This measure was justified as an emergency relief program and was approved over President Hoover's veto. The measure placed a charge of $1,700,000,000 on the public treasury. Congressman Rainey took no active part in the public debate on this legislation. In a private letter, he explained that he had supported the measure although he would have preferred an outright payment of the certificates in full with cash. The compromise was justified on account of the relief it would bring to many veterans in distress.[21] This legislation had proven immensely popular with the veterans' lobby, and the issue was seemingly resolved satisfactorily.

Such was not to be the case and Rainey as majority leader became embroiled in the controversy. In fall, 1931, pressures were building again for the immediate payment of the bonus certificates in cash. By April 9, 1932, petitions bearing 2,240,030 names and supporting full redemption were presented to him and other congressional dignitaries. Rainey promised prompt consideration of the petitions by the Ways and Means Committee. In a few days he issued a statement indicating that this bonus proposal was "uneconomic, unsound, and destructive" because the issuance of greenbacks to pay the bonus would lead to inflation. In a signed article for the New York *Times*, he cautioned that grave consequences would result from the immediate payment of the bonus in full. He feared an inflation such as Germany experienced following World War I. While admitting sympathy for the plight of many veterans, Rainey could not embrace unbalancing the budget to meet this demand.[22] From the perspective of his leadership position and the worsening economic conditions, Rainey now found it necessary to reverse his stand on this question.

In order to press their demands, unemployed veterans organized a march on Washington for May and June, 1932. The Bonus Expeditionary Force grew to approximately 12,000 persons. The object of their support was a bonus measure introduced by Democrat Wright Patman of Texas. Patman was busy endeavoring to secure the 145 signatures necessary for a discharge petition so that the bill could be considered on the floor of the House. Rainey repeated his opposition

to the proposal, but averred that "every one knows that the Bill
can never become law and I think it would be better for all
concerned to have the agony over." By June the discharge petition
had the required signatures and the subject was brought to the
floor of the House for action. Although Rainey had drafted the
report opposing passage, he did not take part in the debate since
he had been designated Speaker pro tem, a rare occurrence
necessitated by Garner's illness. His name was called so that he
could vote against the Patman bill, but it passed 211 to 176.[23]
On June 16 the Senate declined to approve the Patman bill, and the
issue was terminated for the time being. Congress appropriated
monies to help veterans return to their homes. The next session of
Congress and the next administration would encounter similar
pressures.

Rainey's opposition to the veterans' bonus did not mean that
he was unmindful of the need for federal assistance to those
requiring relief. Aid to the unemployed was an important humanitarian as well as political issue. Therefore, he placed in the
hopper a bill designed to broaden the lending powers of the
Reconstruction Finance Corporation (RFC) to include a public works
program. Speaker Garner, a contender for the Democratic presidential
nomination, was co-sponsor of what became known as the Garner-Rainey
relief measure. The bill provided for direct relief to be administered by the President, for additional money for the RFC so that it
might make loans to stimulate employment, and for a bond issue to
support a specific list of public works projects. Actual cash
expenditures were to be financed by a tax of a quarter of a cent
per gallon on gasoline. Upon hearing of the measure, President
Hoover denounced it as a gigantic pork barrel and an unexampled raid
on the public treasury. Rainey countered that the President was
absolutely reversing all his previous positions on public relief.
The Democrats were not deterred from pushing the bill. The Garner-
Rainey relief bill was sped through the legislative process. It was
reported from the Ways and Means Committee without amendment, and
a special rule limited debate to three hours and allowed none but
committee amendments. Rainey opened debate on the bill in general
terms, stressing the need for relief programs. He controlled the
time of those favoring the measure, and at the close of debate he
presented a few minor amendments which were adopted. The measure
then passed 216 to 182.[24] The bill moved to the Senate where it
was referred to the Committee on Banking and Currency. After a
week, the measure was reported with amendments.

Rainey was fearful that Congress would adjourn without doing
anything for the relief of individual sufferers as opposed to the
loans already advanced for railroads, banks, and states. During
debate on the measure, the Senate cut everything out of the House
version except the enacting clause and substituted a bill sponsored
by Democrat Robert F. Wagner of New York. The Wagner measure agreed
upon the total to be spent, but differed as to the allocation of
funds and the manner in which these were to be raised. The
differences between the two measures were submitted to a conference
committee. The measure was considered so important for Garner's

presidential ambitions that he seriously considered the
precedent-shattering step of appointing himself to the conference
committee, but ultimately he placed Rainey on the committee as his
alter ego. In spite of presidential interference, the conferees
were able to effect a compromise. The conference report was agreed
to by both chambers and promptly vetoed by the President. Hoover
objected to the RFC's being permitted to make loans to individuals
and to increasing expenditures on nonproductive public works.[25]
There was no chance of mustering the two-thirds vote necessary to
pass the bill over a veto.

If any constructive legislation were to be passed, the only
available recourse was for Congress to subscribe to the President's
wishes. Rainey urged the Ways and Means Committee to draft another
bill conforming to the President's desires. Within twenty-four
hours a modified bill was introduced. There was no serious
opposition to the measure. The only disputed portion was an amendment introduced by Rainey which called for publicity of the RFC loans.
This was Speaker Garner's pet feature and he was able to cast the
tie-breaking vote in behalf of the amendment. After two conferences
with the Senate, the measure was approved with the controvertible
publicity feature retained. The bill as signed into law provided
RFC loans for self-liquidating projects, for loans to provide direct
relief to the jobless through the states, and for discretionary
public works if the money became available.[26] Even in this modified
form, the Emergency Relief and Construction Act of 1932 placed upon
the federal government greater responsibilities for active inter-
vention to mitigate a depression than any preceding Congress or
President had been willing to assume.

The most controversial feature of this Emergency Relief and
Construction Act was the publicity provision. Rainey argued that
the qualification was necessary in order to assure that the funds
were not administered in such a fashion as to aid the Republican
national or congressional ticket in the campaign. President Hoover
countered that the adverse publicity would shake the public's
confidence in those businesses seeking assistance. Nevertheless the
measure was signed into law with the publicity clause retained so
that expanded relief programs could begin at once. Republican
Congressman Allen T. Treadway of Massachusetts regarded the provision as injurious, but believed that Rainey had conducted himself
well in representing Speaker Garner's interest in the matter.[27] The
prominent role played by the majority leader in the relief legislation became an issue in the presidential campaign.

The general conduct and partisan operation of the Democratic
lower House was condemned by candidate Hoover. In 1928 the
Republican national committee had circulated widely Rainey's
speeches defending Hoover's record as food administrator during the
war period. This spirit of cooperation and support evident between
the two men during World War I was in marked contrast to the tone
of opposition and hindrance which characterized their relationship
during the Great Depression. In 1932 Rainey was criticized for his
partisan approach to the nation's economic ills. In the heat of
the campaign, Hoover charged that Rainey held "honorary degrees

from all the schools of demagoguery." Republican Representative
William C. Hawley of Oregon confided to the President that Rainey
was the least tractable of the Democratic leadership because he
hoped to make political capital of the depression difficulties.
In major campaign addresses in St. Paul and Detroit, candidate
Hoover stressed the Garner-Rainey relief bill as an illustration
of the sabotage being committed by the Democrats in Congress.[28]
While the President endeavored to make an issue of the partisanship displayed in a divided Congress, the voters were more
impressed by the continued downward trend of the business cycle
for which they held the Chief Executive responsible.

The complete reversal of party fortunes in 1932 confronted
the lame-duck session of the Seventy-second Congress with even
greater dilemmas. Between the November election in 1932 and the
inauguration in March, 1933, Congress played a largely negative
role in the legislative process. While President Hoover was
disposed to take several steps to alleviate the depression, the
Democratic leadership looked to President-elect Roosevelt for
guidance. FDR's unwillingness to cooperate without power stalled
the legislative machinery on most measures. In effect Hoover's
term ended the day following the election, but the formal abdication
of authority did not arrive for four months.[29] In that interval,
Majority Leader Rainey endeavored to make a constructive record
for his party and to consolidate his drive for the Speakership.

The interregnum was a trying period in the nation's history.
During the 1920s, Senator George W. Norris had conducted a
continuing crusade for a Constitutional amendment which would
provide for the presidential inauguration in January and eliminate
the lame-duck session of the old Congress. The Senate approved
the proposal five times between 1923 and 1931, but it failed to
secure the approval of the House. Rainey voted for the measure
each time it came before the House. It was not until March, 1932,
that the necessary approval was obtained in both Houses so that it
could be submitted to the states for ratification.[30] By February 6,
1933, the required three-fourths of the states had ratified it, but
it was too late to minimize the difficulties in transition from
Hoover to Roosevelt. The last of the lame-duck Congresses began
meeting on December 5, 1932. During the short session, Congress's
principal constructive preoccupation was the modification of
prohibition.

The circumstances of the early 1930s greatly altered Rainey's
views on the prohibition question. The popular opposition to the
moral decree and the need for revenue served to dilute his dry
convictions. After the 1928 election, in which the wet/dry issue
had been a prominent part of the campaign, Rainey had indicated to
Governor-elect Roosevelt that the country was dry. He predicted
that there would be no change in the Eighteenth Amendment or
material change in the Enforcement Act "as long as any of us who
are now alive live." Inside four years, his assessment was markedly
different. The temper of the times was changing, as indicated by
the 1930 election. Illinois' Democratic senatorial candidate
J. Hamilton Lewis had campaigned successfully on a wet platform.

When speaking at Jacksonville in Rainey's traditionally dry
district, he was urged to soft-pedal any wet statements for fear
of injuring Rainey's chances for re-election. Lewis ignored the
advice and received the loudest ovation when he advocated repeal.
Confirmation that dry sentiment was vanishing in downstate
Illinois was evident in a statewide referendum on questions of
public policy. Referenda results on three issues relating to
prohibition indicated that the sentiment downstate as well as in
Cook County favored repeal of the Eighteenth Amendment, the
Illinois Prohibition Act, and the modification of the Volstead
Act.[31]   Undoubtedly these manifestations of public opinion
contributed to the transformation in Rainey's stand.

Rainey retreated to a position that called for a popular
plebiscite on the controversy. As majority leader in the first
session of the Seventy-second Congress, he construed the House
rules so that the wets could have a roll call vote either on a
referendum to repeal the Eighteenth Amendment or a ballot on the
return of light wines and beer. In either case, the proposal
would have to be brought to the floor by a petition of 145 members
because the House Judiciary Committee was predominantly dry and
would not report either measure favorably. Rainey thought the
referendum would have a better chance of passage because numerous
drys like himself would favor submitting the question to the
people. There were also indications of mounting pressure to
legalize alcoholic consumption in order to allow the federal
government an immense revenue source. By parliamentary maneuvering,
the House managed a vote on both liquor propositions, but they were
turned down in March and May, 1932.[32]   The issue, however, would
not die.

Both political parties found it necessary to make some
pronouncement on the subject. Rainey's recommendation, which was
submitted to the Democratic platform committee in conjunction with
Cordell Hull and A. Mitchell Palmer, called for a prohibition
referendum which would determine the party's policy. In the
interval, the party would be expected to oppose the return of the
saloon and to favor federal protection for dry states. The party's
national convention rejected this suggestion in favor of a forth-
right plank backing complete repeal.[33]   When the Republican platform
declared a desire for some revision, it was obvious that a
policy change was imminent.

The electoral success of the Democratic party renewed pressure
for action on the liquor question. On November 15, Rainey was
reported expressing doubt as to the legalization of beer during the
short session, but he thought Congress would take a step toward
nullification of the Volstead Act by cutting the appropriations for
enforcement. Since a majority of the present Congress was elected
on dry platforms in 1930, he believed there would be no repeal and
no legalization of light alcoholic beverages. The very next day
he reversed his position. Returning congressmen, he said, indicated
they would be inclined to favor a movement for beer. Rainey then
stated that he would not oppose such a bill's advancing on the
calendar since both parties were pledged to altering the dry laws.

If there was to be a change, he said, it might as well be at this time because the revenue was needed as soon as possible. Democratic Representative Emanuel Celler of New York wrote Rainey that his second pronouncement on beer was "well received and should help you." This statement gives rise to a strong suspicion that Rainey may have bargained a wet stand for support of his candidacy for the office of Speaker.[34]

The pressure for legalization of beer and light wines continued to mount. The principal argument in support of such a move was the need for revenue. Rainey doubted that income from beer-for-revenue legislation would be sufficient to balance the budget, but it would help reduce the deficit. Later he feared that legislation to legalize beer would meet opposition from the lame-duck group and also from the President, even if it did pass the House. Nevertheless, the Ways and Means Committee reported a beer-for-revenue bill. Rainey argued that the impelling motive for supporting it was the need for revenue and the additional employment which would result from stimulating this industry. The bill passed the House by a comfortable margin.[35] Under the threat of a presidential veto, the Senate declined to take affirmative action to legalize beer.

The other facet of the prohibition question was the repeal of the Eighteenth Amendment. Here the wet forces had ultimate success during the session. Rainey was still interested in providing a national referendum on the question of revoking the amendment, and in consultation with A. Mitchell Palmer, he introduced a joint resolution calling for repeal through especially convoked state conventions, a method of ratifying amendments never utilized before or since. Debate on the resolution was limited to twenty minutes on each side. A subsequent roll call revealed 272 yeas and 144 nays, so the measure lacked by six votes the necessary two-thirds for passage. In a statement weeks later, Rainey argued that repeal would mean the solution for all the budget problems because of the additional revenue from general liquor taxes. Although the Senate refused to legalize beer, it approved by a two-thirds vote a constitutional amendment similar to Rainey's. The only major difference was the Senate's inclusion of a specific provision safeguarding those states wishing to remain dry. Rainey then brought the measure before the House again and supported its passage. This time the necessary two-thirds majority was obtained. Rationalizing the actions of Congress on the prohibition issue would indeed be a "hazardous enterprise."[36] The initiation of the steps leading to the repeal of the Eighteenth Amendment proved to be one of the few acts of a positive character in the last lame-duck Congress. By December, 1933, the Twenty-first Amendment was officially added to the Constitution.

The last lame-duck session enacted few remedies for the nation's economic ills. At the same time it did nothing in particular which would hamper the solutions to be proposed by the man entering the White House in March. Rainey's final session as majority leader was filled with proposals and studies about the depression, but limited in actual accomplishment. The Congress, as well as the nation, awaited the New Deal that had been promised.

The activities of a lame-duck Congress—divided in control, weakened by the presence of rejected representatives, and led by a defeated President—were less interesting to the politically inclined individual than the contest for the Speakership. The elevation of John N. Garner to the vice-presidency created a void in the House's principal leadership position. The short session was a backdrop for the adroit pulling and hauling of those Democrats who sought to succeed Garner in the Speaker's chair.

Rainey was among those who aspired to this position. After the 1932 election, three different leadership positions became possible for him. It was assumed that he could continue as majority leader if he so desired. The absence of James Collier of Mississippi and the resignation of Charles Crisp of Georgia opened the way for him to become chairman of the Ways and Means Committee, if he wished that position. While it was the Washington consensus that he might prefer the chairmanship, Rainey resolved the matter when he declared "I think I am in line for the Speakership and will be a candidate." His announcement noted that the Midwest deserved recognition since the presidency had gone to the Northeast and the vice-presidency to the Southwest. In this early stage of developments, Rainey indicated that he expected considerable support from the newly elected Democrats in the lower House.[37]

By the time Congress reconvened for the short session, the contest for Speaker was clearly in evidence. Besides Rainey, there were several other candidates. John McDuffie of Alabama, then the Democratic Whip, was Speaker Garner's choice and the candidate of the South's conservative element. Representing the border states was Joseph W. Byrns of Tennessee, chairman of the influential Appropriations Committee. New York's Tammany organization entered Thomas H. Cullen in the lists for whatever bargaining position it might bring. William B. Bankhead of Alabama, member of the Rules Committee and later to become Speaker, was considered to be a candidate. There were also those who believed that Sam Rayburn, destined to become Speaker much later, should succeed Garner.[38] Byrns, McDuffie, and Rainey were considered to be the three most serious contenders for the position.

Numerous arguments were advanced in support of Rainey's selection by the party caucus. First, he was a rallying point for all northern Democrats who were tired of seeing most of the party plums go to the South. Democrats from Dixie would likely hold twenty-six of the forty-seven chairmanships in the next House. Second, he had a liberal outlook which would harmonize with that of the incoming President. On numerous issues, reciprocal tariffs and waterpower for example, the two were considered to be in complete accord. Third, his rural and small town background would help balance a party which drew heavily from the urban areas and the Solid South. In this connection, the *Prairie Farmer* believed that his selection "would add much to the prestige of his party in the Middle West, and would be especially welcome to agriculture."[39]

In addition to these major factors, there were other considerations which supported a Rainey candidacy. A fourth argument in Rainey's behalf was his long congressional experience. His 1920

defeat had shattered his seniority record, but only one member in
either House outranked him in total years of service at the Capital.
North Carolina's Edward W. Pou, chairman of the Rules Committee,
had been in continual service since 1901. Rainey's fourteen terms
in Congress far exceeded that of any of his competitors for the post.
In a legislative body where longevity of service is a major consideration, the Rainey record was a distinct advantage. A very important
fifth factor working for Rainey was precedent. Four of the Democratic Speakers since the Forty-seventh Congress had been elevated
from the post of majority leader and a fifth from acting majority
leader. In all other cases without exception, the Speaker had been
the ranking member of the Ways and Means Committee, a position
Rainey would occupy when the new Congress met.[40] Thus, it was
argued by Rainey supporters that precedent doubly favored his
selection.

A number of intangibles also entered into the discussion. A
less cogent argument was Rainey's striking personal appearance.
Contemporaries observed that his bulky 275 pound frame, flowing
black tie, bulldog pipe, and silvery mane made him look the part of
a Speaker. Another unknown quantity was the balance of power to be
exercised by members newly elected to Congress. The Roosevelt
landslide had carried 129 new members into office. Most of them were
from the North and West. While the Washington *Post* advised the new
members to study the situation before making a pledge, it was considered generally that this group represented a source of Rainey
strength. A third unknown was the deportment of the rival candidates
during the lame-duck session. Each of the three major contenders
held responsible positions which could advance or retard their
candidacy. It has already been suggested that Rainey's increasing
wetness may have been motivated in part by his ambitions for the
Speakership.[41] This combination of influences would operate until
the Democratic caucus met in early March, 1933, to decide the issue.

During the short session of Congress, the behind-the-scenes
activity continued unabated. Congressman Adolph J. Sabath of
Chicago was appointed campaign manager. Rainey also enlisted the
aid of Illinois' governor-elect, Henry Horner, and Chicago's mayor,
Anton J. Cermak. These men agreed to exert their influence for an
Illinois delegation united behind Rainey and for an advantageous
consideration from the Tammany leaders when appropriate. By the
close of 1932, each of the Byrns-McDuffie-Rainey triumvirate
believed that victory was attainable.[42]

As a part of his campaign, Rainey had an appealing pledge
working in his behalf. His announced aim was to make the party
national in scope and to distribute some of the honors of office to
states which had recently elected Democratic members. This was to
be accomplished by internal party reform through the establishment
of a steering or policy committee. The idea had originated in 1919
when certain dissident Democrats, Rainey among them, had balked at
the inept minority leadership of Champ Clark and at the southern
domination of party policy. These Democratic insurgents unsuccessfully proposed a steering committee as the best means of assuring
party harmony. When the Democrats gained control of Congress after

the 1930 election, the policy committee proposal was revived,
but Speaker Garner resolutely opposed it. Rainey now resurrected
the idea and made it a major plank in his campaign. In Rainey's
view, the steering committee would remove arbitrary powers from
the Speaker and return them to the House. He attributed the
failures of the last Congress to the fact that determination of
policy came entirely from the Speaker's chair. He promised under
the new system that the Roosevelt program would be enacted. The
Rainey proposal embraced a committee representing a number of
geographical districts, which was to meet once a week to determine
party policy in vital matters coming before the House. Each
district member was responsible for maintaining contact with his
particular group. The proposal had the effects of diluting the
seniority rule by giving responsible positions to some newer
members and of assuring representation of all sections in the
party's councils. It was the judgment of contemporaries that the
steering committee concept was a leading factor in Rainey's
selection as Speaker.[43] In addition to these astute pledges of
party participation, the Rainey campaign manager Sabath engaged
in the necessary political plotting.

The effective deal that elevated Rainey to the Speakership
combined support from Tennessee, Tammany, and Texas. When the 302
Democratic members-elect met in secret caucus on March 2, 1933, the
three-way trade was readily in evidence. According to the newspaper reports of the secret conclave, the conservatives whom
Garner had hoped would carry on his leadership were unhorsed by the
liberal coalition led by Rainey. The Illinoisan beat McDuffie for
the Speakership by a vote of 166 to 112. Any hope that Garner had
of running the House from the Senate rostrum was shattered. The
pre-arranged deal swept the rest of the slate into office as well.
In exchange for withdrawing from the Speakership contest, Byrns
gained Rainey's support for the position as majority leader.
Tammany's Cullen withdrew with the understanding that he would be
made assistant leader. Rainey had been advocating the creation of
this post since 1923. Numerous votes from the Lone Star State
were involved with the expectation that the elevation of Byrns
would clear the way for Texan James P. Buchanan to become chairman
of the Appropriations Committee. Recognition was given northern
and western Democrats when Arthur H. Greenwood of Indiana replaced
McDuffie as party whip and Californian Clarence F. Lea was elected
permanent chairman of the caucus.[44] Sabath's management succeeded
in removing McDuffie and the conservative element from positions of
party leadership. The climax of Rainey's twenty-eight years of
service in the House of Representatives was approaching.

His official selection as Speaker when Congress convened in
special session on March 9 was merely a matter of formality. On
that date, Representative Lea placed Rainey's name in nomination
and briefly extolled his qualifications. Also nominated were
Bertrand Snell (a fellow graduate of Amherst) for the Republicans
and Paul J. Kvale for the Farm-Laborites. Rainey absented himself
during the roll call in which he received 302 votes, Snell, 110,
and Kvale, 5. Following the announcement of the result, Rainey

was ushered into the chamber and Snell introduced the Speaker-
elect with a few gracious remarks. Rainey acknowledged the great
honor bestowed upon him, assured members of his impartially, and
reminded them of the great responsibility each was assuming. In
the serious business ahead, he urged bipartisan support to relieve
the American people who were "exhibiting a patience and a forti-
tude in the midst of their difficulties unparalleled in the
history of this or any other nation." Following these remarks,
the "Father of the House," Edward Pou of North Carolina, administered the oath of office.[45] For only the second time in the
nation's history, a son of Illinois had achieved the pinnacle of
success in the House of Representatives.

Congress met five days after President Roosevelt's inauguration in the twenty-fifth special session in the nation's history.
Critical legislative times had been faced before, but this
situation was unique. From the Rainey standpoint, the gathering
of representatives before him presented a novel challenge. The
presence of over 150 new members, 129 of them Democrats, presented
difficulties of organization and leadership. Most of the new
members were unfamiliar with the legislative process and problems;
yet very likely each had novel proposals for the nation's ills. The
wide numerical margin of Democrats, 191 members, made severe
regimentation of individual members avoidable, but harmony was
still necessary if that majority was to be effective and responsive
to leadership. Rainey hoped to achieve the cooperation of members
through the newly inaugurated steering committee and by a judicious
use of the party caucus.[46] In the economic crisis which confronted
the nation, Congress as well as the nation turned to the President
for guidance and leadership. The newly elected Speaker served as
intermediary between the White House and Capitol Hill.

Three decades had intervened between the seating of a
fledgling congressman from a traditionally one-term district and the
selection of that same individual for the third highest political
position in the nation. The Illinoisan had used the post of
majority leader as a stepping stone to the Speakership. Rainey,
the Bryanite reformer of the early twentieth century and the
Wilsonian progressive of the intermediate years, was now called
upon to guide a legislative program which represented a culmination
of these principles and at the same time their extension into new
avenues of the nation's life. The climax of Rainey's career was
about to begin.

NOTES

1. George A. Rogers, "President Hoover and the Seventy-Second
Congress" (M.A. thesis), 38–39; Loretta Kehoe, "The Relation of
Herbert Hoover to Congress, 1929–1933" (M.A. thesis), 110–163;
Jordan A. Schwarz, *The Interregnum of Despair.*

2. "Next Tuesday's Upheaval," 5–6; "The Democratic Landslide,"
7–9; "What to Expect from a Deadlocked Congress," 5–7.

3. HTR to Garrett, Carrollton, July 5, 1927, and Garrett to

HTR, Dresden, Tenn., July 11, 1927; Lewis to HTR, Chicago,
Dec. 16, 1930, all in RP.

4. HTR to Lewis, [Washington], Dec. 19, 1930, RP.

5. Texas delegation to HTR, Washington, Jan. 8, 1931; HTR
to Dallman, [Washington], March 4, 1931; HTR to Smith,
[Washington], April 4, 1931, all in RP.

6. "Widening the Democratic Smile," 11.

7. New York *Times*, Nov. 24, 1931, 4:4; Nov. 26, 1931,
20:1; N. T. N. Robinson, "Democrats Claim House on Eve of New
Congress," 289–290.

8. *Patriot*, Dec. 3, 1931, 1:1, 4:3; *Star* quoted in *Patriot*,
Dec. 10, 1931, 1:6; "The Congress: Garner's House," 11; "Rainey
New Party Leader," 20; T. R. B., "Washington Notes," 242; "A
Victim of Minorities," 20.

9. Chicago *Tribune*, Dec. 7, 1931, 2:3–5; New York *Times*,
Jan. 3, 1932, IX, 2:3–4.

10. For differing analysis see Bascom N. Timmons, *Garner of
Texas*, 136; George R. Brown, *The Speaker of the House*, 142–143.

11. New York *Times*, Nov. 10, 1931, 6:2; Nov. 30, 3:4; and
Dec. 6, IX, 8:3.

12. NBC interview with William Head reprinted in *CR*, 72:1
(Jan. 5, 1932), 1298–1300; *CR*, 72:1 (Jan. 9, 1932), 1591–95, 1600.

13. Recollection of HTR, *CR*, 72:1 (July 8, 1932), 14913;
H. J. Res. 147, *CR*, 72:1 (Dec. 18, 1931), 867; Garner–Rainey
rider discussed and reproduced in Lawrence Sullivan, *Prelude to
Panic*, 25; Chicago *Tribune*, Dec. 28, 1931, 15:2.

14. New York *Times*, July 25, 1932, 1:6; Nov. 16, 2:6–7;
Nov. 19, 6:1–3; Nov. 24, 3:5–6; *Business Week*, Dec. 7, 1932, 3.

15. Radio interview over NBC on Jan. 4, 1932, printed in *CR*,
72:1 (Jan. 5, 1932), 1298–1300.

16. New York *Times*, Dec. 28, 1931, 1:6 and 2:4–6; editorial,
"Can the Pill Be Sugared?," New York *Times*, Dec. 29, 1931, 22:2–3;
Dec. 31, 1931, 1:5; T.R.B., "Washington Notes," 242.

17. *United States Daily*, Jan. 25, 1932, 1:5; Blakey and
Blakey, *The Federal Income Tax*, 308–310; House Report 708,
72 Cong., 1 Sess., "The Revenue Bill of 1932," 8–10.

18. *CR*, 72:1 (March 17, 1932), 6353–59; NBC broadcast of
March 17, printed in *CR*, 72:1 (March 22, 1932), 6655–57.

19. "The 'Soak-the-Rich' Drive in Washington," 8–9; Blakey
and Blakey, *Federal Income Tax*, 313–317; Howard Zinn, *LaGuardia in
Congress*, 220–226; Cyrenus Cole, *I Remember, I Remember*, 515. For
the sales tax fight from the Speaker's perspective see Jordan A.
Schwarz, "John Nance Garner and the Sales Tax Rebellion of 1932,"
162–180.

20. New York *Times*, March 25, 1932, 14:2-5; *CR*, 72:1 (April 1, 1932), 7310 and vote on 7329; E. Pendleton Herring, "First Session of the Seventy-second Congress," 866-868; *CR*, 72:1 (June 4, 1932), 12016-18.

21. HTR to R. B. Adams, [Washington], Feb. 17, 1931, RP.

22. New York *Times*, April 9, 1932, 3:1-4; April 12, 1:7 and 12:5-6; and April 17, III, 6:1; "All Uproarious on the Bonus Front," 5-6.

23. HTR quoted in Jack Douglas, *Veterans on the March*, 36; 72 Cong., 1 Sess., Report No. 1252, "Payment of Adjusted-Compensation Certificates," 1-5; New York *Times*, June 14, 1932, 4:5; *CR*, 72:1 (June 15, 1932), 13053-54.

24. H.R. 12445, *CR*, 72:1 (June 3, 1932), 11942; New York *Times*, May 30, 1932, 1:3 and 2:2-6; *CR*, 72:1 (June 6, 1932), 12128; (June 7), 12189-12244.

25. New York *Times*, June 12, 1932, 1:2; for summary of subsequent action see Herring, "First Session of the Seventy-second Congress," 868-872; Gilbert Y. Steiner, "The Congressional Conference Committee: Seventieth to Eightieth Congresses" (Ph.D. thesis), 231-236.

26. *CR*, 72:1 (July 11, 1932), 15042; H.R. 12946 (July 12), 15168; (July 13), 15221-33; (July 14), 15390-91; (July 15), 15468, 15490-92, 15505-6; "Relief at Last," *Time* magazine, XX (July 25, 1932), 8.

27. *CR*, 72:1 (July 15, 1932), 15505-6; New York *Times*, July 19, 1932, 25:3; Allen T. Treadway, "The Amherst Illustrious," 213.

28. Editorial, "Rainey's Defense of Hoover," *Gazette*, Oct. 31, 1928, 1:2; Bascom N. Timmons, *Jesse H. Jones*, 174; Hoover, *The Memoirs of Herbert Hoover*, Vol. III, *The Great Depression, 1929-1941*, 102-104, 262-263, 276.

29. Rogers, "Hoover and the Seventy-second Congress," 56-57.

30. For legislative history see Richard Lowitt, *George W. Norris*, 515-518.

31. HTR to FDR, Washington, Dec. 15, 1928, Roosevelt Papers, DNC, Ill. 1932 Campaign Pre-Convention: R; Townsend, *Illinois Democracy*, I, 348-349; *Illinois Blue Book, 1931-32*, 852-857.

32. "A Wet-Dry Test in Congress," 8; New York *Times*, Dec. 30, 1931, 1:4-5; Herring, "First Session of the Seventy-second Congress," 850-852.

33. "Democratic Platform Suggestions by Hon. Henry T. Rainey, Illinois, Majority Floor Leader," copy in RP, "Farm Relief Bill— Earl Smith" file; New York *Times*, May 29, 1932, IX, 3:4-5; Hull, *The Memoirs of Cordell Hull*, I, 150-151.

34. New York *Times*, Nov. 16, 1932, 2:1, and Nov. 17, 1:6; "The Movement for a Federal Tax on Beer," 354; *Business Week*,

Nov. 30, 1932, 5; penned note added to letter of Celler to HTR, Washington, Nov. 17, 1932, RP, "18 Amendment" file; editorial, "May Not Inaugurate with Bungstarter," *Patriot*, Dec. 8, 1932, 2:2.

35. New York *Times*, Nov. 18, 1932, 1:3 and 15:2; Dec. 12, 1932, 1:2 and 2:3; *CR*, 72:2 (Dec. 20, 1932), 745–748; vote on (Dec. 21), 867.

36. Palmer to HTR, Washington, Dec. 1, 1932, RP, "18 Amendment, Repeal of" file; *CR*, 72:2 (Dec. 5, 1932), 6–8, 12–13; New York *Times*, Dec. 25, 1932, 2:7; *CR*, 72:2 (Feb. 20, 1933), 4508, 4516; E. Pendleton Herring, "Second Session of the Seventy-second Congress," 420–421.

37. Washington *Post*, Nov. 17, 1932, 1:2. For an extensive inquiry into the Speakership race consult Robert A. Waller, "The Selection of Henry T. Rainey as Speaker of the House," 37–47.

38. Chicago *Herald and Examiner*, Nov. 10, 1932, 5:4; Memphis *Commercial Appeal*, Nov. 27, 1932, 16:1; Walter J. Heacock, "William B. Bankhead and the New Deal," 347–359; C. Dwight Dorough, *Mr. Sam*, 224.

39. Editorial, "Illinois for Rainey," *Illinois State Register*, Nov. 28, 1932, 1:1–2; editorial, "Rainey for Speaker," *Prairie Farmer*, CV (Jan. 7, 1933), 8.

40. "The Congress," *Time*, XX (Dec. 19, 1932), 9; New York *Times*, Feb. 5, 1933, 4:1.

41. "The Congress," *Time*, XX (Dec. 19, 1932), 9; editorial, "Selecting a Speaker," Washington *Post*, Dec. 29, 1932, 6:1; *Illinois State Register*, Dec. 15, 1932, 10:2.

42. Chicago *Daily News*, Nov. 16, 1932, 4:4; Horner to HTR, [Springfield], Jan. 13, 1933, and HTR to Horner, Washington, Jan. 17, 1933, Horner Papers, Administration Correspondence, Downstate, Greene County; Washington *Post*, Dec. 27, 1932, 2:1.

43. New York *Times*, March 5, 1919, 9:1; March 7, 12:7; and March 31, 7:2; Bolling, *Power in the House*, 99, 149–150; New York *Times*, March 3, 1933, 3:4–5; Floyd M. Riddick, "The House of Representatives and the President," 89; editorial, "Leadership in the Next Congress," Chicago *Daily News*, March 6, 1933, 10:2; E. Pendleton Herring, "First Session of the Seventy-third Congress," 68–69.

44. New York *Times*, March 3, 1933, 1:5 and 3:4; *Illinois State Register*, March 3, 1933, 1:3–4 and 8:1; Nashville *Tennesseean*, March 3, 1933, 1:2; Washington *Post*, March 3, 1933, 1:1 and 2:1; Chicago *Tribune*, March 3, 1933, 3:6–8; *Labor*, March 3, 1933, 1:5.

45. *CR*, 73:1 (March 9, 1933), 69–70.

46. New York *Times*, March 10, 1933, 4:3; Herring, "First Session of the Seventy-third Congress," 68.

10
Legislative Marshal of the New Deal

The special and regular sessions of the Seventy-third Congress (March—June, 1933, and January—June, 1934) comprise the inaugural period for the Franklin D. Roosevelt era. The same activities embrace the concluding years of Henry T. Rainey's career. During the interregnum months, he had maneuvered himself into a political position which enabled him to become Speaker during the first New Deal Congress. In the new administration, he was the legislative chieftain organizing the congressional forces behind the President's policies. Following the special session, the scientific farmer turned legislator served as intermediary between the people and the program. During the regular or second session of the Seventy-third Congress, Speaker Rainey resumed his task as legislative marshal of the New Deal. The first eighteen months of the New Deal era are examined from the perspective of a participant in a position of legislative prominence.

As Speaker of the House of Representatives during the era, Henry T. Rainey played an important role, but one that is difficult to determine. Democratic control of the House meant largely the formal determination of the legislative procedures. For primary leadership in policy matters, Congress turned to the Chief Executive and his Brain Trusters. Rainey was in an ideal position to serve as middleman between executive wishes and legislative fulfillment. Unfortunately much of the intimate record of that relationship is lost forever because Franklin Roosevelt did not preserve memoranda of his personal conferences and phone conversations. Since most of the key legislative transactions were handled in this fashion, the record upon which to construct the climax of Rainey's career is limited severely.[1] Nevertheless, Rainey's auxiliary role as publicist and interpreter of programs affords some insight into the legislative byplay which comprises a history of the early New Deal.

Banking was the first major crisis facing the new administration. The day following the inauguration, Speaker-designate Rainey was present at a 2:30 P.M. White House meeting at which the circumstances of the banking crisis were outlined. From that meeting came unanimous approval for a special session of Congress. In a press statement the following day, Rainey asserted that the President's declaration of a bank holiday was "the first step toward economic recovery, although the step was drastic." He doubted that it would be necessary to give the President additional

power beyond that in the trading-with-the-enemy law under which
he had acted. Rainey indicated that war-debt negotiations would
be delayed while readjustments were made in the domestic
financial system; however, plans for the World Economic Conference
in London would continue. It was not until nine o'clock of the
night before Congress convened that Joseph T. Robinson, prospective
Senate majority leader, and Rainey had any idea of the program they
would be asked to approve. The new Speaker was at his post during
the unprecedently short forty-minute session when the Emergency
Banking Relief bill was whisked through the House.[2] The measure
was passed by the Senate and was signed by the President that
same day.

The next day Congress was in receipt of another presidential
message, one urging the support of a bill to maintain government
credit by drastic reductions in expenditures. Rainey was in
complete accord with the President on this issue. At a January,
1933, conference with the President-elect, he had urged a two-step
program to balance the budget. The steps were a radical reduction
of expenditures and the passage of a beer tax bill. He stated then
that the people would not stand for more taxes and if they were
voted, it would be inviting revolution. Rainey had previously
inquired about the savings which would result from various government salary reductions. It is generally assumed that the first
New Deal Congress was a rubber stamp, but here is an instance in
which a congressional leader had prepared a complete fiscal program for the President-elect.[3] The economy bill which the
President now recommended gave him wide discretionary powers to
cut the salaries of federal employees by as much as 15 percent
and to reduce as well the pensions and allowances of war veterans.
The measure pleased the disciples of economic recovery through
budget balancing and stunned the veterans' lobby.

The most controversial portion of the proposal was the
optional power given to the President to reduce veterans' benefits.
Rainey tried to bind the party to the entire measure in caucus but
failed to muster the necessary two-thirds approval. Through
Democratic Representative Gordon Browning of Tennessee, the
veterans' lobby urged an amendment so that the President could not
completely discontinue a pension or other allowance or reduce them
by more than 25 percent. The caucus would not be bound by this
limitation either. Democratic unity was shattered by the economy
bill. The bill went to the floor of the House for debate under a
rule providing a two-hour limit, no opportunity for amendments,
and one motion to recommit by anyone opposing the proposition.
The supposition was that Browning would offer the motion to
recommit with instructions that the bill be reported back with his
amendment which the caucus had rejected.

Administration forces schemed to block that move. It was
decided that Democrat William Connery of Massachusetts, an ardent
veterans' supporter, should make a motion to recommit the bill,
which would pigeonhole the entire economy proposal. As his part
in the scheme, Rainey agreed to recognize Connery and did so at
that point in the proceedings when both Browning and Connery

were on their feet demanding recognition for the single motion to
recommit. As expected, the Connery motion for outright rejection
of the entire bill was defeated. Although Browning protested that
he had received a virtual promise in caucus that he would have a
chance to offer his amendment, Rainey coldly replied that he had
no knowledge of a binding agreement. The economy bill was approved
in its original form by a vote of 266 to 139. Ninety-two Democrats opposed the bill, while sixty-nine Republicans crossed the
aisle to provide the margin of victory. Ordinarily the Speaker
never votes except to break a tie, but in this case Rainey asked
to be called and voted aye.[4] In this instance the Speaker used
his right to recognize with decisive effect, and saved the
administration from an embarrassing defeat during its first few
days in office.

Typical of the rapid-fire order in which bills were considered during the emergency session was the docketing of a
proposal modifying the Volstead Act. Even before the Congress
convened, Rainey had given positive assurances that the Democrats would make good their promises and legalize beer at the
earliest possible moment. The measure was recommended by the
President on March 13 and it passed the House the next day by a
3 to 1 margin. Rainey asked to be called during the roll call
on the beer bill and voted yea. Two days later the Senate gave
its approval. After the passage of this bill, Rainey proclaimed
to a New York Board of Trade audience that the budget would be
balanced without resort to any further taxes. To these businessmen Rainey compared the condition of the country on March 4 to that
of the Allies during the darkest days of World War I. President
Roosevelt's daring measures were equivalent to those of Marshall
Foch, he said. In a subsequent press interview, Rainey reassur-
ingly expressed the view that the nation could make ends meet
after the passage of the economy and beer bills.[5] The New Deal
was off to a fast and advantageous start, according to Rainey.

After assisting in the passage of the New Deal's farm program, as previously discussed, Rainey turned his attention to a
bill providing unemployment relief through reforestation and
conservation projects in a Civilian Conservation Corps. When
asked about the measure at a press conference, he explained that
the President contemplated taking men out of the breadlines and
off the dole by putting them to work, under reasonable discipline,
carrying into effect a real and greatly needed reforestation
program. The program, he said, would mean honorable employment and
self-respect to hundreds of thousands of less fortunate citizens.
The funds for this project were to come from money originally
allocated for public buildings and other public works, but for
which no contracts had been let. Rainey pointed out that
reforestation would provide employment many times greater than
could be utilized on the uncontracted building projects.[6] This
bill needed no pushing. The conservation and humanitarian features
were such that the measure quickly passed both chambers by voice
vote.

Rainey used his influence as Speaker to block legislation that

was not a part of the President's urgent program. The Senate
was considering an industrial recovery bill sponsored by Democrat Hugo Black of Alabama which would limit labor to a five-day
week and six-hour day. Rainey predicted that if it should
pass the Senate, it would be sidetracked in the House
temporarily to clear the way for more urgent bills. He thought
he saw in that proposal a lot of "dynamite" and "complications"
which would bear investigating. A New York *Times* editorial
agreed with Rainey since the proposal's infringement upon states'
rights made its constitutionality doubtful. A short time later,
the House Labor Committee favorably reported a companion measure
known as the Connery bill. Rainey was not inclined to give the
matter preferential treatment on the House floor, and supported
the administration in its demand for considerable revision.[7]
During the delay, the presidential staff was able to present
their own bill for industrial planning.

The administration's response to the demand for a planned
economy was the measure which came to be known as the National
Industrial Recovery Act. The proposal embraced the objectives of
Black and Connery for reduced hours by establishing a system of
industrial codes under which maximum hours of work could be
established, minimum wages set, and child labor forbidden. The
demand of industrialists for a relaxation of the antitrust laws
was likewise met through the proposed drafting of codes for fair
competition. In an omnibus appeal to all interested groups, the
measure also called for a program of direct work-relief employment on a variety of federal projects. Once the new measure was
ready, Rainey announced that both the thirty-hour week bills had
been put on ice. Several House committees wanted jurisdiction
over the new bill. The Speaker assigned it to the Ways and
Means Committee, although it was not directly a revenue measure.[8]
Rainey used his discretionary power in assigning bills to committee to foster the Roosevelt program. By the close of the
session, the bill for industrial self-government was ready for
the President's signature. The thirty-hour measures were left
in limbo.

Another important item on the Roosevelt agenda was a greatly
expanded program for the Muscle Shoals project. The President's
recommendation of a Tennessee Valley Authority (TVA) exceeded
the Norris proposal of federal power development and the American
Farm Bureau Federation's support of fertilizer production.
Roosevelt envisioned a program of regional planning for an entire
river watershed which also included flood control, reforestation,
land and resource utilization, soil conservation, industrial
development, and social planning. The House passed a bill on
April 25 which emphasized the fertilizer production aspects; a
Senate version under Norris's guidance placed the emphasis on
public power. The Senate bill then lay on the Speaker's desk
for five days without being referred to a conference committee.
Swift consideration had been expected as an immediate aid to
unemployment relief. Ostensibly the reason for the arbitrary
delay was to allow preliminary unofficial meetings to reconcile

the two measures. On May 9 the bill was taken up and conferees
appointed. The Norris text dominated the conference report,
but ample latitude was provided for fertilizer production
enthusiasts. Few Democrats opposed the Tennessee Valley Act,
but a significant number--thirteen out of twenty-eight--came from
Illinois because they feared the competition of TVA waterpower
with the state's hard-pressed coal industry.[9] The effectiveness
of Rainey's cooling-off period is indeterminable, but the law
provided one of the most far-reaching accomplishments of the first
New Deal Congress.

The remaining programs in the President's emergency legislation
received less attention from the Speaker as he went about his
legislative duties. Eleven pieces of legislation comprise the first
of the New Deal efforts to combat the depression emergency. In
addition to the ones discussed above, Roosevelt gave special
emphasis to federal emergency relief, supervision of stock market
operations, relief of small home owners, and railroad reorganiza-
tion and relief. On these four pieces of recommended legislation,
Rainey's services as master parliamentarian were not needed. The
first hundred days of the New Deal had displayed a honeymoon
relationship between the Hill and the White House. The crisis
situation and the public demand for action resulted in a congressional session which was subservient to presidential wishes. Rainey
had identified himself fully with the President's program. While
the Speaker is not called upon to vote during roll calls, the
Illinoisan established a record by being enscribed as supporting
New Deal measures on twenty-three separate occasions during the
hundred days. At the close of the session, Roosevelt made a
point of thanking the legislators through Rainey for their
cooperation and teamwork in meeting the nation's problems.[10]

The first session of the Seventy-third Congress completed a
gigantic legislative task. A competent political observer noted
that the session was "unparalleled for the speed and discipline
with which Congress was brought to face and finished its task."
The numerous bills presented to Congress were pushed through so
expeditiously that there were occasional murmurs of rubber-stamp
legislation. Rainey was credited with keeping the House in line
"with a gentle but firm touch."[11] He nevertheless could crack the
whip when the occasion demanded—especially by adroit parliamentary
maneuvers. The preponderant Democratic majority and the extreme
economic emergency served, however, to minimize leadership
problems for the Speaker. Elections were far enough removed so
that partisanship was minimal and first-time members were uncon-
cerned about their individual record for re-election. This
picture, however, contrasts markedly with the following session
of Congress. Nevertheless, Rainey could be justifiably proud of
his role in demonstrating that a representative democracy could
rise to an emergency and carry through a broad legislative program in record time.

In addition to Rainey's service as legislative marshal for
the New Deal, he performed in a second capacity as explainer of
the relief and recovery legislation. While Congress was still in

session, he began to assume his role as interpreter of the
policies to the people. Early in the session, he praised "the
patience with which the people of the United States have stood
their sufferings and have remained loyal to the Government."
He urged a little more patience and a vigorous support of the
administration because the sun had already commenced to shine
through the dark clouds enveloping the nation. Confidence
turned to cautious optimism as some of the New Deal measures
were enacted. Rainey explained in mid-May that the administration declined to lie down quietly and permit this great
juggernaut of destruction to crush the nation. Rather, the
enactment of a constructive program was attempting to reverse
the downward trend and direct the return climb to prosperity.
He warned, however, that "too much must not be expected too
soon" because recovery would not be instantaneous, but gradual.
A recurrent theme in these addresses was a deep-seated admiration
for President Roosevelt. This was the eighth President under
whom Rainey had served. Typically he summarized his evaluation
and admiration for the Chief in this fashion: "A superman is
there [in the White House], combining all the idealism and the
initiative of a Wilson with the energy of a Jackson and the
wise statesmanship of a Jefferson."[12]   The veteran legislator
was completely engrossed by the Roosevelt magic, an effect
which helps to explain his prodigious labors in behalf of the
New Deal.

Following a summer of extensive speaking trips explaining
the New Deal programs, especially those relating to farming,
Rainey returned to Washington to tackle the nation's legislative
needs. Two concerns seemed especially to dominate the second
session of the first New Deal Congress. An all-important factor,
as in the emergency session, was the adoption of measures which
would hasten economic recovery. A new factor to be considered
was the desire of the individual congressman and his party to
secure favorable election returns in November. Congressional
leadership was largely sustained by the impetus to action in the
continuing economic crisis; however, Speaker Rainey's mettle was
severely tested when he attempted to curb the pressure for
individual attainment. Each member desired to make his own
impress upon the legislative process so that he could more
effectively campaign in his own district.[13] Marshaling support
among the members of Congress for New Deal measures proved not
to be a sinecure for Roosevelt's Speaker. His handling of the
situation led to criticism in some circles.

Reporters eagerly sought out Rainey for his predictions about
the approaching session of Congress, the first to be convened in
January as provided in the Twentieth Amendment. In December, 1933,
he forecast a relatively short and harmonious session since
economic conditions were generally showing signs of improvement.
He confidently felt that Democrats would follow the lead of the
President in the approaching session. In order to dispose of
rumors that the President would not enjoy the same spirit of
cooperation as the previous spring, Representatives Rainey and

Byrns issued a joint statement that "the country is with the
President and the country runs Congress." With respect to
individual members revolting, the Speaker said every opportunity
would be given for individual expression from members. The New
York *Times* editorially expressed the suspicion that the Rainey–Byrns
observations represented "the triumph of hope over experience."
Rainey stubbornly insisted that there would be no legislative innovations or dramatic incidents for reporters to write
about in that session. It was to be a working session at which
the Republicans had better not snipe because anybody who sniped
would be left at home after November. Over a nationwide radio
network, the Speaker said the Roosevelt program had been so
successful that there was "little for Congress to do but to grease
the wheels and keep the work moving."[14] As a prognostication of
legislative happenings, Henry T.'s pronouncements leave much to be
desired.

The second session of the Seventy-third Congress began
inauspiciously with Speaker Rainey gaveling the House of Representatives into action. The picturesque gentleman in the presiding
officer's chair was described by *Newsweek* as looking "at first
glance like a better nourished, more compact and less discontented
Democratic edition of Senator Borah." Although Rainey predicted
"a short, harmonious and constructive session," *Time* magazine
foresaw that this would not be the case. The rubber-stamp special
session had made a stirring record for the President but added
little glory to individual representatives. In this election year,
said *Time*, each and every representative would be determined to
make an individual record which would justify his being returned
at the November elections. Through the Speaker, the President
expressed hope that Congress would speedily dispose of legislation
and adjourn by early spring.[15] The presidential decision to
outline needed legislation in his annual message and let Congress
iron out the details proved a detriment to a short and harmonious
session, but it was nonetheless a productive term.

Among the reform measures passed during the early New Deal,
legislation guaranteeing bank deposits especially interested
Rainey. A measure extending the features of the Federal Deposit
Insurance Corporation came up for renewal during this session.
The program was to be strengthened and an effort was made to
increase the amount insured. When the bill was sent to conference,
Roosevelt exerted pressure through Rainey so that the bill would
guarantee the very small depositor's money and not aid the 3
percent who had more than $2,500 in any one bank. The figure of
$2,500 had been set in the 1933 act, but the House Banking and
Currency Committee favored a $10,000 limit. Conferees settled
upon $5,000 as a compromise figure.[16] In this form, the bill
passed both chambers.

Rainey was frequently called upon to defend the administration's tremendous financial outlays for relief programs. His
rejoinder to critics was that the government had spent forty
billion dollars to win World War I, while the New Deal contemplated spending only twelve to fourteen billion on recovery.

Characteristically, he noted that "the war in which we are now
engaged is more serious even than the World War." When pressed
he could manipulate the debt figures so that the 1934 situation
was relatively better than at any time under Hoover. The New
York *Times* did not appreciate the prowess in arithmetic by which
Rainey arrived at his conclusions.[17] The incongruity of the
administration's pledge of economy and the huge relief bills
provided a controversial subject. Rainey's services as a staunch
administration supporter were frequently utilized to reconcile
the conflicting policies.

The Speaker and the President were also in complete accord
on the need for tariff reductions through reciprocity. Since
January, 1932, Rainey had been advocating an international
economic conference which would reopen the world markets through
tariff reductions. At the insistence of Rainey and others, the
Democratic platform had contained a plank promising tariff
reductions through reciprocal trade agreements. It was anticipated that the new administration would act quickly in this area,
but tariff questions were held in abeyance during the first
session of Congress while awaiting the outcome of the London
Economic Conference. Rainey was hopeful that the lowering of
tariff barriers and the stabilization of international exchange
would restore world prosperity. As it became evident that the
London conference was unable to agree upon a multination policy,
the Speaker warned against a policy of American economic
isolation. He later defended the President's unwillingness to
be bound by an international currency stabilization agreement.[18]
The inability of the London delegates to reach accord and the
reluctance of Roosevelt to restrict the depreciation of the
dollar were severe blows to Rainey's hopes for economic recovery,
but this disappointment was not mirrored in his public pronouncements. Instead, he began to work behind the scenes for
bilateral rather than multilateral economic arrangements.

The principal manifestation of this effort was the campaign
for tariff reciprocity, a concept being promoted by Secretary of
State Cordell Hull. Rainey attended a White House conference on
February 28 at which the proposed draft of the Trade Agreements
bill was prepared and approved. After the meeting, Rainey
described the proposal as the "most important yet," and emphasized
that this was to be "a change in tariff policy, not in the tariff."
Reciprocity, Rainey said, would end the present paralysis of
world trade. There was no question in Rainey's mind that the
flexible provisions of the bill would be sustained by the Supreme
Court as constitutional. In a press interview, he vigorously
argued against Senate views that the President's flexible powers
to reduce tariffs be limited to three years. Rainey was sure the
House would retain the bill's original form which provided power
to make permanent treaties. During the lower chamber's debate on
the proposal, Republican opponents reminded the Speaker that he
had opposed surrendering legislative power to the executive when
the Republicans controlled the administration. In a radio rejoinder,
Rainey defended the tariff program and indicated that altered

conditions necessitated the allocation of power to the executive.
He expressed the hope that the Tariff Commission he had fostered in
the Wilson administration could be made an effective arm of the
President in these negotiations. The measure passed the House on
a strictly partisan vote in its original form. Rainey privately
hailed the bill as the "key" to the entire recovery program
because normalcy would return only with the re-establishment of
foreign markets.[19] The measure ultimately passed the Senate and
was signed into law on June 12. Rainey, as well as Secretary of
State Cordell Hull, was pleased at this advent of economic
internationalism and at the prospect of tariff reductions.

The second session of the Seventy-third Congress produced
great quantities of legislation which passed through both chambers
with few obstacles. In viewing Rainey in relation to legislative
questions, it should be remembered that he played two roles. On
the one hand he was a representative with his own views on matters
before the Congress, and on the other he was an intermediary of
the President's, therefore, duty-bound to implement the Chief
Executive's wishes. It was generally an easy matter for him to
reconcile these two positions, but occasionally there were times
when the individual viewpoint prevailed over the legislative
leader. Usually the Speaker was able to fill the normal role of
a presiding officer superintending the smooth operation of a
complicated process of decision making and maintaining order.[20]
The ultimate test of Rainey's leadership came during the struggle
over the most controversial issues of the session—silver legislation, veterans' benefits, and the economy program.

One of the most vexatious questions was the desirability of
bringing about inflation. To a large extent this issue was
inherited from the preceding session. During the Hundred Days,
the proponents of silver agitated for silver purchases and
coinage by the government as an artifical means of stimulating
the economy. In 1933 Congress had approved the Thomas amendment
to the Agriculture Adjustment Act. It granted discretionary
powers to the President so that he might pursue a number of
inflationary courses. For the time being, the silver forces
were placated. As congressmen returned for the second session,
Rainey gleaned the impression that there was "an increasing
demand for the broadening of our monetary base." While he
thought the House would favor free coinage, he indicated there
would be no affirmative monetary legislation unless recommended
by the President. Rainey subsequently urged the issuance of
silver certificates against silver bullion deposits as "a very
small bite at the cherry" known as inflation. The New York
Times was editorially sure that ardent inflationists like Rainey
would not be satisfied unless they devoured the whole bowl of
cherries. Just before Congress convened, the silver advocate of
three decades earlier predicted the House would insist upon a
liberal silver remonetization measure.[21] The issue was again in
the forefront of congressional policy making.

Rainey evidently intended to play a minimal role in the
agitation for silver inflation. *Newsweek* observed that he was

an old-time liberal who was now joining the inflationist crowd, yet there were no further statements from Rainey on the subject until March. In that interval, the Senate came within two votes of passing a silver purchase amendment to the gold reserve bill and Democratic Representatives Martin Dies of Texas and William Fiesinger of Ohio each introduced bills advocating special consideration for silver. In support of inflationary policies, Father Charles E. Coughlin filled the air waves with sermons and exhortations that his listeners write their congressmen in support of silver inflation. To one of his correspondents, Rainey indicated that he always listened to the Coughlin lectures and that he had much confidence in the radio priest. On March 10 the House Committee on Banking and Currency reported the Dies bill which provided for the acceptance of silver at a premium from foreign purchasers in exchange for agricultural exports. Rainey now issued a public statement characterizing the measure as a good bill which would likely pass the House and not incur presidential objection.[22] The Speaker evidently had not consulted the administration.

The President and his Secretary of the Treasury were horrified at this bill's implications. In an effort to block further silver agitation, Secretary of the Treasury Henry Morgenthau told the press on March 15 that he was still unconvinced that silver was a cure-all. Further, he hinted that Treasury investigations of silver speculation implicated some of the congressional champions of silver. These remarks backfired, and the next day Morgenthau absolved all congressmen of any involvement; however, the damage had already been done.[23]

Speaker Rainey took personal affront at the secretary's first announcement and unleashed a personal campaign for silver. According to *Newsweek*, Rainey was "infuriated" by the Secretary's statement. The Speaker called the silver bloc to his office for a conference on strategy, and announced that he would exert pressure to call up both the Dies and the Fiesinger silver bills. The latter provided for mandatory government purchase of 1,500,000,000 ounces of silver in monthly installments. Under a suspension of the rules, the measures would require a two-thirds majority to pass. Rainey privately confessed that his purpose was to show the amount of silver sentiment in the House. He was somewhat surprised when the Dies bill passed 258 to 112. Fittingly the measure was approved by the House on the seventy-fourth anniversary of Bryan's birth. In spite of administration "frowns," Rainey materially assisted in the passage of the Dies bill.[24] This measure was sent to the Senate, where the Chief Executive now endeavored to strike a compromise.

Once Rainey became actively involved in the currency question, he maintained his efforts to support the remonetization of silver. In early April he delivered a speech predicting that the United States was headed for bimetallism. The Treasury Department, he said, would soon be issuing silver certificates based on silver bars as a medium of exchange. Just before a White House conference on legislative matters, he referred to "an awful sentiment for silver," but he insisted the subject would not be discussed unless the President first broached it. On coming from the meeting, the only statement about silver elicited by reporters from him was a comment that "the President said he was as much for silver as I am." The following day this was elaborated to indicate that the President preferred a free hand in employing the remonetization of silver. Rainey stated that the President was not very enthusiastic about the Dies bill, but he might not veto it. The next day the Speaker indicated that the chances of silver legislation were discouraging unless the President was converted because he was sure the House would ultimately abide by the President's decision. Roosevelt successfuly compromised his differences with the Silver Senators by agreeing to some mandatory and some permissive features in the proposed legislation. The Speaker called this the most important concession that the President had made during the session. Rainey now confidently predicted that Congress would not adjourn until silver legislation was passed. The adoption of a bimetallic system, he said, would "help increase commodity prices and . . . be a great aid in restoring prosperity."[25] The Silver Purchase Act of June 19, 1934, ultimately satisfied both the legislative and executive branches of government.

The silver inflation debate was the only major occasion on which the Speaker differed markedly with the President. In this case, Rainey led the revolt rather than trying to stifle it. The Speaker evidently wished to vindicate Bryan's earlier crusade to promote silver to an important position in the nation's monetary system. This fact, plus the mounting desire for inflationary policies, was a stronger force than Rainey's extreme loyalty to the party's current leader.

Another measure subject to equally great pressure from voting blocs was legislation to provide benefits for war veterans. The Patman Bonus bill authorized the immediate payment to World War I veterans of the face value of their adjusted service certificates. The House supporters of the veterans' lobby sought to utilize a discharge petition to get the measure out of the Ways and Means Committee and on the floor for debate. When the Democrats took over control of the House in 1931, they had liberalized the discharge rule so that only 145 signatures were needed rather than 218. During the 1933 session and again at this session, Rainey and other House leaders had urged the necessity for stricter discipline by returning to the higher figure. Fifty-nine Democrats, including leaders of the inflation and veterans' blocs, held a rump caucus to protest against the proposed rule change. In the interest of party harmony neither side forced the issue and the liberal discharge rule stayed throughout the Seventy-third Congress. Rainey decided that the minute anybody started an inconvenient discharge petition, the committee could bring in an adverse report and that would end the matter. In the case of the bonus bill, however, it was decided to let nature take its course. By February 20 the veterans' bloc had acquired sufficient signatures for their petition.[26]   A highly vocal minority was succeeding in making its wants known.

The Speaker endeavored to let his and the President's opposition to the Patman Bonus bill be known. Rainey, as well as Roosevelt, was unwilling to expend $2,400,000,000 in order to redeem all the world war veterans' bonus certificates. After the day the last signature was affixed to the discharge petition, the President warned the House through Rainey that this was not the time to approve such legislation. Advocates of the bonus construed this to mean only that Roosevelt would allow the bill to become law without his signature. The Speaker wrote for clarification and received this unequivocal reply: "Naturally when I suggested to you that I could not approve the bill for payment of the bonus certificates I did not mean that I might let it become law without my signature. I don't do things that way. What I meant was that I would veto the bill, and I don't care who [sic] you tell this to." The President's stance was widely publicized due to the public interest in the bonus measure. The press also featured the grammatical error in the last sentence.[27]

Rainey's lifetime interest in veterans' affairs made him especially sensitive on this issue. His files contain numerous letters urging favorable or unfavorable action on the bonus legislation. To those veterans not among his constituency, he referred the inquiry to the appropriate representative since there was an unwritten law which prevented him from interfering in matters of this kind in another man's district. Veterans in his district received a detailed itemization of the Rainey stance and a defense of the need for fiscal responsibility. Typically these letters closed with the admonition to let those friendly to veterans accomplish whatever was possible within the constraints of the economic emergency.[28] In spite of the Speaker's opposition to the Patman bonus proposal and the wide publicity received by the President's note, the House elected to follow an independent course. On March 12 the House voted by a 3 to 1 margin to approve the discharge petition. In this instance Rainey had been unsuccessful in getting the House to follow the President's guiding hand. By a vote of 295 to 125, the bonus bill was approved. The measure was sent to the Senate and reported adversely; it died without a Senate vote being taken.

The veterans' matter was not finished yet for it reappeared during consideration of the major appropriation bill for the government's next fiscal year. After an early January conference with the President concerning the budget, Rainey had pledged that the House would keep "absolutely" within the budget recommendation limits submitted by the President.[29] It was only by an adroit series of parliamentary moves that the House came close to honoring that promise.

Almost immediately after convening, Congress began consideration of the Independent Offices Appropriations bill. In order to uphold the President's economy program, the House leadership prepared a rigid control of procedure to ward off Treasury raids by the amendment process. A special rule was provided which would

disallow all amendments except those offered by the Appropriations Committee. The rule also prohibited amendments to this or
any subsequent appropriation bill that would run counter to the
economy plan voted the previous session. During extensive
debate on the rule, Minority Leader Snell objected that such a
procedure would prevent the minority from offering the usual
motion to recommit with instructions. Speaker Rainey declared
that he would rule in order a motion to recommit so long as its
instructions did not violate the rule on economy. By a strictly
partisan vote, the Rainey interpretation of the rule was validated.
By the narrow margin of 197 to 192, the stringent rule was
approved. Three more defections from the Democratic ranks would
have opened the public treasury to all special interest groups. A
motion to recommit the bill was defeated by a vote of 240 to 141.
The measure then passed on a voice vote.[30]   The House leadership
had successfully weathered this crisis.

The bill passed in a form perfectly acceptable to the
President. The New York *Times* reported that the "heavy administration machine rolled successfully over another House uprising."
This account, however, failed to take into consideration the
extremely thin margin by which a severely restrictive procedural
rule had made the steamroller possible. The Speaker told reporters
the passage of the bill was a distinct administration victory.[31]
Action on the House version of this major appropriation bill had
been so quick that there was little public sentiment for or
against retention of the salary cutbacks and veterans' benefit
reductions of the previous March. Administration forces in the
Senate were not so fortunate in avoiding the pitfalls of these
pressure groups. Senate leaders were unable to keep the Pandora's
box of amendments closed. By a 41 to 40 vote, the senators
approved an amendment providing for full restoration of all pay
cuts on July 1, 1934. A subsequent amendment limited the restored
pay to those receiving less than $6,000 per year. Another House
leadership crisis appeared when the Senate finished with its
version of the appropriation bill.

The House leaders utilized every parliamentary device
available to them in order to sustain the principles of the Economy
Act of 1933. Upon hearing of the Senate bill, Rainey expressed the
thought that the Democrats in the upper House had allowed the bill
to become overloaded in order to bring a veto. Because he felt
sure the people would favor economy in the government's operation,
the Speaker advised "letting Congress hear from the country."
Byrns and Rainey had thought to call a caucus to bind the party's
membership in the House to hold the line on appropriations, but
they changed their minds. There was nothing to confer about,
Rainey rationalized, because the Senate had deliberately assassi-
nated the appropriation bill and there was no use conferring over
a dead body. The House leaders elected instead to employ delaying
tactics. The Senate bill reached the Speaker's desk on March 1.
Custom dictated that the bill be sent directly to a conference
committee by a unanimous consent agreement. Instead, the unusual
procedure was followed under the regular rules whereby the bill

was referred back to its committee of origin in the House for
further consideration. The original idea was that the bill
could be redrafted in a form which the Senate would be "sane
enough to accept." Rainey was sure the Senate version would
receive a presidential veto if it were not modified. He was
equally certain the House would stand by the President in this
conflict with the Senate.[32]

Further efforts were made to forestall a runaway on
expenditures during the interval gained by referring the bill
to the Appropriations Committee. Hopefully, constituent pressure
upon recalcitrant Democratic senators would bring them to their
senses on the need for economy. Troubles increased when the
Appropriations Committee declined to redraft the Senate version.
The House leaders held two caucuses to bind their followers to
ignore the Senate amendments, but they failed to obtain the
necessary two-thirds support. In desperation on March 14, the
Rules Committee reported a special rule authorizing the
appropriation bill to go to a conference committee without
specific instructions from the House of Representatives. The
hope was that the conferees would see fit to remove the objectionable encroachments on the Treasury. When the vote was taken on
the rule, party lines broke and the rule was overwhelmingly
defeated. The bill was now open to amendments from the House
floor, and the veterans' bloc seized the opportunity. The Senate
amendments were voted down. On March 14 the House substituted a
bill embodying an American Legion proposal that all veterans'
benefits reduced by the Economy Act of 1933 be fully restored.
The House was in a state of pandemonium. Ever the wily politician,
Rainey tried to place the onus of repudiating the President's
economy program upon the Republicans. Although this was good
political technique, it seems a bit ridiculous in view of the
preponderant Democratic majority. On March 26 the Senate gave way
to the House amendments which added $228,000,000 to the
President's original recommendations. Roosevelt promptly vetoed
the bill.[33]

The next step was an attempt to override the veto. Rainey
had confidently predicted that if the President vetoed the
Independent Offices Appropriations bill, there was "not the
slightest chance of passing it over his veto." The Speaker
completely misjudged the response of the legislative body. He
left the rostrum in order to vote to sustain the veto. According
to *Newsweek* he "sorrowfully" announced that the House had passed
the bill over the President's veto. The vote stood at 310 to 72.
No fewer than 209 Democrats bolted, while two Republicans joined
70 Democrats in voting to sustain the veto. The Senate vote to
override was by a 63 to 27 margin.[34] In this instance, the proven
magic of the slogan "back the President" failed to work its charm.
The overriding of the veto of the increases in government salaries
and veterans' benefits was the first which President Roosevelt
suffered. The Chief Executive had had to compromise and retreat
on previous occasions, but he had never suffered outright rebuff.

The combination of silver agitation, bonus ferment, and

economy commotion produced a veritable three-ring circus in the congressional halls. During this legislative crisis of March, 1934, Speaker Rainey had utilized every resource at his command to enforce the President's wishes. Midway through the month, it was learned that he was keeping a checklist on how Democratic members were voting. His list indicated those who had voted "wrong" on as many as twenty-one different occasions. Rainey was unwilling to admit that there was any plan of action to be taken against outstanding irregulars, but the implications for patronage were obvious. The following day it was revealed that he kept a similar book on Republicans in the House. Rainey hinted that there was a possibility that Republicans who supported the President's program might find Democratic opposition less strenuous in their districts. Rainey's hometown Republican newspaper was not certain that his extreme loyalty to an "autocratic administration" was desirable since it might ultimately be shown that the "wrong Democrats" were right.[35] The threat of being blacklisted by the administration was an unsuccessful deterrent to House revolts. Neither parliamentary nor patronage maneuvers stemmed the wave of independence which engulfed Rainey's direction of the New Deal's legislation.

The month of March, 1934, represents a period of crisis in Rainey's leadership of the House of Representatives. The three major controversies of the session—silver legislation, veterans' benefits, and the economy program—reached their climax in the span of a few days. Rainey helped to lead one revolt and was unsuccessful in halting the two others. Roosevelt's compromise on the silver question and his defeat on the veteran and salary matters gave rise to disparaging comments on the Speaker's leadership capabilities. In the face of these crises, the *Literary Digest* observed that the Illinoisan was "an easy-going person who is not much of a disciplinarian." The editor marveled at the control which Roosevelt exercised over Congress in spite of this weakness of Speaker Rainey. The Washington *Post* published a dispatch advocating a shake-up in party chieftains after the November elections. Reportedly some administration members foresaw a need for a change in congressional leaders, in the House of Representatives particularly. According to observations appearing in the *Literary Digest*, it was no secret that Roosevelt "sighed for a stronger directing hand over his party majority in the lower House of Congress." Likewise, it was not news that the House leaders had "chafed occasionally at indications of this lack of confidence at the White House." Both Rainey and Byrns vigorously defended their leadership. In an angry reaction, the Speaker denounced the insinuations as untrue and sinister. He said that the House had made a good record in passing twenty-two administration measures. A few days later Rainey and Byrns were at a White House conference seeking reassurance from the President. Upon leaving the meeting, Rainey volunteered this statement to the press: "I asked the President for a job and he told me he wasn't going to give me any because he wanted me to stay where I am." According to the *New Republic*, the reassurances the President gave were by no means complete since Roosevelt had in fact been "disquieted by the

ineffectual nature of the party management in the lower chamber."[36]
There were persisting rumors that Rainey might be spirited out of
the Speakership with offers of attractive appointments in other
capacities, possibly a Supreme Court post if a vacancy should arise.
However, the rift soon blew over and was forgotten.

The restiveness of the House membership as the session neared
its end also contributed to the strain on the presiding officer.
In an effort to overcome the confusion on the House floor, an
experiment was tried of using loudspeakers so that the oratory
could be heard above the din raised by the representatives. Rainey
also approved a circular sent out by the House Committee on
Accounts which asked members to refrain from conference and
conversation, and smoking, on the floor of the House. It was also
necessary for the Speaker to order removed from the *Congressional
Record* notations of "Applause" and "Laughter" inserted in
perorations printed in the official document when the remarks had
not been delivered before the House. In spite of the publicity
given the restlessness of the lower chamber, Rainey stoutly maintained that the business of Congress was "never transacted in a
more orderly way and a more expeditious way." He asserted that
the Seventy-third Congress had passed more bills of a constructive
nature than the last ten Congresses. Soon to be seventy-four years
of age, Rainey showed the strain of the vigorous physical and
mental efforts required in this high office.[37] It had been the
most strenuous session in his thirty-year career.

In the closing weeks of the session, Rainey was additionally
troubled by nonlegislative concerns which also demanded his
attention. Among these interests was the relationship of the
Supreme Court to the New Deal measures. It was speculated that
Roosevelt might soon have three vacancies to fill due to anticipated retirements. It was strongly suggested that one of these
appointments should be accorded a midwesterner since that area
was not represented on the nation's highest court. Although
Rainey's name had been mentioned in this connection, he privately
discounted this possibility. In Illinois, bipartisan support
was being organized for Rainey's former law partner, Norman L.
Jones. After the Rainey-Jones partnership was discontinued in
1914, Jones was elected circuit judge for the succeeding seventeen
years. In 1931 he was elected to the State Supreme Court, and in
1933 was appointed chief justice for that body.[38]

In an exchange of correspondence with Jones, Rainey provided
a perceptive analysis of the national Supreme Court situation. In
Rainey's view, any candidate for the highest federal bench would
have to exhibit strong pro-labor decisions and decided anti-water-
power trust rulings. The Speaker noted that the five to four
decisions upholding the first two tests of. the New Deal legislation
formed a dangerous margin on which to establish a national program.
Thus, he anticipated that only those with liberal records would
receive serious consideration whenever vacancies occurred. Rainey
indicated that the Supreme Court members would be expected to keep
their ears to the ground and yield to popular movements on critical
occasions. Rainey anticipated the Roosevelt court-packing scheme

of 1937 by suggesting that Congress could pass legislation
enlarging the membership on the Supreme Court if the Tory-
dominated court should rule key New Deal measures to be
unconstitutional. Rainey advised Jones to establish a
liberal and progressive record—even a radical stance—if he
wished to be a serious contender for any vacancies which might
occur.[39] Subsequent events were to demonstrate that Rainey's
preoccupation with the constitutionality of a legislative program heavily buttressed with emergency clauses was not misplaced.

Another of the concerns imposing on Rainey's time was
racial discrimination in the restaurant of the House of Representatives. In 1928 Oscar De Priest had been elected as a Republican
from a black district in Chicago. He was the first Negro congressman since the turn of the century. The arrival of Mrs. De Priest
upon the Washington social scene had been the occasion of considerable racial animosities during the first year of Hoover's term.[40]
During the Roosevelt administration, the Jim Crow practice of the
House restaurant was severely criticized by De Priest. The
congressman spoke on the subject and introduced a resolution
calling for an investigation of racial discrimination. Speaker
Rainey was unsympathetic to the resolution and delayed appointing
the Democratic members of the investigating committee. During
Rainey's long legislative career, he was rarely involved with
questions relating to racial problems. Although he was a staunch
supporter of antilynching legislation, there is little in the
Rainey record which bears upon this question.[41] The congressman's
response to the De Priest incident, however, can only be labeled
racist by straining the definition beyond utility and by imposing
upon a previous generation the social and emotional guilt of its
successor.

The third of the diversions which demanded Rainey's time and
attention was a defense of the Brain Trust. In a widely
publicized attack upon the administration, Dr. William A. Wirt
charged that Roosevelt was the Kerensky of America and that the
Brain Trust members were responsible for stopping recovery so that
the public in its despair would accept state regimentation and a
planned economy. Initially the Speaker preferred to ignore the
charges, but ultimately demands for a congressional investigation
could not be squelched. The inquiry was of a perfunctory sort, but
many of the administration's spokesmen took to the hustings to
defend the intellectual corps of the New Deal. In a typical statement, Rainey denied any Communist conspiracy in the administration
and defended the use of experts (many of whom he had recruited)
in the conduct of the people's business. As a loose construction-
ist of the Constitution, Rainey found it easy to justify the
federal government's incursion into social and welfare areas.[42]
Criticism from the right, such as the Wirt pamphlet, would become
an increasing concern to the Roosevelt administration. Rainey
was especially sensitive on this subject and thus exerted extra
efforts to correct any misinformation or misrepresentations.

In spite of the rumblings generated by the constitutional
issues, the racial question, and the conservative/liberal clash,

the second session of the Seventy-third Congress had made an
impressive record for itself. Contemporary assessments of
Rainey as Speaker help to reveal his role in this facet of
twentieth-century history. The Washington correspondent of the
New York *Times* described Rainey on the rostrum as an "'old-
fashioned Democrat,' ever a dependable follower of his party,
patient, kind and tolerant." His departure was regarded in
Washington as a severe loss to the administration because the
Speaker had been a powerful influence and a major factor in
the President's recovery program. In an editorial, the *Times*
placed Rainey as Speaker in the category of a follower like
Speaker Frederick Gillett rather than a leader like Nicholas
Longworth or John Garner. Nearly a score of years later,
Congressman Adolph J. Sabath described his friend as a "great
liberal, possessed of remarkable ability" who was "a tower of
strength in expediting the progressive legislative program
urged and advocated by Franklin D. Roosevelt."[43]

As Speaker of the House of Representatives in the first
New Deal Congress, Rainey was a conscientious, patient, loyal,
and careful presiding officer who was content to do well and
unostentatiously the day's work. In the performance of his
duties he was a master parliamentarian, but not an innovator
of legislative enactments. His role was concerned more with
the process of legislative enactment rather than the product
itself. Each type of leader has a contribution to make within
society, and given the Roosevelt partiality for leadership it
is perhaps better that Rainey was a loyal follower. Henry T.
as Speaker justly deserves the title of "Legislative Marshal
of the New Deal."

NOTES

1. Herring, "First Session of the Seventy-third Congress,"
82; interview with Miss Margaret McMahon, HTR's personal
secretary from 1931 to 1934, on December 6, 1962. Neither the
Rainey nor the Roosevelt Papers contain significant records of
what may have transpired between the two men. In addition, as
presiding officer of the House there is little indication in
the *Congressional Record* of Rainey's influence upon the shaping
of bills or of his views on the resultant legislation.

2. New York *Times*, March 7, 1933, 3:6; *CR*, 73:1 (March 9,
1933), 75-81.

3. New York *Times*, Jan. 2, 1933, 10:1, and Jan. 9, 3:3-4;
Herbert D. Brown (Chief, U.S. Bureau of Efficiency) to HTR,
Washington, Feb. 2 and 4, 1932, as printed in *CR*, 72:1 (Feb. 8,
1932), 3534; Bolling, *Power in the House*, 126-127.

4. Virginia Searls, "Presidential Influence on Legislation,
March 9—June 16, 1933" (M.A. thesis), 29-32; Herring, "First
Session of the Seventy-third Congress," 71-72; *CR*, 73:1 (March 10,
1933), 129-131; (March 11), 198-218; memoir of Gordon Browning in

Columbia Oral History Project, 36–38.

5. New York *Times*, March 6, 1933, 14:4; *CR*, 73:1 (March 13, 1933), 284–288; (March 14), 373–402; New York *Times*, March 17, 1933, 3:3, and March 19, 1933, IV, 4:8.

6. New York *Times*, March 26, 1933, 1:5 and 3:3. After HTR's death the CCC camp outside Carrollton was named in his honor. *Patriot*, Nov. 15, 1934, 1:5.

7. New York *Times*, April 8, 1933, 3:1; in the same issue, editorial, "A Lot of Dynamite," 12:1–2; New York *Times*, April 13, 1933, 2:1.

8. New York *Times*, May 14, 1933, 5:2.

9. King, *The Conservation Fight*, 274–275; Kile, *The Farm Bureau*, 248–250; Aaron Wildavsky, "TVA and Power Politics," 577.

10. For a very convenient chart summarizing useful information about the legislation of the hundred days, see E. Pendleton Herring, *Presidential Leadership*, 44; Thomas H. Coode, "Georgia Congressmen and the First Hundred Days of the New Deal," 144–145; Floyd M. Riddick, *The United States Congress*, 76; FDR to HTR, [Washington], June 15, 1933, Roosevelt Papers, OF 24.

11. Herring, "First Session of the Seventy-third Congress," 65; Townsend, *Illinois Democracy*, IV, 7.

12. Radio addresses of March 13, May 11, and June 6 as printed in *CR*, 73:1 (March 15, 1933), 490–491; (May 12), 3340–41; and (June 7), 5197–98 respectively.

13. Randall B. Ripley, *Majority Party Leadership in Congress*, 70–87.

14. New York *Times*, Dec. 10, 1933, 38:7; Dec. 14, 1933, 1:7 and 2:5; editorial, "What Congress Will Do," Dec. 15, 1933, 24:1; Dec. 29, 1933, 3:1; Dec. 31, 1933, 15:6.

15. *Newsweek*, III (Jan. 6, 1934), 19 (HTR's picture as Speaker appears on the cover of this issue); *Time*, XXIII (Jan. 8, 1934), 15; New York *Times*, Jan. 7, 1934, 29:2.

16. Telegram of Roosevelt to HTR, Washington, March 27, 1934, in Elliott Roosevelt (ed.), *F.D.R.*, III, 395–396.

17. Jefferson Day speech reported by New York *Times*, April 8, 1934, 1:4 and 31:3; editorial, "Mr. Rainey's Arithmetic," April 9, 1934, 16:2. HTR typified those experienced in World War I who drew the parallel with the Great Depression as presented by William E. Leuchtenburg, "The New Deal and the Analogue of War" in John Braeman, *et al.*, *Change and Continuity in Twentieth Century America*, 81–143.

18. *CR*, 72:1 (Jan. 5, 1932), 1299; John T. Flynn (interview with HTR), "The Trap that Jack Built," 12–13, 41–42; "The Congress," *Time*, XX (Dec. 19, 1932), 10; New York *Times*, June 21, 1933, 3:2, and June 29, 1933, 2:3; *Gazette*, July 6, 1933, 1:6.

19. New York *Times*, March 1, 1934, 1:8 and 4:2, March 8, 1934, 2:6; *CR*, 73:2 (March 24, 1934), 5367, and (March 26), 5436; radio address of April 7, 1934, *CR*, 73:2 (April 16, 1934), 6660; HTR to George F. Bauer, [Washington], March 30, 1934, RP, "Tariff Bill-1934" file.

20. For discussion of the leadership problems consult Richard F. Fenno, Jr., "The Internal Distribution of Influence: The House" in David B. Truman (ed.), *The Congress and America's Future*, 52-76.

21. New York *Times*, Dec. 15, 1933, 2:4; Dec. 24, 1933, 2:5; editorial, "Appetite from Eating," Dec. 25, 1933, 22:1; Dec. 31, 1933, 4:1.

22. *Newsweek*, III (Jan. 6, 1934), 19; secretarial note to be used in answering letter of N. J. Wheeler to HTR, Edwardsville, Feb. 24, 1934, RP; New York *Times*, March 11, 1934, 20:1. The Rainey Papers abound with evidence of the effectiveness of Father Coughlin's pleas for silver.

23. John M. Blum, *From the Morgenthau Diaries*, 185-186. For a complete discussion of the silver inflation question, see Herbert M. Bratter, "The Silver Episode," 609-652, 802-837.

24. John A. Brennan, *Silver and the First New Deal*, 119-120; "Revolt: House and Senate Kick Over Administration Traces," *Newsweek*, III (March 24, 1933), 11; New York *Times*, March 19, 1934, 2:2, and March 20, 1934, 1:6; *CR*, 73:2 (March 19, 1934), 4863 (HTR asked that his name be called and voted aye); HTR to H. G. Pine, [Washington], March 21, 1934, RP.

25. New York *Times*, April 8, 1934, 29:4; April 15, 3:1; April 16, 1:8 and 6:2; April 17, 2:1; April 18, 3:6; and May 18, 1:4.

26. Herring, *Presidential Leadership*, 34-35. For a discussion of the electoral impact of the veterans' lobby see V. O. Key, Jr., "The Veterans and the House of Representatives," 27-40.

27. HTR to Marvin H. McIntyre (Sec. to FDR), Washington, Feb. 21, 1934, and FDR memo to HTR, Washington, Feb. 26, 1934, Roosevelt Papers, OF 95-C; "The Presidency," *Time*, XXIII (March 12, 1934), 11.

28. HTR to Roy C. Laibhart, [Washington], April 4, 1934, and HTR to L. O. Cox, [Washington], March 12, 1934, RP, "Veterans' Legislation Correspondence—Answered" file.

29. New York *Times*, Jan. 7, 1934, 29:6.

30. Debate and votes on H. Res. 217 in *CR*, 73:2 (Jan. 11, 1934), 479-512; debate and votes on H.R. 6663 on (Jan. 12), 550-597. For discussion of these parliamentary moves, see E. Pendleton Herring, "Second Session of the Seventy-third Congress," 858-859.

31. New York *Times*, Jan. 13, 1934, 3:1.

32. New York *Times*, Feb. 28, 1934, 2:5, and March 1, 1934, 13:2-3; *Newsweek*, III (March 10, 1934), 8; Herring, "Second Session of the Seventy-third Congress," 859.

33. *Newsweek*, III (March 24, 1934), 11; Herring, "Second Session of the Seventy-third Congress," 859-860.

34. HTR to Hamlet C. Ridgway, [Washington], March 10, 1934, RP, "Veterans' Legislation Correspondence—Answered" file; *Newsweek*, III (April 7, 1934), 5-6.

35. New York *Times*, March 19, 1934, 3:4-5, and March 20, 1934, 5:3; editorial, "Speaker Rainey and 'Wrong Democrats,'" *Patriot*, March 22, 1934, 2:2.

36. Diogenes, "News and Comment from the National Capital," 11; Washington *Post*, April 22, 1934, 1:3 and 8:1; Diogenes, "News and Comment from the National Capital," 13; New York *Times*, April 24, 1934, 4:2; T.R.B., "Washington Notes," *New Republic*, LXXVIII (May 9, 1934), 363.

37. New York *Times*, May 9, 1934, 13:6; *Newsweek*, III (May 19, 1934), 7; HTR to S. T. Williamson (editor of *Newsweek*), [Washington], May 26, 1934, RP; *Newsweek*, III (June 16, 1934), 9; Memoir of Marvin Jones in Columbia Oral History Project, V, 769-770.

38. Chicago *Tribune*, Feb. 26, 1934, 8:1; Jones to HTR, Carrollton, Feb. 28, 1934, RP; Townsend, *Illinois Democracy*, II, 58.

39. HTR to Jones, [Washington], March 2, 16, 1934, RP.

40. Hoover Papers, "Colored Question—Mrs. DePriest Incident (June 1929 to July 1930)," Box 1024; Larry Richey Papers, White House Subject File, Box 7; Melville J. Herskovits, "Race Relations," 1061-62.

41. H. Res. 236, *CR*, 73:2 (Jan. 24, 1934), 1275; (March 21), 5047-49; (April 25), 7359-60; Elliott M. Rudwick, "Oscar DePriest and the Jim Crow Restaurant in the U.S. House of Representatives," 77-82; HTR to Irvin C. Mollison (Pres., Illinois NAACP), [Washington], March 9, 1934, RP.

42. Wirt, "America Must Lose—By a 'Planned Economy,' the Stepping Stone to a Regimented State" (New York: Committee for the Nation, 1934); New York *Times*, April 5, 1934, 3:5, and April 7, 21:3; Chicago *Tribune*, June 30, 1934, 2:2-3.

43. New York *Times*, Aug. 20, 1934, 3:4-5; editorial, "Speaker Rainey," Aug. 21, 1934, 16:1; *CR*, 82:1 (Jan. 31, 1951), 780.

11

Spokesman of Progressive Democracy

Among the most difficult tasks for the student of history and
the social sciences is the determination, with a reasonable
degree of accuracy, of the relation between a political leader
and the forces of his time. It is perplexing to untangle the
extent to which a legislator shapes his environment and is
shaped by it. The span of service embracing the career of
Henry Thomas Rainey compounds the problem by including a
generation of time. Altered conditions may warrant a shift
in principles or practices; nevertheless, it may be said of
Henry T. that he was patient and persistent in the pursuit of
progressive goals. He endeavored to guide his party's and the
nation's thinking away from the nineteenth-century concept of
individualism to a mid-twentieth-century approach to social
welfare. In this transition, there are elements of continuity
and liberalism mixed with components of interruption and
conservatism as evidenced by contemporary and subsequent
appraisal of Rainey's entire career which climaxed in the
Speakership.

Following the adjournment of Congress in 1934, Rainey
embarked upon an extensive speaking trip as an ambassador for
the New Deal as he had done the previous summer. In flitting
about the midcontinent area filling speaking engagements, Rainey
became known as the flying spokesman of the Roosevelt administration. The advent of the air age in politics held no terrors
for him. In three weeks' time he had traveled several thousand
miles in behalf of the policies he had helped to inaugurate.
Following the speaking tour, he was home at Walnut Hall preparing
for his own campaign and for his role in assisting colleagues
who were before the voters. His last official act was to write
a letter to General Hugh S. Johnson, director of the National
Recovery Administration, asking that a crushed stone company in
Eldred, Illinois, be exempt from the minimum salary provisions
of the NRA code. Granting the company's petition, he wrote,
would provide jobs for some thirty to forty men currently
unemployed.[1] It was fitting that his last public act should be
in behalf of a local constituent, for upon this kind of service
Rainey had built his successful career.

The Speaker was suffering from a slight cold when he
returned from several local speaking engagements in early August,
1934. It was not thought to be serious, but on August 10 he was

admitted to De Paul hospital in St. Louis. The diagnosis indicated
a light attack of pneumonia. It was reported that he was recovering
nicely but would remain at the hospital for a few days rest. On
August 19, one day short of his seventy-fourth birthday, the
Speaker unexpectedly succumbed to angina pectoris (a disease
usually accompanying a heart ailment which produces suffocation).
The extreme pressure of the Speakership and the strenuous speaking
schedule plus his advanced years contributed to his death.[2]

The funeral ceremony for Congressman Rainey was the most
memorable event to take place in the town of Carrollton. On
August 22, 1934, the 2,000 citizens of that Illinois agricultural
community were joined in mourning by the state and the nation.
During the four hours that his coffin was displayed in the
rotunda of the Greene County Courthouse, an estimated 12,000
persons filed by in homage. President Roosevelt arranged his work
schedule so that he might personally attend the Episcopal service
at Walnut Hall. Illinois' Governor Henry Horner and a congressional delegation of some twenty-five persons were also present.
While "Taps" sounded, the mortal remains of Henry Thomas Rainey
were laid to rest beside his parents in the local cemetery.[3] For
a short time Carrollton was the capital of the United States and
the center of national attention.

Following the Speaker's death, there were countless eulogies
and tributes to his memory. President Roosevelt, Governor Horner,
congressional colleagues, and numerous administration officials
provided glowing tributes. United States Senator William H.
Dieterich, a long-time friend, expressed the sentiment of many in
these words: "By his death progressive government has lost a
champion, the Nation has lost a leader, the State a servant, and
the district a friend." In behalf of the community, the
Republican Carrollton *Patriot* paid this tribute: "As we knew him,
his poise, his mild manner, his even-tempered nature seemed most
admirable traits of character. His love of home and his efforts
to make it more attractive appealed to us. It was as a fellow
townsman that we most admired him, his neighborliness, his
unassuming approachableness, his wholesome democratic manner."[4]
As a career politician and gentleman farmer, Rainey possessed an
abundance of attributes which endeared him to friend and foe
alike.

Rainey's death created a void in the political slate for the
twentieth congressional district in the November election.
Initially Senator Dieterich suggested that Mrs. Rainey become a
candidate for her husband's seat. In her own right, Mrs. Rainey
was regarded as a competent politician who could campaign well.
About a week after her bereavement, she announced that she would
not run because an elective office was not an inheritance.[5] While
she declined to follow in her husband's political footsteps, she
did resolve to devote her time and attention to civic and
philanthropic enterprises. Mrs. Rainey continued to live at
Walnut Hall and to engage in social and charitable work, particularly promotional efforts in behalf of the Boy Scout and Girl
Scout movements. She died on September 28, 1945, at the age of

eighty-six years, and was buried beside her husband in Carrollton.[6]
A spirit of unselfish service had dominated the life of Congressman and Mrs. Henry T. Rainey.

Since Mrs. Rainey had declined to become a candidate,
Dieterich shifted his favor to Judge James Barnes of Morgan
County. Governor Horner cast his support to Scott W. Lucas of
Havana. Previously Lucas had been national judge advocate for
the American Legion and unsuccessful primary opponent of Dieterich's
in 1932. Lucas was now closely identified with the Horner
administration as chairman of the Illinois Tax Commission and
judge advocate general of the Illinois National Guard. The
struggles between the federal and the state political factions
which were evident during Rainey's career were continuing. At
the district's nominating convention, the state crowd was
victorious.[7] Lucas ran on the Rainey-Roosevelt record in the
1934 election and was successful. He subsequently served two
terms (1935-39) as representative of the twentieth district and
two terms (1939-51) as United States senator from Illinois.

Rainey was only the third Speaker of the House to die while
holding the office. Those preceding him were Michael C. Kerr of
Indiana in 1876 and Nicholas Longworth of Ohio in 1931. The
Illinoisan's two immediate successors as Speaker, Joseph W. Byrns
and William B. Bankhead, also died while executing the functions
of this office. Rainey's death brought immediate speculation
about his successor. Byrns, Bankhead, and Sam Rayburn were
mentioned as likely candidates for the post. In an arrangement
reminiscent of the Rainey deal, Byrns was elected Speaker and
Bankhead became majority leader. Upon Byrns' death in 1936,
Bankhead was his logical successor and Rayburn became majority
leader. At Bankhead's death in 1940, Rayburn became Speaker;
his successor as majority leader was John W. McCormack.[8] Thus,
the hallowed tradition of progression from the majority leader's
position to the Speakership was maintained.

One of the honors customarily accorded the various presiding
officers of the House of Representatives is a memorial portrait
to be hung on the walls outside the chamber. In Rainey's case,
this tradition led to a perplexing problem since Mrs. Rainey could
not say no to the many artists seeking the commission for the
portrait. Ultimately, the Library Committee of the House had
sixteen portraits from which to choose. In June, 1936, the
committee selected the painting by Howard Chandler Christy as the
official portrait to join the gallery of past Speakers.[9]
Subsequently another of the paintings was purchased by an anonymous
donor and given to the State of Illinois for display at Springfield,
where it hangs outside the entrance to the governor's office in
the Capitol building. Years later another of the portraits was
given to the Carrollton Public Library for proper display through
the good offices of Senator Lucas. Still others of the paintings
found their way to such places of honor as the Carrollton Post
Office and the Amherst College Library. In the battle of the
portraits, admirers of the congressman had a plethora of likenesses
with which to perpetuate his memory.

As a permanent remembrance of a distinguished successor to
Lincoln and Douglas, the State of Illinois erected in Carrollton
a monument to honor Rainey's memory and public service. Sculptor
Frederick C. Hibbard created a life-sized figure of the bushy-
haired Democrat, gavel in hand, presiding over the House of
Representatives. The statue, portraying a strong and vigorous
man, stands before a small pedestal symbolic of the House rostrum.
The inscription reads: "One of the Godlike things of this world
is the veneration done to the human worth by the hearts of men."
On August 12, 1937, Governor Horner dedicated the memorial and
eulogized Rainey as a symbol of strength and security. The
monument still stands as an almost forgotten reminder of the
attainments of an unknown contributor to the historic past. In
1965 Rainey's name, along with nine other distinguished Illinoisans,
was placed on the frieze of the addition to the Centennial building
in Springfield.[10] However, few outside the Carrollton community are
now aware of the long legislative record which lies behind the
symbolism of the statue and the inscription.

The extensive public career of Henry T. Rainey provides an
historical perspective on the continuity between the early New
Deal and its antecedents in the Progressive era at the turn of the
twentieth century. In focusing upon a single individual, this
study has endeavored to discover one man's contribution to the
succession of legislative interests which extend from the Theodore
Roosevelt-Taft-Wilson era across the 1920s to the age of Franklin
Roosevelt. This interpretational challenge continues to interest
historians who strive for an understanding of the recent past.[11]
The Rainey record represents one link in this complex set of forces
which blends men, ideas, and institutions into the heritage that
influences posterity's direction, if not its decisions.

Investigations into the continuity of the liberal tradition
are handicapped by a lack of precision in the term's definition and
conceptual framework. In the most elemental fashion, one may
consider a measure as progressive/liberal if it was so identified
in the political rhetoric of the time. Congressman Rainey did
little to assist in unraveling this tangle for he was no theorist
about the philosophical underpinnings of liberalism.[12] In Rainey's
view, the concepts of progressive and Democrat were so entwined
as to be synonymous. In 1911 he wrote a constituent that he
objected to the expression "progressive Democracy" because there
could be no division of Democrats into progressives and non-
progressives. In a simplistic distinction, he wrote that "those
men who are not progressives are not Democrats, although they may
be masquerading as such." The Illinoisan had only contempt for
Republicans with progressive inclinations because he believed they
ought to be Democrats. In 1924 the *Nation* conducted an inquiry
into the disappearance of the prewar radicals. As one of the
respondents, Rainey quipped that "a progressive is a Republican
who thinks his district is going Democratic." In assessing his
own place in the political spectrum, Rainey described himself as
"a liberal and a progressive always." In the twilight of his
career, Rainey enjoyed being called a "radical," which he defined

as embracing change rather than opposing it as a conservative
was wont to do.[13]   In the absence of more precise intellectual
insights into Rainey's concept of the political continuum, one
is forced to rely upon his works rather than his words.

Happily, the congressman was more exact in his approach to
the duties of a representative in a democratic society.   In
keeping with accepted progressive tenets, the key ingredient
was service.   In 1916 Rainey lectured his colleagues on the
importance of constituent service if the people were to be
correctly and properly represented in the Congress.   Later, as
Rainey was leaving the national legislature after eighteen
years, he provided a lengthier analysis of a representative's
duty.   As a frequent member of the minority, he stressed the
need for constructive criticism of the oppositions' legislative
program.   He also emphasized that the debates on the House
floor, personal as they may seem to the general public, are
clashes of ideas and not of men.   In the flowery language of
the orator, Rainey summarized that "I have labored at all times
for the advancement of those measures and for those propositions
which in the best of my judgment made for the prosperity, and
the success, and the perpetuity of this great Government and
for the progress and the happiness of all people who owe
allegiance to the flag."[14]   While advocates of most political
persuasions could fit themselves under this broad umbrella,
the statement reveals a willingness to work within the system,
for the general welfare, and on an independent basis.   These
prescripts governed Rainey's response to the legislative
challenges encountered during thirty years in Washington.

The progression of Rainey from a traditionally one-term
district to the Speakership is a political version of the
Horatio Alger success story.   As a freshman in Congress, Rainey
quickly moved from the obscurity of a single-term district to
the notoriety of an outspoken reformer.   He had been able to
launch his dream for development of the internal waterways.
The idea of tariff reform had been thrust dramatically upon
his party and the nation.   In the Fifty-eighth and Fifty-ninth
Congresses, he presented a record as a proponent of reform.
This was evidenced by his votes in support of railroad regulation,
pure food and drug legislation, and labor measures.[15]   In his
first four years, he earned a creditable record for party
regularity and he surprised his fellow Democrats with the
forcefulness of his arguments and their popular appeal.   At the
same time, he had been able to satisfy sufficiently the personal
demand of his constituency.   The fledgling congressman devoted
himself to the chief legislative problems as he saw them, con-
fident that the political pendulum would provide him with the
opportunity to use his experience.

As a member of the loyal opposition during the years 1907 to
1910, Rainey emphasized the negative in Republican activities.
At the same time, he endeavored to stimulate his own party into a
more aggressive reformist stance.   His own record in the Sixtieth
and Sixty-first Congresses continued to favor the progressive

impulse. On such issues as those relating to conservation, Cannonism, tariff reductions, income tax, and railroad regulation he could be counted regularly among the supporters of reform. He would probably have agreed with the pundit who observed that the only Democratic victory of the period was the party's team winning the congressional baseball game by the score of 26 to 16.[16] In spite of the dearth of personal and party accomplishments, Rainey was a persistent politician struggling to establish a record which the voters could endorse. In these attempts, he incurred the wrath of the Republican presidents under whom he served, but, more importantly, he earned the respect of his Democratic colleagues. The congressional campaign of 1910 marked another segment of Rainey's career.

In the period from 1910 to 1913 Rainey assumed the role of a militant Democrat as he intensified his efforts to encourage the election of a Democratic Congress and Chief Executive. In legislative matters, the "Sage of Walnut Hall" continued his interest in the tariff-trust combine. To his continuing interest in waterways, Rainey added a concern for water conservation. As an aid to embarrassing the majority party, he pursued the investigation of the Panama Canal's acquisition. At the same time, his personal roll call of support for progressive measures included advocacy of tariff, tax, and political reform. It also shows endorsement of anti-injunction legislation for labor, establishment of the Children's Bureau, and an investigation of banking by the Pujo Committee, a House inquiry into concentrations of capital. In Jerome Clubb's assessment of congressional voting records, Henry T. is listed among the Democrats "most favorable" to reform measures in the Sixty-first Congress. While the Sixty-second Congress with a Democratic majority in the House did not make an enviable record in reform legislation due to President Taft's exercise of the veto power, it did serve a partisan end. The first Democratic House of the twentieth century presented a record of sane and constructive leadership along progressive lines and initiated investigations into the complex problems of trusts, tariffs, and banking.[17] While these years of transition between Republican and Democratic regimes were largely devoid of constructive legislation, the 1912 election results vindicated the Democratic strategy. Political considerations leading to a revival of the Democratic party had dominated activities. As a member of the Ways and Means Committee, the congressman could take pride in his contribution to the Democratic victory. Ahead lay his constructive role in the fulfillment of the promises for domestic changes.

The New Freedom of 1913 to 1917 embraced a multiplicity of domestic reforms, and Rainey earned a position as one of Wilson's legislative lieutenants. Henry T. played an influential role in the downward revision of the tariff and assumed the position of leadership in the establishment of a tariff commission. He struggled valiantly for the principles of water conservation on a state and national level. His efforts in behalf of an Illinois deep waterway as a part of the lakes-to-gulf system were continued.

On such reform measures as the Underwood-Simmons bill, the Glass-Owen currency reforms, the Panama Canal tolls repeal, the Federal Trade Commission bill, and the Clayton anti-trust bill, Rainey was counted among the party regulars supporting Wilson's program. Through personal conference and party caucus, the President was able to establish a harmonious relationship between the executive and legislative branches of government. In fact, the teamwork effected in the prewar years established a cabinet system of government characterized by party responsibility without benefit of a constitutional amendment.[18] Rainey operated effectively in this situation of strong executive leadership and majority party status.

World events had not figured prominently in the thinking of most Americans, of their President, or of Congressman Rainey. Nevertheless, events in Europe were to provide the orientation for the next subdivision in Rainey's legislative career. Unlike some persons with progressive inclinations, he had no qualms about a declaration of war when the diplomatic impasse was reached. Because of the aversion of Speaker Champ Clark and Majority Leader Claude Kitchin to the Wilson war programs, Rainey became unofficial champion of the administration during the years 1917 to 1921. His contributions on the home front included the war revenue measures and the inauguration of the Illinois waterway. In the reconstruction years, his interest focused on preserving the earlier progressive gains in tax and tariff matters. He was also a supporter of the League of Nations, with reservations. These years were characterized by extreme loyalty to the Wilson administration's policies and principles.

During the first half of Rainey's career, he had come to have the highest personal regard for two of his mentors, William Jennings Bryan and Woodrow Wilson. With great sincerity following the 1920 election, Rainey wrote William Gibbs McAdoo this assessment of the President's position in the nation's heritage: "History will accord to him the position to which he is entitled—the greatest man the world has produced in a century of time." Although Rainey was cognizant of the fact that Wilson was popularly believed to be cold and unapproachable, he found him to be a man of the tenderest sympathies. The Illinoisan was equally praising of the pioneering leadership of Bryan. Of his lifelong friend, Rainey wrote that he regarded Bryan as "the greatest American of his generation" because he "blazed all the trails for the last quarter of a century which have led to better things and the rest of us have merely followed where he led."[19] Rainey knowingly owed political gratitude to these two giants of progressive democracy. Upon his return to public life following the 1922 election, he subconsciously dedicated his subsequent career to the fulfillment of their political principles.

Since 1903 Rainey had risen steadily in the party's councils until he was one of the top congressional leaders. His defeat in 1920, along with eighty-eight members of his party, decimated the Democratic side of the congressional aisle. When he returned to

Congress in 1923, he did so with a renewed enthusiasm for
progressive ideals. In Arthur S. Link's assessment of the
1920s, the most vibrant vestiges of progressive reform may be
seen in the opposition to the Mellon tax plans, the maturation
of a farm relief program, and the formulation of plans for
public power and regional development.[20] Rainey was in the
forefront of each of these fights as a constructive critic of
the Republican administrations. Agricultural issues dominated
his interest upon returning to the national legislature, but
he also evidenced concern for revenue matters and river regulation
policies. As a "freshman" congressman and yet elder party
spokesman, Rainey returned full of enthusiasm for a reawakening
of Democracy. He continued his identification with the liberal
wing of his party. In spite of the frustrations experienced in
a period of Republican ascendancy, he preferred to strive for
reform from within his party rather than gamble on third-party
efforts, as did some progressive proponents in 1924. Events
were to demonstrate that the "Sage of Walnut Hall" would have an
uphill climb fighting to overcome his loss of seniority and to
revitalize his party.

The constructive critic of the early 1920s became the party
conscience after mid-decade. In the face of expanding prosperity,
the Democratic congressional delegations were becoming increasingly
conservative. Rainey was among the few resisting such ideological
tendencies, but his views were a minority expression within the
party. The divided nature of his party plagued him during these
years. By 1926 Rainey had served longer in the House than any
previous Democrat from a northern state. It was from this vantage
point that he charted an independent course. As an elder politician
in the Democratic ranks, his voice commanded attention but not
followers. Charles P. Stewart, Washington columnist writing for
the New Orleans (La.) *States*, observed that there was no longer an
opposition party in Congress, except for a few independents like
Henry T. Rainey. Illinois' senior Democratic congressman earned
this title by opposing the Mellon tax proposals and the debt
settlements for Italy and France. Eventually, according to
Stewart, some fellow law makers realized this was good campaign
material and rallied to the cause. Stewart definitely aligned
Rainey with the "mavericks" who were expected to resurrect the
Democratic party. William D. Jamieson, former Iowa congressman
turned Washington reporter, suggested that if people would elect
representatives, senators, and presidents of a caliber equal to
Rainey, then "this legislative stealing business would soon be
only a matter of frightful recollection . . . and no longer a
thing of present experience." Rainey was especially praised for
representing all the people all the time by trampling on the
special interests and invisible government.[21] As a Democratic
maverick during the years 1925 to 1931, he was not among the
party's inner conservative clique.

The change in party fortunes with the 1930 off-year elections
also brought a change in Rainey's status within the party. By
virtue of geography and longevity, he was a logical choice for

majority leader. His stint as the Democratic guide in the
lower House coincided with a time of economic and political
crisis for the nation. He concentrated upon budget balancing,
unemployment relief, farm recovery, and tariff reductions as
the principal problems meriting his time and attention. As
majority leader he was partially successful in upholding the
Hoover administration's efforts to combat the depression,
especially in the area of fiscal responsibility, even though
it meant compromising progressive tenets. At the same time,
he attempted to surpass the administration by sponsoring forward-
looking legislation in the areas of farm and unemployment relief.
He operated with one eye on the nation's welfare and the other
on the presidential election situation. Progressive ideals were
becoming fashionable again in the legislative chamber as well as
among the populace as a whole. The proposed New Deal would
reach into the experience of countless individuals—Rainey among
them—for ideas that could be adopted to the economic crisis.
The nation's experiences during World War I provided an
especially fruitful background for plotting the responses to
an equally challenging situation.[22]   The advent of the new
administration meant new responsibilities for Henry T. Rainey,
former Wilson lieutenant.

Rainey's selection as Speaker represented the triumph of
devotion to duty and development of deals. Among contemporaries,
there was some doubt about the leader's place on the political
spectrum. It was observed that his selection as majority leader
had been opposed because he was too radical and would upset the
party's apple cart. Some opponents of his Speakership candidacy
argued that he was too conservative to conform to the ideas of
President-elect Roosevelt. *Time* magazine noted that his outlook
filled "many a conservative with alarm" because Rainey favored
such policies as recognition of Russia, government operation of
Muscle Shoals, publicity of RFC loans, expanded federal job
relief, and farm support through the domestic allotment plan.
One gleam of conservative hope was that he was not "a rabid
currency inflationist." After elaborating on his progressive
views, *Time* devoted an equal amount of space to convincing the
reader that this "picturesquely independent fire-eater" had
mellowed after twenty-eight years in the House. Although he
still had bursts of crusading fervor, he was now subdued by the
responsibilities of party principles. There was no denying that
Rainey combined some progressive and conservative elements, but
the balance of the scales definitely leaned to the liberal side.
Chiefly in the area of fiscal responsibility in his support of
the sales tax and budget balancing, Rainey may be said to have
catered to conservative interests. Since the First New Deal was
modestly progressive in its approach to relief, recovery, and
reform and avowedly conservative in its approach to financial
solvency, Rainey fit perfectly into the new administration's
philosophy.[23]   The headlines announcing Rainey's death shared
the spotlight with front-page stories indicating the birth of
the American Liberty League. One can only speculate about how

he might have responded to ventures into social welfare legislation and Keynesian financing. It is likely that the former would have been embraced readily and that the latter would have been accepted reluctantly but rationalized into a defensible policy.

As legislative marshal for the first New Deal, Rainey acquitted himself quite well. The Illinoisan was the first Democrat since the Civil War from north of the Mason-Dixon line to become Speaker of the House. At the age of seventy-two years, he was the oldest man elected to that post and the oldest to serve in this capacity until Speakers Sam Rayburn and John McCormack. Despite his years, Rainey exhibited remarkable vigor in the fulfillment of his responsibilities. By entreaty rather than command, he followed the practice of parliamentary maneuvering to enact Roosevelt's legislation. While there was some concern about the Speaker's success in 1934, the President yearned for the Rainey capacities when Congress revolted in 1937 over the revamping of the Supreme Court. Among the many schools of New Dealers, the "Little Giant" fitted best with the agrarian element whose heritage dated to William Jennings Bryan. At the same time, he could reach an accord with the Wilson trust-busting element, the Rooseveltian progressives of 1912, the Cleveland fiscal conservatives, and the Smith urban/immigrant liberals. Rainey was noted for democratic acceptance. The first and second sessions of the Seventy-third Congress combined to provide President Roosevelt with the passage of thirty-three major administration measures.[24] No presidential lieutenant ever served more faithfully in the execution of the Chief Executive's will.

The marvel of the Rainey career is not that he was progressive or successful, but that he was able to retain his liberalism and his seat in spite of the basic conservatism of his district. His rural constituency repeatedly endorsed his candidacy and thereby approved a larger role for government in public affairs. The attachment between constituent and representative is best explained perhaps in a personal magnetism which Rainey was able to generate.[25] His idealism and experience were suitable complements to a President who needed followers while providing leadership. Rainey made his impress upon the pages of history as an essential supporter of the Roosevelt program.

As loyal party worker for half a century from local through state to national levels, Rainey bequeathed one major innovation to the political process. That was the institution of the policy or steering committee in 1933. As a part of the deal which elected him to the Speaker's chair, Rainey had heralded the steering committee as an opportunity to share the leadership function and to resolve party differences. While the idea sounded good in principle, it never worked well in practice. During Rainey's occupancy of the chair, there is evidence of only one occasion when the steering committee influenced the course of legislation. Grass-roots support for the Glass-Steagall banking bill gathered by the committee helped to convince President Roosevelt to add the measure to the administration program. While the machinery of the steering committee outlived

Rainey, it never became a viable instrument of party
organization.[26]   Southerners like Sam Rayburn distrusted
such a body as a diminution of their influence in the
party's councils, and it fell into disuse. The chief impact
of this innovation was to solidify support for Rainey's
selection as Speaker, so his parliamentary contribution was
ephemeral.

In determining whether it is man or environment that controls history, the balance of the scales in Rainey's case lies
on the side of the individual. In part this outcome was
determined by his choice of a public profession as national
legislator in the lawyer-statesman tradition. His long membership in a political institution which reveres seniority, longevity
of service, and lock-step advancement to positions of influence dictated that circumstances would play a large part in the
determination of his impact upon the historical record. The
good fortune of a northern constituency with traditional Democratic voting preferences accentuated the impact of Rainey's
surroundings. While admitting the contribution of external
forces in determining his destiny, the preponderant influence
of the man cannot be discounted. Numerous individuals preceding
Rainey as representative from the twentieth congressional
district had been unsuccessful in capitalizing upon these
favorable circumstances. Credit Rainey with the political acumen
to gain and then retain a legislative position which enabled him
to attain the Speaker's post. His talents for constituent
service and constructive statecraft facilitated his climb to the
Speakership. This fortuitous blend of an individual with conditions contributed to his continuance in the legislative chamber.

The span of Rainey's life makes him an important link
between the late nineteenth century and the early twentieth
century. He provides a direct connection between the simple
Bryan agrarianism of the 1890s, the broader Wilsonian idealism
of the Progressive era, and the still more complex economic and
social orientation of Roosevelt's New Deal. There is a continuity
of interest and orientation that is obscured if one examines only
the ideological peaks. Rainey represents a transitional figure, a
connective link, between these reform spurts. To a large degree
he exemplifies the typical middle-class group so dominant among
the progressives before World War I; yet, Henry T. exhibited a
greater concern for the laboring classes than many of his contemporaries and thus presaged the New Deal. On the other hand, his
virtual neglect of the urban masses placed him out of step with
that New Deal concern. Although Rainey favored the major political
reforms which characterized the prewar progressives, his intense
concern was economic matters. In this way he links the first
decade of the century with the third. Rainey's concern for the
farm communities which did not enjoy the prosperity of the 1920s
forecasts the broadened New Deal program for those who suffered
economic deprivation. In the historical debate over whether the

New Deal was evolutionary or revolutionary, the Illinoisan's
career emphasizes the continuity inherent in the program's
absorption and adaptation of earlier approaches.[27] Rainey is
one of the few national legislators whose career spans the years
from the beginning of progressivism at the turn of the century
through the first New Deal reforms. He served as a twentieth-
century spokesman for the humanitarianism of Jefferson and the
equalitarianism of Jackson.

Henry T.'s electoral success in Illinois during years that
were predominantly Republican was phenomenal. He managed the
biennial encounter with the voters by a masterful knack for
providing service to his whole constituency, by an intense
interest in each individual regardless of party affiliation, and
by supporting issues in which the district had an interest. His
endorsement of prohibition and his advocacy of farm relief had
transparent implications for himself, his constituency, and the
nation. On the other hand, he asserted his independence by
showing especially great involvement with national issues in
which his district had no immediate concern—shipping subsidies,
for example. Rainey was able to maintain the delicate balance
between errand boy for his district and public servant of the
nation.[28] For the most part he was not prominently in the public
eye; he was content to serve the citizenry with little publicity
and sparse public recognition. While occasionally mentioned as
a candidate for governor or United States senator, the "Sage of
Walnut Hall" never evidenced any desire for a place other than
in the popular branch of the national legislature. On occasion
he was considered to be a presidential or vice-presidential
possibility. While he was not presidential timber because he
lacked the dynamic leadership capability necessary for twentieth-
century occupants of the office, the modern-day "Little Giant"
could have filled admirably the other positions for which he
was mentioned. Nevertheless, he was content to continue
unostentatiously his labors in the lower House.

Rainey served from Roosevelt to Roosevelt, and a great
legislative mass was enacted during that time. No piece of
legislation bears his name for posterity's remembrance, and only
occasional laws give evidence of his preponderant influence.
During most of his years, membership among the minority diminished
opportunities for that kind of prominence. His most significant
personal legislative accomplishment, the Tariff Commission, has
been neglected as an important contribution to the New Freedom.
The provision for scientific revision of the tariff such as he
fostered was a natural complement to the tariff reform of the
Progressive era. In Rainey's assessment of legislative issues,
there were two sides—the people versus greed. While this may be
analytically unsophisticated, it represents the psychological
basis on which many reformers argued their case for changes within
American society. The people needed disinterested protection, and
it was Rainey's aim to provide that defense. His stubborn fights
on tax policy and war debts are indicative of this tendency to
champion the underdog. Rainey's most permanent monument—the lakes-

to-gulf waterway system—is one for which he receives little or
no credit. He was instigator, developer, manipulator, and critic
of the Illinois component of the program from conception to
completion. Today that barge network should stand as a constant
reminder of his service to district, state, and nation.

In matters of foreign policy, Rainey's horizons were sharply
limited to national self-interest, as he conceived it. His
concern for matters of state was essentially limited to those in
which justice, politics, or economic urgency demanded his interest.
He was an avowed anti-imperialist, and consistently favored
independence for the Philippine Islands. Judicial inclinations
and political considerations led him to support the cause of
Colombia in smoothing the difficulties arising out of the
acquisition of the Panama Canal. Unlike some progressives in
1917, he had no qualms about participation in the Great War once
circumstances forced it upon the nation. An acknowledged internationalist, Rainey favored the League of Nations and the World
Court. His attitude toward the depression was also internationalist in outlook. Reduction in the economic barriers to
trade, he thought, would remove the causes of war and depression.
In both foreign and domestic affairs, he sought to improve, not
to scrap, the ship of state whenever imperfections appeared.

As an individual, Henry T. was a remarkable man. During his
thirty years in Congress, his vitality seemed inexhaustible,
even when he was over seventy years old. His doggedness and
determination were a trademark among those 2,375 individuals who
were his contemporaries in the Senate and the House of Representatives. While others indulged in golf and bridge, he found
relaxation in studying issues and smoking his pipe. Local
tradition credits him with a wondrous memory for facts and faces.
He is said to have given long speeches entirely from memory and
to have varied hardly at all from advance copies given the press.
Constituents marveled at his ability to remember them once he had
made their acquaintance even fleetingly. The warmth of his
personality was infectious. He may be characterized as energetic,
public-spirited, capable, and dependable.

At the same time, he was not without his faults. That same
personality which was buoyant and dynamic was also combative. In
legislative argument, he was frequently tactless, unnecessarily
abusive, extremely stubborn, and overly dramatic. He was an
excellent orator and skilled in debate. Too often he utilized
vitriolic personal attack to make his points, yet his harangues
were immediately forgotten when away from the political arena.
His homespun frankness was a virtue often turned to vice when
reporters enduced him to prognosticate where politicians ought to
fear speculating. The result was countless retractions and
retreats which diminished the impact of his utterances when he had
important pronouncements to make. Essentially he was a loner in
political circles, self-confident and self-sufficient. In spite
of these human failings, his opponents, within and without his
party, respected the genuineness and sincerity with which he
approached his legislative tasks. For posterity, the Rainey

success story indicates the efficacy of patience and perseverance in the pursuit of liberal reforms, a true spokesman for
progressive democracy.

The events of the first third of the twentieth century
have been viewed and reviewed from the perspective of a congressman participant. Henry Thomas Rainey deserves a larger niche in
the state's and the nation's history than has thus far been
accorded him.[29] "The Sage of Walnut Hall" is admittedly not in
the first rank of all the legislative greats of the nearly two
centuries since the Congress began, but at the same time he does
not rate the oblivion of the mediocre who serve and deserve to
be forgotten. His career is sufficiently long and constructive
to deserve rescue from obscurity. Henry T.'s impress on party
and policy during thirty years make him worthy of attention.
This distinguished son of Illinois should be assigned a place in
the second rank among the near great of the nation's congressmen,
and should be accorded a fuller recognition for his sturdy
liberalism and his climb to the Speakership. His role as
representative in a democracy and his service as a legislator
represent a model for posterity to emulate.

NOTES

1. Parke Brown, "Speaker Rainey Here on Aerial Campaign
Tour," Chicago *Tribune*, June 29, 1934, 12:3-4; letter summarized
in Chicago *Tribune*, Aug. 9, 1934, 3:2-3.

2. *Patriot*, Aug. 16, 1934, 1:5, and Aug. 23, 1:1.

3. *Ibid.*, Aug. 23, 1934, 1:5-6, and Aug. 30, 1934, 1:5
and 2:1; New York *Times*, Aug. 21, 1934, 1:1 and 11:4; Aug. 22,
1934, 1:4; Aug, 23, 1934, 3:1-2.

4. *Memorial Services . . . Henry T. Rainey*, 44; editorial,
"We Mourn the Death of Henry T. Rainey," *Patriot*, Aug. 23, 1934,
2:1.

5. New York *Times*, Aug. 20, 1934, 3:5, and Aug. 28, 1934,
9:1.

6. Beginning in 1941 Mrs. HTR began suffering from arterio-
sclerosis (a hardening of the arteries which frequently accompanies
old age). There was also some question of her mental condition
and a court committed her to a mental institution where she
might receive professional care. Several efforts by friends to
have her released to private care were unsuccessful. See the
Gazette of Jan. 15, 1943, 1:1; June 9, 1944, 4:4; June 30, 1944,
1:6; and Aug. 31, 1945, 1:2.

7. *Illinois State Journal*, Aug. 20, 1934, 1:2; Chicago
Tribune, Aug. 23, 1934, 4:4; Aug. 28, 4:2; Sept. 19, 2:8; Littlewood,
Horner of Illinois, 71, 94, 114, 245.

8. Chicago *Tribune*, Aug. 20, 1934, 2:3, and Aug. 22, 1:1;
George B. Galloway, *History of the House of Representatives*,

Appendix A, 289, and Appendix B, 291–292.

9. Chicago *Tribune*, Feb. 11, 1935, 1:5; "Speaking Likeness," *Time*, XXVI (Oct. 28, 1935), 23; *CR*, 74:2 (June 20, 1936), 10566–67, 10615.

10. *Gazette*, Jan. 24, 1935, 1:5; Aug. 12, 1937, 1:6; and Aug. 19, 1937, 1:3–4 and 4:1–2; Wayne C. Temple, "Tribute to G. V. Black," 3–4.

11. For an extensive study of this question involving 168 individuals (HTR not among them), see Otis L. Graham, *An Encore for Reform*.

12. Interestingly many of the nation's most illustrious liberal politicians leave no precise definition of their creed. See, for example, the observations of David Fellman, "The Liberalism of Senator Norris," 27–51.

13. HTR to H. N. Wheeler, Washington, Dec. 6, 1911, RP; William Hard, "What Is Progressivism?," 27–28, and HTR response in "What—After All—Is 'Progressivism'?," 161; HTR to Norman L. Jones, [Washington], March 16, 1934, RP; interview with Virginia Gardner, "Rainey Radical, Not Red, He Says," Chicago *Tribune*, June 30, 1934, 2:2.

14. *CR*, 64:1 (April 27, 1916), 6935; *CR*, 66:3 (March 4, 1921), 4542–4543.

15. Jerome M. Clubb, "Congressional Opponents of Reform, 1901–1913" (Ph.D. thesis), 26–29, 54, 60–62, 68–69.

16. John B. Wiseman, "Dilemmas of a Party Out of Power" (Ph.D. thesis), 61; Clubb, "Congressional Opponents," 75–76, 82–85, 115–116, 119–121, 126–127, 130–137, 157–160, 167–169, 192; *Gazette*, July 22, 1909, 4:3.

17. Clubb, "Congressional Opponents," 237–238, 249–252, 256–260, 264–266, 276–278, 291, 331; Claude E. Barfield, Jr., "The Democratic Party in Congress, 1909–1913" (Ph.D. thesis), 424.

18. Elston E. Rhoady, "Party Regularity in the Sixty-third Congress" (Ph.D. thesis), 311; Ripley, *Majority Party Leadership in Congress*, 52–69; Lindsay Rogers, "President Wilson's Theory of His Office," 174, 181; Marshall E. Dimock, "Woodrow Wilson as a Legislative Leader," 12.

19. HTR to McAdoo, Carrollton, Nov. 8, 1920, McAdoo Papers, Box 243; HTR address at Wilson day luncheon, Pittsburgh, Pa., on Dec. 27, 1924, *CR*, 68:2 (March 4, 1925), 5572; HTR to J. W. Hughes, Washington, Dec. 7, 1923, original in Bryan Papers, Box 38.

20. "The Toll of Leaders," *Searchlight on Congress*, V (Dec. 1, 1920), 5–6; Arthur S. Link, "What Happened to the Progressive Movement in the 1920's?," 841, 845–847.

21. For an analysis of the congressional Democrats in the 1920s, see Burner, *The Politics of Provincialism*, 158–178; Charles P. Stewart, "Rainey Often Licked but Fights On," *States*,

June 21, [1926], 6:1, RP, "Newspaper Clippings" file; William D. Jamieson, "The Window Seat," *Patriot*, June 17, 1926, 4:1.

22. Leuchtenburg, "The New Deal and the Analogue of War," 81–143. HTR's support of the New Deal contrasts with the opposition of the six Wilsonians (Newton D. Baker, Bernard Baruch, Bainbridge Colby, George Creel, Edward M. House, and David Lawrence) studied by Paul L. Silver, "Wilsonians and the New Deal" (Ph.D. thesis).

23. "The Congress," *Time*, XX (Dec. 19, 1932), 10; William Hard, "The Nation's New Leaders," 150; Otis L. Graham, Jr., "Historians and the New Deals, 1944–1960," 133–135.

24. Riddick, "The House of Representatives and the President," 83–85, 89–90; diary entry for June 17, 1937, in Harold L. Ickes, *The Secret Diary of Harold L. Ickes*, II, 151; Arthur M. Schlesinger, *The Coming of the New Deal*, 18–19; "Speaker Rainey, Legislative Marshal of the New Deal, Dies," 6; Ripley, *Majority Party Leadership*, 70–88.

25. Editorial, "Hon. Henry T. Rainey," *Illinois State Journal*, Aug. 20, 1934, 4:1.

26. Ripley, *Majority Party Leadership*, 70–71; Walter E. Beach, "The Democratic Steering Committee in the House of Representatives, 1933–1960" (M.A. thesis), 25–32.

27. Charles A. Beard, "The Historical Approach to the New Deal," 14–15; Andrew M. Scott, "The Progressive Era in Perspective," 685–701.

28. For a discussion of the potential conflict between conscience and constituent, see John F. Kennedy, *Profiles in Courage*, 12–21.

29. Marvin W. Block, "Henry T. Rainey of Illinois," 142–157, is the only published summary of HTR's career.

Bibliography

I. MANUSCRIPT COLLECTIONS

William Jennings Bryan Papers in the Library of Congress.

Albert Sidney Burleson Papers in the Library of Congress.

Herbert Clark Hoover Papers in the Hoover Presidential Library at West Branch, Iowa.

Henry Horner Papers in the Illinois State Historical Library at Springfield.

Claude Kitchin Papers in the Southern Historical Collection at the University of North Carolina Library.

William Gibbs McAdoo Papers in the Library of Congress.

Herbert W. Mumford Papers in the Archives of the University of Illinois at Urbana.

Gifford Pinchot Papers in the Library of Congress.

Henry Thomas Rainey Papers in the Library of Congress.

Larry Richey Papers in the Hoover Presidential Library at West Branch, Iowa.

Franklin D. Roosevelt Papers in the Roosevelt Library at Hyde Park, New York.

Charles Edward Russell Papers in the Library of Congress.

Woodrow Wilson Papers in the Library of Congress.

II. ARCHIVAL MATERIALS

Election Returns, State Officers 1882 [to date], Secretary's Office, Illinois, in Illinois State Archives at Springfield.

The Minutes of the Directors of the Public Library and Reading Room of the City of Carrollton, Illinois, in the Carrollton Public Library.

III. PRINTED SOURCES

A. Federal Government

Biographical Directory of the American Congress, 1774-1961. Washington, D.C.: Government Printing Office, 1961.

Census of Religious Bodies: 1936. Washington, D.C.: Government Printing Office, 1941.

Congressional Record. 57th Cong. (1901)—87th Cong. (1961).

Contested-Election Case of Henry T. Rainey v. Guy L. Shaw from the Twentieth Congressional District of Illinois. Washington, D.C.: Government Printing Office, 1921.

Contested-Election Case of Rainey v. Shaw: Hearings before the House Committee on Elections No. 2. Washington, D.C.: Government Printing Office, 1921.

Fourteenth Census of the United States Taken in the Year 1920. Washington, D.C.: Government Printing Office, 1922.

Memorial Services Held in the House of Representatives of the United States, Together with Remarks Presented in Eulogy of Henry T. Rainey, Late a Representative from Illinois. Washington, D.C.: Government Printing Office, 1936.

Papers Relating to the Foreign Relations of the United States with the Annual Message of the President Transmitted to Congress December 7, 1909. Washington, D.C.: Government Printing Office, 1914.

Treasury Department, U.S. Department of Internal Revenue. *Traffic in Narcotic Drugs: Report of Special Committee of Investigation Appointed March 25, 1918, by the Secretary of the Treasury.* Washington, D.C.: Government Printing Office, 1919.

U.S. Congress, House, Committee on Foreign Affairs. *The Story of Panama: Hearings on the Rainey Resolution*, 62nd Cong., 2nd Sess. Washington, D.C.: Government Printing Office, 1913.

———, ———, Committee on Rivers and Harbors. *Hearings on the Improvement of the Illinois and Mississippi Rivers, and the Diversion of Water from Lake Michigan into the Illinois River*, 68th Cong., 1st Sess. Washington, D.C.: Government Printing Office, 1924.

———, ———, ———. *Hearings on the Improvement of the Illinois River, Ill., and the Abstraction of Water from Lake Michigan.* Washington, D.C.: Government Printing Office, 1926.

B. State of Illinois

Blue Book of the State of Illinois, 1903-70.

Division of Waterways, Annual Report, 1917-45.

Journal of the House of Representatives, 1901-36.

Journal of the Senate, 1901-36.

Report of the Illinois State Planning Commission. Springfield: unknown, 1934 and 1935.

C. Published Papers

Baker, Ray S. (ed.). *Woodrow Wilson: Life and Letters.* 8 vols.

Garden City, N.Y.: Doubleday, Page, 1927–39.

——— and William E. Dodds (eds.). *The Public Papers of Woodrow Wilson.* 6 vols. New York: Harper, 1925–27.

Darling, Arthur B. (ed.). *The Public Papers of Francis G. Newlands.* 2 vols. Boston, Mass.: Houghton Mifflin, 1932.

Morison, Elting E. (ed.). *The Letters of Theodore Roosevelt.* 8 vols. Cambridge, Mass.: Harvard University Press, 1951–54.

Roosevelt, Elliott (ed.). *F.D.R.: His Personal Letters.* 4 vols. New York: Duell, Sloan and Pearce, 1947–50.

Sullivan, William L. (ed.). *Dunne: Judge, Mayor, Governor.* Chicago: Windermere Press, 1916.

D. Miscellaneous

Democratic National Convention *Proceedings*, 1896–1936.

Lakes-to-the-Gulf Deep Waterway Association Conventions, 1906–10. St. Louis: Lakes-to-the-Gulf Deep Waterway Association.

Official Report of the Proceedings of the Democratic National Convention . . . 1920. Indianapolis, Ind.: Bookwalter-Ball, 1920.

IV. BOOKS

A. Autobiographies, Memoirs

Bloom, Vera. *There's No Place Like Washington.* New York: G. P. Putnam, 1944.

Butt, Archibald. *Taft and Roosevelt: The Intimate Letters of Archie Butt, Military Aide.* 2 vols. Garden City, N.Y.: Doubleday, Doran, 1930.

Clark, Champ. *My Quarter Century of American Politics.* 2 vols. New York: Harper, 1920.

Cole, Cyrenus. *I Remember, I Remember: A Book of Recollections.* Iowa City: State Historical Society of Iowa, 1936.

Harrison, Carter H. *Growing Up with Chicago: Sequel to "Stormy Years."* Chicago: Ralph Fletcher Seymour, 1944.

———. *Stormy Years: The Autobiography of Carter H. Harrison, Five Times Mayor of Chicago.* Indianapolis, Ind.: Bobbs-Merrill, 1935.

Hoover, Herbert C. *The Memoirs of Herbert Hoover.* 3 vols. New York: Macmillan, 1951–52.

Hull, Cordell. *The Memoirs of Cordell Hull.* 2 vols. New York: Macmillan, 1948.

Ickes, Harold L. *The Secret Diary of Harold L. Ickes.* 3 vols. New York: Simon and Schuster, 1953–54.

Jones, Jesse H. *Fifty Billion Dollars: My Thirteen Years with the RFC, 1932-1945.* New York: Macmillan, 1951.

Peek, George N. *Why Quit Our Own.* New York: D. Van Nostrand, 1936.

B. Biographies

Arnett, Alex M. *Claude Kitchin and the Wilson War Policies.* Boston, Mass.: Little, Brown, 1937.

Blum, John M. *From the Morgenthau Diaries: Years of Crisis, 1928-1938.* Boston, Mass: Houghton Mifflin, 1959.

————. *Joe Tumulty and the Wilson Era.* Boston, Mass.: Houghton Mifflin, 1951.

Brown, George R. *The Speaker of the House: The Romantic Story of John N. Garner.* New York: Brewer, Warren and Putnam, 1932.

Charnwood, Lord. *Theodore Roosevelt.* Boston, Mass.: Atlantic Monthly, 1923.

Coletta, Paolo E. *William Jennings Bryan.* 3 vols. Lincoln: University of Nebraska Press, 1964-69.

Crissey, Forrest. *Theodore E. Burton: American Statesman.* Cleveland, Ohio: World, 1956.

Davis, Forrest. *Huey Long: A Candid Biography.* New York: Dodge, 1935.

Dennett, Tyler. *John Hay: From Poetry to Politics.* New York: Dodd, Mead, 1933.

Dorough, C. Dwight. *Mr. Sam.* New York: Random House, 1962.

Downs, Winfield (ed.). *Encyclopedia of American Biography.* Vol. XI. New York: American Historical, 1940.

Fite, Gilbert C. *George N. Peek and the Fight for Farm Parity.* Norman: University of Oklahoma Press, 1954.

Gwinn, William R. *Uncle Joe Cannon, Archfoe of Insurgency: A History of the Rise and Fall of Cannonism.* [New York]: Bookman Associates, 1957.

Hutchinson, William T. *Lowden of Illinois: The Life of Frank O. Lowden* 2 vols. Chicago: University of Chicago Press, 1957.

Littlewood, Thomas B. *Horner of Illinois.* Evanston, Ill.: Northwestern University Press, 1969.

McCoy, Donald R. *Calvin Coolidge: The Quiet President.* New York: Macmillan, 1967.

Timmons, Bascom N. *Garner of Texas: A Personal History.* New York: Harper, 1948.

————. *Jesse H. Jones: The Man and the Statesman.* New York: Henry Holt, 1956.

Tumulty, Joseph P. *Woodrow Wilson as I Know Him.* Garden City, N.Y.: Garden City, 1925.

Zinn, Howard. *La Guardia in Congress.* Ithaca, N.Y.: Cornell University Press, 1959.

C.   Secondary Works

American Biography: A New Cyclopedia. Vol. 50. New York: American Historical Society, 1932.

Atkinson, Charles R. *The Committee on Rules and the Overthrow of Speaker Cannon.* New York: Columbia University Press, 1911.

Atlas Map of Greene County, Illinois. Davenport, Iowa.: Andreas, Lyter, [1873].

Barnes, Mortimer G. *Inland Waterways: Their Necessity, Importance and Value in Handling the Commerce of the United States, and Reducing Transportation Costs.* Springfield, Ill.: Department of Public Works and Buildings, 1920.

Bennett, Edward M. *Recognition of Russia: An American Foreign Policy Dilemma.* Waltham, Mass.: Blaisdell, 1970.

Blakey, Roy G., and Gladys C. Blakey. *The Federal Income Tax.* New York: Longmans, Green, 1940.

Bolling, Richard. *Power in the House: A History of the Leadership of the House of Representatives.* New York: E. P. Dutton, 1968.

Brennan, John A. *Silver and the First New Deal.* Reno: University of Nevada Press, 1969.

Browder, Robert P. *The Origins of Soviet-American Diplomacy.* Princeton, N.J.: Princeton University Press, 1953.

Burner, David. *The Politics of Provincialism: The Democratic Party in Transition, 1918-1932.* New York: Alfred A. Knopf, 1968.

Campbell, Christiana M. *The Farm Bureau and the New Deal: A Study of the Making of National Farm Policy, 1933-40.* Urbana: University of Illinois Press, 1962.

Cook, John W. *Educational History of Illinois.* Chicago: Henry O. Shepard, 1912.

Douglas, Jack. *Veterans on the March.* New York: Workers Library, 1934.

Drury, John. *Old Illinois Houses.* Springfield: State of Illinois, 1948.

Federal Writers' Project. *Illinois: A Descriptive and Historical Guide.* Chicago: A. C. McClurg, 1939.

Frost, Thomas G. *Tales from the Siwash Campus.* New York: Appellate Law Printers, 1938.

Galloway, George B. *History of the House of Representatives.* New York: Thomas Y. Crowell, 1961.

Gilman, Agness G., and Gertrude M. Gilman. *Who's Who in Illinois, Women-Makers of History.* Chicago: Eclectic Publishers, 1927.

Gosnell, Harold F. *Grass Roots Politics: National Voting Behavior of Typical States.* Washington, D.C.: American Council of Public Affairs, 1942.

Graham, Otis L., Jr. *An Encore for Reform: The Old Progressives and the New Deal.* New York: Oxford University Press, 1967.

Grassmuck, George L. *Sectional Biases in Congress on Foreign Policy.* Baltimore, Md.: Johns Hopkins Press, 1951.

Haines, Lynn. *Law Making in America: The Story of the 1911-12 Session of the Sixty-second Congress.* Bethesda, Md.: unknown, 1912.

Havighurst, Walter. *Voices on the River: The Story of the Mississippi Waterways.* New York: Macmillan, 1964.

Hays, Samuel P. *Conservation and the Gospel of Efficiency: The Progressive Conservation Movement, 1890-1920.* Cambridge, Mass.: Harvard University Press, 1959.

Hechler, Kenneth W. *Insurgency: Personalities and Politics of the Taft Era.* New York: Columbia University Press, 1940.

Herring, E. Pendleton. *Presidential Leadership: The Political Relations of Congress and the Chief Executive.* New York: Farrar and Rinehart, 1940.

Hicks, John D. *The Populist Revolt: A History of the Farmer's Alliance and the People's Party.* Minneapolis: University of Minnesota Press, 1931.

History of Greene County, Illinois. Chicago: Donnelley, Gassette and Lloyd, 1879.

Hofstadter, Richard. *The Age of Reform: From Bryan to F.D.R.* New York: Alfred A. Knopf, 1955.

Howard, Robert P. *Illinois: A History of the Prairie State.* Grand Rapids, Mich.: William B. Eerdman, 1972.

Howes, Durward (ed.). *American Women: The Official Who's Who among the Women of the Nation, 1937-1938.* Los Angeles, Calif.: American Publications, 1937.

Illinois-Progress, 1921-1928. Springfield, Ill.: Schnepp and Barnes, 1928.

Kefauver, Estes, and Jack Levin. *A Twentieth-Century Congress.*

New York: Duell, Sloan and Pearce, 1947.

Kennedy, John F. *Profiles in Courage*. New York: Harper, 1956.

Kerwin, Jerome K. *Federal Water Power Legislation*. New York: Columbia University Press, 1926.

Key, V. O., Jr. *American State Politics: An Introduction*. New York: Alfred A. Knopf, 1963.

Kile, Orville M. *The Farm Bureau through Three Decades*. Baltimore, Md.: Waverly Press, 1948.

King, Judson. *The Conservation Fight from Theodore Roosevelt to the Tennessee Valley Authority*. Washington, D.C.: Public Affairs Press, 1959.

Link, Arthur S. *Wilson: Confusions and Crises, 1915-1916*. Princeton, N.J.: Princeton University Press, 1964.

————. *Woodrow Wilson and the Progressive Era, 1910-1917*. New York: Harper, 1954.

Lowitt, Richard. *George W. Norris: The Persistence of a Progressive, 1913-1933*. Urbana: University of Illinois Press, 1971.

Mack, Gerstle. *The Land Divided: A History of the Panama Canal and Other Isthmian Projects*. New York: Alfred A. Knopf, 1944.

Miner, Dwight C. *The Fight for the Panama Route: The Story of the Spooner Act and the Hay-Herran Treaty*. New York: Columbia University Press, 1940.

Miner, Ed. *Past and Present of Greene County [,] Illinois*. Chicago: S. J. Clarke, 1905.

Moulton, Harold G. *Waterways versus Railways*. Boston, Mass.: Houghton Mifflin, 1912.

Mowry, George E. *The California Progressives*. Berkeley: University of California Press, 1951.

————. *The Era of Theodore Roosevelt, 1900-1912*. New York: Harper, 1958.

Nourse, Edwin G., Joseph S. Davis, and John D. Black. *Three Years of the Agricultural Adjustment Administration*. Washington, D.C.: Brookings Institution, 1937.

Odegard, Peter H. *Pressure Politics: The Story of the Anti-Saloon League*. New York: Columbia University Press, 1928.

Palmer, John M. (ed.). *The Bench and Bar of Illinois: Historical and Reminiscent*. 2 vols. Chicago: Lewis Publishing, 1899.

Parks, E. Taylor. *Columbia and the United States, 1765-1934*. Durham, N.C.: Duke University Press, 1935.

Paulson, Ross E. *Radicalism and Reform: The Vrooman Family and*

American Social Thought, 1837-1937. Lexington: University of Kentucky Press, 1968.

Pearson, Drew. *More Merry-Go-Round.* New York: Liveright, 1932.

Pease, Theodore C. *The Story of Illinois.* 3rd ed. Chicago: University of Chicago Press, 1965.

Peirce, Clyde. *The Roosevelt Panama Libel Cases: A Factual Study of a Controversial Episode in the Career of Teddy Roosevelt, Father of the Panama Canal.* New York: Greenwich, 1959.

Plat Book of Greene and Jersey Counties, Illinois. Chicago: Hammond, 1893.

Putnam, James W. *The Illinois and Michigan Canal: A Study in Economic History.* Chicago: University of Chicago Press, 1918.

Riddick, Floyd M. *The United States Congress Organization and Procedures.* Manassas, Va.: National Capital, 1949.

Ripley, Randall B. *Majority Party Leadership in Congress.* Boston, Mass.: Little, Brown, 1969.

Romasco, Albert U. *The Poverty of Abundance: Hoover, the Nation, the Depression.* New York: Oxford University Press, 1965.

Schlesinger, Arthur M. *The Coming of the New Deal.* Boston, Mass.: Houghton Mifflin, 1958.

Schwarz, Jordan A. *The Interregnum of Despair: Hoover, Congress, and the Depression.* Urbana: University of Illinois Press, 1970.

Shelton, William A. *The Lakes-to-the-Gulf Deep Waterway.* Chicago: University of Chicago Press, 1912.

Sullivan, Lawrence. *Prelude to Panic: The Story of the Bank Holiday.* Washington, D.C.: Statesman Press, 1936.

Swain, Donald C. *Federal Conservation Policy, 1921-1933.* Berkeley: University of California Press, 1963.

Tarr, Joel A. *A Study in Boss Politics: William Lorimer of Chicago.* Urbana: University of Illinois Press, 1971.

Taylor, Arnold H. *American Diplomacy and the Narcotics Traffic, 1900-1939: A Study in International Humanitarian Reform.* Durham, N.C.: Duke University Press, 1969.

Timberlake, James H. *Prohibition and the Progressive Movement, 1900-1920.* Cambridge, Mass.: Harvard University Press, 1963.

Townsend, Walter A. *Illinois Democracy: A History of the Party and Its Representative Members—Past and Present.* 4 vols. Springfield, Ill.: Democratic Historical Association, 1935.

Tuttle, Charles R. *Illinois Currency Convention.* Chicago: Charles H. Kerr, 1895.

Watson, James E. (comp.). *Federal Commissions, Committees and Boards: List of Federal Commissions, Committees, Boards and Similar Bodies Created During the Period September 14, 1901, to March 4, 1929.* Washington, D.C.: Government Printing Office, 1930.

Wecter, Dixon. *When Johnny Comes Marching Home.* Boston, Mass.: Houghton Mifflin, 1944.

Wiebe, Robert H. *Businessmen and Reform: A Study of the Progressive Movement.* Cambridge, Mass.: Harvard University Press, 1962.

Williams, C. Arch. *The Sanitary District of Chicago: History of Its Growth and Development.* [Chicago: Bentley Murray], 1919.

Willoughby, William R. *The St. Lawrence Waterway: A Study in Politics and Diplomacy.* Madison: University of Wisconsin Press, 1961.

V.   ARTICLES

Abrams, Richard W. "Woodrow Wilson and the Southern Congressmen, 1913-1916," *Journal of Southern History,* XXII (Nov., 1956), 417-437.

Adams, Samuel H. "The Joke's on You: How Your Chosen Representatives Work the Joker Game on Legislation," *American Magazine,* LXX (May, 1910), 51-59.

Adler, Selig. "The Congressional Election of 1918," *South Atlantic Quarterly,* XXXVI (Oct., 1937), 447-465.

————. "Isolationism since 1914," *American Scholar,* XXI (Summer, 1952), 335-344.

"The Administration of Charles S. Deneen, 1905-1912," [Chicago]: Charles S. Deneen Campaign Committee, [1912].

"All Uproarious on the Bonus Front," *Literary Digest,* CXIII (April 23, 1932), 5-6.

"American Waterways," *Annals of the American Academy of Political and Social Science,* XXXI (Jan., 1908), 1-262.

Anderson, William G. "Progressivism: An Historiographical Essay," *The History Teacher,* VI (May, 1973), 427-452.

Ashton, Bessie L. "The Geonomic Aspects of the Illinois Waterway," *University of Illinois Studies in the Social Sciences,* XIV (June, 1926), 1-177.

Baker, Charles W. "What Is the Future of Inland Water Transportation?," *Engineering News-Record,* LXXXIV (Jan. 1, 8, 15, 22, and 29, 1920), 19-28, 85-89, 137-144, 184-191, and 234-242.

Baker, John D. "The Character of the Congressional Revolution of 1910," *Journal of American History,* LX (Dec., 1973), 679-691.

1920), 19–28, 85–89, 137–144, 184–191, and 234–242.

"Ballinger Whitewash Is Upset," *National Monthly*, II (Oct., 1910), 164.

Barrows, Harlan H. "Geography of the Middle Illinois Valley," *Bulletin 15 of the State Geological Survey* (Urbana: Phillips Brothers' Printers, 1910, reprinted in 1925).

Bates, J. Leonard. "Fulfilling American Democracy: The Conservation Movement, 1907 to 1921," *Mississippi Valley Historical Review*, XLIV (June, 1957), 29–57.

Beard, Charles A. "The Historical Approach to the New Deal," *American Political Science Review*, XXVIII (Feb., 1934), 11–15.

Billington, Ray A. "The Origins of Middle Western Isolationism," *Political Science Quarterly*, LX (March, 1945), 44–64.

Black, John D. "The McNary-Haugen Movement," *American Economic Review*, XVIII (Sept., 1928), 405–427.

Bliss, W. D. P. "The Church and Social Reform Workers," *Outlook*, LXXXII (Jan. 20, 1906), 122–125.

Block, Marvin W. "Henry T. Rainey of Illinois," *Journal of the Illinois State Historical Society*, LXV (Summer, 1972), 142–157.

Blythe, Samuel G. "The Soldier in Politics," *Saturday Evening Post*, CXCI (March 15, 1919), 16–17, 79, 82.

Boller, Paul F., Jr. "The 'Great Conspiracy' of 1933: A Study in Short Memories," *Southwest Review*, XXXIX (Spring, 1954), 97–112.

Bratter, Herbert M. "The Silver Episode," *Journal of Political Economy*, XLVI (Oct. and Dec., 1938), 609–652, 802–837.

Brown, L. 'Ames. "Preparedness for Peace: An Authorized Statement of President Wilson's Plans," *Collier's*, LVIII (Sept. 16, 1916), 12–13.

"Bryan! Bryan!! Bryan!!! Bryan!!!!," *Fortune*, IX (Jan., 1934), 60–69, 110, 112, 114, 116, 119–120, 122, 126.

Buenker, John D. "Edward F. Dunne: The Urban New Stock Democrat as Progressive," *Mid-America*, L (Jan., 1968), 3–21.

———. "The Illinois Legislature and Prohibition, 1907–1919," *Journal of the Illinois State Historical Society*, LXII (Winter, 1969), 363–384.

———. "The New-Stock Politicians of 1912," *Journal of the Illinois State Historical Society*, LXII (Spring, 1969), 35–52.

Buswell, Arthur M. "Chicago and the Mississippi Waterway Problem," *American Review of Reviews*, LXXIV (Dec., 1926), 610–612.

Candeloro, Dominic. "*The Public* of Louis F. Post and Pro-
    gressivism," *Mid-America*, LVI (April, 1974), 109-123.

"Candidates for Congress," *Prairie Farmer*, XCVIII (Oct. 30,
    1926), 4.

Carleton, William G. "Isolationism and the Middle West,"
    Mississippi Valley Historical Review, XXXIII (Dec., 1946),
    377-390.

Carlson, Earland I. "Franklin D. Roosevelt's Post-Mortem of
    the 1928 Election," *Midwest Journal of Political Science*,
    VIII (Aug., 1964), 298-308.

Clark, Champ. "What the Democrats in Congress Will Do,"
    Hampton's Magazine, XXVI (Feb., 1911), 205-206.

Clayton, John. "How They Tinkered with a River," *Chicago
    History*, I (Spring, 1970), 32-46.

Coletta, Paola E. "Secretary of State William Jennings Bryan
    and 'Deserving Democrats,'" *Mid-America*, XLVIII (April,
    1966), 75-98.

————. "William Jennings Bryan and the United States-Colombia
    Impasse, 1903-1921," *Hispanic American Historical Review*,
    XLVII (Nov., 1967), 486-501.

"Comment on Congress—Changing Tariffs Quickly," *Collier's*,
    LVIII (Dec. 23, 1916), 9.

"The Congress: Garner's House," *Time*, XVIII (Dec. 7, 1931), 11.

Coode, Thomas H. "Georgia Congressmen and the First Hundred
    Days of the New Deal," *Georgia Historical Quarterly*, LIII
    (June, 1969), 129-146.

Cooper, John M., Jr. "Progressivism and American Foreign Policy:
    A Reconsideration," *Mid-America*, LI (Oct., 1969), 260-277.

Cross, Whitney R. "W J McGee and the Idea of Conservation,"
    Historian, XV (Spring, 1953), 148-162.

Cummins, Cedric. "Indiana Looks at the World War—1914,"
    Indiana Magazine of History, XXXVII (Dec., 1941), 307-344.

Davenport, Eugene. "Twenty-Five Years Hence in Illinois,"
    Country Gentleman, LXXXVIII (April 14, 1923), 15, 20.

Davenport, F. Darvin. "The Sanitation Revolution in Illinois,
    1870-1900," *Journal of the Illinois State Historical
    Society*, LXVI (Autumn, 1973), 306-326.

Davis, G. Cullom. "The Transformation of the Federal Trade
    Commission, 1914-1929," *Mississippi Valley Historical
    Review*, XLIX (Dec., 1962), 437-455.

"The Democratic Landslide," *Literary Digest*, CVII (Nov. 15,
    1930), 7-9.

Deneen, Charles S. "Vast Wealth for the State," *Technical*

World Magazine, IX (April, 1908), 121-129.

Dexter, Lewis A. "The Representative and His District," *Human Organization*, XVI (Spring, 1957), 2-13.

Dimock, Marshall E. "Woodrow Wilson as a Legislative Leader," *Journal of Politics*, XIX (Feb., 1957), 3-19.

Diogenes, "News and Comment from the National Capital," *Literary Digest*, CXVII (March 31, 1934), 11, and CXVII (May 5, 1934), 13.

"Do We Want a Tariff Commission?," *Collier's*, LVI (Nov. 13, 1915), 14.

Eliot, Charles W. "The Achievements of the Democratic Party and Its Leader since March 4, 1913," *Atlantic Monthly*, CXVIII (Oct., 1916), 433-440.

Emery, Henry C. "The Democrats and the Tariff," *Yale Review*, II (Jan., 1913), 193-214.

Fellman, David. "The Liberalism of Senator Norris," *American Political Science Review*, XL (Feb., 1946), 27-51.

Fenno, Richard F., Jr. "The Internal Distribution of Influence: The House" in David B. Truman (ed.), *The Congress and America's Future*. Englewood Cliffs, N.J.: Prentice Hall, 1965, 52-76.

Feuer, Lewis. "American Travellers to the Soviet Union, 1917-1932: The Formation of a Component of New Deal Ideology," *American Quarterly*, XIV (Summer, 1962), 119-149.

Field, Walter T. "The Amherst Illustrious: Speaker Rainey," *Amherst Graduates' Quarterly*, XXIV (Nov., 1934), 22-24.

Filene, Peter G. "An Obituary for 'the Progressive Movement,'" *American Quarterly*, XXII (Spring, 1970), 20-34.

Fitch, George. "Politics in Illinois," *Collier's*, LIV (Oct. 24, 1914), 21-22.

Flynn, John T. "The Trap that Jack Built," *Collier's*, LXXXIX (May 21, 1932), 12-13, 41-42.

Friedlander, Robert A. "A Reassessment of Roosevelt's Role in the Panamanian Revolution of 1903," *Western Political Quarterly*, XIV (June, 1961), 535-543.

Gleason, John P. "The Attitude of the Business Community toward Agriculture During the McNary-Haugen Period," *Agricultural History*, XXXII (April, 1958), 127-138.

Graff, Maurice O. "The Lake Michigan Water Diversion Controversy: A Summary Statement," *Journal of the Illinois State Historical Society*, XXXIV (Dec., 1941), 453-471.

Graham, Otis L., Jr. "Historians and the New Deals, 1944-1960," *Social Studies*, LIV (April, 1963), 133-140.

Grantham, Dewey W., Jr. "The Progressive Era and the Reform Tradition," *Mid-America*, XLVI (Oct., 1964), 227-251.

Gregory, Clifford V. "The American Farm Bureau Federation and the AAA," *Annals of the American Academy of Political and Social Science*, CLXXIX (May, 1935), 152-157.

Hard, William. "The Nation's New Leaders," *Current History*, XXXVIII (May, 1933), 146-151.

———. "What Is Progressivism?," *Nation*, CXVIII (Jan. 9, 1924), 27-28.

Hardy, W. F. "'Mr. Speaker' as the Country Squire" in the *Illinois Magazine* (supplement to the Decatur *Herald and Review* for Aug. 13, 1933), 1 and 3.

Harvey, George. "Will the Democratic Party Commit Suicide?," *North American Review*, CXCIII (Jan., 1911), 1-8.

Hays, Samuel P. "The Politics of Reform in Municipal Government in the Progressive Era," *Pacific Northwest Quarterly*, LV (Oct., 1964), 157-169.

Heacock, Walter J. "William B. Bankhead and the New Deal," *Journal of Southern History*, XXI (Aug., 1955), 347-359.

Herring, E. Pendleton. "First Session of the Seventy-second Congress," *American Political Science Review*, XXVI (Oct., 1932), 846-874.

———. "Second Session of the Seventy-second Congress," *American Political Science Review*, XXVII (June, 1933), 404-422.

———. "First Session of the Seventy-third Congress," *American Political Science Review*, XXVIII (Feb., 1934), 65-83.

———. "Second Session of the Seventy-third Congress," *American Political Science Review*, XXVIII (Oct., 1934), 852-866.

Herskovits, Melville J. "Race Relations," *American Journal of Sociology*, XXXV (May, 1930), 1052-62.

Hill, James J. "Highways of Progress: The Future of Our Waterways," *World's Work*, XIX (April, 1910), 12779-791.

"How Illinois Congressional Candidates Stand," *IAA Record*, II (Oct. 25, 1924), 4.

Huthmacher, J. Joseph. "Urban Liberalism and the Age of Reform," *Mississippi Valley Historical Review*, XLIX (Sept., 1962), 231-241.

"Illinois River Project," *Illinois Journal of Commerce*, IV (Dec., 1922), 19.

"The Illinois Waterway," *Journal of the Illinois State Historical*

Society, XIII (Oct., 1920), 409.

James, O. F. "The Illinois State Society of Washington, D.C.," *Journal of the Illinois State Historical Society,* XXI (Jan., 1929), 569-570.

Johnson, Hildegard B. "The Location of German Immigrants in the Middle West," *Annals of the Association of American Geographers,* XLI (March, 1951), 1-41.

Jones, Alexander J. "The Chicago Drainage Canal and Its Forebear, the Illinois and Michigan Canal," *Transactions of the Illinois State Historical Society, 1906,* 153-161.

Joyce, Isabel. "Women of the Democracy," *National Monthly,* III (July, 1911), 78.

Kabaker, Harvey M. "Estimating the Normal Vote in Congressional Elections," *Midwest Journal of Political Science,* XIII (Feb., 1969), 58-83.

Kaplan, Edward S. "William Jennings Bryan and the Panama Canal Tolls Controversy," *Mid-America,* LVI (April, 1974), 100-108.

Kaufman, Burton I. "Organization for Trade Expansion in the Mississippi Valley, 1900-1920," *Business History Review,* XLVI (Winter, 1972), 444-465.

Kennedy, David M. "Overview: The Progressive Era," *Historian,* XXXVII (May, 1975), 453-468.

Key, V. O., Jr. "The Veterans and the House of Representatives: A Study of a Pressure Group and Electoral Morality," *Journal of Politics,* V (Feb., 1943), 27-40.

"Know Your Friends When You Go to the Polls, Vote Accordingly," *IAA Record,* IV (Nov. 1, 1926), 3.

Kyvig, David E. "Raskob, Roosevelt, and Repeal," *Historian,* XXXVII (May, 1975), 469-487.

Leuchtenburg, William E. "The New Deal and the Analogue of War" in John Braeman, *et al.* (eds.), *Change and Continuity in Twentieth-Century America.* (No. 1, Columbus: Ohio State University Press, 1964), 81-143.

"Light on the Ship Subsidy Proposition," *Commoner,* VII (March 22, 1907), 4-5.

Link, Arthur S. "What Happened to the Progressive Movement in the 1920's?," *American Historical Review,* LXIV (July, 1959), 833-851.

Lippincott, Isaac. "A History of River Improvement," *Journal of Political Economy,* XXII (July, 1914), 630-660.

Livermore, Seward W. "The Sectional Issue in the 1918 Congressional Elections," *Mississippi Valley Historical Review,* XXXV (June, 1948), 29-60.

Logan, Thomas F. "Watching the Nation's Business," *Leslie's Weekly*, CXXII (Feb. 24, 1916), 223, and (March 2, 1916), 257.

Lohof, Bruce A. "Herbert Hoover, Spokesman of Humane Efficiency: The Mississippi Flood of 1927," *American Quarterly*, XXII (Fall, 1970), 690-700.

Lord, Frank B. "The Next Senate and House," *National Monthly*, II (Dec., 1910), 255.

Lowden, Frank O. "Illinois, the New Keystone of the Union," *American Review of Reviews*, LVII (March, 1918), 271-272.

Lowry, Edward G. "The Tariff Revisers: The Democratic Members of the Ways and Means Committee of the House," *Harper's Weekly*, LV (Feb. 4, 1911), 8-9.

Lynde, Cornelius. "The Controversy Concerning the Diversion of Water from Lake Michigan by the Sanitary District of Chicago," *Illinois Law Review*, XXV (Nov., 1930), 243-260.

Maddox, Robert James. "Another Look at the Legend of Isolationism in the 1920's," *Mid-America*, LIII (Jan., 1971), 35-43.

Margulies, Herbert F. "The Election of 1920 in Wisconsin: The Return to 'Normalcy' Reappraised," *Wisconsin Magazine of History*, XLI (Autumn, 1957), 15-22.

Markowitz, Gerald E. "Progressivism and Imperialism: A Return to First Principles," *Historian*, XXXVII (Feb., 1975), 257-275.

Mathews, John L. "Water Power and the 'Pork Barrel,'" *Hampton's Magazine*, XXIII (Oct., 1909), 455-469.

"Mawsh Members," *Searchlight on Congress*, I (Oct., 1916), 1, 8.

Maxwell, Hugh L. "Illinois Waterway Delayed Needlessly," *Illinois Journal of Commerce*, IV (May, 1922), 16.

McClure, W. Frank. "The Chicago-St. Louis Waterway," *Scientific American*, XCVII (Sept. 21, 1907), 209-210.

McFarland, C. K., and Nevin E. Neal. "The Reluctant Reformer: Woodrow Wilson and Woman Suffrage, 1913-1920," *Rocky Mountain Social Science Journal*, XI (April, 1974), 33-43.

McGee, W J. "Our Great River," *World's Work*, XIII (Feb., 1907), 8576-84.

"Millions of Bullfrogs," *Time*, XXII (Nov. 20, 1933), 16.

Morrison, Geoffrey. "Champ Clark and the Rules Revolution of 1910," *Capitol Studies*, II (Winter, 1974), 43-56.

Mott, Rodney L. "Reapportionment in Illinois," *American Political Science Review*, XXI (Aug., 1927), 598-602.

"The Movement for a Federal Tax on Beer," *Editorial Research Reports, 1932*, II, 354.

"Mr. Rainey's Kindergarten for Standpatters," *Commoner*, VI

(April 20, 1906), 6.

"The National Capital," *Illinois Statesman: A Weekly Magazine for Illinois*, I (June 17, 1911), 6.

Newlands, Francis G. "The Use and Development of American Waterways," *Annals of the American Academy of Political and Social Science*, XXXI (June, 1908), 48–66.

"Next Tuesday's Upheaval," *Literary Digest*, CVII (Nov. 1, 1930), 5–6.

"'On Watch,'" *The American Syren and "Shipping" Illustrated* (May 28, 1904), 174–175.

Paullin, Charles O. "Henry Thomas Rainey" in Harris E. Starr (ed.), *Dictionary of American Biography*. Vol. 21. New York: Charles Scribner's Sons, 1944.

"Personalities: The Mississippi's Greatest Riverman [Kavanaugh]," *Hampton's Magazine*, XXV (Aug., 1910), 272–273.

Pinchot, Gifford. "The Democrats and Conservation" in "The Story of the Democratic House of Representatives" (a condensed chapter from *Law Making in America* by Lynn Haines). Copyright 1912. (Pamphlet available in Library of Congress.)

————. "How Conservation Began," *Agricultural History*, XI (Oct., 1937), 255–265.

Polsby, Nelson W. "The Institutionalization of the U.S. House of Representatives," *American Political Science Review*, LXII (March, 1968), 144–168.

Potts, E. Daniel. "The Progressive Profile in Iowa," *Mid-America*, XLVII (Oct., 1965), 257–268.

Rader, Benjamin G. "Federal Taxation in the 1920's: A Re-examination," *Historian*, XXXIII (May, 1971), 415–435.

Rainey, Henry T. "The Legal Effect of the Maximum Provision of the Aldrich-Payne Tariff Law," *Central Law Journal*, LXIX (Dec. 3, 1909), 414–416.

————. "Tariff Law Should Be Vetoed," *Prairie Farmer*, CII (May 10, 1930), 5.

————. "The Thirteenth Census and the Sixty-second Congress," *National Monthly*, I (Oct., 1909), 170–171, 180.

————. "What--After All--Is 'Progressivism'?," *Nation*, CXVII (Feb. 13, 1924), 161.

"Rainey New Party Leader," *Prairie Farmer*, CIII (Dec. 12, 1931), 20.

"Rainey of Illinois," *Commoner*, VI (Nov. 2, 1906), 3:3.

Rainey, Mrs. Henry T. "The Woman's Congressional Club," *New England Magazine*, XL (May, 1909), 265–271.

"Records the Best Guide for Voting," *Prairie Farmer*, XCVI

(Oct. 25, 1924), 7.

"The Report upon the Proposed 14-ft. Deep Waterway from Chicago to New Orleans," *Engineering News*, LXI (June 24, 1909), 686-692.

"The Report of a Board of Engineers on the Illinois Section of the Lakes-to-the-Gulf Waterway," *Engineering News*, LXV (March 2, 1911), 269.

Rhodes, Benjamin D. "Reassessing 'Uncle Shylock': The United States and the French War Debt, 1917-1929," *Journal of American History*, LV (March, 1969), 787-803.

Rice, Stuart A., and Malcolm M. Willey. "American Women's Ineffective Use of the Vote," *Current History*, XX (July, 1924), 641-647.

Riddick, Floyd M. "The House of Representatives and the President," *South Atlantic Quarterly*, XXXIV (Jan., 1935), 79-90.

Robinson, N. T. N. "Democrats Claim House on Eve of New Congress," *Congressional Digest*, X (Dec., 1931), 289-290.

Rogers, Lindsay. "President Wilson's Theory of His Office," *Forum*, LI (Feb., 1914), 174-186.

Roosevelt, Theodore. "Our National Inland Waterways Policy," *Annals of the American Academy of Political and Social Science*, XXXI (Jan., 1908), 1-11.

Rudwick, Elliott M. "Oscar DePriest and the Jim Crow Restaurant in the U.S. House of Representatives," *Journal of Negro Education*, XXXV (Winter, 1966), 77-82.

Rusk, Jerrold G. "The Effect of the Australian Ballot Reform on Split Ticket Voting: 1876-1908," *American Political Science Review*, LXIV (Dec., 1970), 1220-38.

Schwarz, Jordan A. "John Nance Garner and the Sales Tax Rebellion of 1932," *Journal of Southern History*, XXX (May, 1964), 162-180.

Scott, Andrew M. "The Progressive Era in Perspective," *Journal of Politics*, XXI (Nov., 1959), 685-701.

Seligman, Edwin R. A. "The War Revenue Act," *Political Science Quarterly*, XXXIII (March, 1918), 1-32, appendix 33-37.

Shelton, William A. "The Lakes-to-the-Gulf Deep Waterway," *Journal of Political Economy*, XX (June, July, and Oct., 1912), 541-573, 653-675, 765-806.

————. "A Waterway between Chicago and St. Louis: A Study in Freight Rates," *Journal of Political Economy*, XXII (Jan., 1914), 64-78.

Sherman, Richard B. "The Status Revolution and Massachusetts Progressive Leadership," *Political Science Quarterly*,

LXXVIII (March, 1963), 59-65.

Shideler, James H. *"Flappers and Philosophers*, and Farmers: Rural-Urban Tensions of the Twenties," *Agricultural History*, XLVII (Oct., 1973), 283-299.

Shover, John L. "The Farmers' Holiday Association Strike of 1932," *Agricultural History*, XXXIX (Oct., 1965), 196-203.

————. "Populism in the 1930's: The Battle for the AAA," *Agricultural History*, XXXIX (Jan., 1965), 17-24.

Smith, Everett G., Jr. "Twentieth Century Voting Patterns for President in Illinois," *Illinois Government*, 32 (Jan., 1970), 1-8.

Snyder, J. Richard. "Coolidge, Costigan and the Tariff Commission," *Mid-America*, L (April, 1968), 131-148.

"The 'Soak-the-Rich' Drive in Washington," *Literary Digest*, CXIII (April 2, 1932), 8-9.

"Speaker Rainey, Legislative Marshal of the New Deal, Dies," *Literary Digest*, CXXVIII (Aug. 25, 1934), 6.

"Speaker Rainey Mourned," *IAA Record*, XII (Sept., 1934), 4.

Stahl, Rose M. "The Ballinger-Pinchot Controversy," *Smith College Studies in History*, XI (Jan., 1926), 65-136.

Steiner, Gilbert Y., and Samuel K. Gove. "The Legislature Redistricts Illinois," *University of Illinois Bulletin*, LIV (Oct., 1956), 5-32.

Sullivan, Mark. "Comment on Congress," *Collier's*, XLVI (Nov. 5, 1910), 20; (Dec. 17, 1910), 12; (Feb. 4, 1911), 20; and (Sept. 14, 1912), 13.

————. "Comment on Congress: The Tariff Commission," *Collier's*, LI (Aug. 30, 1913), 9.

————. "Looking Forward," *Collier's*, XLVI (March 11, 1911), 14.

————. "The Most Important Thing," *Collier's*, L (Jan. 4, 1913), 15.

————. "The Waning Influence of the Farmer," *World's Work*, LI (April, 1926), 657-661.

"The Sullivan Case," *Commoner*, VI (Sept. 14, 1906), 14.

Tager, Jack. "Progressives, Conservatives and the Theory of the Status Revolution," *Mid-America*, XLVIII (July, 1966), 162-175.

"The Tariff Board," *American Review of Reviews*, LIII (March, 1916), 273.

Tarr, Joel A. "President Theodore Roosevelt and Illinois Politics, 1901-1904," *Journal of the Illinois State Historical Society*, LVIII (Autumn, 1965), 245-264.

Temple, Wayne C. "Tribute to G. V. Black," *Illinois Dental Journal*, XXXV (July, 1966), 2-11.

Thelen, David P. "Social Tensions and the Origins of Progressivism,"

Journal of American History, LVI (Sept., 1969), 323–341.

T.R.B., "Washington Notes," *New Republic*, LXIX (Jan. 13, 1932), 242, and LXXVIII (May 9, 1934), 363.

Treadway, Allen T. "The Amherst Illustrious: The Congressional Leaders—Rainey, '83 and Snell, '94," *Amherst Graduates' Quarterly*, XXII (May, 1933), 210–211.

Trout, Grace Wilbur. "Sidelights on Illinois Suffrage History," *Journal of the Illinois State Historical Society*, XIII (July, 1920), 145–179.

Uhle, Lee. "Gadfly Rainey," *Illinois History*, XXII (May, 1969), 186–187.

"A Victim of Minorities," *Collier's*, LXXXIX (Jan. 23, 1932), 20.

Von Blon, Philip. "The Soldier Vote," *The Home Sector*, I (Dec. 20, 1919), 32–33, 37–38.

Waller, Robert A. "The Illinois Waterway from Conception to Completion, 1908–1933," *Journal of the Illinois State Historical Society*, LXV (Summer, 1972), 124–141.

———. "The Selection of Henry T. Rainey as Speaker of the House," *Capitol Studies*, II (Spring, 1973), 37–47.

Way, R. B. "Mississippi Improvements and Traffic Prospects," *Annals*, XXXI (Jan., 1908), 146–163.

Weinstein, James. "Organized Business and the City Commission and Manager Movements," *Journal of Southern History*, XXVIII (May, 1962), 166–182.

"A Wet-Dry Test in Congress," *Literary Digest*, CXI (Dec. 19, 1931), 8.

"What to Expect from a Deadlocked Congress," *Literary Digest*, CVII (Nov. 22, 1930), 5–7.

White, G. Edward. "The Social Values of the Progressives: Some New Perspectives," *South Atlantic Quarterly*, LXX (Winter, 1971), 62–76.

Whiting, Daniel. "The St. Lawrence Seaway Power Project," *Editorial Research Reports*, II (Aug. 3, 1932), 78.

"Why a 14-foot Deep Waterway through the Mississippi Valley Is Not Worth While," *Engineering News*, LXI (June 24, 1909), 694–695.

"Widening the Democratic Smile," *Literary Digest*, CXI (Nov. 14, 1931), 11.

Wildavsky, Aaron. "TVA and Power Politics," *American Political Science Review*, LV (Sept., 1961), 576–590.

Willey, Malcolm M., and Stuart A. Rice. "A Sex Cleavage in the Presidential Election of 1920," *Journal of the American Statistical Association*, XIX (Dec., 1924), 519–520.

Williams, William A. "The Legend of Isolationism in the Twenties,"

Science and Society, XVIII (Winter, 1954), 1–20.

Wirt, William A. "America Must Lose—By a 'Planned Economy,' the Stepping Stone to a Regimented State." New York: Committee for the Nation, 1934.

Wish, Harvey. "John Peter Altgeld and the Background of the Campaign of 1896," *Mississippi Valley Historical Review*, XXIV (March, 1938), 503–518.

Woodward, Carl R. "Woodrow Wilson's Agricultural Philosophy," *Agricultural History*, XIV (Oct., 1940), 129–142.

VI. SERIALS

A. Newspapers

Amherst Student, Sept. 17, 1881—June 26, 1883.

Carrollton *Gazette*, Dec. 30, 1898—Sept. 19, 1947.

Carrollton *Patriot*, Sept. 23, 1898—Dec. 27, 1934.

Chicago *Daily News*, Nov. 1, 1932—March 10, 1933.

Chicago *Herald and Examiner*, Nov. 1, 1933—March 10, 1933.

Chicago *Record-Herald*, Jan. 1, 1904—Dec. 31, 1912.

Chicago *Tribune*, June 5, 1895—Sept. 29, 1945.

Daily Illinois Courier, March 12, 1906.

Illinois State Register, Jan. 1, 1907—Dec. 31, 1934.

Labor, March 3, 1933.

Memphis *Commercial Appeal*, Nov. 1, 1932—March 10, 1933.

Nashville *Tennesseean*, Nov. 1, 1932—March 10, 1933.

New York *Times*, Jan. 1, 1894—June 30, 1962.

Peoria *Herald-Transcript*, June 1–30, 1908.

United States Daily, March 4, 1926—March 3, 1932.

Washington *Evening Star*, Nov. 1, 1932—March 10, 1933.

Washington *Post*, Nov. 1, 1932—Dec. 31, 1934.

B. Periodicals

Amherst Graduates' Quarterly, Vol. 1 (1911)—Vol. 38 (1949).

Business Week, July 6, 1932—Sept. 1, 1934.

Collier's, Vol. 33 (April 2, 1904)—Vol. 62 (Dec. 21, 1918); Vol. 73 (Jan.—June, 1924); and Vol. 91 (Jan.—June, 1933).

The Commoner, Vol. 1 (Jan. 23, 1901)—Vol. 23 (April, 1923).

The Congressional Digest, Vol. 1 (Oct., 1921)—Vol. 14 (Dec., 1935).

Editorial Research Reports, 1929–35.

Engineering News-Record, Vol. 61 (1909); Vol. 65 (1911); Vol. 84-85 (1920).

Greene County Farm Bureau Bulletin, Feb. 20, 1922—March, 1938. (Called the *News Letter* after 1929.)

Hampton's Magazine, Vol. 23 (July, 1909)—Vol. 27 (Jan., 1912).

Illinois Agricultural Association Record, Vol. 2 (Jan. 5, 1924)—Vol. 12 (Dec., 1934).

Illinois Issue, Vol. 5 (March 4—Dec. 30, 1910).

Illinois Journal of Commerce, Vol. 4 (Jan.—Dec., 1922).

Illinois Statesman: A Weekly Magazine for Illinois, Vol. 1 (June 17, 1911).

Literary Digest, Vol. 26 (Jan., 1903)—Vol. 120 (Dec., 1935).

The Nation, Vol. 106 (Jan., 1908)—Vol. 140 (June, 1935).

National Monthly, Vol. 1 (June, 1909)—Vol. 4 (Sept., 1912).

The New Republic, Vol. 1 (Nov. 7, 1914)—Vol. 85 (Feb. 5, 1936).

Newsweek, Vol. 1 (Feb. 17, 1933)—Vol. 5 (June 29, 1935).

Prairie Farmer, Vol. 95 (Jan. 6, 1923)—Vol. 106 (Dec. 29, 1934).

Searchlight on Congress, Vol. 1 (Feb. 1, 1916)—Vol. 11 (March, 1927).

Time, the Weekly News Magazine, Vol. 4 (July 7, 1924)—Vol. 28 (Dec. 28, 1936).

VII.   UNPUBLISHED MATERIAL

A.   Columbia Oral History Memoirs

Gordon Browning

Marvin Jones

Milburn L. Wilson

B.   Correspondence and Interviews

E. Porter Dickinson, Reference Librarian at Amherst College.

Lisle Hanna, Judge of Clay County, Nebraska

Margaret McMahon, Rainey's secretary from 1931-34.

Mary K. Rainey, Relative

Kurt Schwerin, Librarian at Northwestern University School of Law.

C.   Theses and Miscellany

Baker, William E.   "The Political Career of Henry T. Rainey, 1903-1934."   M.A. thesis, University of Maryland, 1953.

Barfield, Claude E., Jr.   "The Democratic Party in Congress, 1909-1913."   Ph.D. thesis, Northwestern University, 1965.

Beach, Walter E. "The Democratic Steering Committee in the House of Representatives, 1933–1960." M.A. thesis, George Washington University, 1961.

Becht, J. Edwin. "Commodity Origins, Traffic and Markets Accessible to Chicago via the Illinois Waterway." Ph.D. thesis, University of Illinois, 1951.

Block, Marvin W. "Henry Thomas Rainey: Some Major Aspects of His Legislative Career." M.S. thesis, Illinois State Normal University, 1960.

Brown, Leahmae. "The Development of National Policy with Respect to Water Resources." Ph.D. thesis, University of Illinois, 1937.

Clubb, Jerome M. "Congressional Opponents of Reform, 1901–1913." Ph.D. thesis, University of Washington, 1963.

Graff, Helen E. "Henry T. Rainey—An American Statesman." M.A. thesis, State University of Iowa, 1933.

Gutek, Gerald L. "George Brennan and the Illinois Delegation in the Democratic Convention of 1924." M.A. thesis, University of Illinois, 1959.

Jones, Robert H. "The Administration of Governor Frank O. Lowden of Illinois, 1917–1921." M.A. thesis, University of Illinois, 1951.

Kehoe, Loretta. "The Relation of Herbert Hoover to Congress, 1929–1933." M.A. thesis, Loyola University, 1949.

Kenkel, Joseph F. "The Tariff Commission Movement: The Search for a Nonpartisan Solution of the Tariff Question." Ph.D. thesis, University of Maryland, 1962.

Mathews, Alvin G. "How Illinois Will Feed Her New Waterway." M.A. thesis, University of Illinois, 1922.

Mayhill, George R. "Speaker Cannon under the Roosevelt Administration, 1903–1907." Ph.D. thesis, University of Illinois, 1942.

Morrison, Hugh A., and Robert T. Patterson. "Hon. Henry Thomas Rainey, 1860–1934, Speaker of the House of Representatives; Record of Services as a Member and Speaker of the House of Representatives, United States Congress, as Given in the Indexes of the Congressional Record from the 58th Congress to the End of the 73rd Congress, March 4, 1903—June 18, 1934." Washington, 1934. Typescript in Rare Book Room of the Library of Congress.

Philip, William B. "Chicago and the Downstate: A Study of Their Conflicts, 1870–1934." Ph.D. thesis, University of Chicago, 1940.

Plum, Lester V. "The Federal Power Commission: Federal Regulation of the Electric Power Industry, Prior to 1935, in

Theory and Practice." Ph.D. thesis, Princeton University, 1936.

Roady, Elston E. "Party Regularity in the Sixty-third Congress" [1913–15]. Ph.D. thesis, University of Illinois, 1951.

Rogers, George A. "President Hoover and the Seventy-second Congress." M.A. thesis, University of Illinois, 1947.

Schmidt, Royal J. *"The Chicago Daily News* and Illinois Politics, 1876–1920." Ph.D. thesis, University of Chicago, 1957.

Schwartz, Carroll J. "Distribution of the Foreign-Born Population of Illinois, 1870–1950." M.A. thesis, Southern Illinois University, 1959.

Searls, Virginia W. "Presidential Influence on Legislation, March 9—June 16, 1933." M.A. thesis, University of Illinois, 1946.

Silver, Paul L. "Wilsonians and the New Deal." Ph.D. thesis, University of Pennsylvania, 1964.

Slichter, Gertrude A. "Political Backgrounds of New Deal Agricultural Policy, 1928–1932." M.A. thesis, University of Illinois, 1952.

Steiner, Gilbert Y. "The Congressional Conference Committee: Seventieth to Eightieth Congresses." Ph.D. thesis, University of Illinois, 1950.

Werner, Mildred C. "The History of the Deep Waterway in the State of Illinois." M.A. thesis, University of Illinois, 1947.

Whitney, Doris B. "Highlights in the Career of the Late Speaker of the House, Henry T. Rainey." Carbon copy of typescript dated Oct. 23, 1951, in Carrollton Public Library.

Wiseman, John B. "Dilemmas of a Party Out of Power: The Democracy, 1904–1912." Ph.D. thesis, University of Maryland, 1967.

Index